T. of HOLINESS and LOVE

Kenneth E. Jones

University Press of America, Inc.
Lanham • New York • London

Copyright © 1995 by
University Press of America,® Inc.
4720 Boston Way
Lanham, Maryland 20706

3 Henrietta Street
London, WC2E 8LU England

All rights reserved
Printed in the United States of America
British Cataloging in Publication Information Available

Library of Congress Cataloging-in-Publication Data

Jones, Kenneth E.
Theology of holiness and love / Kenneth E. Jones.
p. cm.
1. Theology, Doctrinal. 2. Church of God (Anderson, Ind.)--
Doctrines. 3. Holiness churches--Doctrines. I. Title.
BT75.2.J65   1995   230'.99--dc20   95-23280 CIP

ISBN 0-7618-0035-2 (pbk: alk ppr.)

Unless otherwise noted, all Scripture quotations are from the New Revised Standard Version, copyright 1989 by the Division of Christian Education of the National Council of the Churches of Christ in the United States of America. Used by permission. All rights reserved.

∞™ The paper used in this publication meets the minimum requirements of American National Standard for Information Sciences—Permanence of Paper for Printed Library Materials, ANSI Z39.48—1984

CONTENTS

Preface	v
Abbreviations	vii
1. The Meaning of Theology	1
2. Christian Belief in God's Existence	15
3. God Reveals Himself	29
4. The Bible and Its Authority	45
5. The Nature of God	63
6. Christian Belief in the Trinity	75
7. The Works of God	85
8. Theological Anthropology	101
9. The Nature of Sin	113
10. Original Sin	129
11. God Seeking People	145
12. Christology: Christ the Savior	159
13. Salvation	177
14. Human Holiness	191

15. The Holy Spirit	209
16. Entire Sanctification	223
17. Holy Living	239
18. The Church of God	253
19. The Holy Spirit in the Church	277
20. Gifts of the Spirit	291
21. Church Organization and Work	305
22. Final Things	319
Notes	345
Bibliography	351
Index	357

Preface

Theology is considered by the writer to be an exposition of the truth found revealed by God, written in the Bible, and which we seek to interpret with the guidance of the Holy Spirit. It is true that not all truth is written in the Bible, but no truth is contradictory to the Bible.

This theology is written from the Wesleyan holiness point of view. To say that this theology is Wesleyan is not to say that it seeks to interpret only John Wesley's writings and sermons. We seek to interpret the Bible, but do this interpretation through some of the key insights which Wesley provided. John Wesley did not accept the anthropological pessimism of Augustine nor the optimism associated with the name of Pelagius. That is, he did not accept the idea that man is so depraved from birth that he can be saved only if he is one of those chosen by God. He was convinced that the Holy Spirit so works in each person as to give that person the ability to accept salvation from God, or reject it. He rejected also the idea that anyone can live a holy life without redemption through Christ. Wesley was sure that no one could be eternally lost because of Adam's sin alone, without ever committing sin themselves. Yet he was sure that all are depraved by sin, and that no one can be saved without saving faith in Christ. And he was sure that all the good we do is aided by the Holy Spirit, even before conversion. We shall have to look further at these points later on, but say this much only to point out a major distinction of this theology.

It may be helpful to give some brief account of my own theological development to this point. As a lifelong member of the Church of God (Anderson, IN), I have been strongly influenced by Church of God writers and preachers. The first theology book I read was R. R. Byrum's, which I first read as a boy, and much later used as a college text. The first theology professors I had in college were Earl

Martin and C. E. Brown. Dr. Brown introduced me to the way in which a study of the early Christian writers can aid our theological thinking. In seminary, I was forced by Walter Marshall Horton to struggle with major theologies and write my reactions to them. Still other instructors under whom I have studied, though they are not all Wesleyan, have challenged me. I should mention Donald Guthrie, John Gerstner, Harold Lindsell, and J. Oliver Buswell, Jr.

In addition to the Church of God writers mentioned, I would have to add such persons as W. C. Roark, A. F. Gray, F. G. Smith, and the host of preachers I heard in my youth. The latter would have to include such men as H. M. Riggle, W. T. Wallace, E. E. Byrum, H. C. Heffren, and my own father, T. A. Jones. I learned from all of them, and still have notes I made of some of their sermons.

In my years of college teaching I continued reading all types of theologies which came my way. But I have been most helped by some Wesleyan scholars. One of them who excited my thinking was Mildred Bangs Wynkoop, especially her *Theology of Love*. I have continued to learn from the writings of Albert C. Outler, Richard Taylor, Timothy Smith and Willard Taylor, Paul Bassett and Kenneth J. Collins. The latest Wesleyan scholar to excite me has been Thomas Oden, especially his two editions of *Agenda for Theology*, and his three volumes of Systematic Theology, just completed in 1992. He has emphasized the writings of the Early Christian Fathers, and used them well. His three volumes constitute one of the most exciting theology studies I have ever read.

My colleagues in teaching have influenced me more than they know. Teaching on the faculty with such men as Milo Chapman, Ronald Joiner, Garlin Hall, Walter Doty and Max Gaulke has made my learning most enjoyable. From each of them I have learned. Friends on other faculties have also influenced my thinking: Barry Callen, Gilbert Stafford, Spencer Spaulding, and John Stanley.

My intention in this theology has been to set forth what I believe is the Biblical teaching. I have no great desire to interact with all the modern theologies. Nor do I wish to spend major time explaining differences with Calvinists, Lutherans, or others. These would lengthen the book too much. I am more interested in this book in asserting the Biblical message, and defending it against some who seem to be distorting it.

ABBREVIATIONS

ABC	Asbury Bible Commentary
ASV	American Standard Version Bible
BaDT	Baker's Dictionary of Theology
BeDT	Beacon Dictionary of Theology
BBC	Beacon Bible Commentary
BBR	Bulletin for Biblical Research
DJG	Dictionary of Jesus and the Gospels
DPL	Dictionary of Paul and His Letters
IBC	International Bible Commentary
ISBE	International Standard Bible Encyclopedia, Revised
JETS	Journal of the Evangelical Theological Society
KJV	King James Version
LXX	Septuagint
NIV	New International Version Bible
NICNT	New International Commentary on the New Testament
NIDCC	New International Dictionary of the Christian Church
NIDNTT	New International Dictionary of New Testament Theology
NRSV	New Revised Standard Version Bible
TWNT	Theological Wordbook of the New Testament
UBS	United Bible Society text of the Greek New Testament
WTJ	Wesleyan Theological Journal

Chapter 1

The Meaning of Theology

> "Hold to the standard of sound teaching that you have heard from me, in the faith and love that are in Christ Jesus. Guard the good treasure entrusted to you, with the help of the Holy Spirit living in us." (2 Tim. 1:13-14).

What is theology? Is it necessary for all to study theology? With all the books of theology we already have, why would anyone write another? What is the difference between this book and others?

The word "theology" comes from two Greek words, "theos," meaning "God," and "logos," meaning "knowledge of," or "words about." So theology is words about God. The word is sometimes used in a narrow sense to mean simply the study of what we can know about God. However, it is now usually used to mean the study of what we know about God and human beings in relation to God. It can include the whole universe in relation to God who created it, but the most space is usually given to human beings in relation to God, since that is a primary concern.

If we were to reduce Christian Theology to the bare essentials, and put it in terms a child could understand, it could be something like an expansion of the phrase "God Loves You." It could look something like this:

GOD loves you. God who loves you is the Maker of heaven and earth. He not only created all things that are, but he upholds the universe all the time. He is the Lord of all life, Lord of history, and has all power. He is the Lord of the eternal destinies of all of us. And He is holy. This is the God who loves you.

God LOVES you. He does not love you in some impersonal way, as you may say that you love everybody, but knows you better than you know yourself. He cares about you personally. You are important to God, so that your trouble grieves God, and your love pleases him. He loves you so much that he sent his only Son to die for you rather than give up loving you. God loves you so much that he wants you to live for him and with him forever and ever. Yet God's love is not soft, and cannot tolerate evil nor condone sin. God loves you so much that he hates all sin, as that separates you from him. If you persist in your refusal to live for God and obey him, you must spend eternity without him.

God loves YOU. God loves you individually, personally. He loves you so much that if there had not been any other persons on earth, Jesus would have died for you alone, to save you from your own sin. God showed his love to us when Jesus died on the cross. God loves you just as you are, but wants you to let him change you so that he can show his love to you in ways you cannot yet comprehend. God wants you to love and serve him. Surely, to see the love of God in the cross, is to be changed by it into a new kind of person.

God can put his love in you. His love in you, then, is both love for God and love for others.

You can live with him forever. If you live in Him in this life, and do his will, you can live with him forever. If you do not live for him, you will die and suffer the loss of God and all good forever.

This brief summary leaves much to be desired. It cannot even introduce some of the great truths of theology. Yet, so far as it goes, it is a true summary of the basic idea of Christian theology, which is all bound together by the love, mercy and grace of God which he has shown to all who will see it. This basic concept of theology must not be forgotten as we look at the details of the subject. Never forget that theology is about the love of God, and the God who loves, and the human beings whom he loves so as to save us from ourselves.

Theology is talk about God, and all that is related to him. Christian theology is an attempt to collect, organize and understand all that Christians believe about God and his works and will. The purpose of this task is to clarify what we know and what we do not know about God, and to make clear why some concepts are not true to what we know about God. Theology, then, should help us sort out the truth which we must believe from the ideas we should not believe.

It is true that we can know God without any study of theology, though everyone has some kind of theology, whether good or bad. We can know God without knowing much *about* God. Yet it is far better to know God and to seek to learn more about him. If we truly love God we will seek to know as much about him as we can. The attempt to do this is the study of systematic theology.

THEOLOGY AND EXPERIENCE

A common objection to the study of theology is that it is better to have the experience of being touched by God than to study about God. No doubt this is true. There is no use knowing about God and understanding the words to use in talking about Him, if one does not have the experience of knowing God.

Sometimes this objection is raised by one who says that he has felt God while out in the boat fishing or in the deep woods hunting on a Sunday morning. He insists that the experience he had there in the woods was far more real than the theological preaching he would have heard in church that morning. He decides therefore that he does not need theology at all. This has a little truth in it, but it is far from the whole truth.

C. S. Lewis, in one of his radio talks on "Beyond Personality," compared theology to a map of the ocean. The map is not the ocean, but only a guide to it. Obviously, the ocean is more "real" and exciting than the map. But if you want to cross the ocean and get to the other side, you had better have a good map, or know a guide who does understand the map. If you can be satisfied with standing on the shore a little while, and listening to the waves breaking on the rocks, you do not need a map. And if you can be satisfied to feel the presence and power of God once or twice, then that is probably all you will ever have. But if you want to live your whole life with the assurance of God's continued presence and blessing, then you need to know more theology.

Theology is like a map in that it is a description of our knowledge of God and his will for all humanity. It must be written in carefully chosen words so as to be a safe guide to truth. Many of the words traditionally used in theology are not simple, nor easy to understand. Like other valuable studies, it may be difficult at times. Yet the words which are used point to truths which can change lives and change the world.

Theology is especially important for one who is to be a leader or teacher in the church. If you are to lead anyone else into an experience of salvation and knowledge of God, you need to know all the theology you can. A careful study of Christian theology will help you to a better understanding of Biblical truth, and will help you guide others away from false ideas which can be harmful.

It is for this reason that we find in certain books of the New Testament so many references to "sound teaching" (1 Tim. 1:10; 6:3; 2 Tim. 1:13; 4:3; Titus 1:9, 13; 2:1, 2). The command is, "Hold to the standard of sound teaching that you have heard from me, in the faith and love that are in Christ Jesus" (2 Tim. 1:13). "Teach what is consistent with sound doctrine" (Tit. 2:1).

In Matthew 28:20, we read that Jesus, in his Great Commission, told the disciples that as they went everywhere they should be "teaching them to obey everything that I have commanded you." And though some say that we do not need to do any more than simply believe in Jesus, we read in John: "The one who rejects me and does not receive my word has a judge; on the last day the word that I have spoken will serve as judge" (John 12:48). If we believe in Jesus, we must also accept what he taught.

It must be admitted that in this time there are scholars who insist that we do not know what he taught, since they believe we cannot depend on the written Gospels to be true witnesses to his doctrine. Yet without these Gospels we would not know much about him, and surely not enough to believe in him as Savior. The gospel of Jesus Christ has changed individual lives, and transformed history. So even in this post-modern age, some of us have decided we cannot throw out what has been so significant in our lives. We can unashamedly build our lives on the Bible and its teachings, and trust completely in what we know the Bible to teach about God and his plan of salvation from sin.

Beliefs that make a difference

Let no one imagine that theology is unrelated to life. The word itself means "knowledge about God." But theology is far more than talk about God. It is thinking about God in relation to the universe and everything in it. Most importantly, it is thinking about God and the way he deals with human beings. It is about human beings in our necessary relation with God. Since God created humanity and will decide the fate of every person in the end, there is no person who does not need to know and understand theology. The time will come when you will either know God and his will or wish you had. When Christ comes again, he said that he will pronounce a blessing on those who know God, and send away forever those who do not know him and live for him (Matt. 25:31-46). So what we know and believe about God makes a difference not only in this life but in the life to come.

Integrated theology

Theology is not simply isolated facts or concepts. All the facts about God and creation fit together and belong together. All parts of theology fit together. This means that one cannot discuss any part of theology properly without it being connected to every other part. All aspects of Christian theology are interrelated and inseparably interdependent.

To speak in this way of theology is to speak of an ideal presentation of theology. It is not easy to write an exposition which makes clear the interdependence of all aspects of the subject, but it has to be attempted. This is part of what is meant by "systematic theology. A system of theology ought to show how it all fits together. Karl Barth did not attempt to organize his theology into a system, and declared that it was impossible to do this. Yet, as others have pointed out, he did end up with a systematic presentation of theology, even though he may never had admitted it. Some say that John Wesley was not a theologian at all, because he did not write a book which presented a well-organized system of theology. But that is because Wesley was primarily interested in the evangelistic presentation of gospel truths. He was not most interested in speculation or philosophy, but mainly in what would bring sinners to a saving knowledge of God in Christ Jesus. This is why he did not seek to write a system, but presented truth which came from his systematic study .

It is one thing to know that all the various topics of theology fit together, and it is another to write a description of it in which all the parts are clearly one united whole. It would take a perfect theologian to do that. Yet it is important to recognize the goal of the description, and to do one's best to reach for it.

Why another theology?

If truth is truth, and God does not change, why do we ever need to write another book on Christian theology? Does theology get out of date? Do we discover new truths about God and his ways, so that we need to write new theologies? Such questions deserve an answer, and we can give it by listing a few points in reply.

Words change. Since theology is a study and refinement of words about God, the use of individual words has to be revised. After words have changed in either denotation or connotation, or both, they mislead the reader instead of helping. For example, it has been common in theology to say that the triune God is "one in substance and three in person." Yet these words have so changed their meaning that we get from them a far different idea than they originally expressed. So we find it very easy to misunderstand the ancient creeds and have a false concept of the Trinity. The modern theologian must seek to correct such false ideas by using words with clear modern meanings, and seek to explain the old words.

Our understanding grows. Through the study of the Bible, our understanding of theology should grow. No human being has ever completely understood the whole teaching of all the Bible. As we ask the Bible new questions, we get new answers, which may lead to further questions and more answers. So our understanding grows. The same thing is true as we study the writings of theologians.

New problems bring new questions. New problems and new social situations call for new restatements of theological truths. One of the sad facts of American history is the fact that some Christians defended slavery on the basis that the Bible does not specifically condemn it. This happened also in other parts of the world, as slavery has at various times been almost universal. We now have an understanding of theology which leaves no possible place for approval of slavery, and should not hesitate to make that clear. The truths of the Bible has not changed, but our understanding of it has grown.

The writers of theology have for two thousand years carried on a dialogue with one another in their writings. As each has written what seemed true on a subject, others have seen inconsistencies or problems in the writing, and have so written their own understandings.

These facts are true of the mainstream of theology as it has developed over the centuries since the New Testament was written. However, new books are also written because of the real differences of opinion between theologians. We find then some other reasons for new discussions of theology to be written:

Denominations and cultures differ. This accounts for the differences between Roman Catholic, Eastern Orthodox, and Protestant theologies. In Protestantism there are several main groups of churches with broad agreements in theology, but differences between the groups, such as Lutheran, Calvinist, Wesleyan and Baptist. Each of the groups have many churches within them, each of which tends to write its own theology because of divergent beliefs and emphases, and different understandings of terms.[1]

Within the same denomination, theologians may feel impelled to write on theology because of differing viewpoints. These differences may be on minor points, or they may be vastly different. For example, they may have different philosophical presuppositions, beginning points, or basic assumptions, so that they simply cannot agree on basic issues. In our time, we see basically different views of revelation and reason. If some emphasize reason as a primary source of theology, they can have little in common with those who emphasize the Reformation principle of basing theology on the authoritative Bible. So differing theologies are written.

It is easy to misunderstand what is here said about reason and revelation. We can do no better than to quote Ray Dunning:

> Following John Wesley, Wesleyan theology has always built its doctrinal work upon four foundation stones commonly referred to as the Wesleyan quadrilateral. In addition to the Scripture, they are tradition, reason, and experience. These are not of equal authority, however. In fact, properly understood, the three auxiliary sources directly support the priority of Biblical authority.[2]

Biblical authority is the primary source and test of our theology, but this is interpreted by means of reason, tradition and experience. In spite of the difficulty of doing so, we must keep our priorities straight. We must test tradition, reason and experiences by Scripture. In Chapter three ("Necessity of Revelation") we shall see why it is necessary for God to reveal himself if we are to know him.

Albert C. Outler, who invented the term "quadrilateral," said that Wesley's theological method has "Scripture as its preeminent norm but interfaced with tradition, reason and Christian experience as dynamic and interactive aids in the interpretation of the Word of God in Scripture."[3]

As we work with Scriptures in this way, we will learn. In that learning, we will find ourselves sometimes rejecting aspects of our tradition. We will be reasoning about what we read, and reinterpreting experience. We may find that we have misunderstood Scripture, or overlooked things we should have found there. Because this is such a difficult process, we will never come to a perfect knowledge of theology here in this life (1 Cor.13:12). If any two of us did achieve that perfection of knowledge, we would be in perfect agreement in theology. Even then, we might want to use different words to express our concepts. The meaning and use of words are determined by culture and experience, so we can differ in our understanding of them.

At the same time, even those theologians who are in basic agreement on the content of theology may feel led to write their own explanations for one or another of the following reasons:

Organizing principles differ. They may want to use a different organizing principle, such as love (Mildred Bangs Wynkoop), hope (Jurgen Moltmann), eschatology (Thomas N. Finger), ecumenical consensus

(Walter Marshall Horton), the refutation of cults (Walter R. Martin). It is customary to begin with God, but some want to begin with human beings. Another may emphasize the eschatological nature of all aspects of theology.

Writers have different purposes. Different purposes lead to new expositions of theology. One may be polemic, arguing against one or another false concept. Others may be much more irenic, simply explaining what the theologian believes to be true.

Writing for different readers. The theologian must consider the audience for whom the book is to be written. In a book written for beginning students, there must be simpler language, and much more explanation of terms than in one written for scholars only. And in one written for a particular denomination, the discussion is necessarily different from one written for a more general group of readers. At the end of this book is a list of some theologies written from different viewpoints, and broadly classified.

Some theologies are being written today from a far different perspective than this one, and without considering the Bible as the primary source. At one extreme from this book is what some call "liberal" or "modernist" theology. This theological modernity has developed in the last two centuries. It tends to deny what cannot be scientifically proved. So it often includes a denial of the Virgin Birth of Jesus, His divinity, His bodily resurrection, and His second coming. It tends to look at the Bible as just another humanly produced book. Some feel that we must believe only what we can prove by some non-biblical means to be true. They may therefore deny all miracle and prophecy. Theology built on such a presupposition of the primacy of science as judge of truth is far different from theology built on a strong faith in the Bible as witness to the revelation of God, and centering on Jesus Christ as revealed in the New Testament.

In the twentieth century there have grown up a variety of theologies and ways of expressing them. They include Dialectical theology, liberalism, liberation theologies, modernism, evangelical theology, fundamentalism, Black theology, neo-orthodoxy, postmodernism, process theology, and narrative theology.[4] Some of these overlap, and the last may be not so much a theology as a way of presenting theology. There is no one good way to classify them.

A popular view is to put them on a continuum with liberalism at one extreme and fundamentalism at the other. But there are serious problems with such a classification. One problem is that many of these terms cover a variety of theologies, and some of the terms are so fluid in their use that they are not specific in meaning.

Consider the two which are usually thought of as opposite extremes:

Liberalism and fundamentalism. The term "liberal" should mean one whose mind is open to all truth, no matter where it is found. But some who call themselves "liberal" have minds that are closed to all except their own beliefs. It is sometimes used to refer to a specific kind of beliefs. So the term is misleading. A fundamentalist once meant one who believes in the fundamental beliefs of Bible teachings. But it was used to mean belief in a certain group of doctrines. Now the term has become attached to a certain "literal" method of Biblical interpretation and to dispensationalism, so that it shuts out those who differ with these concepts.

For these and other reasons, classification and definition of various theologies is difficult, and not very useful. For example, to say that a certain theologian is an "evangelical" does not say much without further clarification. In many countries that simply says the theologian is not Roman Catholic. In the United States it has meant various things at different times. It usually means one who is committed to the Bible, and who accepts the atonement for sin in the crucifixion and resurrection of Christ. Yet the word is so unspecific that it is not very helpful as identification. Many of the other terms above have the same problem.

In the last decades or so the holiness movement has been shown to be a dynamic force in the shaping of American theology. The holiness movement, differing as it does from both fundamentalism, though squarely based on the authority of the Bible, is a meaningful and distinctive term of choice. It distinguishes churches teaching Scriptural holiness of heart and life from all others. This is being recognized more widely by historians of the American churches.

THE USE OF THE BIBLE IN THEOLOGY

One of the key points to look for in any theology is the attitude of the person to the Bible, and the use that person makes of the Bible in theology.

The first factor in using the Bible in doing theology is the basic assumption of the theologian as to what the Bible is. In the nineteenth and twentieth centuries, there has grown up a way of thinking which has strongly influenced theology and the attitude toward the Bible. Radical enlightenment thinkers have insisted that autonomous reason can know more surely than any revelation what is truth and what is not.

Reason is a gift of God, and should be used as carefully and universally as possible. But reason must not be allowed to be the sole source and test of truth. If it is, then it becomes something more than reason, and can be called rationalism. This we can define briefly as the belief that the mind, not divine revelation, is the source of religious truth. Thus we must use reason to decide what parts of the Bible are true and valid, and which are not.

Note that we are not at all rejecting or minimizing the role of reason in religion. Reason is necessary if we are to understand the Bible and what it has to say to us. Reason is essential if we are to know God and his will. We are instead insisting that human reason must never be placed above the Biblical revelation as the source of theology. Those who do this have more and more cut up the Bible into little pieces, discarded much of it as either wrong or irrelevant, and made themselves the judges of what Jesus may have said, and could not have said. Those of us who accept the Bible as normative may use the same facts of textual criticism, historical knowledge, archeology, linguistic and philological study, and other aids to Biblical study. But we use these methods, not destructively, but to help us gain a better understanding of God and of his will for us.

The fact that one accepts the Bible as revelation from God does not make that person's theology correct. The Bible must be interpreted and used as a source for theology. Then that theology must be carefully hammered out, using reason, tradition and personal experience with God as guides to an understanding of the Bible and its teaching.

In performing this task of doing theology, no one can avoid seeing the Bible through the spectacles of a tradition, and of personal experiences.

Biblical Criticism

Modern criticism of the Bible is an attempt to apply all that we know to the attempt to understand the Bible. So "criticism" is not necessarily wrong. Textual criticism is the attempt to study all the ancient manuscripts we have in order to decide the exact words originally written. This is necessary since until the fifteenth century, all books had to be copied by hand, or not at all. Since copying by hand is never perfectly done, each manuscript of any part of the Bible may differ in some small ways from all other copies. Many of these differences are of no importance, such as different ways of spelling a name or word. It is true that there are thousands of such variant readings (differences in a word or letter) in the New Testament, but most of them are not important. It has been estimated that of those thousands, only about one out of four hundred would make any difference in our interpretation or understanding, In the Old Testament we find a similar need for textual studies. We owe much to the scholars who have helped us to recover a more accurate text of the whole Bible. This is most valuable, as we cannot study what the Bible means until we discover what it says.

Historical Criticism

Historical criticism of the Bible has to do with the authorship, date and composition of individual books. This kind of study has helped immensely in the understanding of the Bible, and we should be grateful for it. Those who believe the Bible is authentic and inspired by God can use the methods of historical and grammatical study to great advantage.

We need to be aware, however, that there is another kind of radical historical criticism, which assumes that there is no such thing as inspired writing. Such scholars treat the Bible like any other book, and assume that some of it is true and some is not. Those of us who believe the Bible is from God through the instrumentality of human writers can study the work of such scholars, but should do it with full awareness of the source. We can learn to take what is valuable and lay aside the rest.

So Many Kinds of Theology

Each of the approaches to the Bible has its own theology supported by that approach. Some like to classify them by attaching a label to each type: Liberal, conservative, modernist, fundamentalist.

Perhaps the wisest course is to refuse to classify our theological position with one of those four terms, and seek to explain what the Bible tells us of the various aspects of theology. It would be most attractive to this writer to write an irenic theology with no attempt to show how it differs from any other. Yet one of the primary forces in the history of theology has been the attempt to build fences around the truth, and to say that it is wrong to go beyond the fence. Theology has been developed in order to show the falsehood of all other ways of thinking. It will therefore be necessary at times to go beyond "We believe this" and to say "We do not believe that." However, even when a certain amount of polemic reasoning seems essential, we will seek to do it in a Christian spirit, leaving the final judgment to God, who is omniscient and full of mercy.

The Final Test

The Bible is the final test of our beliefs. We should be committed to following truth revealed in the Bible wherever it may lead. Whatever we find the Bible clearly teaching, we must believe. We must keep ourselves open to new truth at all times, yet we must "test everything; hold fast what is good" (1 Thess. 5:21). The Christian should be one who loves the truth, and seeks after it with all diligence (Ps. 119:103). Paul once spoke of "those who are perishing, because they refused to love the truth and so be saved" (2 Thess. 2:10). He warned Timothy: "Follow the pattern of the sound words which you have heard from me, in the faith and love which are in Christ Jesus; guard the truth that has been entrusted to you by the Holy Spirit who dwells within us" (2 Tim. 1:13-14).

The best way to get a grasp of the various kinds of theology found in Protestant churches today is through a thorough study of historical theology. But our purpose here is to give a little guidance toward understanding where this theology stands in relation to the mainstream of Christian thought.

Sixteenth Century Reformation

The sixteenth century reformation marked a break with Roman Catholicism, with its allegiance to the Pope and its teaching that salvation was mediated to the person through a human representative of God who pronounced a person's sins forgiven. Luther and Calvin stand out as they taught that the individual can go directly to God for forgiveness, and needs no priest to intercede with God. Yet Luther taught that we can never in this life live the perfect love which God requires. That has to wait until death. Calvin, too, seemed to have no hope for real holiness before death. These two leaders laid the foundation for the Lutheran and Reformed types of theology, which include the many Lutheran churches, and all the Presbyterian and other Reformed churches.

In the eighteenth century the preaching, writing and singing of John and Charles Wesley marked the beginning of the Methodist and other Wesleyan churches preaching holiness as a possibility in this life. In the period between Luther and Wesley, Arminius had helped clear the way for the theology of Wesley. John Fox had taught holiness in a way very similar to Wesley, but among his followers—the Quakers—holiness was at a low ebb in the England of Wesley. Later, many of the Quakers have come into the mainstream of holiness teaching. Wesley himself learned much from the Pietist Moravians. From Pietism we learn the value of prayer and more intensive Bible study for each individual Christian, and the blessed experience of personal assurance of salvation. We should also learn from our Pietist background the necessity of practicing love for others as well as love for God. We can know God for ourselves, and have a clear assurance of God's presence.

The Church of God

The Church of God (Anderson, IN) is one of the churches which grew out of the nineteenth century holiness movement, with all its love for camp meetings. This group has combined holiness with a search for the unity of all Christians, and with a concept of the church which could make this unity possible.

It is from the background of this holiness group that this theology is written. There is here no desire to present any new theology. The Church of God has all along been determined to preach all the Bible teaches, and nothing else. So we have much in common with all Christians everywhere who have built their concepts on the foundation of a faith in the inspired word of God. Our faith in God as a Trinity, who created the whole universe, and who, through Christ, the Son of God, made salvation from sin possible, and who will one day bring the world to an end and take His faithful to be with him forever, leaving all others to outer darkness. All this we have in common with others, because it is the clear teaching of the Bible.

The Church of God has never intended to invent any new doctrine. The purpose, instead, is to preach the New Testament truths so as to bring as many as possible to salvation. At the same time there has been a determination to emphasize the possibility of holy living in this life, assurance of salvation, and the way out of the divided state of the church.

A Wesleyan Theology

The Church of God, then, is Wesleyan in theology, as opposed to Calvinist or Lutheran. We seldom hear our preachers quote Wesley, and could suspect that most of our preachers never read his works. Sometimes we say "Wesleyan/Arminian" and wonder if we ought to say "Arminian/Wesleyan," because Jacobus Arminius lived before John and Charles Wesley. However, this adds little to an understanding of our theology. Arminius was not Wesley's primary early mentor.[5]. Our theology is more directly related to that of the nineteenth century holiness movement, which is a slightly modified form of Wesleyan theology. One modification is that made by John Fletcher, a contemporary of Wesley. It was more a matter of emphasis on the baptism with the Holy Spirit as the means to sanctification. Both taught the work of the Holy Spirit, but Wesley seldom spoke of the baptism with the Spirit, while Fletcher emphasized it.

A second modification is also a matter of emphasis. Wesley taught that sanctification is wrought by the grace of God in response to the faith of the Christian. Phoebe Palmer, a great nineteenth century preacher in the Holiness Movement, preached that since it comes by faith, it can come suddenly, as soon as the Christian gives the saved self to God and believes that God accepts the gift.

This is the heart of the holiness emphasis in the theology of the Church of God, but another major emphasis has been that the unity of the church must be made real, and that the present divided state of the church into denominations is not pleasing to God. The combination of these twin truths have been the theological contribution of this reformation movement to the church[6]. They are bound together by the conviction that the holiness wrought in the heart by the Holy Spirit is the real secret to the unity of all Christians in one church—God's church.

As a part of the attempt to be free of denominational division, the Church of God has called itself a reformation movement. It has insisted that it is not the whole church, nor a "denomination" among other denominations. It has sought instead to be a movement toward unity in the church as a whole. All Christians are not in this movement, but only a small part of them. There has been an insistence instead that all Christians are in God's church, and have no need to join any other.

This, then, is the background from which this theology is written. It is hoped that it will appeal not merely to those who are in the Church of God reformation movement, but to all who love God, the Bible and the holiness God requires.

CHAPTER 2

CHRISTIAN BELIEF IN GOD'S EXISTENCE

> Thus says the Lord: Do not let the wise boast in their wisdom, do not let the mighty boast in their might, do not let the wealthy boast in their wealth; but let those who boast boast in this, that they understand and know me, that I am the Lord (Jer. 9:23-24a).

Since God is not visible to our eyes, how do we know for sure that God is? What if we were wrong, and there is no God? Since we have never seen God, how can we know him?

Christians believe in God. But that is not a very meaningful statement until we define the word "God." What do we mean by the word? What kind of God do Christians believe in? A full definition must wait until another chapter, but for this purpose we can say that God is the One who was before the world existed, who brought into being the kind of universe he chose to create from nothing (Heb. 11:3), and sustains it at every moment (Col. 1:17). Further, Christians know that there is only one God, and can be no other (Isa. 44:6).

How Do We Know God Is?

So Christians all believe in God. They have to believe in God in order to be Christians, for Christ is the Son of God (1 John 5:2). But what if Christians could be proven wrong on this basic point? What if the whole thing is a delusion, and there is no God after all? Since God is not apparent to the physical senses, it is seemingly possible to live one's life fairly well without believing that there is any God at all. Can we prove that God is?

Christian thinkers have not been unmindful of such questions, and have struggled long and seriously with them. Believing that we ought to face up to the thoughtful objections to Christianity so as to win the objectors to Christ, great thinkers of past centuries have hammered out a whole series of logical reasons for believing in God. But before we give some attention to the reasons for believing in God, we need to make some preliminary observations.

The Bible does not attempt to prove that God is. Strange as it may seem to us, the writers of the Bible did not feel it necessary to give logical proof for God's existence. They simply assumed it as a basic presupposition. They were as sure of God as they were of their families and friends. Only one who was wicked enough to play the part of a fool would claim that "there is no God" (Ps. 53:1). Such a person may *wish* God is not, because he wants to *act* as though there is no God. So the Bible writers, assuming that everyone believes in God, did not seek to prove His existence. They told of things God did, and if believed, these things would cause one to believe in God, but they never consciously sought to lay out logical reasons for believing that God is. The major problem of Israel was that their neighboring nations believed in too many gods.

The Bible also assumes that we can all know, through our own experience, that God is. "Be still and know that I am God" (Ps. 46:10). "The heavens are telling the glory of God; and the firmament proclaims his handiwork" (Ps. 19:1). Speaking of wicked people who reject the knowledge of God, Paul declares:

> For what can be known about God is plain to them, because God has shown it to them. Ever since the creation of the world his eternal power and divine nature, invisible though they are, have been understood and seen through the things he has made. So they are without excuse (Rom. 1:19-20).

It is far different with the believer in God through Jesus Christ. One discovers that God will reveal his presence and blessings to the believer in such a way that there is real assurance of salvation through God's grace and blessing. Then there is no longer doubt. "No longer shall they teach one another, or say to each other, 'Know the Lord,' for they shall all know me, from the least of them to the greatest, says the Lord; for I will forgive their iniquity, and remember their sin no more" (Jer. 31:34). We can know God for ourselves. We then have a strong foundation on which to build reasons which can help overcome the doubts of others who do not yet know.

Yet it is not wrong to seek to prove God's existence. Some conscientious Christians have concluded that it is wrong to seek to reason about spiritual things. They feel that doubt is always sinful. We must simply take spiritual ideas by faith, no matter how unreasonable they may seem to be. But it was not for that reason that the Biblical writers did not seek to reason about God. In their day, atheism was not the problem, but polytheism. The people around them believed in many gods, and it was the task of the prophets to show that God is *one*.

The Biblical writers were not averse to the use of reason. "Come now, let us reason together, says the Lord" (Isa. 1:18). "Always be prepared to make a defense to anyone who calls you to account for the hope that is in you" (I Pet. 3:15). Through Micah, God reasoned with the people about their sins (Micah 6). Malachi's didactic method was that of reasoning with the people about their relationship with God. When Jesus quoted what he called the "greatest commandment," he added one explanatory word and told us to love God with our mind (Matt. 22:37). Paul often used closely reasoned arguments to make his point clear or to prove it. For example, in Acts 17:22-31, when preaching to the philosophers in Athens, he started with their worship of an unknown god, and reasoned with them about the God who made all things. In 1 Corinthians 15, the great chapter on the resurrection, we find some of the most careful reasoning to support what he had preached about Jesus rising from the dead. So it is clear that God gave us our reasoning abilities to use in the search for truth, and in declaring it to others.

We must distinguish between knowing God and knowing about God. There is a fundamental difference between "knowing about God" and "knowing God". As Job said when the Lord revealed Himself to him, "I had heard of thee by the hearing of the ear, but now my eye sees thee" (Job 42:5). It is possible to know many things about God without knowing Him personally. It is also possible to know God without knowing much about Him. Since God is personal, not impersonal, it is possible for us, as conscious selves, to know Him in somewhat the same manner that we know one another. That is, we can have personal communion with God.

We must understand that when we apply words like "personal" to God, we are not saying that God is like human beings. We are saying rather that we human beings are a little bit like God, but in a very limited sense. Or we are taking the good characteristics of human beings and raising them to the infinite power and applying them to God. Otherwise we would have no words with which to speak of God at all. All we know is that God made us enough like himself that he can make possible a personal communion with us. In that we are different from all other creatures we know.

We know God through His works. Just as we can know something of a person by examining the things he has made, so we can learn some things about God by considering the universe which God has created.

> The heavens are telling the glory of God; and the firmament proclaims his handiwork (Ps. 19:1) When I look at your heavens, the work of your fingers, the moon and stars that you have established; what are human beings that you are mindful of them, mortals that you care for them? (Ps. 8:3-4).

When we read such passages, and the questions God asked Job in Job 38—41, we learn that we can see the glory of God in all the universe he has made. We can see in the world around us something of the power, glory and majesty of God who made it all. We can learn about God from looking at what he has made.

Yet it is easy to over-emphasize this fact and feel that we need to do nothing more than study "nature" to have an adequate concept of God. This is simply not so. We can and should be moved to worship by seeing the wonders of nature, but when this happens, we must worship God who made the wonders, and not the wonders themselves. God has created the mountains, the forests, and the rivers, but it would be pagan to think of these things as being worthy of worship. We worship, not the created things, but the Creator.

A second problem with knowing God through His works is that there is not much that we can know in this way. If we had no Bible and no record of Jesus Christ, there are only a few basic facts we could know about God through a study of nature. First, we could know that God works in an orderly fashion. This universe is so orderly that scientists are able to express in precise mathematical formulas the ways in which things operate. We cannot ignore the problems of the New Physics, which has found it necessary to admit a certain indeterminacy in the extremely small particles. Yet this fact does not nullify the concept of order in the universe. As Thomas Oden points out so clearly:

> It remains a premise of scientific inquiry that the world is characterized by intelligibility, which itself is often called the "natural order." Even when physicists discover an odd principle of indeterminacy, such as the Heisenberg principle, when nature at times appears unpredictable, those who have pursued that principle have found that there is, even in the principle of random indeterminacy of atomic interaction, a meaning and order.[7]

The Heisenberg principle deals with subatomic physics, which can be distinguished from the visible universe. If there were no signs of order at all in the universe, or if the signs of order were not prominent, scientific experiment would have no meaning. So we can learn by observation that the world is created with orderliness.

Second, we could know that God has immense power. We see this power in the rivers which we use to make electricity, and in the tiny atom which we harness for bombs and for industrial power. We see it in the force of great storms, which dwarf even our greatest bombs. And when we turn from this earth to the vastness of the interstellar spaces revealed by astronomy, our minds reel as we seek to comprehend. The immensity of God's power is overwhelming.

Third, we could know that God is concerned with the smallest details. When we turn from the telescope to the microscope we do not move out of the area of God's concern. We find the same precision in the atoms that we find in the planets and nebulae. God never neglects details. Fourth, we could know something of God's generosity in providing for us. In the last hundred years there has been an increasing awareness of the possibility that we will run out of some of the things we need to sustain a technological civilization like ours. Yet the problem is not in nature, but is our use of it. God has provided air, water, solar power, and other natural resources in amazing abundance.

This much we can learn about God by a study of nature. But there are truths of basic importance which we could never know in this way. We could not be sure that God is one. We could not know of God's hatred of sin, His justice, or His redeeming love. And we could never know anything of Christ and His salvation. We could not know that God is personal, yet this is one of the most important aspects of God's nature. Nor could we know of His holiness. We can know something about God by a contemplation of His works in creation, but not some of the vitally important aspects of God's nature.

We know God as He reveals Himself to us. God is infinite, but we are limited in knowledge, power and wisdom. God transcends us so greatly that we could never know Him if He did not choose to reveal Himself to us. After God created us, He took the initiative in reaching down to show us Himself and His will. Otherwise we could never know Him, for He is far beyond our reach. When we seek to know Him, our seeking is a response to the redemptive work of His Holy Spirit.

The Problem of Evil

There is another problem with learning about God from what he has made. This comes from the fact that there are so many aspects of the creation that do not seem sensible or just to us. We can call these things "natural evils" as opposed to moral evil. But they constitute a real problem. Why is cancer allowed to kill? Why must earthquakes, floods, lightning, and volcanoes do so much damage? Did God have to make mosquitos? Is this the best of all possible worlds?

A variety of responses have been given to the problem of evil in nature. An old response was to believe in many gods, some good and some evil. This was **polytheism. Dualism** taught that there was that good and evil had always existed in conflict with one another, with neither winning the victory. Dualism was found in ancient Persian Zoroastrianism and in Manichaeism.

Another response is to deny the existence of evil, by saying that some things only *seem* to be evil. This has found some expression is nineteenth-century Christian Science. Yet this is a most difficult position to hold logically, at least in its more inclusive form. Trouble is too much with us.

Some have decided that with so much evil in the world, both natural evil and moral evil, it is impossible to believe in a good God. Some have sadly come to this conclusion after a tragedy has come to some loved one. They have come to feel that if there is a God, he cannot be both *good* and *all-powerful*. One was Hartshorne, who concluded this after the death of his beloved only son.[8]

The Christian Response to Natural Evil

We know that God is good, and that he loves us. We cannot know whether or not this is the best of all possible worlds, but we do know that there was no evil in the Creator who made this world as it is. Some of the ways we imagine would improve the world would not really be improvements. And since this world is a place and time of testing and growth, much that seems to be evil may be the best preparation for God's eventual plan for us. First of all, we can assume that God has plans we can never fully comprehend.

> For my thoughts are not your thoughts, nor are your ways my ways, says the Lord. For as the heavens are higher than the earth, so are my ways higher than your ways and my thoughts than your thoughts (Isa. 55:8-9).

The Christian way is never that of denying the existence of evil, either natural or moral. We know that evil exists, but we also know that God exists and that He loves us. God is able to give us the victory over all evil. "I can do all things through him who strengthens me" (Phil. 4:13). Paul said this after admitting that he had been suffering severe hardships. He meant by this that he was able, by the grace of God, to bear up under all burdens and go on doing God's will.

In writing to the church in Corinth, he wrote: "We are afflicted in every way, but not crushed; perplexed, but not driven to despair; persecuted, but not forsaken; struck down, but not destroyed; always carrying in the body the death of Jesus, so that the life of Jesus may also be made visible in our bodies " (2 Cor. 4:8-11).

Paul was admitting that he was not finding it easy to preach the gospel in new places. Travel was difficult, and there was often severe opposition to his preaching. He did not always have enough money for food, clothing and lodging. But he was not letting anything deter him from preaching the gospel. In Romans 8:37-39, after writing of his great faith in God's providence, and listing some of the hardships we can face, he said,

> No, in all these things we are more than conquerors through him who loved us. For I am convinced that neither death, nor life, nor angels, nor rulers, nor things present, nor things to come, nor powers, nor height, nor depth, nor anything else in all creation, will be able to separate us from the love of God in Christ Jesus our Lord.

Some Do Not Believe in God

Most people who reject God do not doubt His existence, but probably every generation has had some who have apparently convinced themselves that it is not reasonable to believe in God. Such persons give various reasons for their doubt, but in the last century or so several arguments have been most persistently put forward.

"*It is a superstition.*" Like belief in witches, ghosts, and haunted houses, the belief in God should be laid aside in these enlightened times, they say. Is it an accident that in the English language the word *spirit* can be applied both to God and to ghosts? In our day, when there is so much stress on science, but not on theology or philosophy, many ordinary persons have a vague feeling of uneasiness at believing in God when he can no longer believe in haunted houses. Some of this comes from the fact that as we mature, we learn to lay aside many childish beliefs as we learn better explanations, and it may be difficult to decide how much to give up.

This argument also takes more sophisticated forms. One example is that of Karl Marx (1818-1883), who deified the Hegelian interpretation of history. Believing then that progress can only come through revolution, and that both progress and revolution are inevitable, he found no place in his scheme for a supreme being. Rather than call on a nonexistent God for help, he said, people ought to further the revolutions which bring progress.

Another form of this argument is the anthropomorphism of Ludwig Feuerbach (1804-1872), who persuaded himself that man has created God in his own image. Therefore man ought to give up his belief in God and trust only in his own efforts. He should outgrow his belief in God. Others of these "apostles of Atheism" such as Sigmund Freud (1856-1939), Friedrich W. Nietsche (1844-1900), laid the foundation for a "religion of suspicion" or a suspicion of all religion. This direction was furthered by such twentieth-century nihilistic philosophers as Jean-Paul Sartre (1905-1980) and Albert Camus (1913-1960).

This development took another turn in the 1960's with the "God is dead" movement. Some of the leaders of that movement were still searching for God, and felt sad that they were dead to Him. But vast numbers of their readers no longer care. They may use the word "God," but do not mean by that anything real or important. They seek for satisfaction in other powers, whether science or some eastern "guru."

"God is unknowable" There may be a God, but if there is, some feel there is no way to be sure of it. Such philosophers as David Hume (1711-1776) and Immanuel Kant (1724-1804) are thought by some to have proved that we cannot know anything about God with certainty. But what they did was to show that there is no way to prove beyond doubt that God exists. Thus they demonstrated what Paul said in 1 Corinthians 1:21: "For since, in the wisdom of God, the world did not know God through wisdom, God decided, through the foolishness of our proclamation, to save those who believe."

It is not by the wisdom of our human minds that we can prove the nature of God. If we are to know God as loving Savior, He must reveal himself to us.

At the same time, we know that no one can prove by logical argument that there is no God. Actually, not many have tried. It is easier for the opponent of Christianity simply to ignore God, or to insist that belief in God is simply an emotional prop needed by weak minds. Those who are strong and mature do not need such props, they say. Others assume that since one cannot prove by logic or science that God is, then God is not. But this does not follow. We human beings have no absolute proof for anything. Knowledge does not require absolute proof. Scientific knowledge is not that which has absolute proof, but rather theories which make it possible to understand and, to some extent, predict events. So we must not require that someone offer us absolute proof that God exists.

Reasons for Believing God Is

Philosophers have developed what are called "arguments" for the existence of God. They are not final proofs, nor "arguing," but logical reasons for believing that God exists. No one of these classical proofs is final proof for the existence of God, and they are not meant to be such. Fault can be found in one way or another with each of them. Yet the cumulative effect of all of them is great.

The *cosmological* argument is so called because it seeks to show that such a One as God must have existed to bring the universe into being. Anselm stated it in the original form. It is sometimes stated now as an etiological, or "First Cause" argument. In this form it reasons that this universe did not cause itself to exist, and therefore there must have been a cause for it. That cause came before anything in the universe existed, and therefore was a First Cause - God.

The *teleological* argument states that the universe shows marks of planning or design. If it was designed, there must have been a Designer. That Designer must have existed before anything else, and therefore must have been God.

Paley's illustration of the watch has become famous, and telling. Paley suggested that if a person strolling on the beach of an island found a watch, he would study it and know that there was a watchmaker who must have produced it. He would reason from the design of the watch to the mind and work of a watchmaker.

It has been suggested that if he found not only that the watch was well made, but that it contained a full machine shop and could produce other watches as good as itself or better, that would say even more about the one who had designed it. Yet we find aspects of our universe more marvelous than any watch.

Other strong arguments are the *anthropological*, which argues from the higher qualities of human beings, which seem to point to One who is higher and earlier than the universe; and the *ontological*, which seeks to show that the idea of God is a necessary idea, and must be true.

The anthropological argument is like the cosmological in that it reasons from the human being we know to the supreme Creator whom we seek to know. It is a special case of the other.

All of these traditional arguments for the existence of God do not amount to absolute proof. However, they are not therefore useless, for two reasons: We do not have absolute proof of much of anything in human existence. Even in the physical sciences, there is not absolute proof, but only strong probabilities, strange as that may seem to those who have not studied the philosophy of science. So we must not expect absolute proof in theology.

The usefulness of the traditional arguments, which have been sketchily presented here, is that they can help those who have honest doubts about the existence of God. The committed atheist scoffs at them. But the honest doubter may be confused by what one has read or heard, and may be helped by a clear exposition of certain arguments. We cannot prove to a committed atheist that God is, but we may remove some of the rational stumbling blocks of one who is confused. Besides, as Christians, we need to use the minds God gave us, and do our best to "out-think opponents of Christianity, as well as out-love them," as Elton Trueblood said so often in his lectures.

Some False Concepts of God

In addition to considering reasons for believing in God in Jesus Christ, we need to consider the alternatives. The concepts we are about to contemplate have developed in a formal way in the last centuries. Understanding them would help us deal more helpfully with people around us, as these worldviews are influential today.

Deism imagines that God made the world, started it going and then left it completely alone. So the God of the deist has nothing to do with the world or anything in it. He is more like a clock maker who made the clock of the universe, wound it up, and then left it alone to run down of its own accord.

Deism arose during the seventeenth and eighteenth centuries, when it seemed to many that science would be able to discover all that would ever be needed by mankind. Since reason was thought to be all-sufficient some decided that God was therefore unnecessary. God did not control or care about the universe, if he ever had. God was only the First Cause, who then left the universe to its own devices. There was no need for revelation in deism, since human beings could learn all they needed to know by means of scientific exploration. Deism in this classic form did not attract a large following for long, and did not have a unified set of beliefs. Many went on to naturalism, and some felt that some form of Christianity might be helpful. Some deists, like Voltaire, were hostile to Christianity, but others, like Locke, were not. Some believed in God, but not as Christians believe. Buckminster Fuller, for example, talked about God, but thought of God, not as a personal being, but only as superior Intellect.

Deism took many forms, and we have described one of its more extreme forms, for the sake of simplicity. But on the whole it was an unstable sort of belief, and served as a transition to others ways of thinking about the universe and God.

Naturalism went only a short step beyond deism, by deciding that there is no point in assuming that there ever was a God. Why believe there is a God, if he has nothing to do with us or with anything else in the universe? There is nothing but "things." Deism considered God irrelevant and unnecessary, so naturalists decided there was no use in imagining that God ever was. Things have always been. Matter is all that matters. The whole universe has always existed in some form, and was never created. It may have once existed in some such form as a tiny lump somewhere, which somehow exploded into the universe as it is now. Such an explosion is now spoken of as the "Big Bang" by some astronomers, though they never seek to explain the origin of the power in the lump of matter which caused the explosion. Nothing comes from nothing, yet there is so much matter and power in the universe that anyone holding such a theory must explain how it all could come about with no creative power to originate it.

In spite of the fact that naturalism has no explanation of the origin of the universe, it appeals to people in our day who have been taught to have such faith in science.

Naturalism finds another serious problem in the origin of human personality. If there is no higher power and mentality planning the universe and all that is in it, then all things happen by chance. If this is the way new things originate - by chance - then how can anyone explain the difference between plants and animals; much less the difference between animals and human beings? One way is to say that there is no great difference. The developments in comparative psychology led to behaviorism, and the insistence that no religious ideas are needed to explain human nature and actions. Human beings are simply animals which have evolved a little further. Another way is to say that we do not know yet, but we must keep on looking for some explanation. Christians simply believe in the creative and sustaining power and supervision of God.

One form of naturalism is *Secular Humanism*, which must be distinguished from literary humanism and Christian humanism. Christianity has always had a strong interest in human beings, since we cannot love God without loving people (1 John 4:20). But by secular humanism we mean the kind of philosophy which denies God and insists that human beings are the highest beings in the universe. Some feel that there may be higher beings in the universe somewhere, as they may have evolved longer and higher than we have. Carl Sagan has made this view popular.

Another form of naturalism is that which Karl Marx and Max Engels developed, by building on the philosophy of Friedrich Hegel. This has been most influential in some parts of the world. It is true that because of its failures, some Russian leaders have recently renounced it, but it still has strong supporters there, and Communist countries are wondering what to put in its place.

Skepticism is simply doubt that God exists. The skeptic says that she has never seen God, and cannot believe there is such a one. It is possible to live in this world without firm belief in the God revealed to us in the Bible.

Agnosticism may go further than skepticism and insist that God cannot be known by anyone. Other agnostics wish they could be convinced that God is what Christians teach, but are still searching for Him. Whether there is a God or not must remain a total mystery to human beings, say those who are convinced that agnosticism is the only true way. If there is a God, he cannot be known by us. However skepticism and agnosticism tend to be individual decisions rather than established "schools" of thought.

Pantheism says that God is everything and everything is God. Spinoza was one representative of pantheism. This would mean that there is no God such as Christians believe in, who created the world and works in and through it. God would then be nothing more than the world, and the sum total of all that is in the universe.

Pantheism, in the western world, seems to be one way out of nontheistic naturalism. One simply learns that God is everything and everything is God. There is no god beyond the matter of this universe. That is all there is. Yet this seems to leave personality, thought and desire out of it all. And it still leaves human beings as lonely persons, with nothing but matter, plants and animals with which to commune. Some forms of eastern religions are thoroughly pantheistic, but westerners find it almost impossible to understand those forms of thought, with its completely foreign set of assumptions and way of thinking. For several decades it has been popular to try, but without great success.

The New Age as it is called now, is not a unified group, or even a cohesive movement at this time. It is simply a collection of eclectic ideas held by a variety of people in this country, and there is no definition of beliefs which are held by all who use the term of themselves. For some, it is basically a westernized, or Americanized form of eastern pantheism. Like naturalism, some New Agers deny the existence of a transcendent God. It is similar to pantheism, but some of the best-known proponents stress that you are your own god. This is the ultimate idolatry, but it is accepted at face value by many as sober truth which they must try to absorb. The whole teaching is full of contradictions, so that there is no point in trying to describe it here, except to point out that it flatly denies the basic truths of Christianity by denying God and Jesus Christ the Savior of the world. When they talk about Jesus, they declare that he was a *seeker after truth* like the rest of us; and they distort his teaching. When they deny the existence of a transcendent God, the deny the very foundation of the Bible and all that it teaches.

Atheistic Humanism seeks to think of human beings as the highest being there is, and declares that if there is a god, it is us. We must be content to be our own gods, they say. They insist that there is no god out there, so we might just as well get used to the idea that all the solutions to problems must come from within our own selves. There is no use in praying, for we are only talking to ourselves.

Christian Faith in God

Christians know that God is, and that he sent his Son into the world to save us from our sins. We know this through faith in God, the faith which has brought salvation and the blessing of God into our hearts and lives. We have been changed by the power of God, so we cannot doubt that God is. "Whoever would draw near to God must believe that he exists and that he rewards those who seek him" (Heb. 11:6). This faith in God is absolutely essential for a Christian, as it is the basis of all Christian belief. As a doctrine, it is the doctrine without which no other Christian doctrine could subsist.

CHAPTER 3

GOD REVEALS HIMSELF

> Thus says God, the Lord, who created the heavens and stretched them out, who spread out the earth and what comes from it, who gives breath to the people upon it and spirit to those who walk in it: I am the Lord (Isa. 42:5-6a).

Can we really come to know God? If God did not want us to know him, could we discover him anyway? Is it possible to know all about God and his plans by a study of the world? Is it possible for God to tell us about himself? How can we be sure?

The universe is so vast that it is beyond human imagination. We can use numbers which symbolize its size, and we can understand those symbols, but who can comprehend this reality? The nearest star to the earth is about twenty-five trillion miles away. That is twenty-five million million miles! One way to handle such figures is to use a much longer unit of measurement than the mile. So astronomers use the light year as a unit of measurement. This is the distance that light travels in one year - nearly six trillion miles. This helps, since it gives us a much smaller figure. It means that the *nearest* star is 4.3 light years away. If certain stars disappeared fifty million years ago, we would just now be finding out about it!

Some Christians simply refuse to believe such figures about the vast size of the universe. In the same way some refuse to believe that the age of the earth and the universe is as large as scientists believe. They have problems reconciling such concepts with their understanding of the Bible teaching about creation. If the universe was created only six thousand years ago, as James Ussher calculated in the seventeenth century, then it would be most difficult to understand the vast ages and distances of modern astronomy and geology. But that this is not an insoluble problem we shall see more clearly in chapter 7. The universe is vast.

Yet the Bible tells us that God made all of this, and that it is all under His control. The Bible says that before any of these things existed, God was; and that God created all of these things out of nothing. The Bible declares that God made us enough like Himself that He and we can have a conscious, loving relationship. It declares further that when people turned from Him in rebellion, God worked for thousands of years to woo them back to Himself, and then sent His own Son into the world to redeem us for Himself.

When sinful people killed God's Son, God raised Him up from the dead, and promised sinners that He stood ready to use this same resurrection power to overcome the power of human sin (Eph.1:19-20), and to raise people up to a new, living, loving relationship with God in Christ Jesus (Eph. 2:4-7). God had made "the wrath of mortals to praise Him" (Psa. 76:10), and made salvation available to every human being. In brief outline, this is the message of the Bible about God.

Talk About God

It is necessary to say something about the use of language in theology. When we are speaking about God, we have to use human language to speak of One who transcends all human experience. We have no words to apply to that which we have not experienced, so we have to choose words which compare the unknown to something known. A little girl saw a tiny insect light on the outside of a window and called it a "bird." A primitive tribe saw an airplane for the first time and called it a "bird." They used a word they knew to apply to something beyond their experience.

God is not only beyond our present experience, in his absolute existence and fullness of being, he is beyond our full knowledge and comprehension. Further, God is not one member of a class of beings; he is the only one of his kind. We can never know all there is to know about God, and what we do know we are forced to describe in human terms. So we use metaphors to describe what we know of God.

Yet God can never be *fully* known by human experience. "It is he alone who has immortality and dwells in unapproachable light, whom no one has ever seen or can see" (1 Tim. 6:16). Finite human beings can never fully comprehend the infinite God.

Theological language is not angelic language, with special words to describe accurately the being and attributes of God. If it were, we would not understand the words. Ordinary language, which refers to empirical objects, is not sufficient to speak of God. So we have to use symbols or metaphors to speak of God and spiritual matters. The parables of Jesus are excellent examples of this way of speaking, as when he compared God to a loving Father welcoming his prodigal son.

Another way we can use words to describe what God is like is to say what he is not. We say that God is infinite, which is to say that God cannot be fully known or described, as He is beyond any and all words we can use. Some writers are so convinced of the inadequacy of human words to speak of God that they reject theological language as nonsense. Such are the logical positivists. Others fall back on mystical experience as the only way to know anything about God, though what they feel they know cannot be put into words. Either of these extremes leaves us with no possibility of theology. If we go to either extreme, we find that nothing about God can be put into words. Yet we do not have to abandon the theological task.

Still another way of speaking of God is to compare him to the best there is in human beings, and say that God is like that, but infinitely better. All this discussion makes more clear the love of God for human beings, as he cut through all the difficulties and began to reveal to us something of his own nature and work.

What we learn of God we put into words by means of metaphors, analogies and models. One of the Biblical models of God is "Father." He is not literally our Father. Yet he is like the best of loving, caring human fathers in the way he supplies our needs and does his best to help us in all we do for Him. Surely this model has enriched our knowledge of God.

There are two objections to this model of God as "Father," that have been raised in modern times. One is that some people have such unloving fathers, or no father in the home, so that the image is either meaningless, or worse. This is a real problem for some, and we need to be aware of it so as to make helpful explanations to them. Use with such persons other biblical models which express compassionate concern, protection, provision for needs, and loving discipline.

A second strong objection has been made by some radical feminists. Some of them have strongly rejected any reference to God as Father, and refuse to use any masculine pronouns in referring to God. A few like to speak of God as "Father-Mother" or as "Mother." Of this we shall have more to say . In considering this objection to the Fatherhood of God, we should note that "Father" is the third most frequently used term for God in the Gospels. As we consider the way Jesus spoke of the heavenly Father, we come to feel that the revolt against the term is often "a revolt against a caricature of the true God whom we come to know through Jesus"[9]

There are some Biblical texts which compare the work of God to that of a mother (e.g. Isa. 42:14; 49:15; 66:13; Luke 13:34). At the same time, the Biblical writers, being confronted with the fertility goddesses of other nations, shunned any symbolism which described God as a mother goddess. The same attitude was seen in the early Christian writers for the same reason. In modern times the Shakers and Mary Baker Eddy have approved the concept of a Father-Mother God. Yet we use the concept of Father instead, knowing that there are dangers in departing from the language of Jesus in his teaching about God. God is neither male nor female, as he transcends sex.

Our primary aim in this regard is to make sure that we do not depersonalize God by the words we use about him. The use of the term "Father" prevents this depersonalization. At the same time we recognize that the fatherhood of God is not an exclusive term, and can be enriched by other forms of symbol, such as "friend," and "Creator"[10]

More will have to be said later about what God is like. For the present, we mast be careful not to read too much into some of the words we use about God, but seek to use them carefully, and recognize always that we must not bring God down to our human level by the way we speak of him in human terms.

Necessity of Revelation

How much could we know about God without the Bible? How much could we learn from the universe about the One who made it? Quite a lot. We could learn that God loves order, for everywhere we look we see evidence of order and system. It all fits together marvelously, as though very carefully planned. We could learn much about the greatness and wisdom of God. We might even be able to infer that God is personal, since God has to be greater than the persons He has created.

But it is at this very point that we come face to face with the need for some special revelation by God of His own self. God is personal, by which we do not mean that He has a body, but rather that He can think and feel, and that He knows Himself to be Himself. Now a person cannot be known in the same way a thing can be known. A thing can be studied and known objectively, by physical examination. But a person can only be known as she discloses herself in various ways. The thoughts, feelings, hopes, fears and knowledge of a person can only be known by another person if that person reveals them in some way. There are no scientific instruments by which to examine these aspects of a person directly. Without conscious or unconscious revelation, they cannot be known by another person. This is as true with God as with any human person.

Although natural revelation can give us knowledge of God the Creator, it can never show us God the Savior nor Jesus Christ our Lord. Thus it can never show us the gospel of salvation. Reason alone can never be the sole source of Christian truth, since it can never reveal God as Savior.

Unaided (?) Reason

Since Kant, we have known that we cannot prove God by mere reason. Some moved from this to a theology which was anthropocentric, and denigrated divine revelation. We must reject this kind of theology, and insist on the necessity of revelation initiated by God. It is essential for God to reveal himself to us or we will never come to a saving knowledge of him and his love.

Reason is good. Human reason was given by God, and is to be used to the glory of God. There is nothing wrong with reason in and of itself. It is part of what distinguishes us from animals. Reason is to be used in our search for God and his will. Without reason we could not understand God's revelation of himself. Without careful use of reason we would never rid ourselves of false ideas and concepts. Without the use of reason we could have no theology. God intends for us to use reason as we seek to understand him. So reason is good.

Reason has its place. Our point is that reason has its place in the whole process of knowing God and communicating with him, but it is not the primary source of knowledge about God. One cannot believe in God with no comprehension of his existence. So reason supplements God's revelation of himself to us, and gives us the ability to receive that communication.

There is no unaided reason in our search for God. Because of the work of the Holy Spirit in revealing God to us, there is no such thing as unaided reason seeking for God. This means that to speak of knowing God without the aid of revelation is merely a theoretical statement. We have the help of the Holy Spirit, and do not work alone seeking for God. Jesus declared, "No one can come to me unless the Father who sent me draws him" (John 6:44). God draws us through the Spirit. Speaking of this work of the Spirit, Jesus said, "And when he comes, he will convince the world of sin and of righteousness and of judgment" (John 16:8 — see further in verses 9-11). This work of the Spirit is often called "prevenient grace." This most important concept will be considered more thoroughly in later chapters.

What we need to see at the moment is that it is futile to deny the possibility of revelation. God does seek to reveal himself to every human being. The Spirit of God works in every person, as much as he is allowed to do so, to prevent sin. There is no way for us to know what the world would be like without this prevenient grace of God in people, whether recognized or not.

Reason is not Rationalism. The two words "reason" and "rational" are closely related. "Rational" means "able to use reason." Yet we must carefully distinguish rationalism from the use of reason. We must use reason in theology as we do in every other aspect of our living (Isa. 1:18; Job 13:3). But the term "rationalism" in theology refers to the view that reason is in itself a source of knowledge superior to revelation in the Bible. Rationalism amounts to a denial of revelation, since statements of the Bible must be judged true or false by our reason. If we do not consider a statement of the Bible to be reasonable, we reject it—according to rationalism. This puts reason as judge over the Biblical words, whereas the Bible, as God's revelation is our judge (John 12:48).

God reveals himself in his works

Some people live in the world of nature but deny that God exists. They see the marvels of nature, but refuse to admit that it was all created by the omnipotent (all powerful), omniscient (all knowing) God. Such persons deny that God can be known by His works, for they begin by denying that there is a God to be known. However, this denial of the existence of God does not disprove our concept of general revelation - that God reveals Himself in the things which He has made. If some cannot or will not see Him, He is still there, and their blindness does not change the fact.

The fact is that God does reveal something of Himself and His nature in the things which He has made. Just as an artist or builder reveals something of his own ideas, hopes and abilities in what he makes, so God reveals something of what He is like in what He has created. Theologians call this "general revelation". If we seek to analyze it, we find that God has revealed something of Himself and His nature in various aspects of His creation.

An Orderly Universe. We call all creation a "universe" because we are so impressed with the fact that the whole is a unit, in which all the parts fit together marvelously, as though planned by some great intellect. As we have seen in the previous chapter, all the parts are interrelated and interdependent. All the things that exist fit together in a single whole.

The importance and significance of this fact can be seen by contrasting it with the opposite possibility. This would be either that all things came into being by chance without any guiding Intelligence, or that they were made by a multitude of unrelated gods. In either case there would be no overall interdependence of the parts, and there would be no consistency which could be developed into physical and biological sciences. Each of the parts would be independent and unrelated to other parts. The result would be chaos.

The Consistency of the Universe. There is enough order in the universe for scientists to study it with some hope of learning how things work.[11] In the basically consistent operation of the universe, we see how systematically God works and thinks. We see his unity in his works. The world was not created by many minds, nor even by a committee, but by one God.

Beauty and Appreciation. As far back in history as we can go, humanity has demonstrated appreciation for beauty through producing art.

When people lived in rude caves, they scratched or painted pictures on the wall. When they first learned to make tools for themselves, they tried to make them beautiful in shape as well as utilitarian. Soon they began decorating tools in various ways. In the earliest Old Testament times we read of people expressing their love of beauty (cf. Gen. 3:6; 4:21; 12:10).

Both natural beauty and human appreciation of beauty speak of the nature of God. The existence of beauty speaks of something in the nature of God which goes beyond orderliness. And the fact of human appreciation of beauty would be hard to understand apart from creation by God who loves beauty.

Reality of Love. When we consider the whole of creation as the work of God, we must include the human mind and heart as well as other things. When we do, we realize that not only does the existence of beauty speak of God, but human appreciation of beauty also speaks of the nature of God Who created us. He created us in such a way that we could have and develop an appreciation of beauty.

In the same way, God made us in such a way that we have the capacity for receiving and giving love. There are various kinds and levels of human love, and it may be that not all are equally capable of showing love, but it is a universal human experience. Some who scoff at it then show it—almost to their own surprise.

Natural revelation is not enough

> I thank thee, Father, Lord of heaven and earth, that thou hast hidden these things from the wise and understanding and revealed them to babes; yea, Father, for such was thy gracious will. . .and no one knows who the Son is except the Father, or who the Father is except the Son and any one to whom the Son chooses to reveal him (Luke 10:21-22).

We have been speaking of the ways in which God reveals Himself in His works, the revelation which is called "natural revelation" or "general revelation." It is true that God does reveal Himself through the things He has made, but there are two major problems with this revelation: It is obscure, and it is partial.

First, it is obscure. It is possible to look at this world and all that is in it for a long time without ever seeing God or recognizing the works of God. It is possible to see the beauty of the world without once thinking that this was created by a God Who loves beauty. The universe does not speak to everyone of the unity of God, though once it is seen and accepted it is obvious.

The creation does not speak clearly enough of God for it to be the only way we learn of Him. It is true that the "heavens are telling the glory of God; and the firmament proclaims his handiwork" (Psa. 19:1), but many who do not already believe may not hear the message. This is seen from the fact that so many have worshiped parts of the universe rather than its Creator.

But an even more important problem with this natural revelation is the fact that it is only partial, and cannot reveal some of the more important facts about God and His nature. Paul contrasted the wisdom of this world's reasoning with the wisdom of God, and insisted that God's wisdom revealed what we could not otherwise know:

> And my speech and my message were not in plausible words of wisdom, but in demonstration of the Spirit and power, that your faith might not rest in the wisdom of men but in the power of God... But we impart a secret and hidden wisdom of God... And we impart this in words not taught by human wisdom but taught by the Spirit, interpreting spiritual truths to those who possess the Spirit. (1 Cor. 2:4-5, 7, 13).

The Corinthians were excited about the kind of wisdom which the Greek 'mystery religions' claimed to give to initiates. Paul insisted that the true wisdom is that which God reveals through the Holy Spirit. This revealed wisdom goes far beyond anything human beings can discover or understand on their own (Isa. 55:8-9; Job 9:10-11).

At the same time, we must recognize that when we seek of purely human knowledge, without revelation, we are speaking of an abstraction which does not exist. No one is totally without the work of God in the mind or heart. We may think we are working without the help of God, but that is not true. Yet once we know God and seek to learn from him, He can teach us much more.

GOD IS PERSONAL

We can never learn from nature that God is personal, yet that is the most basic fact we need to know about Him. By this we mean that God is aware of Himself as One who knows, feels, chooses, and loves. We mean that God is not merely impersonal, unfeeling Law. He is not blind, unthinking Nature. He has all the good characteristics of personality., but raised to infinity. This is basic to all the best we know about God.

When we say that God is personal, we are saying that God is not impersonal. We are saying that He has created human beings as persons - thinking, knowing, feeling, choosing, loving - and that He must be greater than that which He has created. This means that He must have the characteristics of personality. Otherwise, how could He have created man's personality? We are created in the image of God (Gen. 1:26-27) and are his offspring (Acts 17:29), made by him to search after him and know him (Acts 17:26-27). It is, then, valid for us to speak of God in human terms. We can do so without thinking of God as human.

We are not saying that God is limited to the characteristics of human nature. God's personality must be infinitely more complex than human nature, and infinitely greater and richer. We are saying that God is like the best there is in us, only infinitely greater and purer, and guided by infinite wisdom and knowledge. He has all the good characteristics of human personality, but raised to the infinite power.

Of course, in all of this, we are only stating the obverse of Genesis 1:27, which states that people were made in the image of God. Our own personalities, with self-consciousness, emotion, self-determination and moral discrimination, give us some clue to the nature of the God Who could create such personalities.

We should be aware that it has been traditional in theology to speak of the divine Trinity as three "Persons." This comes from the fact that in early church discussions, the Latin term *Persona* was used of God. But it did not mean just what the English word "person" means today. When we read the term as applied to God by theologians, we can understand it as speaking of the fact that God is not impersonal.

In a personal communication, John Stanley pointed out six ways in which Genesis 1:26-31 indicates that human beings are the acme of God's creation: 1. The space allotted to the description of the creation of humans. 2. God spoke personally to mankind, "you." 3. Emphasized this part of creation by saying "Let us . . ." 4. Sexuality is specifically mentioned. 5. Instead of "good," God said "very good." 6. God made them stewards of creation.

The fact that God is Personal means that He can never be adequately known through the *things* He has made. For example, one can learn much about an artist by examining the painting he has done. It is easy to think of some of the things one might learn in this way about the artist; but it is even easier to think of the many facets of his personality which could never be learned from a study of his paintings. And what of his hopes, his plans, his desires, and his love? The person is more than his works. He is more than can be communicated in his works. So if one is to know the person himself, he should meet the worker. One might then learn much more about him by listening to him explain his own works, but the knowledge would come from the person more than from what he made, or even what he said.

We see then that a person can only be adequately revealed through a person, and to a person. A person can reveal facts about himself in words, but if we are to know the person, we must know more than his words. Now we see how important it is to understand God as a Person. When we recognize this, we understand why we cannot learn enough about God through a study or contemplation of the universe He has created. Natural revelation is not enough to bring us to saving knowledge of God Himself. We need something more.

GOD REVEALS HIMSELF IN CHRIST

An astonishing thing is found in Genesis 1:3, where we read that "God said . . ." God is not human, nor physical. What can it mean to say that God spoke? Yet this statement is found repeatedly in the first chapter of Genesis, and in almost every book of the Old Testament. The "word" of God is the means by which all things were created. And it is by the word of God that God revealed himself to people, whether prophets, kings, or children. How does God speak? And how can we know that it is He?

Certain persons of the Old Testament heard God more clearly, and passed his messages on to others. Sometimes it was through a dream, an event, or a vision. Most of the time we are not told how the message was given. The prophets punctuated their sermons with "Thus says the Lord" but without saying how they knew. Often the message came to them as it does to us, through the written word of the books we call "Mosaic." Then, in the fullness of time,

> The Word became flesh and lived among us, and we have seen his glory, the glory as of a father/ only son, full of grace and truth. . . . From his fullness we have all received, grace upon grace. The law indeed was given through Moses; grace and truth came through Jesus Christ. No one has ever seen God. It is God the only Son, who is close to the Father's heart, who has made him known. (John 1:14, 16-18).

Who could have imagined such a thing! God became flesh, not to see what it was like to be human, for he knew that already, but to show us what he intended human beings to be and do, and to give us grace to fulfill His will.

God reveals Himself most fully to us in the person of Jesus Christ, without Whom there could be no Christianity. John calls him "the Word" as in Him God speaks most clearly to us. In Jesus Christ we have the highest revelation of God. The prologue of John describes the way God, in Christ Jesus, revealed himself to us.." No one has ever seen God. It is God the only Son, who is close to the Father's heart, who has made him known (Jn. 1:18).

This is a higher revelation of God than we have in any other way because it is a personal revelation—revealed in a person. God, the infinite Person, speaks to human persons in the Divine-human person of Jesus Christ more fully, completely and perfectly than He could by any other means.

Persons can speak to persons using impersonal means, such as written messages, smoke signals, paintings and architecture. But there is much that can never be communicated in these ways. There is much that we can know about God by study of the things He has made, but there is also much which can never be fully learned in this way.

Old Testament Revelation

In the Old Testament, God had shown his love in a multitude of ways, so as to teach people how very much he cared for human beings. He had shown his love in his actions, through miraculous deliverances, and through the prophets whom he sent.

Deuteronomy 7:8 points out plainly that Israel was a special people, not because of anything they themselves had done, but because of God's love for them. It was not that God loved only them, but that in them he found reason to hope he could work with them and lead them. He had chosen them so that they could be a blessing to all the nations of the world. He had told Abram "I will make of you a great nation, and I will bless you and make your name great, so that you will be a blessing. . . . and *in you all the families of the earth shall be blessed* (Gen. 12:2, 4, emphasis mine). God's love was not exclusive, but included all nations. It is true that Israel tended to forget this, and often felt that they were the only people God loved, but that is not the message of the Old Testament. God intended for all the world to receive a blessing through the descendants of Abraham, because he loved all nations. When Moses led the people out of Egyptian bondage, various Egyptians and other foreigners went with them and worshiped God. The Book of Ruth tells how a foreign woman became an ancestor of Jesus. Jonah was sent to preach to the Assyrians.

God revealed his amazing grace and love for sinful humanity by means of such prophets as Hosea and Isaiah. God's love was shown by them as too strong to let sin go on unchecked. God had given the law long ago, through Moses, to show what God wanted people to be. Then he sent the prophets to remind the people of the will of God, and to call them to obedience. Yet we hear this plaintive cry of God, "When I spoke to you persistently, you did not listen, and when I called you, you did not answer" (Jer. 7:13). "They have turned their backs to me, not their faces; though I have taught them persistently, they would not listen and accept correction" (Jer. 32:33).

So the unfailing love of God is revealed in the Old Testament, but God had one more messenger to send—his own Son, the Word of God became flesh, to seek after the lost human race.

Through the suffering of Jesus on the cross we learn that God does care so much about us that our sin causes God, in His love for us, to suffer as a natural consequence. Rather than cast sinful people aside and thus be rid of the offender, God enters into our situation, even though that entails suffering, and seeks by every means to save us from our sin. This tremendous fact could hardly have been revealed to us so clearly and effectively except in the person of Jesus Christ.

God reveals himself through his Spirit

We have seen that the supreme revelation of God comes to us in Jesus Christ, but what of the thousands of years which have passed since Jesus' earthly ministry? Must we now be content with a past revelation, which is all in the past tense? On the night before His crucifixion Jesus said to His disciples: "I will not leave you orphaned; I am coming to you." (John 14:18). And again: "It is to your advantage that I go away, for if I do not go away, the Advocate will not come to you" (John 16:7). It is through the Holy Spirit, in His abiding presence, that we experience now the living presence of the risen Christ. The Holy Spirit is not the Christ, but it is through Him that Jesus Christ is working now in the world and in the church. Christ at Pentecost entered into a higher ministry than was possible while He was on earth in a physical body. Whatever the Spirit does is the work of Christ. Whatever Christ is doing in the world today is being done through the ministry of the Holy Spirit, Who works in and through those who let Him live in their hearts.

So it is that God is now revealing Himself to us through the Holy Spirit, who is the Spirit of God, the Spirit of Christ (cf. Matt. 3:16; I Cor. 6:11; I Pet. 4:14 with Rom. 8:9; Phil. 1:19; Acts 16:7; Gal. 4:6). Whatever direct experience we have of God comes to us through aid of the Holy Spirit. When we see God in nature, the Holy Spirit has pointed Him out to us. When we feel the presence of the living Christ, it is because the Holy Spirit makes Him known. When we read the Bible and understand God's will, the Holy Spirit has been teaching us. He is the personal Guide and Teacher of every Christian, and the personal Revealer of God.

We must look at these aspects of God in much more detail later. What we need to see for the moment is that we need something more than nature to show us what God is like. One thing more is the Bible, a written record of revelation.

Because of a recent revival of Montanism we must clearly understand what it is that the Holy Spirit does for us, and what he does not do. Some are teaching today, as Montanus taught in the second century, that the Holy Spirit gives individuals revelations of new truths. This would mean that the Bible is not the final source for truth. Those who are teaching this idea seem to pay more attention to what they and others feel has been revealed to them than to what the Bible says. Some charismatics are insisting that the Holy Spirit is today prophesying through Christians, and giving truth which is supplemental to the Bible.

This concept denies the distinctive authority of the Bible, and leaves us with no assurance that we can know God and his will. What God commands might, according to this theory, be changed at any time by what someone feels is a new revelation from God.

This is not true. Those who believe it should remind themselves of the warnings against adding to the Scripture or taking from it (Deut. 4:2; Rev. 22:18-19). The work of the Holy Spirit in this regard is not to add to the Bible, but to help us understand it. He empowers us to teach, preach, write, talk, witness, think and love. When the Holy Spirit guides us "into all truth" (John 16:13) he does it through what is revealed in the Bible, never beyond it or apart from it. He does not give additional revelaltion of truth. He does not make it unnecessary to study the Bible and search it for truth. Rather, he aids our best, most sincere and prayerful study. The Bible is still the final test of our knowledge of God and his will.

CHAPTER 4

The Bible and Its Authority

> "And beginning with Moses and all the prophets, he interpreted to them in all the scriptures the things concerning himself" (Luke 24:27).
>
> **Why is the Bible different from all other books? In what sense is it the word of God? Why do we believe it is better than the books of other religions? Is it God's final and best revelation of the way of salvation?**

We come now to the Bible as a means by which God reveals Himself to human beings. Here we must do some very careful thinking, if we are to lay the foundation for understanding the Bible and teaching it to others. We must know what the Bible claims to be, and how to understand what it is saying.

Christians have all along claimed that the Bible is the very foundation of our knowledge of God. It is the record of the process by which God has revealed Himself to us through His dealings with the nation of Israel, and through Christ and His earliest followers. It is not a book written in heaven and handed down to earth for our information. The Bible was written by human beings—by persons who wrote down what they knew of God and His ways with them. They wrote down what God had done for them and to them, and what they felt sure God had said to them. Yet they wrote with the guidance of the Holy Spirit in a way that provides for us and for all time a sure guide to a knowledge of God. This guidance of the Holy Spirit is what we mean by the "inspiration" of the Bible, and it accounts for the Bible's authority. It is important to realize that the inspiration of the Holy Spirit extends far beyond the original writing, and includes the canonization and preservation of the Bible books.[12]

SOURCE OF THEOLOGY

The Bible is the primary source of Christian belief. The secondary sources of reason, tradition and experience are subsidiary to the Bible and aid in interpreting the Bible.

Since Albert Outler first used the term "quadrilateral" to refer to "Scripture, reason, tradition and experience" as these four were used by John Wesley to support his theology, the term has been misused by some. The four are sometimes spoken of as though they were equally sources of theology. Allan Coppedge examined the relative authority of Scripture, tradition, experience and reason in John Wesley's writings and shows the latter three to be subordinate criteria for matters of faith and practice in Wesley.[13]

The Bible itself is the primary source of theology, and nothing should be accepted which is contrary to Scripture teaching. A primary reason this is true is the nature of revelation itself. God has revealed himself through events in history and through the interpretation of those events by the guidance of the Holy Spirit. The historical events are not repeatable, and the incarnation of the Word of God in Christ Jesus is a one-time event (Heb. 9:28). The Old Testament pointed forward to this event and the New Testament consists of guidance toward understanding his life and work by those who knew him. So when that was completed, there was no apparent reason for further Scripture.

Since God gave the Bible for our instruction, it is the revealed record of what God has done and planned for us. It includes both the Old Testament and the New Testament. The Old Testament tells of the way God worked with people before the time of Christ, and tells of the preparation for the coming of the Messiah. This preparation was the selection of a special people whom God could instruct in the way of righteousness, and their training in godliness. The purpose of this training was for God to get them ready for his Son to come into the world to save all who would come to believe in Him.

Inspiration

Revelation is the act of revealing a thing or making it known. A revelation is a message made known. Inspiration is the method by which

God guided in the writing and preservation of the message so that we have a dependable Bible today. Authority is a descriptive term applied to the message, describing the responsibility of the recipient to hear, believe, and act upon the message.

Churches, colleges, and seminaries have been torn apart by the arguments over the method of inspiration and the exact words to use to describe it. Yet "inspiration" is hardly a Biblical word at all, since it occurs only once as applied to the written word: "All scripture is inspired by God and profitable . . . " (II Tim. 3:16). The single Greek word (θεοπνευστος) here translated "inspired by God" literally means something like "God-breathed." The word occurs only here.

It is ironic that scholars have expended so much effort on this little-used term, when the Bible does not explain anywhere the exact method by which God accomplished the inspiration. One of the few hints is that the writers, "carried along by the Holy Spirit" (as the Greek can be translated) "spoke from God" (2 Pet. 1:21). The preceding verse also warns us that "no prophecy of scripture is a matter of one's own interpretation." This means that we have no right to invent new interpretations to suit our own whims or ideas. We must pay attention to the church's interpretation of a passage—tradition. We have no right to neglect what other Christians have discovered about the meaning of the Bible through two thousand years. It is wrong to think that we can bypass all that has been written about the Bible and begin from the beginning ourselves. Why reinvent the wheel?

Most of the time the Bible writers do not tell how they became aware of the message God wanted them to write. The expression "God spoke" or "thus says the Lord" or something equivalent, occurs more than four thousand times in the Old Testament alone. Usually the Bible does not tell just how God said it.

The surest thing we can say is that the pagan idea of God taking over the mind of the prophet and speaking or writing through him while the prophet's mind is passive, is not found in the Bible. Paul insisted that "the spirits of prophets are subject to prophets" (I Cor. 14:32).

What we usually see in the Old Testament is the prophet being shown something by God, and then doing his best to describe what he has seen. So we see Ezekiel, in the first chapter of his book, struggling to find expressions as "what appeared to be . . . " and "as it were." In the same way we see Paul trying to be sure he is right, and so correcting himself (I Cor. 1:14-16). Yet in all this we see the work of the Holy Spirit, so that, as 2 Peter put it: "No prophecy ever came by human will, but men and women moved by the Holy Spirit spoke from God" (2 Pet. 1:21).

The statement in 2 Peter makes it clear that the Bible is both divine and human in its production. Human beings were carried along by the Holy Spirit as they wrote. Both God and humans were involved in the writing of the various parts of the Bible. This is the reason we can see differences in style of writing, choice of words, and length of sentences. Each writer was guarded and guided by the Holy Spirit in what was written, but protected from distorting the truth as that person wrote in his or her own way.

A most careful definition of inspiration is that of F.F. Bruce: "Biblical inspiration is that special control exercised by the Spirit of God over the speakers or writers of Holy Scripture, by reason of which their words adequately convey the Word of God."[14]

When we say that we do not know the method of inspiration, we are saying that we know the Holy Spirit did it, but that we do not understand just *how* he did it. That is because we do not always understand how the Spirit works (John 3:8). We know that he can guide us, speak peace to the troubled sinner, apply the blood of Jesus to his heart, and make the sinner a Christian. No one knows just how he does these things. We do know that the Holy Spirit guided the writers of the Bible in a way that produced a book that can lead us to God. But we do not understand the methods by which he did this work. We also know that we do not have to understand God to believe in him and his works.

Continuing guidance of the Holy Spirit

An essential part of the doctrine of God's inspiration is that the Holy Spirit was involved not only in the original production of the Bible but also in its protection through the ages since. It is true that there are differences in the various manuscripts, but they are not the kinds of differences that would make it difficult to find the truth about God and his message. Most of them are differences in spelling or minor differences in the manner of expression. There is better manuscript evidence for the whole Bible than for other ancient writers. We can depend on what we have in our standard translations of it. By standard versions, we mean those done by groups of scholars, such as KJV, NRSV, NIV, and NASB, rather than by some individual. We can trust the Bible to guide us to God.

Bible—Human and Divine

The Bible is both human and divine. It is divine in origin but human in transmission. In and through it God reveals to us those things we need to know to live our lives to please Him. At the center of the revelation is Jesus Christ, who shows us God. By His words God will judge us (John 12:48), so the Word of God has eternal authority over us. This authority we ignore at the peril of our eternal souls. Through the study of the Bible, the Word of God, we can know God and learn to love and serve Him forever.

Purpose of Revelation

The heart of the Christian revelation is that God himself has broken through into human history. God has done this in love, and the result is the gospel of grace. Gospel preaching is proclaiming or announcing what God has done for the salvation of humanity. God has come in the life, death and resurrection of Jesus Christ to reveal to us our condition and to bring about our reconciliation with God. This is the gospel which is presented to us in the New Testament, and for which the Old Testament prepared.

The purpose of the revelation and inspiration of the Bible is to guide us in becoming God's people and in trusting him to save and lead us. When John wrote his gospel, he did not tell all he knew about Jesus in his earthly life, but chose what suited the purpose. He said of the things he wrote, "These are written that you may believe that Jesus is the Christ, the Son of God, and that believing you may have life in his name" (John 20:31; cf. 21:25; 1 John 5:13). He felt impelled by the Holy Spirit to write as he did so that readers would be brought to saving faith in Jesus Christ. This statement clearly applies to the rest of the New Testament as well.

AUTHORITY OF THE BIBLE

By the authority of the Bible we mean that we can depend on the Bible for guidance in our knowledge of God and his will for us. We mean that the Bible is true in what it teaches us, since it is the inspired word of God. It is a safe guide to God and salvation, as it comes from God. God is the one who safeguarded the production of the Bible and its transmission to us.

Christian doctrine is built on the foundational idea of the authority of the Bible as the written revelation of the nature, work and will of God. All of our talk about revelation is useless if we do not have an authoritative Bible. All the discussions about the inspiration of the Bible have the purpose of safeguarding the authority of the Bible as the Word of God. Inspiration is a method by which the divine revelation was authoritatively written. Whether or not we understand the method, we must believe in the revelation by God's initiative and in the absolute authority of the resultant writing.

Revelation and the inspired writing of revelation, so that the result is authoritative, is possible because of God's infinite power. It exists because of God's love. It was initiated by God so that the Bible is not the record of humanity's search for God, but of God's revelation of himself to lost humanity.

The divine self-revelation in the Bible is purposeful, since its aim is the salvation of humankind from sin. The Bible is historical in the sense that it and the events of which it tells were not "done in a corner" (Acts 26:26), but were true events in history. It was progressively given and progressively understood. It is authoritatively written for our protection. The Bible offers us all that we need for salvation. It is unified, harmonious, and centered in Christ.

Unity in Diversity

When we say that the Bible is unified, we must also admit that there is diversity. It was written by many different persons, with divergent understandings and different ways of expressing themselves. They were writing to various groups of readers, and for purposes which varied. Yet we are convinced that, in spite of diversity, there is coherence in the whole message that binds it together in one book.

Much of the diversity is literary in that the Bible contains a variety of literary forms. These forms range from genealogical lists to letters, and includes poetry, sermons, drama, and many others.[15] Another kind of diversity in theological concepts is partly explained by the fact that the knowledge of God and his ways was revealed progressively. This is the only way human beings are able to learn. So there are differences between what was known by early writers and what was known by later ones. The greatest difference is between the Old Testament and the New Testament, and came about because of the life and ministry of Jesus Christ. Yet all through the whole Bible there are variations in knowledge and in understanding.

In spite of the diversity, and the differences in numbers, names and spellings, there is a strong theological unity in the Bible. This has been denied by scholars who have a strong anti-supernatural bias in their historical critical approach to the Bible. Historical critical study, as a method, can be good, but it has been misused by so many that it has been repellent to those who love the Bible. Some of these scholars have insisted that the Bible is just another book, and that the ideas in it are purely human in origin. In the New Testament, the same thing is true of some advocates of source criticism, form criticism and redaction criticism. They have studied certain details of the text so exclusively that they cannot see the forest for the trees! It is possible to become so involved in discovering new differences in wording, that one loses sight of the message.[16]

Yet the message of the Bible has a theological unity which makes it a book, not merely a collection. The message of the Old Testament centers around God's search for a people who would love and serve Him. The message of the whole New Testament centers in Christ, who fulfilled that search. Some of us are so impressed with that unity of message that we see no serious problem in the diversity.

The Bible is a safe guide to a saving knowledge of God. There are passages that no one knows how to reconcile, such as differences in the title over the cross of Jesus, some differences in genealogies, the dating of the Exodus, the exact measurements of the laver in the temple, and the number of angels at the tomb of Jesus.

Two things need to be said about such difficulties: First, none of these difficulties affect any Christian doctrine, unless we include the doctrine of absolute inerrancy. Some difficulties are trivial, such as the measurement of the laver in the temple, in which the Bible writer assumed the value of *pi* to be three, instead of three and one seventh, or 3.14159265+ as modern engineers would do. Harold Lindsell sought to prove that the statement in the Bible was mathematically exact. It might be better to admit a certain rounding off of figures and lack of modern scientific exactness, since this does not affect the truth of what the Bible teaches us. Second, it is wise to admit that there are difficult problems, but we can leave the problems open for future study and further evidence, without calling them errors. Further study has solved some problems, and may solve others. It is better to admit the problems, and leave them for the future, just as we do with lack of understanding of the natural phenomena no one can explain. The unity of the whole outweighs all this.

Authoritative Revelation

Authority must accompany revelation or there is no revelation. Revelation is to someone. God does not simply reveal himself, he reveals himself to human beings. This revelation to human beings is no revelation at all unless it is an authoritative revelation. It must be true and truly revealed. It should be the kind of revelation that demands or commands our respect and our faith.

Authority is personal. It is not the blind, impersonal authority of pure power, but it is the personal authority of the Father, Son and Holy Spirit. Contrary to what some people have said, we Christians do not worship a book--not even the Bible. We worship God only. We bow only to the authority of God. This authority of God is a personal authority.

Authority is based on truth. It is easy for most people to agree that truth carries its own authority. Truth is to be believed simply because it is true. The authority of the revelation of God to us comes from the fact that it is true. What God reveals is true for every person on earth. It is not true that for some there is one God and for others there are many gods. The truth is the same for all. It has universal validity. The authority of the Bible is based on this kind of universal truth.

Biblical authority brings salvation. The authority of the Bible is not the condemnatory authority of some hateful power of justice, but it is the authority of God's love. God seeks to save all who are lost. The authority of the Bible is the authority of God who loves and who seeks to save every individual in the world (2 Peter 3:9). We have every reason, then, to trust the authority of the Bible because we know that it will lead us to salvation.

A new term "inerrant" has been used by some as a test of belief in the authority of the Bible. The Church of God has insisted on the authority of the Bible, and has done this without resorting to this rather new term, and affirmed the Biblical authority before this term was used. The term "inerrant" does not add anything significant to the authority of the Bible, partly because it is used with different meanings by various writers, and is inexact. It is essential that we accept the authority of the Bible for our knowledge of God as Savior. But it is not imperative that we agree on the use of a term to describe it.

Authority of the Old Testament

Christians do not always appreciate the value of the Old Testament, and may feel that most of it does not mean much to them. However, the New Testament quotes the Old Testament 368 times and has more than one thousand identifiable allusions to Old Testament passages. This is a strong indication of the basic importance of the Old Testament to Christians. It is the Bible from which Jesus and the apostles preached, and it has much to say to us. Jesus declared that it spoke of him (John 5:39), and condemned those Jews who read the Old Testament but rejected him.

When Paul was discussing some stories of the Old Testament that could teach us moral lessons, he said, "Now these things happened to them as a warning, but they were written down for our instruction, upon whom the end of the ages has come" (1 Cor. 10:11; cf. Rom. 15:4). If Paul was sure that the Old Testament, even the stories, were written down for Christians, it would be good for us to pay close attention to all of the Bible, and not merely the New Testament, or the parts that are clear and easy.

The New Testament is shorter than it would have to be if the Old Testament had not been written. Much that is fully established in the Old Testament is not emphasized in the New. The fact of the oneness of God is mentioned in the New Testament, but it is one of the central facts of the Old Testament message. This is true also of the creation of all things by God, the working of God in history, the prophetic understanding of the laws and ceremonies, and the message of the Wisdom Literature of the Old Testament. We would be so much poorer in our theology if we did not have the Old Testament, which is two-thirds of the Bible. Christians should not neglect all this.

Claims to Authority

The Bible claims authority. For example, Jesus taught with authority, which was so different from that of the scribes (Mat. 7:28-29). But he did more than teach in an authoritative manner; he claimed that what he said had real and eternal authority.

> Truly, truly, I say to you, he who hears my word and believes him who sent me, has eternal life; he does not come into judgment, but has passed from death to life. (John 5:24).
> He who rejects me and does not and does receive my sayings has a judge; the word that I have spoken will be his judge on the last day. For I have not spoken on my own authority; the Father who sent me has himself given me commandment what to say and what to speak. And I know that his commandment is eternal life. What I say, therefore, I say as the Father has bidden me. (John 12:48-50)

The other writers of the New Testament claim that they spoke with authority and that what they said had authority. Paul gave strong support not only for his own authority, but also for the authority of what he was writing. "But even if we, or an angel from heaven, should preach to you a gospel contrary to that which we preached to you, let him be accursed (Gal. 1:8). First and Second Timothy and Titus make at least eight references to "sound doctrine." The author is supporting not only his own personal authority, but the authority of the whole Bible, including what he has written. This is most clear in Second Timothy 4:1-2: "I charge you in the presence of God and of Christ Jesus who is to judge the living and the dead, and by his appearing and his kingdom: preach the Word, be urgent in season and out of season, convince, rebuke, and exhort, be unfailing in patience and in teaching."

The Bible, the Word of God, is declared to be the standard of teaching (2 Tim. 3:16). Since much of the New Testament had not yet been written, he was appealing primarily to them to preach from the Old Testament and to preach it truly. However, the same kind of authority is claimed for the New Testament (2 Pet. 3:15-16).

Vital Importance of Biblical Authority

It is necessary for us to settle this matter of the authority of the Bible, as we know that our salvation from sin and our eternal destiny depend on what the Bible teaches. The Bible is the primary source of Christian theology, and we can have no confidence in our theology unless we have full confidence in Biblical authority. It is the Bible that tells us of the creation and its purpose. It is the Bible that tells us of the love of God for all persons, and gives us the record of the Savior coming into the world for our benefit. It is the Bible that tells us what God is like, and without it, we could not have much certain knowledge of him and his works. Without the Bible, we would have no gospel.

Here we must insert a clarification. While it is true that without the Bible, we would not have the gospel of Jesus Christ, we might have knowledge of God without the Bible. This is because of the work of the Holy Spirit in all. It is possible to know God without knowing of Jesus or the Bible, because God seeks to reveal himself to every person, as he did to Adam, Noah and Abraham, none of whom had any part of the Bible. Yet the Bible gives us the kind of guidance and instruction we need to know God and his way more fully and completely.

Authenticated by the Holy Spirit

It is sometimes said that the Bible is self-authenticating. This statement is based on the observation that those who read it are often convinced of its truth as they read. However, a better explanation of this is that the Holy Spirit works in the heart of the reader, to make the person feel the true force of the words. The same Spirit who worked through the writers and copiers to produce and protect the Bible, also works in and through its readers.

In the last discourse with his disciples before his arrest, Jesus spoke of the Holy Spirit and his purpose. "He will teach you all things" (John 14:26). "He will bear witness of me" (John 15:26), and not to the disciples only, but to all. "He will convict the world of sin, and of righteousness and of judgment" (John 16:8-11). This last clearly shows that the work of the Holy Spirit is not confined to the followers of Christ, but extends to all the world. He seeks to lead all into the truth. He seeks to convict sinners of the sinfulness of their sin. He does this partly by working through the Bible as it is read. So the same Spirit who worked in the production of the Bible also works in the hearts of those who read it. He convinces readers of the truth of what they read. Thus the Holy Spirit authenticates the authority of the Bible.

We see, then, that the Bible is the authoritative record of the revelation by God. He reveals himself to the whole human race. He shows human beings what they really are, what they were meant to be, and what they can be by the grace of God in Christ Jesus.

INTERPRETATION OF THE BIBLE

Once we decide that the Bible is the primary source for theology, we have to wonder why it is that we cannot all agree on what the Bible means. Unless we can do this, we may wonder what good it does to have an authoritative source.

It is true that there will never be a time in this world when all Christians will agree on the meaning of all Scripture. We often differ because of our partial knowledge, and because the text can often be interpreted in more than one way. The only way to seek the truth in such cases is to compare the statement with all the rest of the Bible. None of us knows all that the Bible says or means. Here we "know in part" (1 Cor. 13:12), and we do not all have the same bits of knowledge. So we often disagree on what the Bible means.

Yet it would be wrong for us to emphasize too much the points of theology on which we do not agree. The topics of Biblical teaching on which we agree are far more than those on which we disagree. All Christians believe that salvation from sin comes through Christ alone. All believe that we ought to live without sin, and that there is a judgment coming which will determine our eternal reward.

Why we differ

So it is with the main topics of theology. We differ as we get technical about details. In the understanding of Scripture, we differ in our understanding of particular passages, and of the way they fit into the whole scheme of biblical teaching. Other reasons for differing interpretations of texts are: Misleading translations, inadequate study of the context, inadequate comparison of texts, different worldviews, various theological backgrounds, personal biases and lack of sufficient study of a particular passage.

It is not easy to overcome these problems and come to an assurance of the correct interpretation of a Scripture. All of us have wrong conceptions of some theological details for these and other reasons. The way out is to learn the best principles of hermeneutics, and to spend a lifetime applying them. Since our lives are not long enough to learn everything, we hope to have time in eternity to come to a more complete understanding. In this life, we need to do the best we can to learn and to do the will of God. In this work we have three subsidiary sources of theology to aid us: Reason, tradition and experience. These need some explanation.

Reason

Reason is a necessary aid to the understanding of revelation. God gave us the ability to reason so that we can think and understand what he wants us to know. We can never fully know the extent of God's knowledge, but he gave us minds capable of knowing what he wants us to know of him and his will.

The understanding of scripture is not to be left to the most intelligent, nor to the scholars who spend all their time at the process. The way of God is so far beyond us that we will never know enough to satisfy our curiosity. Yet even the least capable thinkers will find their way if they are truly seeking God. This is not to say that the poor thinker, or the untrained, can know as much as the wiser, but that such a person need not despair. The Bible is shallow enough for the child to wade, and too deep for the greatest to plumb.

A warning is necessary in regard to reason. It must never be used to judge or modify the Bible, but only to interpret it. If we put so much faith in reason as to place our methods of critical study above the Bible, then we will be making reason our guide rather than revealed truth. Scripture is superior to conscience and reason, but not contrary to reason.

Tradition

By tradition we mean the writings of other Christians as to the meaning of Scripture. This includes the ancient creeds and the writings of the early Christians, but also the commentaries and theologies of modern Christians. This is not to say that we ought to accept uncritically all that has been written, for that would be total confusion. Yet there is a sense in which the history of theology is the history of the exegesis of the Bible. There has been a two thousand year discussion among the great minds of Christianity about the meaning of Bible teaching. The result of the dialogue, which is still ongoing, is that we have come to our present understandings. No one who is serious about Bible study can afford to ignore this vast literature.

Tradition is bad if it takes precedence in our minds over what the Bible says. It must not be considered the last word, but as an aid to understanding the Bible. Why should we ignore what others have learned about the Bible and its meaning? Why reinvent the wheel?

As we read what others have written about the meaning of the Bible, we find that some ideas which seem good at first glance have been rejected by others on good grounds. If we study enough, we will continue to learn to "test everything; hold fast what is good" (1 Thess. 5:21). There is good and bad tradition, and we must learn to discern the difference. Paul told the Thessalonian Christians, "hold to the traditions which you were taught by us" (2 Thess. 2:15). If we are careful, we can learn from any Christian.

Experience

By speaking of experience as a means of understanding theology, we mean the Christian experience of repenting of sin and being converted. Only the person who loves to do the will of God is capable of the highest understanding of the word (John 7:17). We mean the experience of knowing the Holy Spirit as the One who speaks peace to our souls, guides us in living, and authenticates the Word of God. With his help we can say with D. O. Teasley:

> I know in my heart what it means,
> Salvation, that word so divine;
> His Spirit has witnessed to mine,
> And I know in my heart what it means.[17]

Experience alone is not a safe guide to truth, any more than is tradition. These are secondary, and must conform to what the Bible teaches, and confirm it, or they must be ignored. We must not test the Bible by our own experiences, but test our experiences by the Bible.

Beware of any theology which cannot be lived. It is possible to describe salvation in such a way that no one can have such an experience. Divine healing is being preached by some in such a way that it is not experienced. If we claim that every Christian can live in perfect health, we are claiming what the Bible does not teach, and which very few experience.

In considering the interpretation of the Bible, we must recognize that this is not a mechanical process. Only one who is totally committed to learning and doing the will of God can fully comprehend the word of God. When speaking about the teaching of God, Jesus said " If any man's will is to do his will, he shall know whether the teaching is from God or whether I am speaking on my own authority" (John 7:17). "If anyone wills" (Gr. θελει *thelei*) means if the person "chooses, decides, determines" to do the will of God. This determination to obey God is a requirement for knowing the will of God.

Prayer. No one should seek to study the Bible without prayer. As one reads the Bible prayerfully, worshipfully, one can hear the word of God. It is the self-revelation of God and his will, and one must approach it as one would approach God. Only so can one truly accept the truth of what is written and know its meaning for oneself.

Exegesis

Biblical exegesis refers to the process of interpretation. It is both a science and an art, and is far too complex to describe here. Yet it may be wise to outline the process by which it is done. The purpose of the process is to seek to understand: (1) What the text meant in its original historical and literary setting, and (2) what it means to the contemporary reader in terms of its subject matter. The full process of exegesis uses all the methods of Biblical criticism: textual, philological, literary, form, tradition, redaction and historical. But all we can do here is outline the basic method which can be used by one who is not yet trained in the use of more technical methods.

With this in mind we can define exegesis as a thorough, analytical study of a Biblical passage done so as to arrive at a useful interpretation of the passage. This interpretation can then be used to make a practical application to current life.

Study the words. Exegesis must begin with lexical study, as any message is made up of words. The best exegesis must begin with the study of the words in the language in which they were written: Hebrew, Aramaic, Greek and a few Latin words. Those without this ability must work with translations. Remember that words in any living language change in meaning, and that the various parts of the Bible were written over a period of more than 1,000 years. So we must study the words of the text etymologically, comparatively, historically and thoughtfully.

Study the grammar and syntax. How are the words put together in sentences and paragraphs? What is the subject? What is stated about the subject of the sentence? How do the various parts of the statement fit together syntactically?

Study the cultural context. The cultural context consists of all the aspects of life in the times of the writer: Political, religious, economic, legal, agricultural, architectural, clothing, social customs, geographical and military. Increased knowledge of any and all of these can throw light on passages we are studying.

Consider the literary type. The Bible includes a variety of literary types: Commandments, history, poetry, prophecy, drama, sermon, letter, biography, proverb, and parable. Knowing the type we are dealing with is a step towards its correct interpretation.

Figures of speech are common in the Bible, as in most writing. Some of the more common ones are: Simile, allegory (Gal. 4:24), ellipsis, metaphor, paradox, irony (Job 12:1-2; 26:1-3), and hyperbole (Mat. 7:3-5). Failing to recognize

Study the Biblical context. This begins with the verses before and after the one we are considering. Beyond this immediate context is the book or section of a book in which the text is found. Since the broad context of the statement is the whole Bible, we need to use cross references to find other statements which may help us see the meaning of the text. Since these references are limited, they must be supplemented by study of concordances, commentaries and word study books which will help us learn more of the total context.

These six aspects of Bible study are not all there is to it, but they are an outline of what must be done. Further, any Bible reader can begin to use these six steps to understand the Bible with a growing comprehension. And no one will live long enough to get beyond these. Nor should any individual imagine that she can learn it all alone. We need to learn from others, whether in person or through what has been written by Bible scholars.

The Holy Spirit

The same Holy Spirit who inspired the writers and guarded their writing, then protected its transmission through twenty centuries, is the One who can help us to understand and accept the word for ourselves. He works with all of us all our lives, seeking to turn us toward God. Yet, until we yield ourselves to his guidance, he can never make us understand and do the will of God. The point of his work is to bring the person to the point of submission to God's will, and when the person yields, the Spirit is able to work in and through him or her effectively. Only then can the Spirit lead one into a knowledge of the word and will of God.

Obedience, prayer and the Holy Spirit work together as one reads the Bible, and leads into a knowledge of the truth of God. The Holy Spirit cannot do his best work until we are prayerful and obedient as we read the words. We can find God, but only as we seek him with all our hearts (Jer. 29:13).

Chapter 5

THE NATURE OF GOD

"Make me to know your ways, O Lord; teach me your paths. Lead me in your truth, and teach me, for you are the God of my salvation; for you I wait all day long" (Psa. 25:4-5).

How can we human beings know what God is like? Can we find in the Bible enough guidance to understand what he wants us to be and do? He is so far above us in every way; can we ever understand him?

When a theologian is asked to explain the nature of God, he responds by giving a list of the *attributes* of God. That is, he lists some of the characteristics of God. The words he uses may seem incomprehensible, such as "aseity", "immutability", and "omnipresence". Yet each of these words has a long history, and is used for a good purpose. Most of them were known to the ancient Greek philosophers before the time of Christ. Since it is important to know these things about God, we will consider them briefly, calling them the *general* attributes of God. We will then give more attention to the specifically Christian aspect of the nature of God.

GENERAL ATTRIBUTES OF GOD

Unity. The Bible strongly emphasizes the unity of God. "The Lord is God; there is no other besides him" (Deut. 4:35). "Hear, O Israel: The Lord our God is one Lord" (Deut. 6:4). See also: I Samuel 2:2; 1 Kings

8:60; Psalms 86:10; Isaiah 42:8; 44:6-8; 45:22; Mark 12:29, 32; John 17:3; Ephesians 4:6, and a host of others. It is true that in their early days, the descendants of Abraham often yielded to the temptation to be like their pagan neighbors in worshiping false gods, and that the great prophets of the eighth and seventh centuries before Christ had to speak out against idolatry. But after the fifth century exile in Babylon, this was never a problem again. They knew only one God from that time on. And even before then, the unity of God was the consistent message of the great religious leaders. The one-ness of God was one of the most settled convictions of the Jews by the time of Christ.

The unity of God is utterly opposed to both polytheism and dualism. Polytheism, of course, is the belief in many gods, or at least more than one god. It could include some interpretations of the Trinity. In other words, it is possible to explain the Christian idea of Trinity in such a way as to result in an idea of three gods. We will see later how this is possible, but false.

Dualism can take many forms, but probably the most troublesome is the idea that both good and evil are eternal, or that both God and Satan have always existed. The puzzle of the existence of evil in a world made by a good God is so serious that it is easy to decide that Satan must have existed from the beginning, like God. But that cannot be. There is only One Who is from everlasting to everlasting. All else is secondary to God, and even evil exists and operates only as God permits it.

Satan has not existed forever, and will not continue his work forever. He was not created evil, but good, as people were. In some manner analogous to the fall of Adam and Eve, Satan fell and became evil. We do not know why God permits him to work evil in the world, but we do know that this is only by the permission of God. He is a defeated enemy (Luke 10:17-19; John 12:31; Rev. 12:9-12). Only God is eternal.

Spirit. "God is spirit, and those who worship him must worship in spirit and truth (John 4:24). This is the clear teaching of both the Old and New Testaments, but it is not so easy to explain exactly what is meant by this. The chief problem is that spirit is beyond the direct experience of our senses, so that we do not know by experience what it is or how to describe it. But of course, we have never seen a thought or an emotion either, yet we know that they are real.

One of the things we mean by saying God is spirit, is that God does not have a physical body, as we have. "A spirit hath not flesh and bones, as ye see me have" (Luke 24:39). God transcends matter, space, and time. By this we mean that God is not physical; He is not bound by the limitations of matter, space, or time. He is beyond all of these. He cannot be limited by them, and must not be identified with them. God is not nature, and nature is not God.

Yet when we say that God transcends all nature, we must carefully guard against two false conclusions which can be drawn from this statement. One is that God is so far beyond this universe that He cares nothing for it. In reply to this we must remember that the Bible insists not only that God is beyond the universe, but that He is at the same time its Creator. God not only created the world in the beginning, but He continues to uphold it each moment, and involves Himself in all the operation of the world. In other words, God is both transcendent and immanent. He is both beyond the world and in it.

The other mistaken conclusion is that God is nothing but an impersonal force or energy from which the universe derives its energy. When some of the ancient Greek philosophers spoke of God as spirit, they meant by this that God is simply impersonal force, with no plan or will. Both the Old and New Testaments show a personal God, so that Christians can believe in nothing less. In Christ we have the supreme revelation of God who loves us, hates sin, and plans for the salvation of all. God is personal Spirit. There is a sense in which this fact can be called the basic foundation stone of Christian theology. Unless we accept this, there is no way to make sense of Christian beliefs. So we will return to it later.

Eternity. God is called "eternal" or "everlasting" (Gen. 21:33; Exod. 15:18; I Chron. 16:36; Neh. 9:5). He is called "the First and the Last" (Isa. 44:6; 48:12; Rev. 1:17; 2:8; 22:13). He transcends time (Ps. 90:2-4). He was before things were created, and will be after they are gone (John 1:1; Heb. 1:10-12). He always has been, and always will be. He is not limited in time or by time. To God, "one day is as a thousand years, and a thousand years as one day" (II Pet. 3:8) "or as a watch in the night" (Ps. 90:4). Yet God, being infinite in knowledge and wisdom, knows what time is like to us.

Immutability. "I am the Lord, I change not" (Mal. 3:6). "...with whom there is no variation or shadow due to change" (Jas. 1:17). This unchangeableness is in the character of God. He does not change His character of holiness, justice, and love. We can depend on Him always to be the same. We must not, like Aristotle, think that God never moves or does anything, for that would be changing. The Bible is a record of the actions of God. Neither must we think of God as a machine which always works in the same way no matter what the circumstances. God constantly adjusts His will and plans to the actions of men, but always in perfect accord with His holy character. "Jesus Christ is the same yesterday, and today and forever" (Heb. 13:8). We can depend on Him forever.

Omnipotence. (All powerful). The Bible does not use this technical term, but speaks of God's ability to do whatever He pleases. "Our God is in the heavens; He does whatever He pleases" (Ps. 115:3). "I know that you can do all things, and that no purpose of yours can be thwarted" (Job 42:2). "For he spoke, and it came to be: he commanded, and it stood forth" (Ps. 33:9). "For with God nothing will be impossible" (Luke 1:37).

The Biblical statements do not concern themselves with speculative questions about the meaning of omnipotence, but simply say that God has all the power there is, and can always do what He chooses to do. Questions such as "What would happen if an invincible force (God) met an immovable object?" and "Could God make something too heavy for Him to lift?" are self-contradictory, and therefore meaningless. The Christian faith is simply that God has all power there is, so that nothing can prevent Him from doing His ultimate will. God made all that is, and therefore has supreme power over all (John 1:1-3). Not even the devil has any power except what God temporarily permits him to use. When the proper time comes, God will bring an eternal end to Satan's power (Rev. 20:10). In the meantime, God lets Satan work in the world, but has power to deliver us from his evil dominion, so that we can live with victory even in this evil world.

Omnipresence. "Behold, heaven and the highest heaven cannot contain thee" (I Kings 8:27). The classic Biblical description of the omnipresence of God is in Psalms 139:7-12. Here the Psalmist declares that there is no place he can go where God is not! If we go up to heaven like astronauts, down into the deepest mines, or to the most isolated region of the earth, we cannot get beyond the love and presence of God. The Bible does not speculate about the nature of God's Spirit which makes this possible, but simply states the marvelous fact. At least this is marvelous for the Christian who loves God. At the same time, it is frustrating to the sinner who wants to get away from God's judgement on his sin.

Omniscience. As God is everywhere, so He knows all things, and nothing can be hid from Him. Here again, the classic passage is in Psalm 139 (verses 1-6). The Psalmist does not speculate about God knowing everything, but simply marvels that God knows all about *him*. It really is not important for us to try to understand God's knowledge of the future and its relationship to man's freedom. All that we need to know is that God knows all that is knowable. God knows all about us, and all about everything that can possibly affect us and our future. God knows our thoughts, our plans, and our hearts. This fact of God's omniscience could be frightening to anyone but a Christian. But the Christian knows that God not only knows us, but also loves us. His knowledge is knowledge plus love. He cares.

MORAL ATTRIBUTES OF GOD

In a general way all of the above characteristics or attributes of God were known by the Greek philosophers before the time of Christ. Those pagan thinkers spoke of God, and reasoned that God must be omnipotent, omniscient, etc. But they denied that God was in any sense personal. For example, Aristotle thought of God as the Prime Mover of the universe, pure energy, the source of all change. Yet Aristotle was sure that God was not conscious of the world nor of people, and could never possibly care what hap
pens to anyone. Since God is perfect, he reasoned, God can never desire anything, and therefore He never does anything. Such a God is so far from the God revealed in the Bible that we wonder if the same word should be used for both of them. Aristotle's God was simply a logical necessity, and could not accept worship nor prayer.

As revealed in the Bible, God is entirely different from this. His uniqueness can best be described by saying that He is a Person, He is holy, and He is love.

God is Personal.

This statement can be easily misinterpreted, but it is so important that Christians have insisted on using it during most of the church's history. By applying the term "person" to God, we are not saying that God is like people, but that people are like God! We are definitely not trying to bring God down to our human level. But how else can we talk about God, except in terms of our own experience? If we knew a higher term to apply to God we would do it. But since we do not, the best we can do is to study persons, with their will, their self-consciousness, and reason, and insist that God cannot be less than that. The biblical conception of God is always strongly personal; never impersonal.

To say that God is Personal is to say that He is not an "it." He is not merely the "Prime Mover" of the universe, nor the impersonal Source of all energy and power. He is not merely the "ground of being" (Paul Tillich's term). He is not merely the Ultimate Cause which wound up the universe in the beginning, as some deists thought. Both Jews and Christians have always insisted that the Creator of all things is One Who must be spoken of in personal terms. He had a purpose in making all things as they are. He looked at them and saw that they were good (Gen. 1:4, 10, 12, 18, 21, 25, 31). He revealed Himself to the people through Moses by means of His personal name, "Yahweh". Persons introduce themselves by telling their names. So God revealed Himself to us through His name. The Bible refers to God as "He" and never "it".

This helps us to pray - and to understand why we do not always get what we pray for. Praying is not like putting coins in a vending machine. If it were, we could always get what we wanted by praying in just the right way. Then we could work out a system of rules of prayer and be sure that by following them, we could be healthy and wealthy, if not wise. Prayer is *not* like that. Prayer is communicating with the Creator of heaven and earth, Who loves us, and Who wants us to have what is eternally best for us. Prayer, then, is not merely asking God to give us things we want, but asking Him to teach us what to want and how to use it. Understanding this raises prayer far above the level of searching for the particular time or place or way of praying which will guarantee the answer. Instead we open our minds and hearts to God and let Him teach us His will and lead us in His ways.

God is holy.

"Holy, holy, holy is the Lord of hosts" (Isa. 6:3). "Holy, holy, holy, Lord God Almighty, who was, and is, and is to come!" (Rev. 4:8). "Who is like thee, O Lord, among the gods? Who is like thee, majestic in holiness, terrible in glorious deeds, doing wonders?" (Exodus 15:11). "For thou alone art holy" (Rev. 15:4). "Holiness becometh thy house, O Lord, forever" (Ps. 93:5). "Who is able to stand before this holy God?" (I Sam. 6:20). Thus the Bible speaks of God's holiness. But exactly what does it mean to say that God is holy?

It is not easy to put into words a good definition of "holy", for several reasons. One is that we can speak of God only with words which are inadequate to express the full truth about any aspect or characteristic of God. Yet we must speak of Him, and of what He reveals to us. Another problem is that the word "holy" does not bring to our modern minds the same idea as the Bible writers intended. And a third problem is that the word must be used in a slightly different way when applied to man, than when it is applied to God. God alone is holy in and of Himself. Man's holiness is derived from God, given by God, and described in terms of a relationship with God.

The Hebrew word קדש (*qadosh*) and the Greek word ἅγιος (*hagios*) have similar histories. Both of them originally carried connotations of "separateness". In the Bible, both of them are primarily applied to God. God is separate from all else. God is separate and distinct from all created things and persons. God is not a part of this universe; He is above it, in the sense that He created it by His word, and sustains it each moment by His will. God is not involved in this world in the sense that He must struggle for existence. If it ceases to be, that will not affect God in any way. In our struggle against evil, we know for sure that God is not a "victim" of evil; He has complete power over it. God transcends the whole universe. God is ruler of the universe. Far from being a part of the structure of things, He is totally separate from it, since He made it.

This "otherness" of God which is part of what is expressed by the word "holy". Through Moses, the people learned of this holiness, or "otherness" of God which meant that there was no form on earth which could properly represent God. So they made no images, or idols so long as they were truly worshiping God. God is not a "thing" to be imitated by an image, or He would be part of the universe of things. He is a One Who is totally other than this universe. He alone is in this sense holy. "For thou alone art holy" (Rev. 15:4). "Who is like unto thee, O Lord, among the gods? Who is like unto thee, glorious in holiness, fearful in praises, doing wonders?" (Exodus 15:11).

The fifty-three times the word "holy" is used in Exodus refer mainly to things associated with God. The same is true of many of the 92 occurrences of the word in Leviticus. However, a most instructive statement is found more than once: "Speak to all the congregation of the people of Israel and say to them: You shall be holy, for I the Lord your God am holy" (Lev. 11:44,45; 19:2; 20:7, 26).

In these first books, the holiness of which they speak was first of all a ceremonial holiness. Yet there were the beginnings of an ethical content, especially in Leviticus 19-26. The people are here told to avoid sins because they are to be holy, since their Lord is holy. This is the message which was emphasized and expounded in some detail by the major and minor prophets.

When Isaiah had his great vision of the throne of God in the Temple, the thing that first impressed him so deeply was the call of the Seraphim, "Holy, holy, holy is the Lord of hosts" (Isa. 6:3). From that time on, he called God "the Holy One," or the "Holy One of Israel." Although God is often called holy in the Bible, this specific term is used 25 times in the Book of Isaiah (1:5; 5:19, 24; 10:20; 12:6; 17:7; 29:19; 30:11, 12, 15; 31:1; 37:23; 41:14, 16, 20; 43:3, 14; 45:11; 47:4; 48:17; 49:7; 54:5; 60:9, 14), and only five times elsewhere in the Old Testament (Psa. 71:22; 78:41; 89:19; Jer. 50:29; 51:5). Ezekiel speaks repeatedly of the "Holy name" of the Lord, and of his "holy things."

When John saw a similar vision of the throne of God in heaven, he too heard the cry, "Holy, holy, holy, Lord God Almighty, which was and is and is to come" (Rev. 4:8).

So "holiness" was not primarily an ethical term in its earliest uses. The primary meaning was that there is a line of demarcation between God and man. God is God, and man is man. Holiness means that we must never try to weaken this line. Theology must be reverent, God-centered. We must never seek to *use* God for our own ends. Faith in God must not be measured in terms of success or happiness. We must not seek, as do

Oriental mystics, to be absorbed into God. We can never be God. We can never even know all about God. God is infinite; we are finite. This distance between man and God is the primary denotation of the word "holy" when we apply it to God.

Yet nothing is more clear than that the Bible puts moral content into the word "holy". God is morally perfect, and this moral perfection cannot be separate from his holiness. But if we define God's holiness as meaning His moral perfection, we will define human holiness as moral perfection, and will think of sin as anything which falls short of God's infinite moral perfection. But this would make all human beings sinners by definition, and would make holiness an impossibility. It would make sin merely the failure which man cannot prevent. The Bible definition of sin is much deeper than this. Sin is personal, willful rebellion against God. Sin is choosing to turn away from God, refusing to belong to Him. Human holiness, on the other hand, means belonging to God, by means of the covenant relationship of grace through faith in Jesus Christ. God's holiness means that God is eternally separate from all created things, and distinct from man; yet God chooses to offer to mankind a personal covenant relationship with Himself. This is because God also is love.

God is Love.

Once we know something of the holiness of God, we find it absolutely astonishing to read that "God is love" (I John 4:8, 16). Emil Brunner called this "man's boldest statement!" He said this because the idea of a loving God is utterly foreign to all non-Christian religions. The closest a pagan has gotten to this is to say that "God loves himself." The ancient Greek philosophers, for example, could not conceive of the Prime Mover of the universe loving anything other than himself. To love man would be degrading to God, they were sure. But their idea is the direct opposite of the Christian concept and doctrine.

The Christian view of God is that God is holy love. It is not a distortion to say that the love of God is at the heart of the whole Bible. In both the Old and New Testaments we learn of the marvelous love of God for us. Those who say that the Old Testament teaches that God is holy, and the New Testament teaches that God is love, are missing the mark. If there is a difference, it is a difference of emphasis and clarity. We might say that in the Old Testament we learn of God's Loving Holiness, and that in the New Testament we find God's Holy Love. The difference in emphasis is made by the demonstration of God's love for mankind by Jesus Christ. In Him we see the love of God in living color. The climax came when He allowed Himself to be crucified, put to death, and buried. Here is the ultimate love. He allowed men to kill Him rather than use His divine power to stop them, because He loved them too much to cancel their power to choose. This act of God revealed to mankind once and for all the depth of God's self-giving love for man.

Yet God's love is truly revealed in the Old Testament. Look at Deuteronomy 7:7-8: "It was not because you were more in number than any other people that the Lord set his love upon you and chose, for you were the fewest of all peoples; but it is because the Lord loves you." "Know therefore that the Lord Your God is God, the faithful God who keeps covenant and steadfast love with those who love him and keep his commandments, to a thousand generations" (vs. 9). Hosea 11 could serve as a commentary on the statement of John that God is love. "When Israel was a child, I loved him, and out of Egypt I called my son. The more I called them, the more they went from me....I led them with cords of compassion, with the bands of love...How can I give you up, O Ephraim! How can I hand you over, O Israel!...My heart recoils within me, my compassion grows warm and tender." (Hosea 11:1, 2, 4, 8, 9). We can sum up the Bible teaching on the love of God in four aspects:

God's love is voluntary. This means, first of all that God's love for mankind is personal. God is more than a human person, as we have seen, but God is certainly *not less than* personal in His love for us God chooses to set His love upon us, as in Deuteronomy 7:7. His will is involved. His love is not impersonal good luck, but is Person to person love. He can then be selective as to the persons to whom He shows His mercy. His love is spontaneous, and comes from His nature, rather than being caused by any loveliness in us. He loves sinners, not at all because they are lovely, but because of what He knows He is capable of making them become.

God's love is affirmed by a covenant. The covenant of God with man is the basis for the divine-human relationship. God makes promises which are conditioned on the behavior of man, and man promises to obey the covenant requirements. The basic promise of God in both the old and new covenants is that He will continue His redemptive love to man. God's love can be depended on. God will be loyal to His own. His love is not fickle. He has affirmed this through His covenant. "He remembered for their sake His covenant, and relented according to the abundance of His steadfast love" (Ps. 106:45).

God's love is holy. There is no way to separate the love of God from His holiness. Shallow thinking may lead up to feel that if God truly loves us He will not under any circumstances punish us for anything we do, or blame us. Amos saw this clearly when he reminded the people of God's love in leading them out of Egypt and then declared the word of God: "You only have I known of all the families of the earth; therefore I will punish you for all your iniquities" (Amos 3:2). *Because* God loves us, He causes us to suffer for our sins, since He wants to lead us to Himself and away from our sinfulness. So God's holy love judges and forgives. But the harshness of punishment is never separated from tenderness (Hosea 11:1-8; Isa. 63:9). Because God loves us so much, He hates the sin which hurts us and separates us from Him and from eternal life. God's love cannot help being holy, because it is the holy God who loves.

God's love is universal. The fact is that the Old Testament stresses the love of God for the people of Israel, but the New Testament makes it crystal clear that God loves all men alike, and does not play favorites. Yet even in the Old Testament we see that God's love is not limited by racial or national boundaries. God chose Abraham and his descendants, but did not hesitate to reveal Himself to others, such as Melchizedek and Balaam. Amos pointed out that God showed His love to the Philistines and Syrians as well as to Israel (Amos 9:7). Rahab of Jericho and Ruth of Moab both became ancestors of Jesus. The point of the Book of Jonah is that God loved the Assyrians. Isaiah saw this clearly also (Isa. 19:19-25; 42:1-6; 49:6). The New Testament, of course, makes the universality of God's love explicit (see Mark 7:24ff; Matt. 8:5ff; Eph. 2:5, 11ff; Gal. 3:28, and Acts 10).

Some False Beliefs

Christian faith in God is incompatible with such beliefs as religious humanism, Satanism, astrology, occultism and modern forms of idolatry. One who believes in God may come to accept one of these common deceptions without being aware of their incompatibility, yet these are no proper part of true Christian faith in God.

Religious humanism takes many forms, but is quite common today as a faith that man, through science, can solve all his problems, including moral evil. We may feel that psychology or sociology will learn how to make criminals into good people. Or maybe we will find a pill which will do the trick. But all of this is to worship man as being all sufficient. It is to make man independent of God, so that God is no longer needed. A Christian is thankful for all that science can do to make life easier and richer, but he puts his ultimate trust in God, not science.

It is astonishing that Satanism has again become popular, after being dead for centuries. To one who understands the history of ideas it is almost unbelievable that in these days of scientific enlightenment, even the most highly educated have dragged out such outmoded and disproven concepts as Satanism, occultism, fortune-telling, and astrology by which to guide their lives. We know that God is all-powerful. Satan's power is limited so that any Christian can successfully "resist" him (Jas. 4:7). Furthermore, the devil is a defeated enemy and knows the end for which he is destined (Luke 10:18; Matt. 25:41; Rev. 20:10). So we must follow the example of Jesus, who refused to worship Satan (Matt. 4:8-10).

To guide your life by use of your astrological horoscope is to worship the created planets rather than God who created them. To seek for some occult knowledge of the future by which to guide your decisions or gain power to carry them out is to trust in spirits rather than the Holy Spirit. To base our security in money, job, or home ownership is to trust in things rather than in God who made all things. This is idolatry just as truly as was the ancient Canaanite worship of images.

CHAPTER 6

CHRISTIAN BELIEF IN THE TRINITY

> ... In the name of the Father and of the Son and of the Holy Spirit (Mat. 28:19).
> The grace of the Lord Jesus Christ, the love of God, and the communion of the Holy Spirit be with all of you (2 Cor. 13:14).
> **What is meant by saying that God is Three in One? Do we have three Gods or one God? Why is such an idea considered so important? Can't we just leave it to some professors to talk about a Trinity? How could such an idea make any difference to us?**

The idea of a Trinity is found only in Christianity. One can be a Christian without knowing the term or the doctrine, but if one is to organize carefully and precisely the Bible teaching about God, there is no way to avoid the concept of the Trinity of God. It is a difficult, but necessary concept.

It is a mystery, not only in the Biblical sense that it could not be known except for revelation, but in the sense that we cannot comprehend it or make it fully comprehensible. Yet we should not be astonished that God is in some sense a mystery to us. Surely finite mortals can never fully understand the infinite Creator of all things! If God is God, He is beyond our ken. Yet, because He is God, He can reveal to us enough of what we need to know about Him, to know Him, love Him, and serve Him.

The term "trinity" does not occur in the Bible. Yet the church has found it impossible to explain the clear teaching of the Bible about God without resort to some such idea, and has struggled hard and long to put it into words which all Christians can accept. The purpose of the term (first used in the second century) is to guard us against two opposite false concepts: The idea that Jesus Christ and the Holy Spirit are not God, and the belief in three Gods. The word itself means "three in one," and is used to mean that God is in some sense three, and in a most important sense one.

Since Tertullian, in the early Third Century, first used the word, Christians have said that God is three *persons* in one *essence*, or *substance*. In the words of the Westminster Confession of 1647: "In the unity of the God-head there be three persons, of one substance, power, and eternity: God the Father, God the Son, and God the Holy Ghost" (Chap. 2, Sec. 3). This definition is quoted as it is brief, but contains the important ideas and expressions on which Christians have agreed since the Fourth Century.

Because of the difficulties of the doctrine, one is apt to feel that it must be an invention of theologians who delight in confusing plain subjects. But this is not so. The doctrine of the Trinity is not the heart of the gospel, and one may be a Christian without knowing the word. But if one is to think deeply and logically about what the Bible teaches about God, the inevitable result must be the idea of Trinity. It is the only way to accept the Biblical teaching that the Father, Christ and the Holy Spirit are God, yet God is one.

God Is One

This is a basic concept of the Old Testament, and is assumed in the New. "Hear, O Israel: The Lord our God is one Lord" (Deut. 6:4). The Old Testament presents the earliest men as monotheists - knowing that there is only one God. But by the time of Abraham, we hear of people worshiping many gods, without being told how this came about.

The Old Testament prophets called the people to leave off their worship of false gods and serve the one true God, Lord of heaven and earth. "I am the first, and I am the last; beside me there is no God" (Isa. 44:6). "I am the Lord, and there is no other; besides me there is no god" (Isa. 45:5). By the end of the Babylonian Exile in the Sixth Century before Christ, the problem of idol worship by the Jews had been settled once and for all. In the New Testament, this settled monotheism is taken for granted, and sometimes clearly stated as in Mark 12:29, where Jesus quoted Deuteronomy 6:4.

The unity of God as taught in the Bible is important because it leaves no place for any eternal force or will but that of God. There is no place for any other god or devil who is eternal. God alone is without beginning or end. God alone has ultimate dominion over all. Satan has power, but it is limited, and will come to an end in God's own time. He will not share His glory with another (Isa. 42:8; 44:20, 25; 48:11). "I am the Lord, and there is no other" (Isa. 45:5).

Jesus Is God

It is the explicit teaching of the New Testament that Jesus is God. This is stated in various ways. For example, we are told that Jesus existed before He came into the world (John 1:1-14; Phil 2:9-10; I Cor. 15:47; Col. 1:17-18; I John 1:1). Jesus Himself implied that He had always been (John 8:56-57; 17:5). This means that He was eternal, and thus God (I Tim. 6:16).

Christ is spoken of as the Creator of the world, and thus God (John 1:3; Col. 1:16; Heb. 1:2, 10). Divine attributes are ascribed to Him, such as omnipotence, omnipresence, eternity, and omniscience. He is called Lord, and is a proper object of worship. All of this praise of the risen Lord Jesus Christ comes to a tremendous climax in the Book of Revelation, in which He is portrayed in all His divine majesty and power.

The Holy Spirit Is God

The Holy Spirit and his work is seen in the Old Testament from the very beginning. The Old Testament tells of the work of the Holy Spirit in action, beginning at the creation (See Chapter 15). The Spirit of the Lord is the great power of the Lord, working in a multitude of ways on things and persons, to reveal and to do the will of God.
Yet Jesus taught much about the personal aspects of the Holy Spirit that was not clear in the Old Testament.

After Pentecost the church understood more clearly that God is Spirit, and that the Spirit who lives in all Christians is God. Not only that, but the Spirit is always spoken of in personal terms, not a mere thing, or object. The personal pronoun, "he" is applied to Him, and personal acts of choice and purpose are ascribed to Him (Acts 13:2-4; 15:28; Rom. 8:26; I Cor. 12:11).

Three, Yet One

So the Bible clearly states that the Father is God, the Son is God, and the Holy Spirit is God; that each of these is distinct from the others; yet that God is one. The Christians of the First Century were sure of all these statements, but they were too busy with persecutions and with the problem of the Gentiles to be concerned about the paradox they presented. When in the Second Century they began to puzzle over the problem, they first concentrated on the relationship of Jesus Christ to the Father, and then on the divine-human nature of Jesus Christ. After settling the fact that Jesus is God, but is not the Father, and the balancing fact that Jesus is not only fully God but fully man, Christians finally began to puzzle over the resulting paradox. How could God be one and three at the same time?

During the Fourth Century the church slowly worked out the doctrine of the Trinity and its wording. The word itself is a combination of the Latin words for *three* and *one*. The real problem was to work out a statement which would protect the church against the two opposite dangers: Unitarianism, which would protect the oneness of God but would deny the divinity of Christ and the personality of the Holy Spirit; and polytheism, which would protect the latter two doctrines but would result in the worship of three gods, not one.

As we have seen above, the statement finally worked out during the Fourth Century after Christ says that "God is one in substance and attributes, but three Persons." This statement does not answer all the questions, but it does protect both the threeness and oneness of God. In fact, it may be said to raise as many questions as it answers, and Christians have not been able to agree on the meaning or use of the key words involved. When it is said that God is "one in essence and three in persons," what is meant by "essence"? What is really meant by "person"?

At this point there are two extremes to which we can go. One is to wade through the morass of literature on the subject and seek to understand and evaluate the many attempts to define the terms in details.

But this would literally take a lifetime, and would chiefly prove that human beings can never fully understand God. The other extreme would be to deny that the whole idea of the trinity is a necessary part of Christian faith. This would be a fatal mistake. The Christian way lies between the two extremes. First of all we need to admit that the essential nature of God is beyond the full comprehension of our finite minds. If God could be fully comprehended, He would not be God. Second, we must keep firmly in mind the real purpose of the doctrine of the trinity, and that is to protect us against the opposite extremes of Unitarianism and of polytheism. The doctrine builds fences on both sides of Christian belief, beyond which we must not go. We must not so emphasize the unity of God that we deny that our Lord Jesus Christ is God or that the Holy Spirit is divine. On the other hand, we must not so stress the three-ness of God as to worship, in effect, three gods rather than one. Between these fences there is room for speculation and differences of opinion.

We have already seen the Scriptural support for the unity of God, and for the divinity of Jesus Christ and of the Holy Spirit. We need to see now that the New Testament repeatedly speaks of the three Persons of the Godhead in one breath, putting the three on the same level.

In what is called the "great commission" Jesus told His disciples to baptize "in the name of the Father and of the Son and of the Holy Ghost" (Matt. 28:19). Somewhat similar is the benediction at the end of II Corinthians, "The grace of the Lord Jesus Christ and the love of God and the fellowship of the Holy Spirit be with you all" (13:14).

Typical of another class of passages is I Peter 1:2, which says that Christians are "chosen and destined by God the Father and sanctified by the Spirit for obedience to Jesus Christ." All three members of the Trinity are mentioned here in the one passage. Others like this are: Rom. 8:9 I Cor. 6:11; 12:4-6; 2 Cor. 1:21-22; 13:14; Eph. 1:3-13; 2:18; 4:4-6; Col. 1:6-8; 1 Thess. 1:3-5; 5:18-19; Titus 3:4-6; Heb. 9:14; I Pet. 1:2; Jude 20-21; Rev. 1:4-5.

It is clear from these Scripture references that the Trinity is an explicit teaching of the New Testament. The problem we have is in putting in unambiguous words the description of the Trinity and the relationships between the three Persons. Not only is this difficult, it has so far proved impossible. God, in His infinitude, is to us a mystery. We can only know what He has chosen to reveal to us of Himself.

Illustrations Of The Trinity

In an attempt to explain the Trinity, Christians have used many illustrations. One of the favorites for a long time was the shamrock, in which we see one whole divided into three parts. A different kind is that of water, ice, and snow. These are three different forms of the same water. So they are all water, yet they are different. There are two problems with this illustration: First, a chemical oneness is a poor comparison to the dynamic oneness of Persons. Second, it would say that God simply appears at different times in three different forms, which is not true. God is Father, Son, and Holy Spirit at one and the same time; from eternity to eternity.

Another illustration is mathematical. We can see that one plus one plus one equals three. But if we change the mathematical relationship of the numbers, we have one times one times one equals one. If the illustration can help someone see that we can have three ones and yet have one whole, it is useful for that person. If it helps us see that the key to the unity of the triune God lies in the relationship of the Persons to one another, then it is helpful. Yet there are both mathematical and theological reasons for this being an inadequate and misleading illustration. Ultimately, we must recognize, numbers are poor analogies for the divine nature.

In one respect, the best illustration seems to be the nature of man himself. Man is body, mind, and soul; yet he is one person. The dynamic interaction of body, mind and soul in one whole can illustrate the interpersonal relations of the Father, Son, and Holy Spirit in one God. If taken as an illustration only, it is good. But if taken as a perfect analogy of the Trinity, it can lead one in several false directions. It speaks of one person and three parts or kinds of being; but in the Trinity we have three "Persons" and one being or essence.

It must be said that this word "person" is the traditional word which has been used in defining the doctrine of Trinity. Yet it was not used with the modern meaning, and has caused much misunderstanding and debate. In the classic creed it was the Latin *persona*, which did not mean what "person" means to us. But since it has been used for so long, anyone reading theology must be aware of it.

Once more we come back to the fact that God is a mystery to us. We cannot fully understand Him. But we can know Him, trust Him, and love Him all the more. And we can worship the Triune God.

Denial of the Trinity

Besides the naive denial of the Trinity by those who simply do not understand the doctrine or its importance, there are three ways in which Christians deny this doctrine in practice, if not in theory. These are, first, the denial which results from emphasis on the Father only; second, that which results from emphasis on the Son; and third, that which results from over-emphasis on the Spirit. The result in each case is a form of Unitarianism which denies the Trinity in practice, if not in words.

Emphasis on the Father only. The Unitarian Church, which has now ceased to call itself "Christian," holds firmly to God the Father, and denies that Jesus Christ is God, and that the Holy Spirit is in any sense a Person of the Godhead. Unitarians thus flatly deny the doctrine of the Trinity. This denial makes a wreck of the Scriptural doctrine of Jesus Christ as our divine Savior from sin. "By this you know the Spirit of God: every spirit which confesses that Jesus Christ has come in the flesh is of God, and every spirit which does not confess Jesus is not of God." (I John 4:2-3).

Many of the groups which are often called "cults" because of their subchristian teachings deny that Jesus Christ was in any real sense divine. They thus explicitly or implicitly deny the Trinity. Among these are Christian Science, Jehovah's Witnesses, Spiritualism, Unity, and Science of Mind. All of these are present in most of our large cities, and their ads appear on the same newspaper reports as Christian churches. Yet they deny that Jesus is the Christ in the sense taught in the New Testament. They deny that the Holy Spirit is more than an impersonal force in the universe. So they deny the Trinity. Mormons make the same denial about Christ.

A third class in this category would include those radical critics of the Old and New Testaments who deny that it is possible to know more about God than reason itself can reveal. They deny that the Bible contains objective revelation from God. So they deny that Jesus was more than a man, thus cutting the heart out of the doctrine of the Trinity.

Emphasis on Jesus only. There are not many who formally aspouse the doctrine of Jesus as the only member of the Godhead, but there are some. What little they have written shows the difficulty they have in finding Biblical support for their peculiar doctrine. There are so many passages they must leave out!

However, there are many Christians now who do so emphasize their love of Jesus as to leave out of their thinking the Father and the Spirit. This comes from a misunderstanding of the Trinity, and may prevent the person from receiving some of the blessings to which he is entitled. Jesus is "exactly like God" (Col. 1:15, Laubach's translation). "He who has seen me has seen the Father" (John 14:9), as Jesus put it. If we love Jesus, we must love God as well. Remember that John (3:16) states that *God* so loved the world that He gave His Son Jesus. Some Christians almost seem to feel that the Father is prevented from punishing us by the loving Christ Jesus. This would be heresy indeed.

Emphasis on the Holy Spirit. Here again we have a view which is formally held by very few, but which is implicit in the view of those who so overemphasize the person and work of the Holy Spirit that they have an unbalanced theology. There is real danger of this in the so-called "charismatic" movement, and some of the leaders are becoming aware of it. Christians can easily get so wrapped up in their search for, and pleasure in an exotic manifestation of the Spirit, that they lose sight of the great truths of the Bible.

The chief point of John 14-16 is that as Jesus was leaving the disciples, He would be sending the Holy Spirit to continue doing the work which He has been doing. The Spirit did not come to do some totally new and strange thing, but to continue and complete the work of Jesus Christ. He gives us power to witness understandably and effectively for Christ.

Importance of the Trinity

One can be a Christian without knowing the doctrine of the Trinity. But if he is to think deeply and rationally about the teaching of the New Testament, he must come to some such doctrine eventually. The Father is God, but is not the Son nor the Spirit. The Son is God, but is not the Father nor the Spirit. The Spirit is God, but is not the Father nor the Son. We cannot understand the how or why of this nature of the one God, any more than we can understand the how or why of gravitation; but we know that it is so. Jesus our Savior must be truly God. The Holy Spirit must be

God, and do the work of God in saving, sanctifying, healing, and keeping us.

How Can We Understand the Trinity?

We cannot fully understand the Trinity any more than we can understand fully any other aspects of God. "For my thoughts are not your thoughts, nor are your ways my ways, says the Lord. For as the heavens are higher than the earth, so are my ways higher than your ways and my thought than your thoughts ." (Isa. 55:8-9).

However, we believe other things without full understanding of them. We are made to wonder sometimes if we fully understand anything at all. And this doctrine of the Trinity is not simply a theoretical concept. It has to do with our salvation. There is an ancient drawing which is a good illustration of what we know of the Trinity. It presents these truths:

> God is One. The Father is God, but the Father is not the Son nor the Spirit. The Son is God, but the Son is not the Father nor the Spirit. The Spirit is God, but the Spirit is not the Son nor the Father.

The gospel of salvation is built on this foundation of the Trinity. If it is not true, then the Son of God is not God and cannot be our Savior. Then the Spirit of God is not God and cannot be the kind of Guide, Helper and Teacher that Jesus said he is. Yet we serve one God, not three. So we can trust the One God to lead us safely into eternal salvation. The Father, Son and Holy Spirit all agree (John 10:30). Jesus prayed for his followers "that they may all be one. As you, Father are in me and I am in you, may they also be in us, so that the world may believe that you have sent me (John 17:21). Summarizing the doctrine of the Trinity in relation to our salvation, H. Orton Wiley wrote: "The doctrine of the Trinity . . . is intensely practical. With it is bound up our eternal salvation. . . . God the Father sent His Son into the world to redeem us; God the Son became incarnate in order to save us; and the Holy Spirit applies the redemptive work to our souls. [18]

Summary

In spite of the difficulties in the wording of the doctrine of the Trinity, this doctrine is essential for our salvation. The wording of the doctrine is a human attempt to protect us from false ideas of God. It tells us not to believe in two or three Gods, as there is only one. It warns us that our God does not appear in different forms in different times in history. It tells us that the Son and the Holy Spirit are each truly God, not partly God, nor appearing to be God, but fully God.

CHAPTER 7

Works of God

> In the beginning was the Word, and the Word was with God, and the Word was God. He was in the beginning with God. All things came into being through him, and without him not one thing came into being (John 1:1-3).
>
> He is the image of the invisible God, the first-born of all creation, for in him all things in heaven and on earth were created, things visible and invisible. . . all things have been created through him and for him. (Col. 1:15-16).
>
> **What is the Christian to believe about the origin of the universe? Does it matter when the universe came into being? Does it matter how it all began? Can a Christian believe what science discovers about the beginning of all things? Or is there a basic conflict between science and Christianity?**

These two passages are clear statements that the Triune God created everything which exists which is not God. John began his story of the gospel of Jesus Christ with this record of his work in creation. And Paul, in order to make clear the transcendence of Christ, also pointed out his work in creation. So we see the importance of the Christian doctrine of creation.

The first thing the Bible tells us is that God created the heavens and the earth. It begins with the words: "In the beginning God created. . ." This majestic statement marks the beginning of a book unlike any other. It puts God before all things and apart from all things. God is not a part of the universe, nor the whole of it, but created it, separate from himself, by his word (Heb. 11:3).

GOD CREATED

"In the beginning God created the heavens and the earth." The Hebrew word translated "create" is ברא, which is never used in this form for shaping previously existing material. For that, the word עשה is often used. Thus the word ברא is fitting for the idea of creation *ex nihilo* - from nothing. God started with nothing and made all that is. The word "creation" has been used to refer both to the activity of God in bringing the universe into existence, and to the result of the activity, which is all that is which is not God.

It is not important when the creation of the universe took place, or how long ago. The age of the earth is of no theological significance, so the Bible gives no hint of it. The universe was made before people, so no person was present to recognize the time. It may even be that we would have no comprehension of the time involved if we were told. Edward J. Young, who was Professor of Old Testament at Westminister Seminary, and who believed every word and letter of the Bible, said, "The Bible does not state how old the earth is, and the question of the age of the earth is not the heart of the issue."[19]. The Biblical record of creation is not contradictory to whatever science may finally prove to be true about the age of the universe and of mankind. In the meantime, we are not responsible for adjusting our biblical exegesis and theology to every new theory. In the early part of the nineteenth century, theology would accommodate itself to the Nebular hypothesis. Later it would have to change as that theory was shown to be inadequate. It would have to change repeatedly to fit Gamow's "big bang," Hoyle's "steady state," and then the "oscillating universe" of Opik. It is sufficient for us to know that however the universe began, God did it.

Science has to do with things, while all theology has to do with God who made the things. If it is not about God, it is not theology. All that is was made by God. He did not choose to tell us more details.

Date of the Creation

Some Christians are uneasy about the statements just made about the time of creation. One reason for this is that some Bibles still print the date 4004 B.C. for the creation. This date was calculated by James Ussher in

1654, and was based on some of the genealogies in the Old Testament, as he interpreted them. It has been shown that this is not a solid basis for any chronology, so that the date has been discredited. The importance of his work is that he was the first to seek to formulate a Biblical chronology. He used the genealogies in the Hebrew Bible. He would have given a far different date if he had used the same genealogies in the Septuagint, which is the Greek translation of the Hebrew Old Testament.

The genealogies of the Bible are not meant to list all the individuals who were in the line of descent, but rather to show in general that a person was from a certain line.[20] Further, the Hebrew word for "father" means "ancestor," and the word for "son" means "descendant." So the various genealogies in the Bible, being made for different purposes, are not all the same. Since they are intended to give the line of descent, they do not include every person in the line. Some add names others do not give, and omit names which others list. No one of them is complete in giving every generation, as we would like to do today. Thus the Bible does not provide the kind of data we need to date early events. For further discussion of this aspect of Old Testament dates, one should read the first two sections of J. N. Oswalt's article on "Chronology of the Old Testament" (ISBE, I, 673-676).

What is Vital?

What matters is: Did things make themselves, or result from accidental development? Or did God create everything from nothing? Is the universe the result of pure chance? Or was it planned by a loving, intelligent God. Is the world running itself? Or is God in charge of the whole universe?

Such questions are not merely concerned with the date of the beginning, but have relevance to us in this stage of history. In fact, the whole doctrine of creation tells us how to feel about some things we see going on in the world right now. We shall consider this more fully later in the chapter, as we consider God's providence.

What Is In The Bible Record?

Genesis provides two accounts of creation. These two are so different in form that some literary critics have decided they were not written by the same person or persons, and not at the same time. We can easily see the differences, but need not agree with these theories which seek to explain the differences.

The first account is in Genesis 1:1--2:4a, and the second is Genesis 2:4b-25. The first is a concise statement of the creation of all things, beginning with the material universe and closing with the creation of human beings. The second says nothing of the order of creation, but stresses the creation of human beings. Both accounts emphasize the supremacy of humanity over the rest of the whole creation. Neither record is given to satisfy our curiosity about when and how things began. Both are theological interpretations of God as supreme Creator of all that is. As soon as we see that their purpose is theological, we see that they are not contradictory in any way. They are telling us about God, and what they are telling us about God is the same, though the forms of the stories are different.

Both Genesis stories of creation emphasize the work of God in it all. Both of them say that it was at the beginning of all things. Both of them stress the supremacy of mankind over all other creatures. The first is the only one which divides the time into "days."

How Long is a Day?

There has been much discussion of the meaning of the days, some thinking they were twenty-four hour periods, and others agreeing with Augustine that they were long periods of time. The word translated "day" is used in three different meanings in the first two chapters ("daylight," "twenty-four hours" and "six creation days"), and is used in other ways in the rest of the Old Testament, where it occurs 1,480 times. These occurrences are translated by more than fifty English words in the King James Version. Much of the discussion over this word is caused by attempts to reconcile "six days" with the astronomical figures of modern science. Part of the interest is caused by our modern fascination with dates in history. But the length of time involved is not important. God could have created everything in a millisecond or less. He chose not to tell us how long he did take. The basic fact we need to know is that all that was made, was made by God, in his own way, and in his own time.

What matters most to us, is that God created human beings, in his own way and for his own purposes.

Creation denies false concepts

Creation denies Polytheism, which is the belief in more than one God. This was the most important fact to the early Israelites, as all their neighboring peoples believed in many gods. They believed that each god had its own responsibilities and powers, and that each must be placated in particular ways. It was a bold step for any prophet of God to say that one God made everything.

Creation denies Dualism in all its forms. One form of dualism which Israel had to face at one time was that good and evil are both eternal, and have been locked in an eternal struggle which neither is able to win. But their belief in one Creator of all things leaves no room for an eternal struggle with evil. There was a time when nothing existed but God, and nothing exists without him.

Creation denies devil worship. God is the Creator and Sustainer of this whole universe. The forces of evil are not in control, even though it may seem so, with our limited vision. Jesus declared to his disciples that Satan is a fallen enemy (Luke 10:17-19) and that God is his judge (John 12:31). Any Christian, through the grace of God in Christ Jesus, has power over Satan (James 4:7). The biblical doctrine of God creating all things makes the service of Satan and evil worse than useless, and even the excessive fear of Satan wrong. God is the one to whom we owe fear and love.

Creation denies atheistic humanism. We must not think of mankind as being all alone in the universe. We are not God. "There is a God in heaven" (Dan. 2:28), and we are to worship and serve Him alone. The Bible does not seek to prove that God is, and that the atheists are wrong, since the problem was that in their neighboring countries, people believed in too many gods, rather than in none. Atheism is a modern problem.

Creation denies pantheism. This is the concept that the universe is God and that God is things. Creation insists that God made all things, not out of his own person, but out of nothing. Pantheism is found today in some oriental religions, and has been adopted from them by some "New Age" writers.

Creation denies astrology. The belief that the stars and planets control our lives is totally false. It is not the stars or planets which make us, but God. God made the stars, planets, and all that is, and gave them none of his power. We must worship the Creator, not what he created.

Creation denies naturalistic evolution. This is a modern way of denying creation by God, just as ancient polytheism denied creation by a single God. If we argue that creation denies evolution, we must be sure that we mean naturalistic evolution, which denies anything supernatural. There are other meanings of the word "evolution," and some of them are compatible with creation. The word can be used to mean any process of change, and does not in itself include any denial of creation by transcendent God.

In the sciences of biology and botany it is possible to observe rather quick changes within species. This is evolution, and there is no reason to deny it. It is micro-evolution, and must be distinguished from macro-evolution, which would mean a change of something from one species to another. This is necessary if one seeks to prove naturalistic evolution.

Naturalistic evolution is the concept that all developed to its present state without God or any supernatural force being involved anywhere in the process. It is, then, a denial of God and creation. This is what the Christian cannot accept, for the Christian has faith in God. The Christian knows not only that God exists, but that he is working today in the world for good.

Doctrine of Creation Affirms

1. God was *before everything.* Nothing is older than God.
2. All that is, was made *by God.*
3. Everything was created *from nothing.*
4. Everything was created *good.*
5. Everything suited *God's purposes.*
6. *Human beings* were created good.
7. Everything is *sustained* by God.
8. *One* God made everything and holds it in being.
9. *Marriage* is good, since God created it.
10. *Work* is good. God worked, and commanded us to do it.

In explanation of the last two points, it is wise to note that God commanded both marriage (1:28; 2:24) and work (2:15) before sin was committed. Both became more difficult as a result of sin. Sin makes work laborious, and marriage burdensome. In a later chapter we shall look further at some of the effects of sin.

Some Limitations of Science

We will never understand the mystery of creation, so as to know when and how it took place. Reason can discover a few things about the universe as it is, and by the methods of sciences such as geology, archeology and astronomy seeks to learn something of the origin and nature of things. But there are limits to what we can learn about the past. And there are limits to what sciences can do.

Modern science has made tremendous changes in the way we live in the world, and has contributed to the welfare of people in marvelous ways. However, scientific knowledge is not all-inclusive, and cannot deal with some aspects of reality. It is limited to what can be studied by the tools and techniques of science. Each science is limited to its own field and has its own techniques for investigation. All science is limited to things, not spirit. So science, no matter how advanced, can never be the *only* source of knowledge. It can never lead to answers to teleological questions (ultimate purpose), and must never seek to be theological.

The physical sciences deal with things, and cannot know about the origin of things, as they can only deal with things after they come into existence. We have no way to study the beginning of time. Augustine argued that the creation did not take place in time, since time could not have been before there were things. So Augustine insisted that there was no time before creation, and that time came into existence at the creation of the universe.[21] Thus, no matter how far back we go in our study of the universe, we have a point beyond which we cannot go. We can only study what exists, not its point of coming into existence.

Science cannot deal with *purpose*. Scientists can discuss and investigate the uses of something, but not the purpose for which it was made. Why is there a universe? Why is the universe like this? Questions about purpose, science, as such, cannot answer.

Science cannot ask about *values*. Science seeks to determine what is, not whether or not it is good. A botanist can know what is the largest flower, but not the most beautiful. The botanist can like one more than another, but he does this as a person, not as a botanist.

Scientific knowledge, in its very nature, is constantly changing and growing. Much has been learned about the world and the universe, but even more remains to be learned. When it comes to problems such as the age of the universe and its beginning, there are a variety of theories. All these theories which show promise of being true must be tested. Facts discovered, such as the rocks and dust on the surface of the moon, and the astronomical discoveries, can demonstrate the truth or falsity of some theories, so scientists continue to analyze all such evidence, and change their theories as the new facts seem to require.

All that scientists eventually prove to be facts, will be capable of being reconciled with all that the Bible teaches. Facts do not contradict facts. Yet they may seem to do so, if we misunderstand either the facts and their implications, or the Bible. We need then, to learn to be patient in our search for truth, and hold some questions in abeyance for the time being. The problem of the time of the prehistoric origin of the universe is one of those questions. It is a mystery for both science and Bible believers. Russell Byrum put it this way,

> Truth is always consistent with itself. Truth in the Bible never contradicts truth in nature. God is the author of both. And as the man of science errs in advancing unproved theories that are opposed to the plain statements of the Scriptures, so also does the theologian err who refuses to regard the facts of science in interpreting the Scriptures, as has been too often done.[22]

Science cannot deal with *supernatural*. A scientist may believe in God, and many of them do, but there is no technique or set of techniques for studying God. Science can neither prove nor disprove anything about God. For knowledge of God we must turn to the Bible. Creation is a theological concept, not open to scientific proof or disproof. To go beyond science we must have revelation from God. And that is exactly what we have. It does not settle all the problems, nor satisfy all our curiosity. But that is not the purpose of revelation. The purpose is to show us the way to God and heaven, and that it does quite well.

Providence

If creation is simply an event which took place in the far distant past, we do not really need to know any more about it than that God did it. But creation is much more than the beginning of all things.

The word "providence" refers to ways in which God provides for necessities. It is of two kinds: General and special. The general providence of God refers to the way God sustains what he has created, and applies to the whole universe (Col. 1:17). Special providence has to do with the needs of individual persons. God sees our future before it comes to pass, and provides for it. He sees what he wants us to do and be, and what we will need, and provides for all.

Deism taught that God created the universe, started it running like a clock, and then left it to run on its own, with no further supervision from him. It implies that God no longer has any interest in the universe or in anything or anyone in it, and is off doing something else or nothing.

If deism were true, there would be no use in prayer, or faith in the helpfulness of God. All we could do is make the most of the universe as we have it, working on our own with no help from above. Deism did not last long as a major worldview, and it is easy to see why. If we have to live as though there is no God, why believe there is a God at all? So deism moved rather quickly to an antisupernatural view which is totally naturalistic or materialistic. It does not matter whether there is a God or not, if he has nothing to do with the world, or with us.

General providence

"He makes his sun rise on the evil and on the good, and sends rain on the just and on the unjust" (Mat. 5:45). The Bible is clear that God continues to work in all of nature. This work is celebrated in Psalm 104, in which we are told that God provides water and grass for all the animals of the earth, which are said to look to God for their food. Psalm 19:1-6 reminds us that the sky, with the sun, moon and stars, tells us of the glory of God, as he keeps them in their places. In Job 38—41 we find God asking Job a wealth of questions about Job's inability to do what God does all the time in his working in the universe and in all the world. Isaiah (40:26) speaks of God bringing out the host of stars by calling them each by name, so that not one is missing.

God is not merely transcendent, greater than the whole universe, but he is immanent, working in and through the whole universe. He not only created it, but is working all the time to conserve it (Heb. 1:3). "He himself gives to all life and breath and all things" (Acts 17:25). "For in him we live and move, and have our being" (Acts 17:28). "For from him, and through him, and to him are all things. To him be glory forever. Amen." (Rom. 11:36). Psalm 104 is a long hymn of praise to God for the way he preserves all living things. Verses 27-30 says:

> These all look to you
> to give them their food in due season.
> When you give to them, they gather it up;
> when you open your hand,
> they are filled with good things.
> When you hide your face,
> they are dismayed;
> when you take away their breath,
> they die and return to their dust.

Jesus insisted that this care of God for all things extends to the small details, "Are not two sparrows sold for a farthing? and not one of them will fall to the ground without your Father's will. But even the hairs of your head are all numbered" (Mat. 10:29-30). Why can't we remember that when we are worried and anxious about things?

Special Providence

Special providence of God has to do with his concern for individual persons. If there is no special providence, we have no reason to think God will answer our prayers and meet our particular needs. This is what was on the mind of the psalmist when he looked at the heavens above and asked, "What are human beings that you are mindful of them, mortals that you care for them?" (Psalm 8:4). How can the same God who designed and runs the universe be concerned with one person on this little planet, revolving around one of the smaller stars?

The answer to such a question depends on how big a God we believe in! We know how limited we human beings are. We find it hard to do many things at a time. Yet we would be wrong to attribute to God the limitations under which we suffer. The Bible encourages us to enlarge our faith to match whatever we find in our telescopes and microscopes. The same God who calls the stars of the most distant galaxies by name, also understands the mysterious ways of subatomic particles/waves. He has no problem knowing your name and address, and your desires.

Can God Break "Natural Laws"? It is common to think that the universe works according to "laws." We cannot break the law of gravitation or the law or the laws of cause and effect. So there are some things which are impossible because they would break natural laws. If we drop a ball, it falls down, not up. If one dies, we bury the body because dead bodies do not live on. This is the problem with miracles. Miracles break natural laws. So we wonder, "Are miracles possible?" Can God break natural laws? This is a serious question, and causes many to have trouble believing in miraculous events. Maybe they do not really happen. How does God work in this world in which we live?

God works in the world in such a consistent way that we can depend on the major things. What we call gravitation always works the same way. Plants and trees grow up, not down or sideways. The sun, moon and stars stay where they are supposed to be. In fact, God so consistently works in the universe that we are able to describe his workings in what we call "laws."

But these are not laws at all. They are only human descriptions of the ways God usually works in the universe. The "laws" have no power over God or over things. God is not in any sense bound to work in those ways. For his own good reasons he can work in other ways as the circumstances require. When he works in some extraordinary way, we marvel, and may call it a "wonder" or a "miracle." We have already seen that the principle of order in the universe is not abrogated by the discoveries of the New Physics (Above, Chapter 2).

These "laws" are not useless or wrong. Being able to describe some of the working of God in mathematically exact statements is a valuable work. We can learn how to protect ourselves from some troubles, and improve our lot by learning to cooperate with our environment. If this were not an orderly universe, we would be constantly surprised and dismayed by what goes on around us. We would not be able to make sense of a disorderly universe. God has put us in a world which makes sense. Then he said for human beings, in their God-given wisdom, to "have dominion (Heb. רדה *radah*) over the environment (Gen. 1:28). God never intended this dominion to be destructive, but constructive. It is the command to be wise and responsible environmentalists.

Is God Fair?

Theology uses the word "theodicy" in discussing the question of the fairness of God. Theodicy comes from the Greek words meaning "the justice of God." The term is used in theology to mean the problem of God and suffering. If God is both good and omnipotent, why does he allow suffering and evil in the world he made.

We ask: "If there is a God, why does he not stop this terrible war?" "If there is a God why does he let a child be murdered?" "If God is good, why does he allow such terrible floods, earthquakes and volcano eruptions?" "If God is good, why does he allow serial killers, wicked rulers and 'ethnic cleansing'?" "If God loves people, why did he allow the Holocaust?"

As a result of such questions, some have decided that there really is no God. One philosopher did not become an atheist when his son died, but he decided that God is good but not omnipotent. His reasoning was that if God had all power, he would have made this boy live. Still others have decided that God is not really good. But if God is not good, what is the source of any goodness in the universe? These choices leave us with more serious questions than ever, and a real problem to solve. Fortunately, Christians have been thinking seriously about the whole problem of theodicy for two thousand years, and have come up with some answers, though the full truth will not be known in this world.

Reasons for Suffering

First we should make a distinction between what we might call natural evil and moral evil. Under natural evil we can include all the suffering caused by diseases, natural catastrophes, and such. Moral evil includes all the things which people do when moved by the wickedness of their hearts. We shall leave the discussion of moral evil to a later chapter on sin. For the moment we shall look at the problem of what we can call "natural evil."

When we consider natural evil as a cause of suffering, we can see that it is only partially controllable by us. Some suffering is caused by our ignorance or carelessness of the way things are in this world. Living on a river bottom can be pleasant most of the time, but invites damage from a flood. Building on a fault line puts one in danger of losing it all in an earthquake. Building a home on the side of a dormant volcano puts one in jeopardy. Bad health practices may bring sickness or death. Yet one may do all these things in ignorance. Or we may do some of them because we want to, hoping for the best.

When troubles come, and we find that we have acted carelessly or in ignorance, the trouble itself may bring good by forcing us to learn what we can of the reasons for the trouble. We may learn how to build dams, plant trees, and do a variety of things which can help prevent flood damage. We may learn not to build on known fault lines. We may learn how to avoid many of the natural disasters.

Some suffering comes to us, then, because of our partial knowledge of how things work, and of the causes of suffering. But the tension between partial knowledge of the causes of suffering, and the strong desire to have all the answers, leads some to trust in strange gods, such as Nature, Chance, Fortune-telling, Drugs; and Astrology. But these are false Gods. To worship them or to believe in them is to worship what has been made, rather than the Maker of all.

Why does God permit such things to be in this world? Can we consider this a good world when such disasters can cause trouble and suffering for so many? When we are doing the suffering, we tend to feel that the whole world is bad, and that God is not good for allowing such things to happen. Yet we have no right to decide that this is not a good world. For even these troubles can help us. If there were no suffering, we could never learn patience and faith in God. If nothing ever went wrong for us, we would never develop some of the capabilities God has put within us. Troubles challenge us, and we need some challenge to grow and develop.

Does the Bible Help?

The Book of Job could never have been written if Job had been in a world where no one ever suffered. What a loss it would have been not to have this great book! Almost every book of the Bible has something to say about the whole problem of suffering.

Two great Psalms on the subject are 37 and 73. In Psalm 37, David grapples with the problem of good people suffering, and says some important things. Jesus quoted a verse or two from this chapter, and all Christians can gain insights from it.

In Psalm 73, written by Asaph, we find even more help in suffering. We learn first of all that we are not alone in our discouragement, for Asaph frankly tells us that he almost gave up his faith in God in the midst of his suffering. He says that his difficulty was made even greater by the fact that he saw wicked persons who did not seem to suffer, and felt that he had been good for nothing. "All in vain have I kept my heart clean and washed my hands in innocence. For all the day long I have ben stricken, and chastened every morning" (vss. 13-14). Yet he realized that he could not afford to tell others this, for this kind of testimony would tend to discourage others. But he did not know how to solve the problem. His worry over it wearied him. Then, in worship, God helped him to see a partial answer. He saw that the wicked would not live forever, and would die and lose all. Then he lost all his bitterness in suffering, and saw that it was best for him to trust in God to bring him to something better after this world was ended.

Paul tells of one way in which suffering helped him. He does not tell us anything about the cause or nature of his suffering, but simply says that "a thorn was given me in the flesh" (2 Cor. 12:7). He continues: "Three times I besought the Lord about this, that it should leave me; but he said to me, 'My grace is sufficient for you, for my power is made perfect in weakness.' I will all the more gladly boast of my weaknesses, that the power of Christ may rest upon me. For the sake of Christ, then, I am content with weaknesses, insults, hardships, persecutions, and calamities; for when I am weak, then I am strong" (vss. 8-10). Paul put in these words the way in which we need to face suffering and trouble in the spirit of Christ. Even if we do not see what the point of the suffering may be, and cannot see how it can help either us or others, we can trust in God to take us through it all with victory, and make something good of both us and others. God's ultimate purpose is not to grow weak babies, dependent on others, but to grow mature adults, strong and able to face difficulty.

In this world, we will never have the perfect answer to all the questions we ask about God permitting suffering. God has never promised to take all suffering away from us.

How Can A Christian Respond?

The highest Christian answer to suffering is in two parts: First, suffering can be of such a kind that it is helpful to others—as was the death of Christ on the cross. Second, the grace of God is sufficient to bring us through suffering with victory, and will make more of us as a result of it. In suffering the grace of God is sufficient to keep us, and to make us stronger as we look to him in faith and confidence. So the Christian answer to personal suffering cannot be seen except through the eyes of faith. Without that faith in the preservation and care of God, we have nothing but a puzzle and a discouraging question about the goodness of God and of the world he has made.

A central passage in the New Testament is Romans 8:28: "We know that in everything God works for good with those who love him, who are called according to his purpose." The King James Version made "all things" (Greek παντα) subject of the sentence, but it can be translated as the accusative of reference as above. God is the one who brings good out of evil.

God can bring good out of any circumstance, no matter how bad it may seem to us. In some human act wrecks Plan A, God always has Plan B. For every contingency, God has a plan which will achieve his purpose of making those who love him to be "conformed to the image of his Son" (vs. 29). If we continue to love and serve him, he will work in all things for good.

In connection with that great passage, we should remember also Phil. 2:12-13: "Work out your own salvation with fear and trembling;; for God is at work in you, both to will and to work for his good pleasure." We must do our best in every circumstance to cooperate with God, who is working in us to do his will in our lives. If God is working in us, and we work with him, we cannot fail to achieve his ends. Much of what we do may look like failure to us, but it cannot be failure if we are working in harmony with God. If we ever doubt this, we need to go back to Romans 8 and read verses 31-39. Nothing can separate us from the love of God unless we ourselves turn away from God to serve our own interests. We can leave God, but God will never in this life leave us.

What Have We Learned?

In this chapter we have considered the fact that God not only created all things that are, but that he continually watches over it all, preserving it and working in and through it all for his own ultimate purposes. If creation were only something that happened once at the beginning of time, and nothing more, it would not matter all that much whether we know about it or not. However, if we understand that God is still in the universe and concerned with working out his own will in and through us, this becomes vitally important.

Chapter 8

Human Beings: Theological Anthropology

> When I look at thy heavens, the work of thy fingers, the moon and stars which thou hast established; what is man that thou art mindful of him, and the son of man that thou dost care for him? Psalms 8:3-4
>
> **Where does humanity fit into the universe? If God is so great, how can he be concerned with human beings? Did God create human beings good? Or bad? If he made us good, how could there be so much evil in the world?**

Anthropology is the study of human beings. Theological anthropology is the study of human beings in relation to God. Science studies people from a variety of viewpoints: Size, chemical composition, physical characteristics, comparison to other animals, social activities and relationships with one another, mental activity, nervous system, and emotions.

However, there is no science of God and no way for science to study man-in-relation-to-God. The best that science can do is to study the ways human beings think about God and ask how such thoughts or opinions affect the way a person lives. No science can put God in a test tube or on analytic scales. No science can control God so as to perform experiments on Him. No experiments can use the standard scientific process of using control groups to find out how people are different if God is working in and through them, as it cannot use a control group in the experiment.

If there is no way to gain scientific knowledge of human beings in relation to God, we are left with several logical alternatives. We might say that man is all alone in the universe, since there is no scientific proof that there is a God for us to be related to. This is the way of *atheism*, and leaves human beings with no higher being to which to look. Some who take this way feel that they must search the starry heavens to see if they can find any greater beings than God. Their primary ways of searching are with special telescopes and the new radio-telescopes, seeking for some message from the far reaches of space. A fortune is being spent on such research.

Others tell us to look within our own souls for God, and that each person can be God. All we have to do is to get in touch with ourselves and know that we are our own God. This is the way of the so-called "New Age" movement, and still leaves the person with no outside guidance and no superior power to whom to look. Some such thinkers say that we can become "one with the universe" and have all the creative power of the universe to guide and help us. Others, going all the way with Hindu reincarnation, insist that we can get in touch with great persons of the past, from whom we can gain help and guidance for life. Yet all of this, like all such pagan concepts, leaves us with nothing but other people and some impersonal force. They believe there is no one "out there" who loves us and wants to help us. New Age thought tells us to keep searching, and that either in this life or in some far-distant future rebirth, we might find something wonderfully helpful. Some of the lecturers claim to have arrived at such contact with power, but their lives are not convincing.

We are left with the Bible, which is God's loving revelation of himself to us. It is the record of the revelation which centers in Jesus Christ, as we have seen. What does it tell us of the nature of mankind, and of the relationship with God which we can have?

HUMAN BEINGS ARE CREATED

The first thing the Bible says about human beings is that we are created by God, from whom our life comes. But this fact of our being created is not a past event only. We are dependent on God for our very existence. We are dependent on God each day for our continued existence. Not only is our dependence stated in the first chapters of the Bible, but it is stressed all the way through the Old and New Testaments.

God warned Israel not to forget him when they had plenty: "When you have eaten and are full, and have built goodly houses and live in them, and when your herds and flocks multiply, and your silver and gold is multiplied . . . Beware lest you say in your heart, 'My power and the might of my hand have gotten me this wealth.' You shall remember the Lord your God, for it is he who gives you power to get wealth" (Deut. 8:12-13, 17-18).

Wealth so often makes people forget their dependence on God and to feel that they can now get along without him. It is all too easy to call on God for help only when we are at the end of our rope, whether in money or health. The prophet Hosea used a story of unfaithful marriage to show Israel that they had done the same thing. The unfaithful wife had finally decided to come back to her husband, "and she did not know that it was I who have her the grain, the wine, and the oil" (Hos. 2:8). And God said to Israel: "When Israel was a child, I love him, and out of Egypt I called my son. The more I called them, the more they went from me; they kept sacrificing to the Baals, and burning incense to idols. Yet it was I who taught Ephraim to walk, I took them up in my arms; but they did not know that I healed them" (Hos. 11:1-3).

We like to feel that we can do things for ourselves. We want to be independent. So it is easy for us to fool ourselves into thinking that we can do for ourselves whatever we really need to do. So we can easily lose our feeling of dependence on God for all that we have. Yet it is God who gives us life and health and the ability to do whatever we do. As Paul declared to the philosophers in Athens, "In him we live and move and have our being" (Acts 17:28).

A wealth of knowledge can have the same effect as economic wealth, whether the knowledge is correct, or imagined. This is exactly what has happened to some in this day of the growth of scientific knowledge and technology. It is easy for us to feel that since we have done so much for ourselves, we can do whatever else we need to do, so we do not need God. This temptation is strong in our age, but we must resist it. We must not feel that since doctors can do so much to help us, we no longer need to pray for healing. It is God who does the healing, even when doctors know how to help. Just as the greatest of doctors quickly get to the end of their knowledge and ability to aid the patient, so all science has its limitations. Technology can do great things, but technology is only able to use what God has created and put into the world. Medical science can aid the healing power which the body has through God's creating, and that is great, but there are severe limits to what medical science can do.

One Race

The Bible insists that all human beings are descendants of one original pair (Gen. 1:27) Paul used this to preach in Athens that God "made from one every nation of men to live on all the face of the earth" (Acts 17:26). Some Greek texts add the word ʹαιματος (blood) after "one," but this would not change the meaning. We are one race.

We are all members of the human race. We are all equal at the foot of the cross. All human beings alike need salvation, and all alike find it in Christ. This is clearly seen in a study of the following passages: Matthew 25:31-46; 28:19; John 1:9; Acts 2:17; 10:28, 34-35; Romans 3:9-30; 11:16-23; 1 Corinthians 1:24; Galatians 3:28; Ephesians 2:11-17; 1 Timothy 2:1-6; and Revelation 7:9-10.

What is a Person?

The common way of speaking of a person as being made up of body, mind and soul (and spirit?) is inaccurate and misleading. It is true that there are passages which refer to some of these, but not in a way as to support the division of a human being into certain parts. "And you shall love the Lord your God with all your heart, and with all your soul and with all your might" (Deut. 6:5). But when Jesus quoted this verse, the Gospels record that he added the word "mind" (Mark 12:30; Luke 10:27; Matt. 22:37 — Matthew omits the word for "strength"). 1 Thessalonians 5:23 lists "spirit and soul and body." Hebrews 4:12 speaks of "the division of soul and spirit, of joints and marrow." This should probably be taken as stress on the accurate judgment by God through his word, rather than a comment on the nature of persons.

From the stories of creation we learn some important facts about human beings. By being contrasted with all other animals, human beings are shown to be superior. Persons have a will, self-determination, and can make considered decisions. Persons can be more creative than animals because of superior thinking ability, and appears to have a more complex emotional constitution than the lower animals. All of these characteristics are related to the concept of being like God, but are not that likeness.

The likeness to God has to do with the person being in a free and open personal relationship with God. But the whole makeup or constitution of the person is what makes that relationship possible. That is why God gave persons minds capable of complex reasoning, and the ability to make chosen decisions about what to do and how. God wanted persons, not robots. God wanted persons to love and serve him, by returning his love for them.

What is the Image of God in People? Wrong question! Nowhere in the Old or New Testaments does the Bible say anything about the image of God in humans. Instead, it always speaks of human beings as "made in the image of God." There is an important difference. We are wrong if we look in human beings for the thing which is the image of God. The image of God is not a thing.

In The Image of God

It is startling to read that we are created in the image and likeness of the Creator of the whole universe! How can that be? Are we like God? In what way could it be said that we are like God? The basic passage in the Old Testament is Genesis 1:26-27: "Then God said, 'Let us make man in our image, after our likeness; and let them have dominion over the fish of the sea, and over the birds of the air, and over the cattle, and over all the earth, and over every creeping thing that creeps upon the earth.' So God created man in his own image, in the image of God he created him; male and female he created them."

The other two Old Testament passages are Genesis 5:3, where it is said that Adam had a son "in his own image," and Genesis 9:6, where murder is condemned "for God made man in his own image." It must be noted that the word "man" (Heb. אדם *adham*) refers here to both male and female, as the two are "in the image of God."[23]. It is humanity as both male and female that is created in the image of God. Except for these two passages, the word "image" is used in the Old Testament for idols, but they are condemned, as God has no physical likeness to be imitated.

James 3:10 echoes the Old Testament use when he speaks of the tongue, "With it we bless the Lord and Father, and with it we curse men, who are made in the likeness of God."

Nature of the Image of God

We must be careful in seeking to define the image of God in humans, since our understanding of this point is so intertwined with the concepts of sin, depravity, salvation and sanctification, and with the nature of human beings. A wrong concept of any one of these leads to wrong concepts of the others.

If we think of sin as some thing which is born in a person, and which can be removed, then the image of God is the lack of that thing. Depravity would then be the outworking of that thing, and salvation and sanctification would be the removal of it. Further, this view of sin leads to the question of how it is passed on from parents to children. This question, then, has led to the development of various theories of transmission of depravity. These theories try to account for the inheritance of the sin of Adam. The purpose of such theories is to explain why it is that everybody falls into sin, after God made human beings in his own image. We shall deal with this more fully when we come to consider the nature of sin. For the present we need to give careful attention to the *imago dei* — the image of God.

The first thing we must note is that the likeness to God is not the absence of some thing. The image of God is not something which could be destroyed. It is not a *thing* at all. Understanding at this point will affect our understanding of what happened when Adam and Eve sinned, and will affect our concept of our human need, and what God does for us in salvation.

It is clear that human beings are not physically like God, as God has no physical appearance to be imitated. In some Mormon writings God is said to have a physical body, but this has no Biblical support.[24] Jesus declared that "God is spirit, and those who worship him must worship in spirit and truth" (John 4:24). The point of Jesus here is that God is not physically limited to one place, and must be worshiped in spirit anywhere one happens to be. Paul made a similar point when he told the Athenian philosophers that since God is "Lord of heaven and earth (he) does not live in shrines made by man" (Acts 17:24). God is not spatially limited to a body.

God warned strongly against making any kind of image of God (Exod. 20:4; Lev. 26:1; Deut. 5:8). These commandments were eventually taken by Israel very seriously, so that after the Babylonian Exile, they shunned all such idols. But this negative definition of the image of God as not physical leaves something to be desired. Is it possible for us to know what is meant by the term?

John Wesley spoke of the image of God as having three aspects: Natural, political and moral[25]. By the natural image, Wesley meant the human power of understanding, the will, and freedom to exercise the will by choosing. By the political aspect, he meant the ability and responsibility of exercising some protective control over the created ecological system. This can be seen as human beings acting in such a way as to mediate the grace of God to all creation. Wesley often stressed the *moral* aspect of the image of God, as it manifested itself in "righteousness and true holiness" (Eph. 4:24).[26]

The most important thing we can say about the image of God, then, is that a human is capable of knowing and loving God so as to live for His glory. This capability has been well described by H. Ray Dunning in terms of four freedoms: "(1) Freedom for God; (2) Freedom for the Other; (3) Freedom from the Earth or World; (4) Freedom from Self-domination." [27]

Freedom for God. This is seen in the free communion Adam and Eve had with God, as seen in the implication that they were in the habit of walking with God "in the cool of the day" (Gen. 3:8). They had nothing of which to be ashamed (Gen. 2:25), and nothing to keep them from God. There was no disobedience to make them want to hide from God (Gen. 3:8). This freedom for God — openness to God, was the very opposite of sin. They had nothing in their hearts or lives to keep them from loving God with all their being. They freely did what they thought would please God, and obeyed him out of love. His will was their freely chosen will, chosen in love for Him. He had made them like himself.

Freedom for the Other. We note that God used the plural when he said, "Let us make man in our image, after our likeness; and let them have dominion . . ." (Gen. 1:26). Christians have long felt that the plural form relating to God supports the New Testament concept of the Trinity. We must recognize that it does not teach that God is three in one; all it does is show that the Old Testament does not contradict the New Testament teaching.

The analogy between the threeness of God and the two-ness of human points to the social nature of humans as one aspect of the likeness to God. Genesis stresses that God make human beings both male and female, as he did other animals. But surely it means something more in humans. God made us social beings, and declared that it was "not good that the man should be alone" (Gen. 2:18). Since they had nothing to hide from one another, and no guilt or shame to keep them from full and free communication, their friendship was unhindered. They were free for each other — open to one another. They had something analogous to the unity of the Father, Son and Holy Spirit.

The love Adam and Eve had for one another was unhindered by self-love, which is lust. It was pure love, which caused each to seek the well-being and pleasure of the other. This love bound them together in true fellowship, and made all their interaction a joy. They pleased themselves by pleasing each other.

This freedom for one another affected every aspect of their being. It is what caused them to be unashamed of their lack of clothing. Dunning has a valuable insight when he states that:

> The openness of man for woman and vice versa as well as each human to the other revolves around the body. The body is the means by which one human being relates to the other.
> This insight provides a solid theological basis for the admonitions regarding physical adornment found in 1 Pet. 3:3-5 and 1 Tim. 2:9-10. Clement of Alexandria spends a great deal of space admonishing against the decoration of the body with clothes, jewels and cosmetics because it is basically an attempt to present a false picture of the self, thus not true openness of person to person.[28]

This helps us see that God made us to be social, not loners. It is good for us to have close fellowship. Friends not only help one another, but the friendship itself is good for each. And although we have used the marriage of a man and a woman to illustrate the social aspect of humans, the importance lies not in the sexual aspect, but in the personal. Whether the friendship is in male/female marriage, which is the closest possible human relationship, or a less intense friendship, it must be based on honesty, concern for one another and for God, and full submission to the will of God. There must be no deceit between the persons, or anything which would cause guilt or shame in the relationship. The persons must be open and free with one another.

Freedom from the Earth or World. The first humans were told to have dominion over the rest of creation. That is, they were not to be bound by their environment, but were to care for it, cultivate it, and use it wisely, and to the glory of God who made it. God gave them responsibility for doing their best with what God had created. In this way, God gives mankind a share in the responsibility for all creation. Whether we call this a part of the image of God or not, it is truly a part of what it means to be fully human. And it can be an aspect of our likeness to God the Creator. In our present time, when the explosion of world population has forced the ecological problems of existence upon our consciousness, we must think through the implications of this responsibility.

Freedom from Self-domination. In one sense, this freedom from self is a part of all that we have been saying. Either we are God-centered, and thus free for God and others, or we are self-centered and find it impossible to relate to God, and difficult to relate to others as we should. Self-centered persons cannot easily be motivated to take care of the environment properly. So this freedom from self is basic to being like God.

Adam and Eve were created good

The first man and woman were created holy. "Behold, this alone have I found, that God made man upright, but they have sought out many devices" (Eccl. 7:29). God did not create sin and evil, but created human beings who were holy and good, with no sin at all. Adam and Eve had a free and open relationship with God who made them. He loved them, and they loved him in return. They had good minds, but besides that, they had the constant love and guidance of God, with no hindrance to communication with him. They were made in the likeness of God.

Christ, the Image of God

Other New Testament passages add two more perspectives: First, that Christ is the image of God (Col. 1:15; 2 Cor. 4:4; Heb. 1:3). Second, that we Christians are being renewed in the image of God day by day (Eph. 4:24; Col. 3:10; 2 Cor. 3:18). The latter passage states it beautifully:

"And we all, with unveiled face, beholding the glory of the Lord, are being changed into his likeness from one degree of glory to another; for this comes from the Lord who is the Spirit." Christ came and died for us so that we might be changed into the "image of his Son" (Rom. 8:29).

As we become more Christlike through the ministration of the Holy Spirit working within us, we are being conformed to the image of God. This is the goal of the Christian life. We are promised that this goal will be reached finally, in eternity (1 Cor. 15:49). This is also what John meant when he said, "Beloved, we are God's children now; it does not yet appear what we shall be, but we know that when he appears we shall be like him, for we shall see him as he is" (1 John 3:2).

Human Probation

Adam and Eve were created to know God and to live for him. Yet God did not want them to be unthinking, unwilling slaves. He wanted them to love and serve him because they willingly loved him. He wanted all of us to choose to serve him. So God gave us the ability to choose. Yet there can be no choice if there is only one thing to choose, so God gave human beings a test. This testing is what is meant by the theological term "probation." God put Adam and Eve on probation. He gave them a test. In the case of Adam and Eve it was a simple test of their obedience, so that they could prove ("probation" comes from the Latin word for "proving" or "testing") their willing obedience. It meant that they had a real choice. They could go on obeying God, or they could disobey, by eating of the tree of which the fruit was forbidden. The species of tree is not important, nor is the kind of fruit. They could obey and live, or disobey and die. Their personal relationship with God would die. They could never again be the same as before.

The First Sin

When Adam and Eve first disobeyed God, they fell from the condition of holiness in which God had created them. Since then "all have sinned and come short of the glory of God" (Rom. 3:23). Because this sin has had consequences on the whole human race, it is called "the Fall." This term is not found in the Bible, but it fits what the Bible has to say about this first sin. People have not since been what God intended. This is the clear message of Genesis, that it was not in any way a step upward to divine knowledge, as the serpent suggested, but a fall from the grace of God.

There are serious questions about the Fall which are not answered in the Bible. How could sin have gotten into the hearts of the two persons whom God had created holy? If the devil tempted them, where did he come from? How could God permit such an awful thing to happen? How did the sin *of Adam lead to the sinning of all his descendants? Are we born sinful? Are we born guilty of Adam's sin? What is there about the soul of each person which leads that one to sin?

Note that Paul insisted on the universality of sin. That is, all human beings have sinned (Rom. 1:18--3:18). In support of this he refers to such passages as Psalms 5, 10, 14, and Proverbs 10:7, as well as other Old Testament passages. He could have referred also to Genesis 6:5-7, which tells of the wickedness of people being so great that God decided to destroy all of them except Noah and his immediate family with the flood. He could have used almost every book of the Old Testament to support his statement of the universality and binding power of sin. He did not need to prove it to his readers, as they could see for themselves that this was true.

Chapter 9

Nature of Sin

> See, the Lord's hand is not too short to save, nor his ear too dull to hear. Rather, your iniquities have been barriers between you and your God, and your sins have hidden his face from you (Isa. 59:1-2).
> **What do Christians mean by sin? Does it really matter in these days? If everybody sins, what is the use of worrying about it? Isn't it impossible to live without sin in a wicked society?**

That branch of theology which deals with the doctrine of sin is Hamartiology. Calvinists and Wesleyans differ in their concepts of sin, especially when they speak of sin in Christian believers. No matter what our theological orientation, we can agree on the beginnings of a definition of sin:

1. "Sin" is a theological concept - not legal. One can sin without breaking any laws.
2. Knowingly breaking a commandment of God is sin.
3. Ignoring or transgressing the covenant of God is sin.
4. Sin cannot be attributed to things.
5. Sin is against God, primarily.
6. Hurting another person is a sin against God.
7. Sin is primarily a person against the personal God.

Sin is a theological concept. Sin cannot be defined without reference to God. Sin is always against God. Even when it is against other people, it is primarily against God. When David had sinned against Bathsheba, against Uriah, and against the nation; he declared to God that he had sinned against God "only" (Ps. 51:4). He felt rightly that the sin he had committed was ultimately and primarily against God. His relationship with God had to be set right if his relationships with others were ever to be right.

Sin has to do with being and doing what displeases God. Failing or refusing to please God is the essence of sin. But we could never know what it is that would please God except as God reveals to us what he wants us to be and do. We could never know God's will except through divine revelation, any more than we can know what is in the mind of another person unless that person reveals it to us in some way. He does this through his Holy Spirit who works in the hearts of all people from the beginning.

Thus God shows his love for all nations and for the individuals in them. Noah served God while his neighbors would not, even after his preaching (Gen. 6). How did God reach him? Terah and Abram lived in a pagan nation when they answered God's call (Gen. 11:31--12:9). Balaam learned something of God in a pagan land, though he was not always faithful (Num. 22-24). All through the rest of the Old Testament we read of pagans who responded to the Spirit's leadings and served God. When Paul preached to the pagans in Lystra, he declared that God "did not leave himself without witness" to them (Acts 14:17).

The best study of this universal aspect of the Old Testament is the survey made by Johannes Blauw.[29] God loves all nations equally. He did not love the nation of Israel more than others. Yet they had the kind of leaders who were able to receive the will of God in a special revelation. The Bible is a record of divine revelations of His will and ways with human beings.

God could have revealed that he wants us to: Obey 625 laws, obey ten commandments, or be perfect human beings, never making mistakes. If he had taken one of these three ways, then sin would be breaking one of the 625 laws, breaking one of the ten commandments, or being less than perfect. If sin were defined in one of the first two ways, it would be conceivable that one could memorize the rules and seek to avoid breaking any of them. If it is defined in the third way, there is no way that any person on the face of the earth could be without sin, since no one is perfect in all that he is or does.

What did God reveal about his will for people? Primarily he revealed a covenant he wished to make with human beings. "Now therefore, if you obey my voice and keep my covenant, you shall be my treasured possession out of all the peoples. Indeed, the whole earth is mine, but you shall be for me a priestly kingdom and a holy nation." (Exod 19:5-6). "And I will make my abode among you, and my soul shall not abhor you. And I will walk among you, and will be your God, and you shall be my people" (Lev. 26:11-12).

Thus it is clear that what God wants is to have a personal relationship with the human beings he created. Sin, then is anything that breaks or hinders that relationship. The essence of sin is not to be defined as breaking a rule, but breaking this God-mortal relationship. "So now, O Israel, what does the Lord your God require of you? Only to fear the Lord your God, to walk in all his ways, to love him, to serve the Lord your God with all your heart and with all your soul, and to keep the commandments of the Lord your God and his decrees that I am commanding you this day for your own well-being". (Deut. 10:12-13).

So the will of God includes the keeping of his commandments, but this obedience comes as the result of love for God. What God wants is for us to love him and serve him (Deut. 10:12-14). The commandments show us the way to do this. They guide our relationship, but the commandments themselves are not the primary aim of God in relation to us. So breaking a commandment is not the essence of sin

THE NATURE OF SIN

Holiness is primarily an attribute of God, and only God is holy in and of himself. Only God is holy in essence. Yet the Bible teaches us that God graciously draws human beings into such a relationship with himself that he calls them "holy." Those who belong to him in this special sense can be said to have a derived or reflected holiness. They are "separated to" God. The negative aspect of this holiness of human beings is separation from sin. The positive aspect is God-given love "poured into our hearts through the Holy Spirit" (Rom. 5:5).

The question of the nature of sin arises when we seek to be free of it. The problem of definition becomes acute when we seek to define holiness as it applies to human beings. If holiness includes victory over sin, the nature of holiness is bound up with the nature of sin. This means that if we are to understand the Biblical commands to be holy people, we must first seek to understand the nature of sin. A wrong definition of sin causes a misunderstanding of holiness.

Being human is not sin. Genesis 1--3 makes it clear that human beings were created in a state of innocence. God did not create sinners. After they were created, they committed sin and became sinful, but this was a fall from the original state in which God had made human beings. Sin, then, cannot be excused on the basis that it is only natural, and part of what it means to be human. Being human is not sin. God never condemns a person for being what he himself had created. For "he knows our frame; he remembers that we are dust" (Ps. 103:14).

Finitude is not sin. To think of sin as being anything less than divine perfection may be considered a high view of sin. It may seem to exalt God and holiness. However, it has the opposite effect. It is saying that to be human is to displease God. It makes God the kind of being who would make people human, and then condemn them for being what he made them. It would mean that there is no possible way for a human being to gain the victory over sin and live a life pleasing to God. So no one living can ever be anything but a miserable sinner before God. It is not biblical to consider finitude as sin. If we think of sin as any falling short of the perfection of God, then of course all of us are sinful and we must remain so as long as we live. None of us can hope to reach the perfection of God's knowledge, wisdom, and justice. We are not God and cannot match his infinite love, understanding, or any other divine perfection. If this is sin, then all of us sin every day. And this is what is meant by many who oppose the concept of holiness. They keep insisting that none of us match the perfection of God. But that of course is not what is meant by the terms "sin" or "holiness" in the Bible. John did not say that sin is any lack of perfect obedience to all the laws of God. What he said was that sin is lawlessness (1 John 3:4). He states flatly that "sin (ἁμαρτὶα) *is* lawlessness (ανομια)." Sin is despising the law, knowingly breaking the law. Sin is breaking the covenant with God, which is the worst thing that could be done, as it breaks the very basis of the God-human relationship, and cuts the sinner off from God. "Your sins (ἁμαρτηματα) have separated between you and God and your sins have hidden his face from you" (Isa. 59:2).

If sin is self-alienation from God, then repentance is turning back to

Nature of Sin 117

God, confessing that one is a sinner, asking for forgiveness on the basis of the self-sacrifice of Jesus Christ, and trusting in God for that forgiveness and mercy.

Etymology (the study of the history of words) is a fascinating study, but a most deceptive guide to Biblical exegesis. Etymology may suggest that sin is either the result of poor aim or of inability to walk a straight line, but the uses and contexts show that it is the result of choosing to disobey. Writing of the various Hebrew and Greek words for sin and their etymologies, Erickson says that "Whereas to the modern person these Hebrew and Greek verbs may indeed suggest a mistake rather than willful, conscious sin, in biblical usage the terms pointed to a voluntary and culpable mistake. [30]

Sin, then, is much more than simply missing the mark through ignorance or failure of aim. Sin is not poor aim, but aiming at the wrong target, one which displeases God.

Ignorance is not sin. "Hamartiology" comes from the generic Greek word for sin. Ἁμαρτια was used in Classical Greek as almost equivalent to "mistake," which was made through ignorance. So if is the way we interpret the New Testament, sin is the result of ignorance. But it is not so used in the New Testament, nor even in the Septuagint. To begin with the latter, we see that when David had sinned so grievously with Bathsheba, he told Nathan, "I have sinned (ἡμαρτηκα) against the Lord" (2 Sam. 12:13, LXX). He was not saying that he had made a simple "mistake" or "error in judgment." He had sinned grievously against God, and knew it. Though the Greeks had not thought of sin as being lawlessness, or breaking a sacred covenant with God, the Hebrews did so, as did the Christians.

Hebrew did not develop a single generic term for sin, but used a variety of words to express different ways of sinning. Though (חטא) is the most common, and is usually translated by ἁμαρτια in the LXX.[31]. Nor did the Old Testament have such a highly developed concept as we find in the New Testament. The deepest understanding of sin could not come until Jesus brought the final solution to the bondage of sin. "Until there was forgiveness of sin in Christ, it was not possible to understand the full depth of sin."(Ramm 1985, 89). Thus grace helped reveal the full scope of sin.

Sin is not merely "falling short of the glory of God." Falling short of the glory of God may not be sin at all in the Biblical sense of the word. If sin is "anything short of the glory of God" then it is hopeless to consider the possibility of any human person being holy, for all human beings are less than God, and "lower than the angels. "So if this is sin, God made us sinful.

Sin comes short of the glory of God. But that is a non-reversible statement. It is not true that "anything less than the infinite glory of God is sin." Paul addresses many of his letters to "the holy ones - saints. (Rom 1:7; 1 Cor. 1:2; 2 Cor. 1:1; Eph. 1:1; Phil. 1:1; Col. 1:2). Peter declared that the command of God is to "be ye holy" (1 Peter 1:15). And Jesus is said to have told the woman caught in adultery, "Sin no more" μηκετι αμιρτανε (John 8:11). But lest we argue that this is a much disputed passage, he said the same thing to the man lying by the pool (John 5:14). Would Jesus command one to do what was not possible to any human being?

Sin is freely chosen. Sin is not something that happens to persons against their will, but is chosen by the individual in freedom, and that individual is responsible for his or her choice. The sinner did not necessarily think about the act or the attitude a long time, weighing all the consequences before making a choice. But sin is from the heart--the will. Yet we do not mean that the "will" is some part of the person which is bad. The will is nothing and does nothing. We mean rather that the person is "willing" or choosing to do wrong. It is the total person who is making a decision and doing something.

In Matthew 5:28 when Jesus declared that the man "who looks (gazes) at a woman to lust after her has committed adultery with her already in his heart," he was saying that the act is not the beginning of sin, but rather the beginning occurs in the heart, in the desire, in the intention of the person.

"Out of the heart come evil thoughts, murders, adulteries, fornications, thefts, false witness, slanders. These are the things which defile the man" (Matt. 15:19-20). The whole person is facing in the wrong direction.

This is what we mean by speaking of sin as being from the heart, and in the will of the person. The person is facing away from God. I take the Biblical terms "heart, soul, mind, body" as each referring to the whole person, as this helps explain their rather fluid use in the Bible. They are not used in a Platonic sense, which would separate the person into a higher part (soul) and a lower part (body). The whole person chooses to sin or not to sin. The whole person should be loving God above all else.

Sin is not some *thing* inside people that causes them to do as they do, but rather sin is the whole person oriented in the wrong direction. William Temple put it well:

> The center of the trouble is not the turbulent appetites, though they are troublesome enough, and the human faculty for imagination increases the turbulence. But the center of the trouble is the personality as a whole, which is self-centered and can only be wholesome and healthy if it is God-centered. This whole personality in action is the will; and it is the will which is perverted.[32]

This is why a chief way of describing salvation is "conversion" which is a turning around to face in the opposite direction.

HUMANS AS SINNERS

By this time we ought to see the truth of the statement of Ray Dunning that "One cannot properly speak of sin in isolation as an abstract concept. Sin does not exist independently of man." (Dunning, 275). What God had planned for human beings is a personal relationship with Him, consciously chosen by each person. "No real relation is possible unless it is freely chosen, and apart from the possibility of violating it, it cannot be affirmed. . The decision to obey or to not obey is more profoundly a decision to either maintain or violate a personal relation[33]. Sinfulness is the person's alienation from God.

Sinning is a person turning away from God, and deciding to please himself or herself rather than God. When Adam and Eve sinned, we see the essence of sin in their separation from God. God came seeking for them. But God knew exactly where they were. They no longer wanted to face God. They had separated themselves, not from God, but from any personal relation with God. They no longer wanted to talk with Him, or to hear what He might have to say to them. They hid. They now wanted to be their own god, and wanted no god beside themselves. This sinning has been seen then as stemming from unbelief, hubris, disobedience, and sensuality. But the essence of it is the person turning from the Person. The result in the life is that the person goes on committing sins - sinful actions - and drifting farther and farther from God, into bondage to sin, as described by Paul in Romans

Freedom from Sin

The problem of the definition of sin becomes acute when we seek to speak of freedom from sin, victory over sin, and holiness. As is well known, John Wesley spoke of holiness as "perfect love for God, and sin "properly so-called" as "a voluntary transgression of a known law." This is equivalent to the statement of 1 John 3:4 that "Sin is lawlessness." He was convinced that this was the primary Biblical use of these words. John 9:39-41 implies that guilt is determined by light, or knowledge of what is right to do. Romans 5:12-13 declares that sin is not imputed, or charged against a person *as sin* when there is insufficient light. Thus there is a clear distinction between unknown transgression and sin which brings imputed guilt.

In answering six questions about Christians needing the grace of God even though they have the love of God in their hearts, Wesley said:

> 1,2. Not only sin properly so called (that is, a voluntary transgression of a known law) but sin improperly so called (that is, an involuntary transgression of a divine law, known or unknown) needs the atoning blood, and without this would expose to eternal damnation.
> 3. I believe there is no such perfection in this life as excludes these involuntary transgressions, which I apprehend to be naturally consequent on the ignorance and mistakes inseparable from mortality.
> 4. Therefore "sinless perfection" is a phrase I never use lest it should *seem* to contradict myself.
> 5. I believe a person filled with the love of God is still liable to these involuntary transgressions.
> 6. Such transgressions you may call sins if you please. I do not.[34]

When asked how perfect love could be consistent with mistakes, he replied that mistakes are not necessarily sin: "Many mistakes *may consist* with perfect love. Some may accidentally *flow from* it:--I mean, love itself may incline us to mistake. The pure love of our neighbor, springing from the love of God, thinks no evil, believes and hopes all things [1 Cor. 13:5,7]. Now this very temper--unsuspicious, ready to believe and hope the best of all men--may occasion our thinking some men better than they really are."

Wesley did not think that a Christian was so far past sinning that he never made a mistake or broke any command of God. He made room for human imperfections, mistakes, and unconscious sins or sins of ignorance. The fact that he used the term "perfect" love, as did Jesus in Matthew 5:48, has led to misunderstandings. In fact, he became so tired of explaining what he meant by the word that he wished at one point that it was not Scriptural so that he could omit it entirely.

This is the reason for the continuing intercession of Christ as High Priest for the "unwitting" sins of Christians. Just as the sanctuary was cleansed on the Day of Atonement from the defilement caused by unconscious sin (Num. 15:24-29; Heb. 9:7), so the "temple" of the soul (2 Cor. 6:19) is continually cleansed by the intercessory work of our Great High Priest (Heb. 7:25; Rom. 8:26-34). This work of Christ we can trust in completely, as John said in 1 John 2:1-2. (Dunning 1988, 258-259, 381-384).

Paul pointed out that the Holy Spirit enables one to love beyond mere human ability (Rom. 5:5). This is the basis of Paul's great hymn of love in 1 Corinthians 13. The love he describes is perfect love, which is seen only in God. However, the Christian is enabled to surpass ordinary human ability to love, and to grow in love so as to be more and more like God.

The love of God which the Holy Spirit pours into the soul is the "expulsive power of a new affection" and tends to drive out the desire for all lesser things, making us love God and his ways. Jesus said, "If a man loves me, he will keep my words" (John 14.23). So Jesus said that the first and greatest commandment is to love God completely (Mark 12:30; Luke 10:27). It is this completeness of love to God which Wesley meant when he called holiness "perfect love."

A primary focus of this discussion has been that sin is personal, individual. Sin cannot exist without the freedom to choose and personal responsibility for that choice. Actual guilt, whether felt or not, rests upon the sinner for his own sinful choices, feelings, and actions. For sin is more than infirmity, it is that which makes one blameworthy in the sight of God, and for which God will condemn the person at the Judgment.

Corporate Sin

The concept of corporate sin is not one with which the Church of God is comfortable. The primary reason is that we emphasize the individual, personal relationship with God which is the beginning of holiness. So when we think of sin, we think first of personal rebellion against God and his will. But love for God cannot be separated from other relationships of the individual.

John Wesley himself taught us to be concerned about social needs and issues. He recognized the social problems of injustice, man's inhumanity to man, and war, and regretted them as much as anyone. John Wesley sought to improve the lot of the working people, taught them better health practices, set up health clinics, and published a book on medicine, to help the poor. He played a significant role in the fight to abolish slavery in the Empire.

We follow Wesley in this desire to alleviate suffering and to establish social justice in this world. We dare not be so concerned about the world to come that we ignore the troubles of this present world. We are constantly troubled by having to live in a sinful, godless world like this. The problem comes from our reaction to the use of the term "Corporate Sin." We seek to reserve "sin" to its common biblical meaning.[35]

If sin is turning away from God, or the refusal to serve God, and sins are the actions, thoughts or decisions which result from this alienation from God, then sin brings personal guilt. No corporate injustice can bring that kind of guilt upon the individual member of society. The individual does not have that kind of responsibility for what the group does. The individual cannot act for the society in which he lives, and cannot control the actions of society; he does not bear the same guilt he would bear for his own actions.

Corporate Sin in the Old Testament?

Several passages in the Old Testament have been thought to give strong support to the concept of corporate sin. One is the story of Achan in Joshua 7. Achan sinned in taking valuables from Jericho and burying them under his tent. When this was discovered, Achan and his whole family were apparently stoned to death. Yet, as many commentaries point out, it would have been difficult for Achan to bring these things from Jericho, and bury them under his tent without the knowledge, if not cooperation, of his family. There is the further fact that the sin involved the breaking of "ban" (חרם), which made the sin one of the greatest which could be committed. Such a sin had to be rooted out of the nation if they were to be a people God could use.

We read of Isaiah in the temple vision which set the stage for his long ministry. When he heard the seraphim calling out the holiness of God, he exclaimed: "Woe is me! For I am lost; for I am a man of unclean lips, and I dwell in the midst of a people of unclean lips; for my eyes have seen the King, the Lord of hosts! " (Isa. 6:5).

This is a clear example of a godly person feeling his participation in the sin of the people among whom he lived and worked. Yet God gave him assurance that his lips were cleansed and then sent him out to preach among the people the holiness of God. He did not take Isaiah out of the people, but assured him of his own acceptance before God. Any personal sin of his would have robbed Isaiah of the assurance that he was pleasing God. But there was no personal guilt resting upon him.

The same thing is true of Daniel, who in chapter nine began confessing the sin of his people. But while he was speaking and praying "confessing my sin and the sin of my people Israel" the angel came from God and assured him that God was well-pleased with him, and was answering his prayer. The guilt of the people did not rest on Daniel.

Ezekiel 18 is a high point in the Old Testament as the prophet spells out our *personal* responsibility to God. We shall not die for the sins of others. If we die, it is because of our own sins. If we live, it is because of our own personal commitment to the will of God.

Sin is that which entails guilt, whether that guilt is sensed or not. Neither Isaiah nor Daniel could repent of the sin of the people, as they had no responsibility to stop that sin. It was out of their hands, and brought no guilt on them. They regretted the people's sin, but such did not affect their own personal relationship with God. Thus it can be misleading to call this "sin."

"Be Not Partaker of Her Sins"

Revelation 18:4, reminiscent of Isaiah 52:11, calls for departing from sinful Babylon: "Come out of her, my people, lest you take part in her sins, lest you share in her plagues." Paul had said something like this to the Corinthian church also (2 Cor. 6:17). We can be in the world, but not of it. Paul made this all the more clear in 1 Cor. 5:9-13. He insisted that they did not have to "go out of the world" to keep themselves clean from the sin of the world.

The Individual and Corporate Sins

Although I am convinced that all that I have said about personal sin is true, I sometimes feel keenly the disturbing fact that we cannot live in this kind of world without partaking to some extent in the sins of our society. So we have to make the best choices we can, avoid as much participation as possible, and ask God to forgive us.

Thus, Reinhold Niebuhr was right to speak of "the double focus of the moral life. One focus is in the inner life of the individual, and the other in the necessities of man's social life."[36] Yet Jesus prayed for us to be kept holy while in this wicked world: "I do not pray that thou shouldst take them out of the world, but that thou shouldst keep them from the evil one. They are not of the world, even as I am not of the world. Sanctify them. . ." (John 17:14-17).

It is possible then, for us to live holy lives in this wicked, pagan world. The very command not to participate in the sins of others (Rev. 18:4; 2 Cor. 6:17; 1 Tim 5:22; 2 John 11) is a clear indication that it is possible to live in a sinful society without sharing the guilt of that society.

Personal Relationship with God.

Fortunately, my relationship with God does not depend on my living in a perfect nation or a perfect congregation. However, I can and must keep my relationship with God sure. I must seek always to "keep the way clear" between "my soul and the Savior" "with nothing between."

This can be done in spite of all the social evils which may surround Christians. The individual person must keep up-to-date in the relationship with God. This, of course, includes keeping the relationships with other persons clear also, as the love of God demands and facilitates the love of others.

We Wesleyans, then, do not wish to use the word "sin" for anything but what the Bible implies is sin. It is the willful alienation of the self from God, and sins are those actions performed because of this alienation. This is the reason we can speak, as the Bible speaks, of being "free from the law of sin and death," and of having victory over sin instead of slaves to sin. We are deeply disturbed by the sin in our environment, and even more disturbed by anything which seems like participation in the sin of the world. We ask God to forgive us, so that we can live in peace with God, even in a world like this.[37]

Peace with God

The good news of Christ is that we can live in peace with God even while we seek to grow in our love for God and for others. "Therefore, since we are justified by faith, we have peace with God through our Lord Jesus Christ" (Rom. 5:1). Whether Paul intended the indicative (as I believe) or the subjunctive, the inference is clear that such peace with God is possible in the grace we have in Christ Jesus.

In the next chapter Paul speaks of dying to sin, and rising, by the power of God, to "walk in newness of life" (Rom. 6:4). There could be no dying to sin if sin is defined as social or political. It is only in the sense of personal sin and guilt that the whole of Romans 6 can have any experiential meaning. Only on this basis can Paul write, "Our old self was crucified with him so that the sinful body might be destroyed, and we might no longer be enslaved to sin. For he who has died is freed from sin. . .Let not sin therefore reign in your mortal bodies, to make you obey their passions" (6:6-7, 12). The Christian then can refuse to go on living in sin as a slave to sin, and yield the self to God "for sanctification" and "eternal life" (6:13-22).

If sin is the irresistible power of sinful society, then there is no hope for us to imagine freedom from the guilt and condemnation of sin. Yet Paul boldly declares that "there is therefore no condemnation for those who are in Christ Jesus. For the law of the Spirit of life in Christ Jesus has set me free from the law of sin and death" (8:1-2). In 7:14-24 Paul showed what it is like to be a slave to sin, unable to do the will of God. Yet in 8:1-17 he describes the wonderful Christian freedom of one who is no longer a slave to sin, but a son of God, living by the Spirit a life approved by God, with no more condemnation. This is only possible on the basis of sin as personal and relational, not social/political. Jesus lived in this world in a very wicked age, and was tempted as we are, yet without sin (Heb. 4:15).

Yet that relationship with God is only one aspect of human holiness. As 1 John 4:20 tells us, we cannot love God if we do not love others. The love of God brings about the love of others. This fact brings us to the ways in which sin becomes a problem much bigger than the individual. We would be terribly wrong to imagine that an individual Christian can live in a world like this without being concerned with anything but self.

War

Consider war. Here we find a situation where we cannot obey both God and the nation without conflict. Jesus told us to love our enemies, but in war, the government tells us to kill our enemies. Some wars are more unjustified than others, but all war is terrible. Even if a war is fought to prevent killing, it involves killing. It is ironic to argue that we must fight another nation to force it to treat its people more humanely. War makes more problems than it can solve.

Each Christian must seek to solve the dilemma as well as possible. One will feel that obeying the government cannot involve personal sin. One may feel that it is wrong to kill, but not wrong to serve as a medic. One may seek to avoid the military service, but work in a factory which makes war material. Still another may refuse to do even that, and work in a factory which does not make war material, but finds that the factory's product is used in some way to further the war. Then the Christian realizes that since part of the taxes supports the war effort, so that there is no way to live in a country at war without being a part of the war effort.

Sin in the Church

Even in the church, there are sometimes serious problems for the Christian who is serious about pleasing God. In the local congregation there may be a situation where a person living in open sin is accepted as Christian by the congregation. This was the kind of situation Paul addressed in 1 Corinthians 5. Paul insisted that this condition should not continue. The congregation as a whole was allowing a sinful condition to continue without rebuke. Yet the individual Christians were not sinful beyond their individual responsibility. The church as a whole was surely sinful in this and missing some blessings from God as a result. Yet it was possible for Christians to be in such a congregation and still have victory over their own sin.

Another example is the way the Church of God in the United States is divided into mostly black and white congregations. It is thus continuing in the church the segregation which has been made illegal in the nation as a whole. It did not begin in this way, but allowed itself to be divided "for the sake of peace." Yet there comes a time when the church must act against this sinful division. Christians must speak their convictions about this and bring it to an end. Such action is neither easy nor cheap, but it is necessary if we are to continue to please God.

Summary

Sin, in the strictest Biblical sense, is that which brings guilt to the individual and separates the sinner from God. It is the whole person facing away from God. "They have turned their backs to me, not their faces" (Jer. 32:33). To speak of "social sin" is to change the use of the word, as the sins of the nation do not bring personal guilt on the one who does not participate in them. Since sin separates one from God, it is most vital for us to understand it and abhor it.

Chapter 10

Original Sin

> For all have sinned and come short of the glory of God (Rom. 3:23).
>
> **What causes all people to sin? If sin is so great an evil, why are we unable to live our lives without it?**

The Bible clearly teaches the universality of sin. The biblical teaching that all have sinned is clear, abundant, and explicit. Yet the Bible does not say *why* all have sinned. It simply does not explain what causes every person who has come to sufficient maturity to make a responsible moral decision, to turn to sin. The Bible says it does happen but does not tell us why.

ALL HAVE SINNED

As early as Genesis 6:5 we read: "The Lord saw that the wickedness of humankind was great in the earth, and that every inclination of the thoughts of their hearts was only evil continually." This introduces the story of the flood. A Psalmist wrote, "There is no one who does good, no, not one" (Ps. 14:3; 53:3; quoted by Paul in Rom. 3:10). It should be noted that the Psalms just quoted begin with the words, "Fools say in their hearts, 'There is no God.'" "Surely there is no one on earth so righteous as to do good without ever sinning" (Eccl. 7:20).

The prophets often spell out the sinfulness of human beings. "All we like sheep have gone astray; we have turned every one to his own way" (Isa. 53:6). In Job, Eliphaz asked him, "What are mortals, that they can be clean? Or those born of woman, that they can be righteous?" (Job 15:14)

In the New Testament, we have already noted Romans 3:10. The ninth verse declares, "We have already charged that all, both Jews and Greeks, are under the power of sin." And verse 23 states, "All have sinned and fall short of the glory of God." Ephesians 2:3 says that all, without Christ, are "by nature children of wrath." For this reason, God calls for all people everywhere to repent (2 Pet. 3:9).

Why Do All Sin?

So the Bible teaches the universality of sin——that all human beings have sinned. But we ask ourselves, why is this true? Why does it seem impossible for a human being to live all his life without turning from God to live in sin?

Answers have been given, and most books of theology discuss one or more of the reasons given, and refer to Scriptures to prove them. Yet these reasons for the universality of sin are not explicit in Scripture. They have to be read in, so that they can be read out of the Bible.

As we shall see, those passages that are used to support a theory concerning why everyone sins, do not say why. They simply say that all human beings, except Jesus Christ, have sinned. All, without exception, need redemption by the blood of Jesus Christ. Everyone since Adam has sinned against God and must be redeemed. The only exception is the Savior himself.

Original Sin

The common explanation for this universality of sin is that of "original sin." This term is often used to mean that we are all born with some sort of sinful nature, so that we cannot help sinning. This sinful nature is said to have been inherited in some mysterious way from Adam. Since the Bible says nothing about this inheritance, several theories have been given as to the method of it. The Bible neither asks nor answers any questions about it.

G. C. Berkouwer, in his book on sin, points out that our very determination to search for the ultimate cause of our sinning may be a search for someone on whom to put the blame for our own sin.[38] There is a natural tendency of human beings to seek to put the blame for guilt on someone else or on something else. Adam, when he had sinned, sought to put the blame on God. "The woman whom you gave to be with me. . .

.(Gen. 3:12). It is true that he was blaming Eve, but he was putting the ultimate blame on God, who made Eve. And when we seek for the ultimate source of sin, we are looking outside ourselves for somewhere to put the blame for our own sin. We are trying to excuse ourselves.

This is what people do when they are accused of a sin or a crime. They often say, "I am only human." "This proves I am human." "Everybody sins." These are only attempts to make excuses for sin.

The attempt to excuse ourselves for our own sin in any way is the attempt to escape our guilt. This is not the way of salvation, but the way of death. It is not the sin which Adam committed which makes us sin. If I sin it is because I do not love God, but am turned away from God. We do not need to know the origin of sin in the world. All we need to know is that we have sinned and that we must bear the guilt for our own sin.

Yet it is natural for us to seek for the origin of sin, just as we seek to understand the ultimate origin of other things. We do not have to know in order to belong fully to God. We may have to content ourselves to live our lives without knowing all the answers.

When people speak of "Original Sin" they often use such terms as "Adamic nature," "depravity," " innate depravity" or "inborn sin." None of these terms are found in the Bible. Since they are widely used in theological discussions, it is necessary to know what is meant by them. But in seeking to understand the Bible it is better to use biblical terminology.

The three terms, "Adamic nature," "innate depravity," and "inborn sin" all refer to the same thing. They all refer to the idea that since Adam sinned, we are all born with a sinful nature in us, which makes it impossible for us to please God, and which makes us sin from birth. His first sin was the first sin of the human race, and the concept is that each person born into the human race is born with a sinful nature inherited from Adam. This sinful nature is called "depravity," a term that is not used in the Bible. Depravity is the effect of sin on the personality of the sinner. It is called "innate" to signify that it is born into the infant. Innate means exactly the same as "inborn."

Original sin is a theological term that is not found in the Bible but has been used in theology with a variety of meanings. It is used by many as though its only possible meaning was the same as *Adamic nature* or *innate depravity*. This is not true, however. We shall see that there is another historic meaning.

Depravity

Even though the word is not used in the Bible, it is used by theologians to mean the result of sin in the personality of the sinner. Both from our experience and from the teaching of the Bible we know that sin has an effect on the sinner, and makes the sinner more and more sinful. Jesus said that "Very truly, I tell you, everyone who commits sin is a slave to sin" (John 8:34). The sinner is a slave to sin because of the depravity the sin works in the heart or personality of the sinner.

Not only does the sin affect the sinner, but the sin of Adam had an effect on all the human race, since he was the first man, and we are all descended from him. John Wesley spoke of the effect of the original sin of Adam when he was asked about its effect on the human race:

> Do you mean [by original sin] the sin which Adam committed in Paradise? That this is imputed to all men, I allow; yea, that by reason thereof 'the whole creation groaneth and travaileth in pain together until now.' But that any will be damned for this alone, I allow not, till you show me where it is written. Bring me plain proof from Scripture, and I will submit; but till then I utterly deny it.[39]

Note Wesley's insistence that this "depravity," or "original sin," does not bring condemnation to any infant born since Adam. Wesley explained in another place that original sin cannot be called sin in the proper biblical sense because sin, properly speaking, is a willful transgression of God's will or a willful turning away from the will and way of God. This point is a reminder that the term "original sin" can mislead us into a false concept of the nature of sin and a wrong way of thinking of human nature.

However, Wesley did insist that, while there was no guilt attached to being born a descendant of Adam, even an infant requires the grace and mercy of God if he or she is to be accepted by God. He simply suggested that the grace of God automatically was applied to the infant.

Before we look at the Biblical evidence, let us seek to be clear as to what we are saying. We are not denying the existence of depravity as the result of sin. We are not denying that there was a Fall when Adam sinned. We are not denying that the sin of Adam had an effect on all who have been born since Adam - except Jesus Christ. But we are asking if depravity is the correct word for that effect on the newborn infant. Is it proper to say that an infant is born as a sinner? If it were true that babies are born sinners, why would Jesus say that "it is to such as these that the kingdom of heaven belongs"? (Mat. 19:14). And why would Jesus be so insistent that the man born blind had not sinned before birth (John 9:3)?

Innocent, but not Holy

The answer to such questions is easier if we remind ourselves that sin is the person facing away from God, not toward Him. Sins are actions of disobedience to the will of God, and can only be committed by a conscious person. Holiness is best defined in relational terms, not as a thing or a state. To be holy is to have a personal relationship of love to God.

The infant is not born sinful but is innocent of sin. However, neither is the baby born holy, since holiness is a positive, personally chosen love for God. Holiness is a consciously chosen relationship of love with God. We could not choose either God or sin until we were capable of choosing responsibly.

Adam was made holy, as God intended all human beings to be. But when he sinned, he lost that for all of us. So we are born deprived of that holiness — that personal relationship with God through the indwelling Holy Spirit, who pours the love of God into our hearts (Rom. 5:5). So what has been called "innate depravity" "inbred sin" or "inborn sin" is more properly "innate deprivity" or deprivation. As H. Orton Wiley put it, "The generally accepted theory of theologians, both Calvinistic and Arminian, is that of privation — a depravity which is the result of deprivation"[40]

C. E. Brown, writing on this point, sought to clarify the meaning of what he called "inbred sin."

> This question as to whether sin is something, like a cancer, or whether it is nothing, like blindness, being, as it is, the absence of something, has puzzled theologians for ages. Undoubtedly it is easier to understand the doctrine of inbred sin as being a reasonable consequence of Adam's transgression if we think of it as the loss of something — just as blindness is not the addition of something, but the loss of something, i.e., the loss of

sight. Inbred sin is the loss of the image of God.[41]

The absence of something which the person should have can have serious consequences. The absence of calcium in the bones can cause frequent fractures. The absence of sight can lead to falling, running into things, and inability to do many things. The absence of a capable immune system can lead to early death. So this way of looking at inborn deprivity is capable of explaining serious consequences.

It is no light matter to say that the newborn person is deprived of a loving relationship with the Spirit of God. Adam had this from the beginning, as God had made them. But when he gave that up to sin, we have all been born without it. We are born without that loving relationship with God. We are born without a freely chosen covenant with God. There is no commitment to God's word or will. There is no understanding of right or wrong. And there is no decision to do right. This is more than enough to account for the fact that all human beings sin.

Not Condemned for Adam's Sin

The Bible does not say that we are born guilty of the sins of our ancestor or of Adam, our most ancient ancestor. Yet this is what some have taken the idea of original sin to mean. Augustine seems to have done this in his argument with Pelagians. He said that "in Adam" we all sinned, meaning that we were all in Adam when he sinned, and thus participated in his sin. He based this on a mistranslation of Romans 5:12, a passage which we shall consider a little later.

Ezekiel had some strong words to say about the idea that anyone dies because of the sins of others, even their own fathers or ancestors: "The person who sins shall die. A child shall not suffer for the iniquity of a parent, nor a parent suffer for the iniquity of a child; the righteousness of the righteous shall be his own, and the wickedness of the wicked shall be his own" (Ezek. 18:20).

This passage clearly says that a person is not guilty of the sins of his or her ancestors. No person is born guilty of the sin of Adam. If one is guilty of sin, it is because that person has sinned. If we could be born guilty of the sins of others, they we would be dying, not because we had sinned, but because we were born into the human race. Ezekiel declares that this would be unfair and unlike God. God knows who has sinned and who has not and does not blame the one who has not sinned.

It is not the teaching of the Bible that infants are born guilty of the sin of Adam. Richard S. Taylor put it this way: "Wesleyanism has consistently rejected all forms of realism which affirm the personal participation of infants in Adam's sin" [42]. If a person is guilty of sin, it is not because of the sin of Adam, but because that person has sinned.

When we look in the Bible for support for the idea that we are born guilty of Adam's sin, or that we sinned before we were born, we find that two have been most widely used. The strongest Old Testament passage is Psalm 51:4-5. The basic New Testament passage is Romans 5:12-21. Without the latter passage it is safe to say that there would be no such concept. We will consider the Old Testament passage first.

Psalm 51:4-5

This psalm is ascribed in the heading to David, after he had sinned against Bathsheba, and after Nathan the prophet had caused him to feel the heinousness of his sin, so that he was ready to repent. Even though this cannot be proved to be true, we will interpret it in this way, as it gives poignancy to the background, and does not in any way distort the meaning. It may have been written by someone else about David. So we will consider it as David's prayer for forgiveness. Note verses 3-5: "For I know my transgressions, and my sin is ever before me. Against you, you alone, have I sinned, and done what is evil in your sight, so that you are justified in your sentence and blameless when you pass judgment. Indeed, I was born guilty, a sinner when my mother conceived me."

How do we interpret a passage like this? Is it meant to be taken as basic doctrine? Or is it, like much of the poetic literature of the Bible, to be interpreted as poetry? Is this a careful doctrinal statement, like Paul's letters? Or is it the prayer of a man grieving over his own sin?

David began this psalm by crying out for the mercy of God upon him because of his sin. His own sin was all he could think of at the moment. He was under the conviction of the Holy Spirit and knew that he wanted forgiveness — the forgiveness of God — more than he wanted anything else in the world.

"Against you, you alone, have I sinned." Is this really true of David when he had sinned with Bathsheba? We know for sure that it is not the literal truth, for he had sinned against himself. He had sinned against Bathsheba and her husband, Uriah, the Hittite. He had sinned against her family, all his court, and the nation as a whole. But does this mean that this statement in the Bible is not true? Not at all. For one thing, this is the prayer of one who is properly thinking of the way he has sinned against God. Compare this with the reply of Joseph to Potiphar's wife, "How then could I do this great wickedness, and sin against God?" (Gen. 39:9). Further, the word "you alone" signifies here, as it often does, "primarily."

The first thought anyone ought to have when tempted to do evil is that the sin would be a sin against God. Every sin is a sin against God. It is also a sin against the sinner and a sin against others, but it is first and most of all a sin against God. David knew that he had sinned greatly against himself and the whole nation; but he knew that the most important consideration was that he had sinned against God! If he could not get the forgiveness of God, then the forgiveness of all others would not help him.

What have we done with this statement? We have not taken it as a careful doctrinal statement. Nor have we taken it to be false. We have not sought to twist its meaning or explain it away. We have interpreted it as a poetic statement of a heart full of grief for sin. The use of hyperbole is to emphasize the basic concept that sin is against God. What was said in this manner truly emphasized the most important and serious aspect of sin. It is just what we need to know.

"Indeed, I was born guilty, a sinner when my mother conceived me" (v. 5). Here again we need to ask some of the same questions. Is David teaching us that we are born in sin? Is he teaching us that in conceiving him his mother committed sin? Is he saying that marriage is a sin?

Clearly the rest of the Bible does not support such ideas. God invented sex and marriage and said that they are good. Sex is holy within marriage (Heb. 13:4), so it is not true that his mother sinned in conceiving David. Yet that is the literal meaning of the words of this passage. And the literal meaning of verse 5 is either that David was born sinful, or that he was born sinning. If he meant that he was born sinning, he could have said it much more clearly. And if so, he was not using the word *sin* in its usual biblical sense. An infant cannot commit willful sin against God, as the infant is not yet capable of responsible choice.

David was not putting the blame for his own sin on his mother for conceiving him in sin. Neither was he putting the blame on God for letting him be born sinful. Quite the contrary. David was insisting that this sin of adultery was not his first sin. Many other sins and sinful thoughts came before this and led him step by step to this monstrous sin. It is as though he were saying, Lord I do not remember when it all started. I have sinned as long as I can remember — all my life. I was born into a sinful world and am part of it. Lord, I am no better than this sinful world of sinners.

If this passage is taken to mean literally that David sinned from the moment of his birth, or before, then this would contradict the biblical use of the word *sin* as the willful turning away from God or the willful transgression of the will of God. God does not hold one responsible for what one cannot prevent. "Sin is not reckoned where there is no law" (Rom. 5:13). An infant cannot have any concept of right and wrong and is therefore not sinning at all.

This is why Christian theologians have insisted that if the word *sin* is applied to newborn infants in any way, it cannot include the concept of personal guilt. Guilt includes responsibility and responsibility requires knowledge. So if this passage is taken to mean that infants sin, it is unique in Scripture.

Notice carefully that we are not saying that this scripture is not true. We are not saying that it is false. We are not saying that David was wrong when he wrote this. We are simply seeking to understand what he meant to be saying and implying.

Scripture must always be interpreted in the light of other Scripture. A basic rule of biblical exegesis is that no passage must be interpreted in such a way that it contradicts other passages. Another basic rule is that difficult passages must always be interpreted in the light of simpler passages. This passage in Psalms is not simple. Some ways of understanding it would contradict much of the rest of the Bible. Those ways cannot be correct. We are bound to seek to understand this passage in such a way that it harmonizes with what the rest of the Bible teaches. No Christian can afford to be shallow in his or her consideration of such a passage or simply to take the first idea that occurs to one as he or she reads it. No one has a right to insist on an interpretation of any passage if that interpretation does not harmonize with other clear biblical concepts.

This point of the proper interpretation of Scripture is imperative. It is difficult for anyone to change the concept of the proper meaning of a verse. Yet if we study the Bible as we should, we shall all have to change our minds rather often. This is what Bible study is all about.

We are naive if we imagine that our first thought concerning the meaning of a text must be the truth, the whole truth, and nothing but the truth. Language is not that simple. And the Bible is not that simple. God has given us writing which can show the most simple-minded person the way to God and heaven, but that is profound enough to challenge the greatest minds of all ages. Therefore we must continue searching for the truth God has made available and keep searching for more truth, even when we believe we have found it.

With this thought in mind, let us cook carefully at the New Testament passage that is often said to teach a common concept of original sin as inborn depravity, Adamic nature, or innate depravity.

Romans 5:12-14

> Therefore, just as sin came into the world through one man, and death came through sin, and so death spread to all because all have sinned— sin was indeed in the world before the law, but sin is not reckoned when there is no law. Yet death exercised dominion from Adam to Moses, even over those whose sins were not like the transgression of Adam, who is a type of the one who was to come.

This passage is the origin of the concept of Adamic nature or innate depravity. If this passage does not teach this, then the doctrine cannot be found in the Bible.

Now let us ask Paul a few questions and see how this passage answers them. Why do all human beings sin? But Paul does not give an answer to this questions. His subject is not why all sin, but why all die. We ask again, What is the connection between the sin of Adam and my own sin? Again, Paul gives no answer. What effect does Adam's sin have on a baby's nature? Nothing is said about this. Did I sin when Adam sinned? No. I only become guilty when I sin through my own choice. Am I born sinful or sinning because Adam sinned? Paul does not discuss this at all.

What, then, does Paul say? He simply states that Adam sinned and the death penalty was passed on sinners. Therefore all human beings die. Not that Paul does not seek to explain why all sin, but he simply says that all die because all sin. He assumes that we can see and know for sure that all sin, and he shows that this is the reason that all die.

It may be thought logical to thing that we are born with an inheritance from Adam of some innate tendency to sin. But this is not what Paul said in Romans 5:12-21. This idea would hinder the though of Paul here. Paul was not seeking to explain why all sin, but why all die. His subject was not sin and salvation in this chapter, but death and life. Dr. Wilbur Dayton, who taught at Asbury Seminary and Wesley Biblical Seminary writes:

> This section is regarded by many as the most difficult passage in the New Testament. However, much of the difficulty is probably caused by reading into it views never intended by the Apostle . . . What Paul takes for granted as a basis to illustrate something else becomes, in their minds, the central argument. Then, having spent their energy on the assumed universality of sin, they seldom give equal attention to the real point of the passage——the supreme adequacy of redemption.[43]

Dr. Dayton continues by pointing out five things Paul did not say here, but which are often read into the passage by eisegesis:

a. Paul did not say that sin was imputed to all because of Adam's sin.

b. Paul did not say that all were present in Adam and sinned when Adam sinned.

c. He did not mention any preexistence of all in Adam, during which guilt was acquired by all.

d. He did not say that all die because Adam sinned. He said that all die because all sin. He says that the death penalty was passed on sinners because of Adam's sin.

e. Paul did not say why all sin. It seems then, that it would be safer for us not to seek for the answer.

All five of these ideas have become a part of one theology or another, and that makes it necessary for us to consider them briefly, as we have. But this passage is not such a problem unless we ask it a question that it does not answer, or even discuss. Paul did not seem to have any problem with the cause of the universality of sin, or he would not have taken it for granted here. He assumes that we all know that and will not argue about it. He then uses that as a basis for his reasoning about death.

Paul does the same thing in 1 Corinthians 15:22, "For as all die in Adam, so all will be made alive in Christ." This is in the chapter on the resurrection of Christ and of all. It is in a discussion of physical death and resurrection, not sin and salvation. The idea of inheriting sinfulness from Adam could not have originated in the reading of this verse, if it has not already been read into Romans 5:12.

When Adam sinned, he turned away from his wonderful, loving relationship with God. He had known him personally, and had daily communion with God. But now that was gone. That was the Fall of the whole human race. Now we are all born into the world without a conscious knowledge of God and with no personal relationship with Him through the indwelling Holy Spirit.

When Adam sinned, he brought upon himself the result God had predicted. He died. It was not until much later that he died physically. But he died in reality the very day he sinned. Life is true life only in God. Without him we are dead. Paul stated this very clearly in Ephesians 2:1-3, when he spoke of all sinners as being "dead in trespasses and sins" (also Col. 2:13; Eph. 5:14; John 6:53). 1 Timothy 5:6 is speaking of widows, but could apply to anyone: "The widow who lives for pleasure is dead even while she lives." To be living in sin is to be dead in reality even though alive physically.

To be alive to God is the only true living. We are born without that spiritual life, even though innocent of personal sin. Watson described this condition as "the loss of spiritual life, followed by estrangement from God, moral inability . . . and enmity to God" (Institutes, 2:124).

When we become responsible persons, we choose to do our own will rather than God's will. Through these wrong choices, we incur personal guilt before God, and become more and more depraved. Each sin makes it easier to sin again, so that we become increasingly sinful. This growing depravity is the result of individual sin against God. Those sins resulted from the person being born deprived of personal communion with God.

When we add to this the prevalence of sin in the world and the temptations of Satan, we see why all sin. Who can resist sin without the power of the indwelling Holy Spirit? The Spirit works in sinners, but can only do what the person will let him do, which is not much until He can bring the sinner to repentance. Whatever goodness there is in this sinful world is due to the work of the Holy Spirit; for he is working in all to bring them to a saving knowledge of Christ and to prevent them, if possible, from going deeper into sin.

The Power of Sin

It is easy to underestimate the power of sin if we are simply thinking in abstract terms. But if we read the newspapers, watch television, listen to the radio news, or just look around, we are often shocked at the evil in human beings.

Notice what the neighbors often say when a person is arrested for a crime, such as embezzlement or murder. "He could not have done what they say. He is so nice and friendly." "She is so helpful in the church, she could not have done it." But the evil comes from the heart, which we cannot see. And once a person lets sin into the heart, there is hardly any limit to what the devil can lead that person to do. You cannot tell by looking at a person what is in the heart.

Sin depraves. Any sin depraves. There is no such thing as "a little sin." Sin leads to more sin. The evil around us can help us to believe what the Bible teaches about the devil, who seeks to lead us away from God and all that is good.

Satan is the source of temptation, and brings it to us in a multitude of ways. Jesus himself was tempted by Satan (Mat. 4:1; Heb. 4:14-15). Judas, one of the Twelve disciples, was led astray by Satan (John 13:2). The best of Christians are warned against the wiles and temptations of the devil: "Like a roaring lion your adversary the devil prowls around, looking for someone to devour (1 Peter 5:8). We must remember always that since Jesus was tempted, no one is safe from the power of temptation (Luke 22:40). Yet God is able to keep us from the power of temptation and give us the victory. "The Lord knows how to rescue the godly from trial" (2 Pet. 2:9).

If the Christian is faithful in resisting the devil, he will find victory in the grace of God. "Resist the devil, and he will flee from you. Draw near to God and he will draw near to you" (James 4:7-8). In fact, the victories over temptation will, by the grace of God, strengthen the Christian (James 1:2-4, 9-11). The secret of victory is trust in God and being watchful. "So if you think you are standing, watch out that you do not fall" (1 Cor. 10:12). It would greatly help every Christian to memorize 1 Corinthians 10:12-13, and repeat them daily!

Relational Terms

As we saw in the previous chapter, sin and holiness are best understood in the Bible as relational terms, and must be seen in personal terms. Sin is committed by a person against God. Sin is not a thing, but a choice of a person. Sin is a person turning away from God—not a thing within the person. It is the whole person turned in the wrong direction.

If sin is the orientation of the whole person away from God, then holiness is the whole person turned in love to God. It is not merely the absence of sin, but the presence of the God-given love for God. It is given by God, but can only be given when the person voluntarily chooses to respond to God's call to turn wholly to Him. This is what caused Luther to prefer the term "personal sin" rather than merely "sin." It makes sense out of the view of Arminius that original sin is deprivation rather than depravation. Actual sins of the individual, whether in word, thought or deed, bring about a depraved personality, but these sins grow out of the original deprivation of the person.

The New Testament says nothing about the eradication of inborn depravity. It speaks instead of the Holy Spirit filling us with the love of God (Rom. 5:5) and of our yielding our "members to righteousness for sanctification" (Rom. 6:19). Instead of saying that we have no carnality (flesh) in us, Paul says that we "are not in the flesh" but "in the Spirit" (Rom. 8:9).

Some careful thought is required to make the change from a depersonalized theology to a personalized theology, but when this is accomplished, it becomes easier to make sense out of the teaching of the whole New Testament. One is no longer required to read so many ideas into the New Testament. One no longer has to infer that Paul had certain ideas that he did not express.

Effects of Sin

Sin Enslaves. Because of the sin which depraves every person who lives long enough to know right from wrong, all human beings need salvation from the power of sin. If one decides to quit the old way of living, and follow a good life, great obstacles are found in the heart. Such a change is found to be impossible in one's own strength. This habit can be broken, and then another change can be made, but the enslaving power of sin is unbreakable in one's own power. This is what Jesus meant when he said, "Everyone who commits sin is a slave to sin" (John 8:34).

Sin is death. Not only is the sinner a slave to sin, but the sinner is dead in sin. "You were dead through the trespasses and sins in which you once lived, following the course of this world, following the ruler of the power of the air, the spirit that is now at work among those who are disobedient" (Eph. 2:1-2). To live in sin is to be dead to God, the only source of real life. "Whoever has the Son has life; whoever does not have the Son of God does not have life" (1 John 5:12). Even if one is comparatively happy in this life of sin, the end is death. "There is a way that seems right to a person, but its end is the way to death" (Prov. 14:12).

Sin will be judged by God. Jesus told his disciples about the coming judgment on those not serving him: "For the Son of Man is to come with his angels in the glory of his Father, and then he will repay everyone for what has been done" (Mat. 16:27). "For all of us must appear before the judgment seat of Christ, so that each may receive recompense for what has been done in the body, whether good or evil" (2 Cor. 5:10).

The Wrath of God. It is often said that the Old Testament shows us the wrath of God, and the New Testament shows His love. This is not true. The Old Testament reveals his love, and the New Testament includes his wrath.

John the Baptist declared that the only way to avoid the wrath of God was to repent (Luke 3:3-17). Jesus warned us that "whoever disobeys the Son will not see life, but must endure God's wrath" (John 3:36). Paul pointed out that sinners are living under the present wrath of God: "All of us once lived among them in the passions of our flesh, following the desires of flesh and senses, and we were by nature children of wrath, like everyone else" (Eph. 2:3). Everyone who has not come to God in repentance is living under the wrath of God, which will eventually come "on those who are disobedient" (Col. 3:6).

The wrath of God is not to be thought of in terms of human anger. God never "loses his temper" nor acts irrationally. The wrath of God is simply the other side of his love for all people. God loves us so much that he hates whatever keeps us from him, and prevents us from becoming what he intends us to be. The wrath of God is God's settled attitude toward the disobedient and sinful. But until the Day of Wrath, which is the Day of final Judgment, or until we die, He is lovingly and graciously waiting for us to turn from sin and come to him for forgiveness. If we do not, there remains for us nothing but the wrath of God (Heb. 10:26-27). "It is a fearful thing to fall into the hands of the living God" (Heb. 10:31).

Who can deliver us from sin? And death? And judgment? And the wrath of God?

Need for Salvation

The previous discussion of sin shows why it is that all human beings need salvation. The need is for salvation from the power of sin to wreck our characters, or present lives in this world, and separate us from God both now and forever. It must be emphasized that without this understanding of the seriousness of sin we can have nothing but a very shallow theology. Sin is that which separates us from God, and without God we are "dead even while living" (1 Tim. 5:6). Nothing could be more central to our study of God than that.

If we make of sin some light thing, a mistake which all human beings do, and which makes little difference, we will have no theology at all, since we would see nothing much wrong. If we considered sin to be a natural part of human existence, salvation would be useless and not really necessary. If sin is like a grammatical error, who cares?

The concept of sin, then, is one way by which to test any theology. Some speak as though sin is just part of being less than God. On the other hand, there are those who make a definition of sin which is so broad that it is inescapable. Richard Taylor pointed out that the Biblical view is distinguished from . . ."the Calvinist and Lutheran views, which so stress the legal concept of sin that it is overextended to include amoral shortcoming; and which also so stress man's irremediable depravity that no deed can ever completely escape sin's taint."[44] The trouble with these concepts is that they make people feel less guilty for their sins, and assume that sin is just part of being human.

One of the common views of sin at the end of the twentieth century is gnostic, since it considers sin to be ignorance, or poverty. If it is ignorance, it can be cured with education. If it is poverty, all we need is to see that everyone has money. Such views are shallow and seek to avoid the real problem.

Chapter 11

God Seeking People

> I myself will be the shepherd of my sheep, and I will make them lie down, says the Lord God. I will seek the lost, and I will bring back the strayed. . . . (Ezek. 34:15-16a)
> **Do we find God by seeking him? Or by responding when he seeks us out and finds us? What kind of God would seek for those who rebel, in order to save them?**

If human beings cannot save themselves, how can they possibly break the power of sin and become what God had intended when he created them? God himself had planned all along to show that he had not only created human beings, but was well able to solve the problem of sin. He began at the first sin to reveal his plan of salvation.

GOD'S PLAN OF SALVATION

Since sin has to do with God, and brings our communion with God to an end, the solution to sin must come from God. He alone set the rules to fit his own character and his plans for creation. Since all sin is against God, only God can find a way to bring us back to himself.

In response to the first sin, the sin of Adam and Eve, God made a hint of his plan to bring salvation (Gen. 3:15). God did not give up on his creation. Three chapters later, we read that people had become so sinful that God set a flood to destroy them. But not all of them—he saved eight persons for a new start because of the obedience of Noah and his family (Gen. 6:9—9:17).

The next step in the redemption of the world was to call Abram to be the founder of a people with whom God would work to prepare for the coming of salvation (Gen. 12:1-3).

The Old Testament begins with the creation of human beings, and almost immediately tells of the fall of the human race into sin. But it does not end there. The overarching theme of the Old Testament is *God's search for a people* who would love and serve him and be his special people in this world.

God's Search for a People

The story of creation is not just a story which was told to satisfy our curiosity about the beginning of things. It is a narrative which shows us the reality of God's work in his world. It shows us how things really are. It sets the stage for the story of God working with people to make the kind of persons he can bless and help. The record of creation, told in the first two chapters of Genesis, shows that God had a purpose in this world. He had a purpose in making humans "in his image and likeness." He made a social being, male and female, with freedom to respond to God in faith and love.

If God had given up when the first two people sinned, there would have been no story to tell, and no one to hear it. But God did not give up. To the serpent, who was the catalyst in the sin of the people, God promised ultimate subjugation by one born of a woman, a promise fulfilled by Christ (Gen. 3:14). This was the first hint of God's solution to sin.

Prophetic History

When we speak of the Old Testament as a "story," we are not implying that it is not true, or that it is just a tale that is told. We mean that it is a prophetic way of showing us the true meaning of what has happened in history. None of the history of the Bible is told as a simple record of events. It is prophetic in the sense that it is told by persons with a prophetic vision of the way God has worked in people.

It was the recognition of this fact which caused the Hebrews to divide the Old Testament into three parts: Law (God's instruction), Prophets, and Writings. In the Prophets they included what we call the historical books, and which they called the Former Prophets (Joshua to Chronicles). Those books we call the Major and Minor Prophets, they called the Latter Prophets. In this way they showed their recognition of the fact that the history was told from a prophetic viewpoint.

The writers of these books did not seek merely to tell of events, but of what those events revealed of the will and work of God. The same thing is true of the first division—-the Law, which includes the history from Creation to Joseph, who led the way to Egypt. It is all told from the point of view of God's activity and his relationships with human beings.

The whole history of the Old Testament moves from Creation to the last centuries before Christ. It is divided into three parts by two great events: The time in Egypt and deliverance from it, and the Exile in Babylon. This is not the place to review the whole story. A quick survey can be seen in Chapter Ten of my book *The Word of God*.[45] .

Highlights of the Story

The first eleven chapters of Genesis are pre-history, in which there are no datable events. The creation of all things is told in such a way as to show something of God's purpose in making human beings on this planet. They rebelled against God's will and life became harder. Yet God continued to seek after every person through the Holy Spirit. A few stand out as those who feared God—-Abel, Enoch and Noah. But on the whole, it is a sad story of the growth and fruits of sin.

Beginning in Chapter 12, we have the stories of Abraham, Isaac, Jacob and Joseph. These men had faith in God and sought to live for Him. Ever after this, the Hebrews liked to refer to themselves as the descendants of "Abraham, Isaac and Jacob." And God is referred to as the "God of Abraham, Isaac and Jacob" (thirty times in the Bible).

Joseph, one of the twelve sons of Jacob, led the way to Egypt as a refuge from famine. But the refuge turned into captivity and hard labor for the many generations until the time of Moses. This period in Egypt had much that the Hebrews hated, but did give the nomadic shepherds time to multiply greatly. And when Moses led them out of the land, he had learned from the Egyptians how to organize.

Egypt to Babylon

With the guidance of God, Moses led the people first to Sinai where they received the Law, or Instruction of God as to the way they should live and worship. After years of wandering they found courage to enter Canaan, where they made their home. They drifted regularly into idolatry, from which they were recalled by Judges and prophets.

They set up a kingdom, which split into two, with both good kings and evil. The Northern Kingdom fell to Assyria and the Southern Kingdom to Babylon.

At the end of this thousand-year period one could say that the people of Israel, the descendants of Abraham, Isaac and Jacob had completely failed. But this is not the whole of the story. In that long period God had been working with them. He would not leave them alone, but sent prophets to them with word of what they ought to do and believe. He told them the reason they were being sent into exile in Babylon was: "They did not heed my words, says the Lord, when I persistently sent to you my servants the prophets, but they would not listen, says the Lord" (Jer. 29:19).

We know now that there were at least two great results of the Babylonian Exile. One is that the people who returned from Babylon had no desire for idolatry, and were determined to worship the one true God alone. Another is that we have the writings of the great prophets whom God had sent to them to make sure they understood his will and what was happening to them. These things were not written for the nation of Israel alone, but for us (1 Cor. 10:11).

Further, the kingdom itself, which did not last, became a symbol of the rule of God which Jesus came to set up in our hearts. In the same way, the tabernacle in the wilderness, and the temple in Jerusalem became symbols of the way God dwells in the hearts of his people.

Babylon to Christ

Some did return to Jerusalem from Babylon, as God had promised. But they were never again able to establish a truly independent kingdom. They rebuilt the city, a small temple, and homes. But they were a small country located in such a way that they were a political football between

Egypt on the south, and the strong nations to their north. Much of this time they were ruled over by Greece and then Rome.

During this time, God sent more prophets, to remind them of the Law and the Covenant with God, and to tell them there was still hope for the future. All the prophets of the Old Testament looked forward to a better time to come, in the will of God.

One aspect of the prophetic vision for the people was that even though many would never live for God, there was a Remnant of the people who carry out the plans of God (Isa. 6:13; 7:3). Through this faithful remnant God would do his will. He wished to work with the whole of the nation, but was able to work with only the few.

Purpose of the Old Testament Period

During the whole period from creation to Christ, God was preparing the people to understand the message and work of Christ in saving his people from their sin. We can see many ways in which various events, people and messages prepared for the coming of Christ. God was working in marvelous ways to carry out this climax of his plan of salvation in Christ.

At the same time, we must not imagine that there was no salvation in the Old Testament. God forgave sin, and healed the bodies, minds and hearts of people before the coming of Christ into his earthly life. God refused to leave all salvation and forgiveness for some distant time. So we read in the earliest parts of the Bible about godly people. "Enoch walked with God; then he was no more, because God took him" (Gen. 5:24).

Consider the heart of the one who wrote Psalm 23. He knew God and loved Him, or he could not have written as he did. Look at the author of Psalm 119, the longest, which tells of the writer's love for the words of God. Listen to the exclamation, "Oh, how I love your law! It is my meditation all day long. . . . How sweet are your words to my taste, sweeter than honey to my mouth!" (Ps. 119:97, 103). What more could a Christian say?

When we look at the Old Testament persons, named and unnamed, who willingly died rather than give up their faith in God, we begin to see that these pre-Christian people had a faith in God which we can only admire. We who know God in Christ must not despise what some had long before Christ. God revealed himself and his love to them, though not as fully as we have an opportunity to know if we will.

THE PROVIDENCE OF GOD REVEALED

One of the great aspects of the Old Testament story is that it reveals so wonderfully the providence of God. We discussed this in one aspect in Chapter 7, but need to take another look at the way it is revealed in the Old Testament.

The whole Old Testament can be seen as the providential work of God with the people of Israel. But it was not with a nation as a whole only, but he worked through individuals. In a sense, he began with Abraham, as we see in the story of his call in Genesis 12:1-3. This call is most important for understanding the whole story: "Now the Lord said to Abram, "Go from your country and your kindred, and your father's house to the land that I will show you. I will make of you a great nation, and I will bless you, and make your name great, so that you will be a blessing. I will bless those who bless you, and the one who curses you I will curse, and in you all the families of the earth shall be blessed."

It is possible to count here seven things God promised to do for Abram and his descendants. But these things are not merely blessings on Abram, later named Abraham, but Abraham was called by God to be a blessing to all the nations of the world. The promises are for all. God does not often give blessings for personal gratification of the one receiving them, as we can see in this call of Abram.

An exciting illustration of faith in providence is the way in which Joseph explained to his brothers who had sold him into slavery what he believed: "And now do not be distressed, or angry with yourselves, because you sold me here, for God sent me before you to preserve life" (Gen. 45:5).

He was sure that God had overruled their evil purpose, and had used their action to save them from starvation. Joseph had learned to trust in God's providence.

Such Psalms as 104, 105, and 106 review some of the history of Israel in order to show how God was working with them through good times and troubled times. The writer of Psalm 139 expresses some of the same faith, but states it as a personal trust in the omniscience, omnipresence and providential care of God for the individual. Even before birth, God knew and cared (139:13-15). Jeremiah wrote that God had appointed him before his birth to be a prophet to the nations (Jer. 1:5).

In the New Testament, Hebrews 11 reviews some of the highlights of God's work in individual lives, by reminding us of some of the many individual persons who trusted God, and whose faith kept them faithful in spite of all the evils that happened to them. What a thrilling story it is of men and women who had firm faith in God and refused to give up their faith in his care. Romans 8:28 sums it all up in a statement: "We know that in all things God works for good for those who love God" (Author's translation).

Many versions make "all things" the subject of the sentence, which has two problems. First, it makes it sound as though all things are good. All things are not good. So this is misleading. Second, it ignores the context, which speaks of the way God helps us live our lives in such a way as to please him, in spite of our ignorance. The two previous verses explain that when we do not know how to pray, or what to pray for, the Holy Spirit is able to pray for us, as he knows all about what we really need. Verse 28 then explains that God helps us in all things. He can work in all things that happen to us so as to bring good to us by overruling the evil.

With this kind of faith in God, we can face any kind of problem or trouble, with peace in our souls. We know that God is able to work in and through us in such a way as to bring about something good.

Once more we ask why God permits trouble. We will never in this life know all the answer to this question. But we can know God. We can know that God is with us. And "if God is for us, who is against us?" (vs. 31). As Christians, we remember how the chapter ends: "No, in all these things we are more than conquerors through him who loved us. For I am convinced that neither death, nor life, nor angels, nor rulers, nor things present, nor things to come, nor powers, nor height, nor depth, nor anything else in all creation, will be able to separate us from the love of God in Christ Jesus our Lord." (Rom. 8:37-39).

This does not mean that God will give us everything we want, or that nothing bad will ever happen to us. Trouble will come, but no matter how bad it may seem to us, God will use it to help bring about his own final result.

Bad things do happen to good people, and most of them are not signs of God's displeasure at all. We live in a world in which troubles can come to all of us. Sickness, accidents, bereavements and poverty are common problems. Listen often to Paul in 1 Corinthians 10:13—"No testing has overtaken you that is not common to everyone. God is faithful, and he will not let you be tested beyond your strength, but with the testing he will also provide the way out so that you may be able to endure it."

Like physical exercise, testing can make us stronger. And we can trust God not to let anything come upon us which he cannot make us able to bear. He will give us power to endure and to stand up under all the troubles which come to us.

Faith is the Key

It is by our personal faith that we can see the providential care of God for us. It is not something which can be proved to all, but like the persons mentioned in Hebrews 11, we can by faith stand all the troubles which come, and glorify God by the way we bear them.

The Christian attitude about trouble is not like "Polyanna" who refused to see anything but good. Christians recognize that evil is all around us, but trust in God to make us overcomers. Biblical revelation never denies evil, as do some religions, but offers victory over it.

Christian faith is victorious. "And this is the victory that conquers the world, our faith" (1 John 5:4). This victorious trust in the power and care of God gives one assurance that nothing can separate from the love of God.

God's Ultimate Purpose

When we are trying to understand why God permits trouble, we should consider two things. First, we may not ever understand fully in this life, for we can see neither the future, nor all the circumstances of the present. Second, we concentrate our thinking on the present and our own plans and hopes. God's ultimate purposes are beyond our knowledge.

Yet there is something we can know about God's plans. We can understand by faith that God is not seeking to spoil us by giving us everything we desire, but rather preparing us for experiences and work about which we can know nothing now. As someone has put it, "God is not in the business of spoiling babies, but growing mature persons with strength to overcome." Strength is developed by being used. And the troubles we face exercise our faith, our obedience, and all our spiritual abilities. Each victory will help us some other to win.

God has plans for us which he may never fully reveal to us. It might spoil his plans for us to know them. But we can trust him to do what is best for each of us, and what will help to make us what he wants us to be and do. We Christians need to learn to sing with Charles W. Naylor:

> God's way is best; if human wisdom
> A fairer way may seem to show,
> 'Tis only that our earth-dimmed vision
> The truth can never clearly know.
>
> God's way is best, I will not murmur,
> Although the end I may not see;
> Where'er he leads I'll meekly follow—
> God's way is best, is best for me.

The Old Testament Looked to Christ

The Old Testament prepared in many ways for the coming of Christ as Savior from sin. It was a long period of instruction in the ways of God.

Law. At the heart of this instruction was the Law as given through Moses. The Hebrew word is usually translated "law" but literally means "instruction." God's instruction has the force of law to the one who loves God.

The formal instruction of Israel had its beginning with Moses at Sinai, as described in Exodus 20-23. God laid down some conditions the people must meet if they were to be his special people. In the preparation for receiving the special commandments of God, they were told: "Now therefore, if you obey my voice and keep my covenant, you shall be my treasured possession out of all the peoples. Indeed, the whole earth is mine, but you shall be for me a priestly kingdom and a holy nation" (Exod. 19:5-6; cf. Lev 20:26).

God sought to have a people who would love and serve him alone, so that he could call them his own special possession, and use them to bring his mercy and grace to all the nations of the world. Such people had to obey his commandments, which gave them religious and ethical instruction.

Ceremonial Worship. The Tabernacle in the wilderness and the Temple in Jerusalem symbolized the presence of God in the midst of his people. Here they offered sacrifices and offerings of various kinds, including thanksgiving, peace offerings, sin offerings, etc. (Lev. 1—7). The sin offerings helped the first Christians to understand the death of Jesus as a sin-offering for the whole world (Heb. 9:10-14). Here too they celebrated some of the special feasts (Lev. 23).

Covenant. We have noted that the beginning of God's "law" or instruction is found in Exodus 20—23. In Exodus 24, we see how the people made a covenant that they would obey God. This sacred covenant is the heart of the Old Testament religion. Other commandments of God which are included in the covenant are found in Leviticus and Deuteronomy.

What we call the historical books (Joshua to Esther) tell the story of the people from the death of Moses until near the time of Christ. This includes the period of Judges, the establishment of the kingdom, During this time the kingdom was established, but was divided after less than a century into two kingdoms. The Northern kingdom fell to Assyria and later the Southern kingdom fell to Babylon. Some returned from Babylon to rebuild the city of Jerusalem and the temple, but they were never again an independent kingdom.

During all their history, the covenant was regularly broken by many. God sent judges and prophets to call the people back to the covenant with God. In spite of some success, the prophets were never able to get all the people to be true to God.

Considered by itself, then, the Old Testament ended in failure. God was not able to make of the people a great nation of people who were true to the covenant he had made with them. But the Old Testament is not the end of the story. The prophets pointed forward, in a variety of ways, to a time when God would do something better in the world. This hope is the core of the predictions of the prophets. They helped to prepare the way for Christ by the message they proclaimed. So the Old Testament was not a failure, but only a time of preparation for the culmination of all in Christ.

Prediction

The predictions of the Old Testament are not merely to satisfy human curiosity, or simply some kind of fortune-telling. They are not as common as is sometimes thought, and are given for specific purposes.

There is a sense in which the Old Testament itself is a prediction of Christ. It is incomplete if not completed by the coming of the Son of God. God was working through all those ages to prepare a people who would have an opportunity to understand who and what the Christ would be and do when he came. This can be better seen if we look briefly at some of the key ideas of the Old Testament which point forward to Christ and his work. Three times the New Testament calls these things shadows of things to come in Christ: Colossians 2:17; Hebrews 8:5; 10:1.

Shadows of Good Things

Festivals, New Moons, Sabbaths. Most of these were celebrations of historical events, or agricultural feasts. But Yom Kippur, or Day of Atonement was one of spiritual renewal. The Passover was a remembrance of deliverance from Egypt. This deliverance later became a paradigm of God's power to deliver (Acts 7; 13:17). Egypt then became a symbol of spiritual bondage (Hosea 8:13; 9:3), which is slavery to idolatry. Other deliverances in the Old Testament were measured by the deliverance from Egypt (Isa. 11:11; Hos. 11:11; Zech. 10:10).

The Sabbath of the Old Testament is used in Hebrews 4:1-10 as being fulfilled in the rest from sin through Christ. This gives a basis for the argument in Romans 14:5-9 that no one should judge another as wicked for not keeping a particular day of the week.

Tabernacle/Temple. The Tabernacle in the wilderness was a tent which was specially made to represent God in the midst of his people. Its description fills the bulk of Exodus 25--40, with its dedication in the last chapter. In the New Testament Paul declares that Christians are the "temple of the Holy Spirit within" (1 Cor. 6:19).

Sacrifices for sin. In Leviticus 1--8 we find descriptions of the various kinds of sacrifices for different occasions and purposes. The sin-offering was offered as confession of sin and a prayer for forgiveness. Jesus became our sin-offering, fulfilling that aspect of the Law.

Shepherd. Ezekiel complained that false shepherds had deceived the people and had delivered them over to spiritual wolves. So, in a fascinating chapter, he declared that God himself would be their Shepherd and would lead them to safety (Ezek. 34). This chapter and the well-loved Psalm 23 are the background for Jesus' declaration in John 10 that He is the Good Shepherd. In Ezekiel 34:7-16, the Hebrew strongly emphasizes the often repeated "I" or "I, myself" since God himself will repair the damage done by the false prophets. God is the "good Shepherd." This promise was fulfilled when God sent Jesus into the world to save the people from their sin.

King. David became the idealized king, and the people of Jesus' time were eagerly awaiting a king like him would conquer the Romans and drive them out of the land. This is what they associated with the coming Messiah. This fact may be the reason Jesus did not introduce himself as the Messiah. The people would have thought he would be a military leader and king. This role Jesus emphatically rejected.

Suffering Servant. The "Servant Passages" of Isaiah climax in Isaiah 52:13—53:12, which describes the humiliation and later exaltation of the Servant of the Lord. He was born to die for the sin of the nation (53:5-12), but his death would not end his living. This made it easy for the church of the New Testament to see Christ in this passage (Acts 8:30-33 and 13:34). Yet they found it difficult to see this until after the resurrection, and Peter even argued with Jesus about the idea of a suffering Messiah (Mk. 8:31-33; Mat. 16:21-23). It was hard for them to reconcile the ideas of "king" and "suffering."

Confirmed by Jesus

It can be seen that almost all the predictions of the future in the Old Testament are concerned with the coming of Christ, or the preparation of the people to receive and accept him. The latter included some which facilitated the building up of the kingdom so as to preserve a people through whom Christ could come.

The Old Testament message of hope is consummated in Jesus, who declared, "For the Son of Man came to seek out and to save the lost" (Luke 19:10). It is illustrated in the stories Jesus told of the Lost Sheep, the Lost Coin and the Lost Son (Luke 15). In each case we see the sorrow of the one who has lost the loved sheep, coin or son. This seeking love is the astonishing love of God for sinful people.

These three parables tell of the love of God which does not cease when the person sins, but is ready to forgive. The first two emphasize the seeking by the one who has lost something. The third is told from the point of view of the sinner, and says nothing about the seeking father, because of this point of view. However, Jesus did emphasize the real repentance of the son which made it possible for him to be forgiven. The father was ready to forgive, but could not help the son until the son repented and returned from his sin. God has no cheap grace. God's forgiveness of sin is not easy, and required the death of his Son. If there had been a better or easier way, God would have chosen it.

Chapter 12

Christology—Christ, the Savior

> In the beginning was the Word, and the Word was with God and the Word was God. . . . And the Word became flesh and lived among us. (John 1:1, 14).

Who was Jesus Christ, who is called Savior? Is it possible that he was really God? Was he God, or was he human?

We have come now to the very heart of Christian theology, for without Christ there is no Christianity. Since this is true we need to do some serious thinking about who and what Jesus was, and what he said and did.

Christianity is nothing but a delusion If we are mistaken as to the person and work of Jesus Christ. He announced at one point: "Come to me, all you that are weary and are carrying heavy burdens, and I will give you rest" (Mat. 11:28). "Believe in God, believe also in me" (John 14:1). Such statements would have no value if made by any other person. He could say such things because he was not just a man.

When the jailer asked Paul and Silas what he must do to be saved, they replied, "Believe on the Lord Jesus, and you will be saved, you and your household" (Acts 16:31). He did not say we must have the same kind of faith Jesus had. Nor did he tell us to believe the message Jesus gave. He said it is necessary to believe in Jesus Christ for salvation.

Jesus himself is the gospel of God. The heart of the first preaching of the gospel was the declaration that "Jesus is Lord." "Because if you confess with your lips that Jesus is Lord and believe in your heart that God raised him from the dead, you will be saved" (Rom. 10:9). Faith in Jesus Christ as Lord of life and death is the primary requirement for salvation. Paul insisted that Jesus is what we must preach. "For we do not proclaim ourselves; we proclaim Jesus Christ as Lord and ourselves as your slaves for Jesus' sake. (2 Cor 4:5). To preach Jesus as Lord is to preach the gospel of salvation. To be saved, we must believe in Jesus Christ. We must trust in him as our Savior.

Christology, the study of the identity and nature of Jesus, is vital, then, because it is the basis of our belief in Jesus Christ. If we are to understand the good news about salvation, we need to consider who Jesus is, and seek to understand why he qualifies as Savior.

THE PERSON OF CHRIST

Christology primarily discuses two aspects of Jesus—his person and his work. By his work we mean what he did to make salvation possible for us. By his "person" we mean who he was and what we can know of his nature. Was he human, or was he God? Was he half human and half God? Was he human but seemed to be God? Was he God and seemed to be human? Was he born a human, but became God?

Such questions occurred to Christians very early in the history of the church. It is easy to see why this was so. Jesus was born into the world as a human baby, and "increased in wisdom and in years, and in divine and human favor" (Luke 2:52). In those growing years we do not read that he gave any impression of being other than an ordinary person. Luke explicitly states that he was obedient to his parents (Luke 2:51), just as any Jewish boy was expected to be. He was human.

The disciples had first known him as a human being, but it was not long before they began to realize that he was more than just another man. The church of the first centuries was sure that Jesus was the divinely sent Messiah, the Son of the Living God (Mat. 16:16; Mark 8:29; Luke 9:20; John 6:69). Peter was the first to put into words the growing conviction that Jesus was the Messiah, fulfilling the expectations expressed in the Old Testament that God would send him. He stated, according to Matthew: "You are the Messiah, the Son of the living God." It is worth noting that the repeated use of the Greek article that this statement is made as definite as words can make it. Mark simply says, "You are the Messiah." Luke: "The Messiah (Anointed One) of God. John explains, "We have come to believe and know that you are the Holy One of God."

It took many years and much discussion before the church could put into clear words their conviction that Jesus Christ was both God and human. He was not part God and part human. Neither did he fit into may other descriptions which were suggested by some in those first centuries, but which were rejected by the church as not being faithful to what they had learned about Him.

Before we consider some of the details of these proposals, we will consider first the claim that he is God, and second his human aspect

.Fully God

A chief part of the Christian doctrine is that Jesus was more than human. He was God. Fundamental teachings of Christianity fall apart if this is not true. So this is not simply an idea which we can accept or not as we please. Look at these passages in 1 John: "By this you know the Spirit of God: every spirit that confesses that Jesus Christ has come in the flesh is from God" (1 John 4:2). For Jesus to come in the flesh, he would have had to be more than human before coming into the world. It would be unusual for a mere human being to say "I have come" in speaking about his being born into the world (twelve times in the Gospels). But if he was in heaven before being born, it is the most natural thing for him to say. To "come in the flesh" is one way to express the incarnation of Christ. It is saying that he became human, in his physical being. "God abides in those who confess that Jesus is the Son of God, and they abide in God" (1 John 4:15). "Everyone who believes that Jesus is the Christ has been born of God . . . Who is it that conquers the world but the one who believes that Jesus is the Son of God?" (1 John 5:1, 5).

We must note that there is a vast difference between being "a son of God" as Christians are, and being "the Son of God." Jesus is the Son of God in a sense which cannot ever be applied to any other person in all the universe. He is the "unique" Son of God.

"Unique" is the real meaning of the Greek word *monogenês*,[46]. It is used nine times in the New Testament. Six times the King James version translated it "only-begotten" (John 1:14, 18; 3:16, 18; Heb. 11:17; 1 John 4:9). Three times it was translated "only," (Luke 7:12; 8:42; 9:38), as it should have been when used of Christ. The idea of "only-begotten" can be traced back to Jerome, who felt it was one way to combat Arianism, which taught that Jesus was created. But the term itself has been misleading to some. Jesus did not become the Son of God by being born of Mary, though some have rather naively thought this was the point of "only-begotten."

He is the "unique" Son of God, or "the only one of his kind." No one else can be the Son of God in the same sense Christ is the Son of God. He is able to make us "sons of God" but not in the same sense that he is. He is the "eternally begotten" Son of God. He has always been, and he has always been the Son of God.

Eternal Son of God

John puts the divinity of Christ at the center of his message about Jesus Christ. This is because he states that his purpose in writing is that he might confirm the reader's belief that "Jesus is the Christ, the Son of God" (Jn. 20:31). Further, John speaks of the "Son" twenty-nine times, and refers to God as "Father" more than one hundred times. So he strongly emphasizes the relationship of Christ with God the Father. In this Gospel we have two clear statements by Jesus that he did not have his beginning when he was physically born into this world. The first is John 8:56-58, where some were boasting of being blessed by being descendants of Abraham. Jesus said: "Your ancestor Abraham rejoiced that he would see my day; he saw it and was glad." Then the Jews said to him, "You are not yet fifty years old, and have you seen Abraham?" Jesus said to them, "Very truly, I tell you, before Abraham was, I am." Note that his last statement began with "Very truly" (Greek, Αμην, αμην). This emphasizes the importance of the statement. A second point to notice in this statement is that Jesus used two different tenses in speaking of Abraham and himself. In the Greek, two different verbs are used. The statement can be translated, "Before Abraham came into being (γενεσθαι), I am (ειμι)." The expression, "I am" is used by Jesus in this absolute sense three times in this chapter (vss. 24, 28, 58). This is a strong reminder of the name by which God told Moses to identify the Lord God (Exod. 3:14). It is one translation of Yahweh (Heb. יהוה. some versions say "Jehovah"). God often said "I am" (Deut. 32:39; Isa. 41:4; 43:10, 46:4 and elsewhere). In these places, the LXX (Septuagint, Greek translation of the Old Testament) uses the same words (εγω ειμι) which Jesus used here in John. On this phrase, Leon Morris remarks correctly that "It is the style of deity, and it points to the eternity of God according to the strictest understanding of the continuous nature of the present ειμι. He continually IS.[47]

No wonder some of the Jews were so angry at apparent blasphemy that they took up stones to kill Jesus. The other Gospels do not include this statement in the same form and manner. But by John it is given emphasis, and shows that Jesus Christ eternally IS. John's prologue to his book is a strong statement of the existence of Christ from the beginning:

> In the beginning was the Word, and the Word was with God, and the Word was God. He was in the beginning with God. All things came into being through him, and without him not one thing came into being. . . . And the Word became flesh and lived among us, and we have seen his glory, the glory as of a father's only son, full of grace and truth (Jn. 1:1-3, 14).

By such an introduction to his Gospel, John sets the life of Christ against a cosmic background, and helps us see the life and work of the Son of God in its true light. Matthew and Luke had begun with his conception and birth as a human being, and Mark began with his baptism. Thus they emphasized his birth and growth as a human being, and this was good, as we shall see. But John stresses the divine aspects of Christ. All four Gospels describe both the human and divine aspects of Christ, but differ in some of the ways they emphasize one or the other.

In Philippians 2:6-7 we have a basic passage on the preexistence of Christ with the Father: "(Christ Jesus) Who, though he was in the form of God, did not regard equality with God as something to be exploited, but emptied himself, taking the form of a slave, being born in human likeness."

On the whole, this passage is one of the most important on the nature of Christ, yet it raises some problems so difficult that scholars have spent much time on its exegesis. We shall have to look at it again as we discuss the incarnation later. For now, we can see that it clearly teaches the preexistence of Christ. He did not come into being when he was born into the world as a baby. He existed before that in the "form" (μορφη) of God. It is difficult to know for sure what this means, but it seems to be correlative to "equality with God." As to the meaning of the word for "form," the meaning is the same as in Colossians 1:15, where Paul is content to say of Christ, "He is the image of the invisible God." In regard to that passage,

Frank Laubach used to say, "He is exactly like God."

Much speculation has clouded this passage in Philippians, as though Paul was presenting his speculation about the nature of Christ before his birth on earth. When we look at the whole passage, and see that Paul is here dealing with a matter of practical ethics, we can get his point more clearly. He was saying that just as Christ humbled himself so as to become a human being in this sinful world, we should humble ourselves to serve others. Though he was God, he became human, for our sake. The point to note here is that Christ was God, divine, and chose to be born as a human being for our sakes. (It must be noted here that in popular speech, the word "divine" has degenerated so that it means simply something the speaker approves. It will be used here in its proper sense of "being God, or pertaining to God.")

2 Corinthians 8:9 has the same self-giving in mind as the Philippians passage. "For you know the generous act of our Lord Jesus Christ, that though he was rich, yet for your sakes he became poor, so that by his poverty you might become rich." He was rich when he was with the Father in eternity, but chose to become poor, a human being in the world he had made, and did it for our sakes. This is the heart of the gospel.

The same message may be found in other passages which speak of God sending his own Son, such as Galatians 4:4; Romans 8:3; 1 Corinthians 15:47; Ephesians 4:8-10.

Divine Titles Applied to Christ

Matthew 1:23. ". . . And they shall name him Emmanuel, which means, God is with us." It is interesting that Matthew uses "Jesus" 150 times and "Christ" 17 times. Jesus was the name given to him, his personal name as a human being. Christ is the Greek word for Messiah, and is a title. It means "anointed one" and was used of the hope of Israel that God would send a deliverer. It therefore refers to his divine mission. But the fact that he is not often called "Christ/Messiah" does not mean that Matthew is less interested in his divinity. But during the life of Jesus, he discouraged even the disciples from calling him "Messiah" (Matt. 16:20, for example, and its parallels, Mark 8:29-30, Luke 9:20-21). The reason seems to be that the term meant so many different things to the people of that time. The concept of many was that the Messiah would be a military leader to deliver them from the Romans, as the ancient Joshua (Hebrew form of "Jesus") had delivered from the Canaanites.

Mark used the term "Christ" only seven times (eight in some texts). Luke uses it twelve times. Two questions arise: If Jesus was the Messiah, did he show that he knew this? If he was the Messiah, why did he not say so? Wrede's "Messianic secret" concept has been answered in many ways.[48]

If Jesus came to fulfill the Old Testament promises of an anointed one, the Messiah, but the people expected that Messiah to be military deliverer to drive out the Romans, he could not openly claim to be the Messiah, or Christ, without raising false hopes. He could neither claim to be the Christ, nor deny it. So, as we have seen, even when the disciples came to believe he was the Christ, he told them not to tell it to others until after the resurrection.

John 1:1,14. Here we find the term "Word" (Greek $\lambda o \gamma o \varsigma$), Who is called "God" in verse one, and in verse fourteen is said to have become human "flesh." With the possible exception of 1 John 1:1, this is the only time the idea of "Word" is clearly applied to Christ. Yet it has been thoroughly discussed and argued about by theologians and philosophers. The important point for us here is that John is speaking of Christ as existing before the creation.

Isaiah 9:6. This passage is applied to Christ in Luke 1:32, and gives four titles which can be shown to be applied to God: "Wonderful Counselor, Mighty God, Everlasting Father, Prince of Peace."

Hebrews 1:8. In a somewhat similar fashion, this passage quotes Psalm 45:8, "Your throne, O God, endures forever and ever" and applies it to Christ. The author of Hebrews uses this passage and others to show that Christ is superior to the angels, and is God

It is worth noting here that eleven of the epistles open with phrases which put the Father and Christ on the same level. Two passages in the epistles call Christ "God" (Rom. 95 and Titus 2:13).

Christ is Omnipotent

The Power of God is clearly manifested in the work of Jesus Christ, both during his lifetime and since his ascension. He not only healed the sick but even raised the dead. He went beyond these physical things and showed his power and authority in forgiving sin, which only God can do.

There are some passages which go beyond describing what Christ did, and claim divine power for him. Jesus himself spoke of his power when he said to Martha, "I am the resurrection and the life" (John 11:25). And after he had risen from the dead by divine power, he declared to the disciples, "All authority in heaven and on earth has been given to me" (Mat. 28:18). It makes no difference that he used the word "authority" and not "power." One cannot have all authority without having all power. Not that he used this authority and power of his as the reason that they should go teach everyone to obey all his teachings.

The power to raise from the dead is the same power he will use to subdue all things and make all subject to his own will (Eph. 1:19-22; Phil. 3:21; Col. 1:18). Paul declares that by this power of God in Christ he is able to meet all troubles that can come (Phil. 4:18).

Omnipresent

As God the Father is everywhere present, Christ is also. He promised that wherever we go, he will be with us (Mat. 28:20). What an encouragement that can be to all Christians! In speaking of the prayer of his followers, Christ said, "Again, truly I tell you, if two of you agree on earth about anything you ask, it will be done for you by my Father in heaven. For where two or three are gathered in my name, I am there among them" (Mat. 18:19-20).

Because of his leaving the limitations of the physical body, he is able to be wherever he is needed, everywhere at the same time. He is present in every local assembly of his people, to hear and answer their prayers, and to exercise government. He is always with us to know us, guide us, and help us do his will.

Created all things

As we have noted already, Matthew and Luke began their gospel stories with the birth of Jesus as a baby, but John began by saying that Jesus Christ was "in the beginning with God" and "was God" (John 1:1). He went further and stated, "All things came into being through him, and without him not one thing came into being" (vs. 3).

This was stated in the Gospels, but in the epistles we read further: "For in him all things in heaven and on earth were created, things visible and invisible, whether thrones or dominions or rulers or powers——all things have been created through him and for him. He himself is before all things, and in him all things hold together (Col. 1:16-17).

In Hebrews we see that a major theme of the book is the way Christ and the New Covenant far surpasses all in the Old. The book begins with a statement that Jesus Christ created all things: "Long ago God spoke to our ancestors in many and various ways by the prophets, but in these last days he has spoken to us by a Son, whom he appointed heir of all thing, through whom he also created the worlds" (Heb. 1:1-3).

Jesus is to be Worshiped

The Bible everywhere represents God alone as being the proper object of worship, and condemn most severely the worship of others, which is idolatry. Yet Jesus Christ is described in the Bible as being worshiped with approval, and even by command of God. Therefore he is God.

Again we can see in Hebrews that Christ is highly exalted: "When he brings his firstborn into the world, he says, 'Let all God's angels worship him.'" (Heb. 1:6). If the angels in heaven should worship him, then we should do so also. Supporting this are such passages as John 5:23; Acts. 7:59-60; 1 Corinthians 1:2; Phil. 2:10 and Rev. 5:13.

Jesus is Divine

In spite of the lowly birth of Jesus, it became more and more clear that he was not like any other person. After his resurrection, the disciples began to see with growing clarity that he was the Son of God.

While among them he had called himself the "son of man." This puzzling term had a variety of meanings, depending on its usage. These meanings ranged all the way from "mortal human" in Ezekiel to something more than this in Daniel. Scholars have long discussed the term without agreement. Jesus may have used it so that he would not be called a blasphemer by the religious leaders, yet he would not be false to his own identity. [49] He was a son of man, though he was also Son of God.

Fully Human

In the early life and ministry of Jesus, what was seen first was his humanness. He was born as a baby and grew up like other boys. He was seen as a human being, and that he was a male, born of a virgin.

Of the four Gospels, only Matthew and Luke tell of the birth of Jesus. Matthew writes from the viewpoint of Joseph and Luke from that of Mary. Mark and John do not tell of his birth and early life, though John, in his prologue, tells of his pre-existence.

The fact that he was born of a virgin is fully attested in the New Testament. Both Matthew and Luke make clear that the Virgin Mary conceived by the creative word of the Holy Spirit without any human male. This is not to be construed as some sort of parthenogenesis such as is known in biology, but as a miracle. The purpose of the miracle is not that the lack of a human father would prevent inheritance of depravity, as some have taught, since depravity itself is not inherited. That concept itself is based on the supposition that depravity is inherited, and that it is inherited only through the father!

If God were to be born into the world, it is natural to expect that it would be by means of a miraculous conception. (Note that it is the conception which is miraculous, and not the birth. Yet the term "virgin birth" has always been used in this way, and can continue to be.)

Jesus was a Male. Was God wrong to have Jesus born as a male? The story is told by Paul: "But when the fullness of time had come, God sent his Son, born of a woman, born under the law" (Gal. 4:4). Paul does not say, "born of a woman and man" but simply "born of a woman." This is one of the indications that Paul believed in the Virgin Birth of Jesus. He was born of a woman without assistance from a male. Was God showing bias against females? Augustine declared that in this way God showed honor both to men and to women.[50]

> "If one takes the premise that the incarnation required birth and that giving birth cannot be done by males——there is no way physiologically——it forms a plausible hypothesis for explaining why the Savior was male: *If the mother of the Savior must necessarily be female, the Savior must be male, if both sexes are to be rightly and equitably involved in the salvation event.*[51]

So there was no anti-female bias in the maleness of Jesus. Neither was there in his teachings, nor in his treatment of women. He treated all women with the highest respect, even those whose life or nationality was not respected by other Jews. In this way he rose above the culture in which he was born.

Jesus called himself human

Jesus called himself "a man" (John 8:40), and others called him "a man" (Acts 2:22; Rom. 5:15) or "a human being" (1 Cor. 15:21; 1 Tim. 2:5). Since the writers of the New Testament did not hesitate to state that he was human, neither should we.

Jesus had human feelings and lived as a human being. He was hungry (Mat. 4:2), thirsty (John 19:28), weary (John 4:6), needed sleep (Mat. 8:24), felt love (Mark 10:21), compassion (Mat. 9:36), anger (Mk. 3:5), anxiety (Heb. 5:7); fear (John 12:27), weeping (John 11:33), prayer (Mat. 14:23). He even suffered and died as a human being. Yet he was a perfect human being, yet without sin (Heb. 4:15).

Jesus did not merely appear to be human; he *was* human. This has not always been understood or carefully stated, but it is important.

A century after the death of Christ there were Christian churches here and there who thought of Jesus as a heavenly spirit who had merely assumed the appearance of a human body (docetism). Some people believed this before the New Testament was completed. And that is what 1 John 4:2 was denying so positively: "By this you know the Spirit of God: every spirit that confesses that Jesus Christ has come in the flesh is from God." So the Christian must believe not only that Jesus is God, but that he became "flesh" — he became human.

Crucified, Dead, and Buried

Not only was Jesus a human being, but he was crucified, died, and was buried (1 Cor. 15:3-4). Not only did he suffer some of the same troubles, trials, and temptations we mortal suffer, but he "tasted death" for us, just as we must do (Heb. 2:9). Note that the author here says that Jesus died "by the grace of God." He did it for our good and for our salvation.

Suffering Servant

The Jews of Jesus' time were expecting a Messiah to come, but they expected him to come as King, who would drive the Romans out of their country, and set them free. However, when Jesus said to them that "the truth will make you free" (John 8:32), they protested that they were not slaves, and never had been, so they did not need to be set free. But Jesus explained that he meant to set them free from their slavery to sin. A few minutes later they wanted to stone him to death. They did not want a spiritual leader or freedom from sin. They wanted a king to free them from the Romans. Two chapters earlier John told how they wanted to make him their king by force (Jn. 6:15), but he refused.

Even the disciples had trouble understanding the role Jesus was to play. They expected a kingdom to be set up by him, and could not conceive of him as servant, and certainly not as a "suffering servant" as predicted in Isaiah 52-53. How could the king suffer? How could the king be a servant? Jesus found it most difficult to talk with the disciples about this (Mat. 16 and parallels). They could not accept the fact that Jesus was to suffer and die. So they did not understand when he told them of the resurrection.

Resurrected on the Third Day

The resurrection of Christ from the tomb gave new meaning to his death. He died as others die, but the grave could not hold him. There is nothing more essential to Christian faith than the resurrection of Jesus Christ. Without the resurrection, the death of Jesus would have been just another death. It was in coming out of the grave that Jesus demonstrated the power of God to raise us up from our death in sin to live a new life in his power. And the same resurrection demonstrated that this life does not end at death, but that there is truly life after death. We must leave for a later chapter further consideration of our personal death and resurrection, but for now we can see that our faith in eternal life is based on the resurrection of Jesus Christ.

Ascended into Heaven

The ascent of Jesus brought to an end the post-resurrection appearances of Jesus to his disciples, and was finally parted from them in his physical presence. The ascension of Jesus was the reversal of his incarnation. In his incarnation, he descended from his glory with the Father to become for a time a human being in this sinful world. At his ascension, he returned to that exalted state of glory with the Father.

According to John, Jesus spoke on three occasions of his ascension (3:13; 6:62; 20:17). Luke describes the ascension in two places (Luke 24:51 and Acts 1:9). Otherwise it is referred to in various places (Eph. 4:10; 1 Tim. 3:16; 1 Pet. 3:22; Heb. 4:14). Paul also exhorted the Colossian believers to "seek the things that are above, where Christ is, seated at the right hand of God. Set your minds on things that are above, not on things that are on earth." (Col. 3:1-2).

The passage just quoted from Colossians helps us to see that what is meant is not that Jesus went up through the stratosphere, but that he is above us in power, glory, wisdom, and knowledge. He now transcends us in every way. With our modern understanding of the universe, we may feel with Westcott that the change was not a change of place so much as a change of state.

The great truth of the ascension is that Christ is no longer limited in space and time, but can be with every person in every place at the same time. In his last long talk with his disciples before his death, he said to the disciples: "I will not leave you orphaned; I am coming to you. In a little while the world will no longer see me, but you will see me; because I live, you also will live. On that day you will know that I am in the Father, and you in me, and I in you" (John 14:18-20). He does go with us everywhere, through the ministration of the Holy Spirit (verses. 16-17). This is part of the reason he told them it was better for him to go away.

FULLY GOD AND FULLY HUMAN

We have shown that Jesus is God, and that Jesus is human. This was the conviction of the majority at the end of the long Christological controversies in the first five centuries after Christ.

The Christian faith is that Jesus Christ is *Fully God* and *Fully Human*.

He was not partly God and partly human, which was the belief of the Apollinarians. He was not created by God, as Arianism and modern Jehovah's Witnesses believe. He was not some creature between God and humanity, as ancient Gnosticism asserted.[52] He was not just an unusually great man, as was believed by the ancient Socinians and some modern "liberal" theologians. He was not a man who became God, as in some writings of the Church of Jesus Christ of Latter Day Saints. He is God incarnate.

Though Jesus Christ was fully God and fully human, it must be remembered that he was one person, not two. He was not half God and half human. He was not schizophrenic—a split personality. It is difficult to comprehend how this could be, but it is also difficult for us to understand a human person. We are physical, mental, emotional, volitional and spiritual, yet we are single persons. Are we spirit in human flesh? Are we half spirit and half flesh? When the physical dies, what happens to the spirit? We may have some answers to such questions, but not complete answers. If we cannot understand ourselves, why imagine that we must fully comprehend God?

The Incarnation

By the Incarnation is meant the process by which the eternal Son of God became a human being. This process involved the virgin birth, and is the most amazing act of grace we could imagine. Why would God so love us as to take upon himself the form of a human being to live in this wicked, depraved world among us? How could he care that much about our salvation from sin?

The fact that God did care enough to do this is the central fact of the gospel, and this is what makes it good news. God's love for human beings reached down to the depths of sinful humanity, and seeks to lift us up out of our degradation.

The incarnation defies our full comprehension because all that we know how to say about God is beyond human comprehension in its fullest sense. Our statements about the Trinity, of which Jesus Christ is involved, are paradoxical. There is no way for human minds to resolve these paradoxes, yet we must believe them as they help to guard us from false concepts.

Donald M. Baillie compared the impossibility of comprehending the divine reality behind these paradoxes to the impossibility of adequately representing the world map on a flat sheet of paper).[53] We can draw such maps in various ways, using either the Mercator or some other projection. But all such maps contain inaccuracies and falsify the true shape. Yet such maps are necessary and helpful. So it is that we must say what we can understand about God and recognize that the description we give is not the full truth. God is in some sense three in one. Jesus Christ is Fully God and Fully human.

The incarnation is really unique to Christianity. No other religion has ever dared to say that the Creator and Sustainer of the universe loved human beings enough to become human for the sake of the persons he made. Some pagan religions have believed that this or that god *appeared* to be human for a while. But they did not really become human, and they did not take human appearance because they loved humanity. They came to gain their own selfish ends. Note the message of Paul: "All this is from God, who reconciled us to himself through Christ, and has given us the ministry of reconciliation, that is, in Christ God was reconciling the world to himself, not counting their trespasses against them, and entrusting the message of reconciliation to us" (2 Cor. 5:18-19).

Consider what this means. God, who inhabits eternity and has unlimited power, subjected himself for thirty-three years to the limitations of space and time. Like us, he was only in one place at a time. He lived in a tiny country, and probably never was as much as 200 miles from his birthplace. He lived and worked for only thirty-three years. He was so conscious of the limited time he had that he refused to settle down in one place, but went about the country, urging the disciples to keep going on to other villages and cities to preach.

Purposes of the Incarnation

To show us what God is like, and how much God loves us.

To show us how much God cares about our situation. He did not become human to find out what it was like, but to show us that God already knows and cares very much.

To show what God intended for human beings to be, and to make it fully possible for them to be just that. He showed that it is possible for us, by his power, to live as human beings who do not rebel against God, but rather serve him wholeheartedly.

Jesus came to die as a sin-offering for us, and to rise again to give us new life in him. We sing with John Newton:

> "Amazing grace! how sweet the sound,
> That saved a wretch like me!
> I once was lost, but now am found,
> Was blind, but now I see."

Atonement

In the next chapter we shall see atonement as an aspect of salvation as it is received by the individual. Here we need to consider what it was that Christ did when he died for our salvation. There are four theories of the atonement which have been developed over the centuries, and stand out from all others. They are the ransom, satisfaction, moral influence and governmental theories of atonement.

At first, Christians did not ask themselves how Jesus was able to save them, but by the fourth century Gregory of Nyssa was teaching that sinners belonged to the devil as his slaves, and that Christ paid the ransom price to buy their freedom from him. This ransom theory, involving a payment to Satan, and some trickery by God, nevertheless was taught for centuries.

Anselm, in the eleventh century, worked out a satisfaction theory. The concept was that the merit of Christ was placed to the account of sinners, by some divine accounting plan, which made their salvation possible. God's justice was satisfied.

Peter Abelard's moral influence theory denies that Christ did anything objective for the salvation of human beings, since it denies mankind's utter sinfulness. Human beings can break the power of sin by themselves as soon as they recognize the moral influence of the loving Christ on the cross. There is moral influence in the life and death of Jesus, but this subjective concept of atonement with God is unsatisfactory.

Hugo Grotius, an Arminian, worked out what is called the governmental theory of atonement. The basic idea is that God's righteous government must be upheld, so that sin cannot be easily and cheaply forgiven. Only through the death of Christ can God be both just and the justifier of wilful sinners (Rom. 3:26).

Each of these theories of atonement has some truth in it. None is completely false. Probably our objection to each of them is not so much what they say as what they omit. They are not equally helpful, nor are they equally false. But no one of them, nor all of them together, tells the whole blessed story. Jesus died for the salvation of all human beings. He did this in a sense that is beyond our logic and philosophy.[54]

However Christ did it, he fully met the need of us for salvation from sin. It is not necessary for us to understand fully all that Christ did, and how he did it. What we need to comprehend is the way to accept that salvation by faith in him. His saving grace is beyond our full comprehension. It is simply amazing grace!

Chapter 13

Salvation

> "See what love the Father has given us, that we should be called children of God; and that is what we are. . . .Beloved, we are God's children now" (1 John 3:1a, 2a).
> **What do we mean by such terms as "salvation," "conversion," "adoption" and "being born again"? Why is this so important? Is it necessary for everybody, or only for the wicked people of the world?**

Salvation from sin is the result of the marvelous love of God. No one can justify oneself in the eyes of God, the only hope of salvation is to trust in God's grace and mercy.

There are a variety of words used in the New Testament which express what happens to a person who is converted.

Save(σωζω--*Sozo*, 99 times in NT). This familiar word is usually translated "save," though it can also mean heal. An interesting thing about this word is that *only once* in the New Testament is it used with "sin", though that is the implicit meaning in most cases. "He shall save his people from their sins" (Matt. 1:21); "Be saved from this corrupt generation" (Ac. 2:40); "Saved through him from wrath" (Rom. 5:9). But it is usually used absolutely, with no statement of that from which one is saved or delivered.

Λυτροσις and απολυτροσις (22 times in NT). "Redemption." 1 Pet. 1:18). Represented by two words, one of which means the buying back of a person, and the other means the price of the purchase.

The meaning of this important word is not fully comprehended by a study of its etymology. Neither is its original meaning to be taken literally. There is something wrong with saying that if Jesus paid the price of our salvation, then we need to know to whom the price was paid. The biblical emphasis of this word is on our deliverance from sin, not on any "deal" with the devil or with God.

The price Jesus paid for our salvation was his death on the cross. He substituted his own death for ours, so that we do not need to die for our sins, as we richly deserved. He died for us, in our stead, and for our sake.

The substitutionary aspect of Jesus' death for our redemption or ransom is clear in scripture (Mark 10:45; Mat. 25:47-48; 1 Tim. 2:6; Titus 2:14). These texts echo Isaiah 53:10-11, which so beautifully depict the way he died for us, in our place.

When Jesus died for our redemption, Paul states that "For our sake he made him to be sin who knew no sin, so that in him we might become the righteousness of God" (2 Cor. 5:21). Yet Jesus did not become sinful, as a casual reading has led some to suppose. The word for "sin" is sometimes used for "sin-offering" as is the Hebrew word in Isaiah 53:6, 9. So Christ's death was a sin-offering for us (Rom. 8:3; Heb. 7:27; 9:12; Jn 1:29).

Αφιημι (Send away) χαριζομαι (forgiving by grace), απολυω (66 times). The first means sending away the sin and its memory. The second means "being gracious" about the sin. The third means "to cut loose and send away, or to pardon. The first and third words are applied to our sins, which are "sent away." The second word is applied to us - God is gracious to us in spite of our sins, and forgives. By grace we are saved (Eph. 2:5, 8).

Three things need to be said about the forgiveness of sins by God. First, there is no bargaining for God's forgiveness, as there is in almost all other religions. The forgiveness comes to us by the grace of God, not by our earning it working for it. God forgives us because of his grace and mercy, not because of anything we do to please God. "If we confess our sins, he who is faithful and just will forgive us our sins and cleanse us from all unrighteousness" (1 John 1:9). When we confess that we have sinned against God, he faithfully keeps his promise to forgive. Not only that, but God has taken the initiative. He prepared the plan of salvation and forgiveness, and has done what he can to get us to accept it.

Second, when God forgives, he gives power to overcome sin. He does not intend for us to go on sinning so long as we live, but by his grace we are able to overcome the power of sin and temptation.

Third, God's forgiveness is not merely overlooking or ignoring the sinfulness of sin. Under the influence of some modern psychology, we are led to say "It was nothing." Sentimentality, not forgiveness, passes sin off as inconsequential. Sin is considered simply a sign that we are human, and therefore less than perfect. But sin is serious, and God never considers it to be less than serious rebellion against him. So Paul says that he was not sorry that he had made the Corinthians sorry by his strong words against their laxity (2 Cor. 7:8-10). God never minimizes sin, but he can and does forgive those who repent.

Δικαιοω (Justify) This is the act of God's love by which he pardons and receives the individual into fellowship with himself. This is both the declaration that one is no longer guilty, and also the making of one to be righteous. God, knowing all things, cannot declare this to be true unless he first makes it true.

Herein lies the great disagreement among theologians about justification. Does God make us just, or does he declare us to be just even though he knows we are not. In other words, does the Greek word mean "to declare righteous" or "to make righteous?" Does God merely impute righteousness to the sinner, or does he impart righteousness to him?

Justification is primarily a Pauline word. The verb is found twenty-seven times in the Pauline Epistles, and the noun form twice (Rom. 4:25 and 5:18). If this were the only word for salvation it would be difficult to understand, but it is only one of the models for what God does in and for us. No one word can express it all.

Another significant point is that "justify" is used as the opposite of "condemn." So it is a relational term, and has to do with the relationship of a person with God. Its forensic significance, then, has to do with God's accepting the person as righteous. But at the same time, the person is regenerated—reborn by the renewing power of God, so that he truly is just. The sinner has been brought into a right relationship with God, which is justification, and he is made righteous at the same time through regeneration.

Καταλασσω "Reconciliation" "Atonement" The relationship is the key to the word. Sin had broken the relationship with God, and God in this way restores it. God is not reconciled to man, but man is reconciled to God. This reconciliation is closely related to justification.

A most important aspect of reconciliation is that it is initiated and carried out by God. God reconciles us to himself (Rom. 5:10; Heb. 2:17). We cannot reconcile God to us, as some religions have sought to do. There is nothing we can do to make God love us and accept us. He loved us as were continuing in sin, and made the sacrifice necessary to reconcile us to himself. God is the subject, and we are the object of reconciliation.

God, in Christ Jesus, did all that was necessary to atone for our sins so that we could be in right relationship with God (Col. 1:21-22). He has reconciled both Jews and gentiles to himself in the death of Jesus (Eph 2:15-16). So we are all one body if we are trusting in him for our salvation. We ought, then, to be reconciled to one another as we are to God.

Just as sin separated us from our relationship with God, so God is determined to seek to reconcile us with himself, thus reestablishing the relationship for which he made us.

Υιοθεσια "Adoption." This is the ordinary word for legal adoption of a child into the new family. The word is not common, and is primarily used by Paul in the context of the salvation of gentiles, who by adoption become children of God. Paul states that God sent Jesus "in order to redeem those who were under the law, so that we might receive adoptions as children. And because you are children, God has sent the Spirit of his Son into our hearts, crying, 'Abba! Father'" (Gal. 4:5-6). "Abba" is Aramaic for father—not the childish "papa" or "daddy," and "Father" translates the Greek word πατηρ. The other important use of the word is in Ephesians 1:5, which makes the same point.

All of the above words have to do with a change in relationship - with God.

αναγενναω "Born again" "Regeneration." To be born into a new life in Christ. This is not merely a change in relationship, but a change of nature. As Jesus told Nicodemus, "What is born of the flesh is flesh, and what is born of the Spirit is spirit" (Jn. 3:6). The new birth is not simply a change of mind, or a coming to believe that Jesus was a great teacher or a good man. It is not merely deciding that one ought to be a better person. It is more than joining a church and claiming to believe in God.

The new birth is a real change wrought in the heart through the power of God. This is the process by which God makes one able to live a new kind of life, and marks a radical change in the way one lives and acts. The new birth is the fulfillment of the promise through Ezekiel: "I will sprinkle clean water upon you and you shall be clean from all your uncleanesses, and from all your idols I will cleanse you. A new heart I will give you, and a new spirit I will put within you; and I will remove from your body the heart of stone and give you a heart of flesh. I will put my spirit within you, and make you follow my statutes and be careful to observe my ordinances" (Ezek. 36:25-27).

All these are not different experiences, but different ways of referring to the one experience of being saved.

Prerequisites for conversion

Only God can save us from sin. There is no way for us to save ourselves, through psychology, sociology, or any other science. Nor can we do enough good things to be acceptable to God. We must be converted by God, in his own way, or not at all. The important thing, then, is for us to know how God has planned to save us from sin through Jesus Christ. This way is made clear in the New Testament, so we must make sure we understand what it says.

Look at what is necessary if a sinner is to become a child of God. The sinner has by sinning broken the relationship with God who created all. This relationship must be made whole. The sinner must be reconciled with God. It is not that God must be reconciled with the sinner. God still loves the sinner and seeks to bring that one back to Himself. But the sinner must be willing to be reconciled with God.

Further, the sinner has been depraved by the sins committed, and is no longer the kind of person who is able to serve God. So the very nature of the sinner must be changed if one is to be converted. Thus we see that salvation is not simply deciding to turn over a new leaf and do better. It is not anything the person can do. It must be done by God. Yet God will not save a person against the sinner's will.

Steps to conversion

This is not a matter of simply reading a list of steps by which to be saved. There is no place in the New Testament which lists the twelve, or three steps to conversion. Yet the way is so clear that we do not have to be brilliant scholars to find God and his salvation. Speaking of the "Holy

Way" Isaiah said, "No traveler, not even fools, shall go astray" (Isa. 35:8). The following list is one way to analyze steps on the way to God.

Awakening, conviction of sin, righteousness and judgment (John 16:8). This is the work of the Holy Spirit, aided by the Word of God, the preaching of the truth, the lives of Christians, and worship.

Repentance - turning away from sin. No one can be saved from sin without first consciously seeking to turn away from it to face toward God. If the essence of sin is turning from God to commit what is displeasing to God, then to be saved, one must turn back to God. "Seek ye the Lord while he may be found, call upon him while he is near. Let the wicked forsake his way, and the unrighteous man his thoughts, and let him return unto the Lord, for he will have mercy, and to our God, for he will abundantly pardon" (Isa. 55:6-7). "Repent ye therefore, and turn around, so that your sins may be blotted out" (Ac. 3:19).

Faith for salvation. Repentance and faith are closely associated. Jesus first preached: "Repent and believe in the gospel" (Mark 1:15). Repenting is what a person does when convicted of sin, and when one comes to point of believing in the grace of God in Christ Jesus. Repentance is an act of the person, but it is done in response to the grace of God in bringing the person to that decision. God has the initiative, always.

Repentance is a gift of God. Acts 11:18, "They glorified God, saying, 'Then even to the gentiles, God has given repentance with the result of life.'" Romans 2:4, "Do you not know that God's kindness is to lead you to repentance?" 2 Timothy 2:25, "God may give them repentance to a knowledge of the truth."

Saving faith is that faith in Christ which brings salvation to the person. "He that believes on the Son has everlasting life: and he that believes not the Son shall not see life" (John 3:36). "Believe on the Lord Jesus Christ, and you shall be saved" (Acts 16:31). "For by grace are you saved through faith" (Eph. 2:8).

C. E. Brown sought to explain the relationship between faith and repentance in this way:

> Repentance is simply one aspect of faith, for faith does not move very far until it makes repentance inevitable or dies in its failure to do so. The very moment a man begins to believe in God as his loving Father, at that moment he begins to see his own sinfulness and appalling need. That is

the beginning of repentance.

"At the beginning this faith is a gift from God, yet a gift which the sinner has the power to reject. If exercised, faith will lead him through all the experience of repentance and acceptance to the full knowledge of the grace of God and the full joy of eternal life.[55]

The fact that conversion is a gift from God is emphasized by the statement of Jesus that "No one is able to come to me except the Father draws him" (John 6:44), and "No one is able to come to me unless it be given him from the Father" (John 6:65).

Nature of Saving Faith

All this indicates that faith is more than the result of logical proof. Faith is not merely intellectual belief in facts. It is not merely belief in correct theology, or belief in a proposition. It is more than a decision to believe, for it is in the beginning given by God. It is not something which a person can do alone. Saving faith is a response to the work of the Holy Spirit, who takes the initiative.

Saving faith is trust in a Person, rather than belief in a fact. The person to Person aspect must never be forgotten. It thus leads to a new relationship with our personal Lord.

A vital aspect of saving faith is that it is an ongoing trust in God, who alone can save and keep. The opposite of faith is pride, or a feeling of self-sufficiency. If one does not feel the need of God, then it is not possible for that person to have this trust in God.

Faith is not the Result of Being Given a Sign. Though we have stressed the fact that God takes the initiative in conversion, we must not imagine that one must wait for a sign of God's willingness to save. God takes the initiative, but he calls all to repent. The offer of salvation is for all human beings to come receive this gift (Titus 2:11). This call to conversion comes to each person through the work of the Holy Spirit. He works within the heart and mind of the person, and he works through the Bible, other Christians, and various circumstances. God "commands all people everywhere to repent" (Acts 17:30). If a person understands the need for salvation or has a desire to be saved, that is all the sign one needs to be saved.

We can sum up this process of coming to the point of having saving faith in Christ briefly. One believes that Jesus died for the sins of all, so one then recognizes his own sinfulness in the light of Jesus' love for him. When that one comes to the point of repenting of sin, forsaking sin, then it is possible, with the help of the Holy Spirit who has led him this far, to have saving faith in Christ Jesus. One is then born again, converted. And it all comes about through the work of the Holy Spirit within.

Conversion is Both Crisis and Process

We insist that both conversion and sanctification are crisis and process. Not either/or, but both/and. A crisis means "that at one dramatic moment in a man's life he will make a choice for evil or for good." [56]. It is not that this crisis is not preceded by a long process, but that there is a moment in which the decision is final. The amount of emotion which may accompany such a crisis is unimportant to the reality of the crisis. The emotion is increased if there is a long period of struggle before the crisis, and may be so nearly absent that one wonders just when it happened. But the fact is that there is a crisis experience. The Church of God considers conversion to be a first crisis in our experience of God, and entire sanctification (1 Thess. 5:23) is considered to be a second crisis. Conversion marks the beginning of a Person-to-person relationship with God.

Wesley sometimes spoke of two "moments" of grace. Following Phoebe Palmer and some other nineteenth century Wesleyan theologians, we have used the terms "first and second *works* of grace." This is admittedly rather inexact terminology, as God performs countless works of grace on all of us. In our best moments, we speak more exactly of two crises in Christian experience. Even this could be misinterpreted, as could any other theological terms. I have dealt with this more thoroughly elsewhere by delineating the Biblical, theological and psychological reasons for the two crises.[57] To summarize briefly:

Biblical Reasons for Two Crises. 1. Those in Acts who were filled with the Spirit were already godly believers. 2. Jesus said he would give to us "the Spirit of truth, whom the world is not able to receive" (John 14:17). 3. The Thessalonians were converted (1 Thess. 1), yet Paul prayed that they might be "sanctified entirely" (1 Thess. 5:23).

Theological Reasons. Only a holy. acceptable person is fit to be given to God as a sacrifice, in order to receive the fullness of the Spirit (Rom. 12:1-2). This is amply supported by the requirements for Old Testament sacrifices in Leviticus 1—7. It is further made clear by the Hebrew word חרם *cherem*. Wrapped up in the use of this word is the concept that the person or thing dedicated to any pagan god could not be dedicated to God. If it were a thing of such material that it could be purified by fire, it could then be given to God. Otherwise it had to be "utterly destroyed." A person who belongs to sin cannot be dedicated to God without a previous cleansing. So conversion is the necessary prerequisite to preparation for giving one's self to God so as to be filled with the Spirit.

Psychological consideration. When a person is deeply enough convicted of sin to want forgiveness from God, it is difficult for that person to consider the need for dedication. The sinful self is not fit to give to God, and also the person is not ready to consider that next step.

Conversion and the Holy Spirit

Conversion gives one the *witness of the Spirit*. One can know for sure that God has worked salvation and forgiveness in the heart (Rom. 8:15-16; Gal. 4:6; 1 John 5:10; 1 John 3:19). All this is the witness of the Holy Spirit within us, witnessing to our acceptance by God.

Conversion is not the baptism of the Spirit. There is a difference between being born of the Spirit in regeneration, and receiving the baptism of the Spirit. The sinful person has a dual need, for forgiveness, and for full consecration to the work of the Holy Spirit. The latter is necessary for one to be filled with the Spirit (Rom. 12:1-2). Since there is cleansing in salvation, we have sometimes called it "initial sanctification."

After conversion, one must continue to follow the guidance of the Spirit in life, so as to grow in grace. It is growth *in* grace, not growth *into* grace. One cannot grow into salvation, but after receiving this grace of redemption, one can and must grow in the knowledge and fear of the Lord. One must become more and more Christlike (2 Cor. 3:17-18). We must grow in love, both our love for God and our love for others. We must even grow in our love for spiritual growth, and all the means by which we can help ourselves to grow. So conversion is both crisis and process of growth.

RESULTS OF CONVERSION

We must never imagine that everyone reacts emotionally in the same way when converted. Yet there are similarities in what is done by God in the person. Emotional reactions or the lack of them have nothing to do with the reality of God's work in the person. Such reactions tell more about the person than about what God has done. If one has been struggling hard against the growing conviction that he ought to yield to God's will, then there may be a strong feeling of release which results in weeping, shouting out, laughing. Another may move so easily into conversion as to wonder if anything at all has happened. But the strength or weakness of emotion has nothing to tell us about what the reality of the conversion. But we can list some of the things which become real in the heart and life of the converted person.

Assurance of the Spirit

1 John 4:13 states, "By this we know that we abide in him and he in us, because he has given us of his Spirit." God does not leave us with no witness to the reality of conversion, but witnesses within us that we are accepted by him. The strength of this witness is not the same in all persons. And it should grow as the person continues to live the new life in Christ. This is the heart of the person witnessing to one's own sincerity and to the faith in God which brought it about. But there is more to it than that, for God adds his own witness to ours. "For you did not receive a spirit of slavery to fall back into fear, but you have received a spirit of adoption. When we cry, "Abba! Father!' is that very Spirit bearing witness with our spirit that we are children of God" (Rom. 8:15-16).

Note that the RSV and NRSV take the marginal punctuation of Westcott-Hort to show the close connection between verse fifteen and sixteen. Since our system of punctuation was not known when the first manuscripts were written, the punctuation of the New Testament is a matter for editors to decide. However, whether we put a period or a comma at the end of verse fifteen, there is a close connection between these two verses. This can be discerned by a study of the context.

When our own spirits witness that we are children of God, and can look to God as our Father, then his own Holy Spirit is a co-witness with our spirits that this is really true. We may not have any clear idea of the way in which this comes about, but it is very real to the Christian, and becomes more and more clear and indisputable as the Christian advances in obedience to God's will.

> Blessed assurance, Jesus is mine!
> Oh, what a foretaste of glory divine!
> Heir of salvation, purchase of God
> Born of his Spirit, washed in his blood."
>
> (Fanny J. Crosby)

Joy of Being Forgiven

The witness of the Spirit to the love of God for the individual person brings about a firm confidence that the person's faith in God's promise was not in vain. It is far more than some emotional response. It changes the intellectual faith of the sinner to an inner conviction of God's personal love. And it gives a firm conviction that God has forgiven sin, as he promised. "If we confess our sins, he who is faithful and just will forgive us our sins and cleanse us from all unrighteousness" (1 John 1:9).

Now the one who has come to God knows that "No one who conceals transgressions will prosper, but one who confesses and forsakes them will obtain mercy" (Prov. 28:13). The confession of sin and faith in God's forgiveness brings out the singing of the Psalmist: "Happy are those whose transgression is forgiven, whose sin is covered. Happy are those to whom the Lord imputes no iniquity, and in whose spirit there is no deceit" (Ps. 32:1-2)

The forgiven sinner now knows the meaning of such passages as Isaiah 55:6-9, and feels that verse twelve has come true in a marvelous and wonderful way. "For you shall go out in joy, and be led back in peace; the mountains and the hills before you shall burst into song, and all the trees of the field shall clap their hands" (Isa. 55:12).

The person who has been transformed by this experience of forgiveness feels that there is something wrong with any theology which speaks only of intellectual persuasion of the truth of the Bible. Those who have come to this conviction that God has truly forgiven feel a certainty which could never come from logical reasoning alone, but is confirmed by the Holy Spirit himself. John Wesley in the famous evening at Aldersgate said that he felt his heart "strangely warmed." Such persons want everyone else to feel this same joy of forgiveness.

This experience of personally being forgiven by God is a large part of the beginning of Christian experience. But this is only the beginning. As the new Christian continues to grow in faith and understanding, the joy of Christian experience grows more and more as Christians are led to have certain knowledge of many other blessings of the atonement.

1. Knowledge of salvation (1 John 3:14; Luke 1:77; Isa. 12:2). 2. Knowledge of adoption (Rom. 8:16; 1 Jn. 3:2). 3. Of God's unfailing love (Rom. 8:38-39). 4. Of peace with God, perfect reconciliation (Rom. 5:1). 5. Of being kept safe (Ps. 3:6,8; 27:3-5; 46:1-3). 6. Of a crown of life waiting at the end (2 Tim. 4:7-8; Jas. 1:12). 7. Of belonging to God (1 Jn. 4:6-7; 5:19). 8. Of eternal life (1 Jn. 5:13).

Two Warnings About Assurance

First, a person may be truly forgiven by God and not be sure of it. Because of false expectations, it may be difficult for a person to accept an assurance of forgiveness. God may accept such persons before they are willing or able to accept themselves.

Wesley struggled long in his early years with this problem. He found it hard to believe that a person in this life could have the inner assurance of salvation by faith. So he tried hard to believe, but his struggle was not soon followed by assurance. But when he finally came to believe that this was the right of every repentant sinner, he found peace with God and with himself. Until then he was seeking to trust in his own goodness rather than in God's grace and mercy. When Peter Bohler helped him to see this, he then found a sure trust and confidence that God saved him from sin by his faith in Christ.

Second, John Wesley guarded against a false emotionalism which could easily mislead some people into feeling that they had the witness of the Spirit when they did not. For it is much more than a feeling. He warned that the true witness of the Spirit of one's faith in God must be preceded by genuine repentance, and followed by Christlike living. There must be a real change in the life, or the person is wrong in claiming conversion, no matter what feelings the person may claim to have had. Wesley recognized clearly that the witness of the Spirit is not to be separated from the fruit of the Spirit. If the fruit of the Spirit is not manifested in the life, the witness the person claims is false. On the other hand, if the person seems to manifest some of the fruit of the Spirit, if that fruit is truly from the Spirit, he should have the witness of the Spirit within.[58]

One cannot be saved by doing good works, but neither can one be saved without then doing good works. The works we do for God can never earn salvation for us, and we can never be good enough to be saved. But when we are saved by faith, we begin to do all that we can for God, by his grace.

The Tenses of Salvation

We need to be reminded quite often that the verb "save" is used in three tenses in the New Testament. In Greek the three tenses are perfect, present and future. Greek perfect tense is represented in Ephesians 2:5,8 "By grace you *have been saved*." We can think of the Greek tense as stating that something happened in the past which has continuing results. We are saved because we have been saved at some time in the past.

The present tense can be seen in 1 Corinthians 1:18: "For the message of the cross is foolishness to those who are perishing, but to us who *are being saved*, it is the power of God." Note that both "perish" and "save" are in the same Greek present tense. Those who are not in Christ are not only going to perish in the end, but they are now perishing. We who are saved because we have been converted in the past, must go on living for God to the end, and so we are being saved. Moment by moment we are being kept by the power of God from sin, and must persist in living the will of God to the end.

This fact leads directly to the future tense of the word, as we find Jesus using in Matthew 24:13, "But the one who endures to the end *will be saved*." It is not merely beginning the Christian life of faith in Christ which takes one to victory in heaven, but continuing faithful moment-by-moment to the very end.

Final perseverance

Calvinists traditionally emphasize their concept that if one is once saved by the grace and predestination of God, that person can never backslide. Christians are sure to be Christian all their lives.

Arminians and Wesleyans have stressed the ability of Christians to go back into sin if they are not careful. Otherwise, what would be the value of all the warnings against falling away? What would be the use of Jesus telling us to endure to the end in order to be saved (Mark 13:13)? "By your endurance you will gain your souls" (Luke 21:19). It is not by beginning, but by beginning and enduring to the end.

Calvinists like to stress the Scripture passages which emphasize the power of God to keep one from falling. Wesleyans stress those which speak of the need for endurance. G. C. Berkouwer recognizes that the Christian life is not simply a gift which is received once for all, but that salvation is a dynamic concept. One must keep on going and growing in the grace of God. He believes, however, as a Calvinist that God will keep the person from falling, and preserve the life which has been begun.

In the most scholarly study done in recent times by a Wesleyan, I Howard Marshall concludes that Wesleyans need more emphasis on the keeping power of God, while recognizing that it is possible to yield to temptation and lose salvation.

> It is possible for the believer, even though he knows of the possibility of apostasy, to be confident of persevering because he puts his trust in God. . . . Exultant confidence and anxious fear must be held together in a paradox, although the normal progress of the Christian should be towards an increasing confidence which removes the fear of apostasy.[59]

This is about as well as it can be put. This conclusion is well supported by the thorough study made of all the passages in the New Testament bearing on the subject.

God does not make it impossible for us to fall, but makes it possible for us not to fall. If we could not fall, that would mean that once we are saved, we lose our power to make decisions. We would have lost our freedom of choice.

Chapter 14

Human Holiness

> For I am the Lord your God; consecrate yourselves therefore, and be holy, for I am holy . . . You therefore shall be holy, for I am holy (Lev. 11:44-45, RSV).
>
> But as he who called you is holy, be holy yourselves in all your conduct; for it is written, you shall be holy, for I am holy (I Pet. 1:15-16).
>
> **Since we are not God, how can God tell us to be holy as he is holy? What would a holy person be? Is such a person possible in this world? Would it mean that if we were holy, we would never make any mistakes? If we cannot be holy, does that mean we are all miserable sinners?**

In the Scriptures quoted above, we note that the second is in the New Testament and is a quotation from the one in the Old Testament.

These passages make clear that God"s word commands us to be holy. Yet the holiness of God consists of his utter transcendence, his shining glory, and his perfect moral purity. The first two of these are totally unique to God, and third seems out of reach of human beings. So how can human beings be holy?

To put the question in another way, can we be saved from sin before death? Is it possible to live in this world in such a way as to please God at all times? Or are we doomed to be the miserable sinners some proclaim us to be, as long as we are in this physical world? Are we to go on sinning every day, with every breath we take, so long as we live? Must we always come to God begging him to forgive us all the sins we have committed since we prayed a few hours ago?

Put the matter in still another way. If sin is anything and everything which is less than God, then we can never in this world be anything but sinful. We will never be God.

But, as we have seen in Chapter Nine, sin is not being less than God, but rather separation from God, rebellion against God, or the lack of love for God. Sin is turning away from God, and neglecting or refusing to live for him. In that earlier chapter we discussed sin and mentioned holiness. Now we need to give some thought to the nature of human holiness.

MEANING OF HUMAN HOLINESS

Biblical scholars have long sought to discern the meaning of the term "holy" by tracing its etymological origin, that is, by finding out what the root form of the word originally meant, either in Hebrew, Greek, or one of the cognate languages. The most common etymology seeks to trace the word to a root that meant "to cut" or "to separate." So it has been common to say that the root meaning of the word "holy" is separation.

N. H. Snaith took a definite step forward when he insisted that it means "separation *to* (God)," not "separation *from*" something else.[60] However, the etymology of this word is very doubtful in any case. And recent advances in linguistics have shown that etymology is never a very sure guide to the meaning of a word. If we are to learn the meaning of a biblical word, we will have to study the Biblical usage of the word.

The first use of "holy" in the Pentateuch is when Moses met God at the burning bush, and God said to him, "Come no closer! Remove the sandals from your feet, for the place n which you are standing is holy ground" (Exod. 3:5). So the first use of the word is of a holy *place*. But the important thing to see in this passage is that "holy" is here used of an encounter with the holy God. The place was not holy of itself, but was called holy because it was where Moses encountered God, who is holy. The fact that Moses was in the presence of God made the place holy.

Holy Things

Later, the Tabernacle and the things in it were dedicated to God and were to be used only in worship, not for common, ordinary uses. These things were called holy because they were considered to belong only to

God. They were holy in that they belonged to God alone. The same was true about the Temple which was built later, and that objects used in it. Besides these, the Sabbath was holy (Exod. 20:8; 35:2) the tithe (Lev. 27:30) and offerings (2 Chron. 35:13). All these were called holy because of their special relationship with God. They were to be used exclusively for God.

In this gospel age, we do not think of material things as being holy in this sense, because we know very well that the whole universe belongs to God. Everything and every day is holy, as it all belongs to God, so we no longer feel compelled to call only certain things holy.

The word "law," which was applied to the teachings of the first five books of the Bible, really translates the Hebrew word "Torah" which means "instruction." It is not laws passed by God or people, but God's instruction of his people in the things that would enable them to understand Christ and what he was to do in the world. It was a "guide" (Gr. παιδαγογος, Gal. 3:25) to lead Israel to Christ, so that they could understand him and his work. Now that Christ has come, we are no longer under that kind of guidance. Yet the instruction of the Old Testament is a most valuable guide to us in seeking to understand the fullness of the gospel to which it pointed.

From the Old Testament we see that the idea of things being holy because of their special use by God, or relationship to him, was a most valuable and necessary step toward understanding the deeper meanings of holiness. For these objects to be holy, they had to be kept *separate to* God, who is holy.

Holy Persons

In the Old Testament, priests and Levites were both called holy (Exod. 29:1; Lev. 8:12, 30) because they had been separated for special ministry to God. Nazarites were called holy because they had separated themselves to God (Num. 6:5). The whole people of Israel were to be holy to the Lord (Exod. 19:6; cf. Lev. 20:24) because they had separated themselves unto the Lord. In every case, these people were called holy, not because they were separated *from* something, but because they were separated *to* God. They belonged to God in some special sense. This is what caused them to be called holy.

In the New Testament the word "holy" is applied to God (John 17:11; Rev. 4:8; 6:10). It is regularly applied to the Spirit of God (as in Matt. 1:18; Acts 1:2; Rom. 5:5, for example) so that he is normally called the Holy Spirit. It is applied to Christ (Mark. 1:24; Acts 3:14; 4:3). And it is supplied to the Scriptures (Rom. 1:2), the Law (Rom. 7:12), the Mount of Transfiguration (2 Pet. 1:18), and the New Jerusalem (Rev. 21:2).

Yet the primary use of the word "holy" ($\alpha\gamma\iota o\varsigma$) in the New Testament is of the people of God, Christians, who make up the church. This characteristic use in the New Testament is distinctive and important. Christians are regularly called "saints" (holy ones, or holy people). It is applied to all born-again believers in Christ, whether they are spiritually and ethically mature or not. So to call them holy does not imply that they are morally mature, but that they are separated to God, and that they have started on the road that must lead to that ideal as soon as possible. It is possible to call someone holy who does not yet measure up to the standard of Christ in many respects. Such a new-born Christian may be compared to a baby, who is a human being, but is far from being physically or intellectually mature. A perfect baby cannot be measured by the standards applied to an adult.

There must be no misunderstanding. The word "holy" is not so broad in meaning that it can be applied to almost anyone. But the primary meaning of the word is that one belongs especially to God. The New Testament leaves no room for holiness divorced from high ethical standards of obedience to God.

We must live holy lives because we are separated to God, wholly committed to Him and His will. We are not holy because of all that we have separated ourselves *from*, but because we are *separated to* the holy God. As soon as we have separated ourselves from sin to God, we are holy, even though we have much to learn about God's specific requirements.

Holy To The Lord

God is holy in a sense in which no human being can ever be. God is transcendent with shining glory, and he alone is absolutely perfect morally. Yet God tells us to be holy, for he is holy.

All the objects and persons called holy had been dedicated exclusively to God. These things were not to be used for ordinary purposes, but only for worship. The objects were no longer considered ordinary or common, because they belonged to God in a special sense.

In the same way, persons were considered holy, no longer ordinary or common, because of their special contact and relationship with God. They belonged only to God. There totally set apart for him and his service. So they were no longer common or ordinary, but holy to God.

Clean, Unclean

"You are to distinguish between the holy and the common, and between the unclean and clean" (Lev. 10:10). This command in the Old Testament had to do with ritual or ceremonial cleanness and uncleanness. It had nothing to do with dirt of physical cleanness. It dealt with the things which God said were acceptable for use in worship and those which were not.

A careful study of the uses of "holy" in the Old Testament shows that a strong contrast is drawn between objects and persons that are holy, and those that are not. Objects that are unclean may or may not be sinful, since uncleanness is often ceremonial uncleanness alone, not ethical or moral uncleanness. A person who was ceremonially unclean for some reason was unfit to be dedicated to God or to go into sacred places until he or she did whatever forms or ceremonies were required to be cleansed. Then he or she was fit to come into sacred places or to worship. God used this concept to teach the people that worshiping God and being his people were no light matters. God will not accept anything sinful or unfit. God will have only the best.

The point of the ideas of "clean and unclean" was that it emphasized human separation from God. It helped keep people aware that there were conditions to be met if they were to approach God or seek to be reconciled with him. In this way it was a step in the instruction of the people, and a guide to the understanding of the gospel which would be revealed.

In the New Testament, we find that Jesus repudiated the whole concept of clean and unclean food as defiling a person. He said that it was not the food one ate which defiled a person, but evil words coming from a sinful, defiled heart (Mk. 7:14-23).

Cherem

An even stronger term used in contrast with *holy* is חרם (*cherem*). This Hebrew word is difficult to translate because it expresses a concept which was common in Old Testament times but which is not used today at all. Not only was it used in Israel in the time of Moses, but also was common in the nations around them.

One of the translations of the word is "devoted." Yet it does not mean simply "devoted," but "devoted to some foreign god." This could be said of a thing or a person. To be *cherem*, then was far worse than to be "unclean."

Some objects that were חרם (*cherem*)could be made clean (undevoted), and therefore made fit to dedicate to God. Gold vessels from Jericho, for instance, were *cherem* because they had been dedicated to the gods of Jericho. But gold could be purified by fire and by ceremonies and dedicated to God. They could not be used for ordinary purposes, but had to be dedicated to God (Deut. 20:10-18; Josh. 6:15-19). Objects that were *cherem* and could not be cleansed *had to be destroyed.* This is why the word *cherem* is sometimes translated "utterly destroyed" (Josh. 6:18; Jer. 25:9; Josh. 2:9; Dan. 11:44).

If persons who were *cherem* because they served other gods, chose to serve the Lord, they then had the right to go through the ceremonies of cleansing. They could then dedicate themselves to God and thus become holy to the Lord. If they did not so choose, they were to be destroyed.

This is the background for such commands as Deuteronomy 20:10-18. It is the reason the people of Jericho and other such cities and nations were to be utterly destroyed. God was teaching the people that there was to be no compromise with idolatry or paganism. If they were to be his people they had to be utterly and permanently separate from false gods.[61]

Unclean not sinful

"Clean"does not mean holy, and "unclean" does not mean sinful. Whatever is clean is capable of being made holy, and whatever is unclean is incapable of being made holy unless it could first be made clean. Any person could be rendered temporarily unclean by a number of things, such as touching a dead person (Num. 5:1-2; 19:11ff). Such a person was not sinful, but could not participate in the religious ceremonies until he or she had been cleansed by the process outlined for such cleansing (Num. 19). It was not a sin to touch a person who had died, but it simply rendered the person ceremonially unclean for a time and made it necessary for him or her to go through a cleansing ceremony. The washing involved in the cleansing ceremonies makes sense in the light of modern medical knowledge of transmissible diseases. But the vital aspect of this is that the uncleanness was ceremonial, not moral. An unclean person or thing could not be dedicated to God until cleansed.

The Pharisees distorted the ideas of clean and unclean in the time of Christ. They condemned Jesus because he did not wash his hands in their special ceremonial way before eating. But Jesus explained that "it is not what goes into the mouth that defiles a person, but it is what comes out of the mouth that defiles. When the disciples, who had been taught otherwise, were slow to understand, Jesus explained further:

> Are you also still without understanding? Do you not see that whatever goes into the mouth enters the stomach, and goes out into the sewer? But what comes out of the mouth proceeds from the heart, and this is what defiles. For out of the heart come evil intentions, murder, adultery, fornication, theft, false witness, slander. These are what defile a person, but to eat with unwashed hands does not defile (Matt. 15:16-20).

The Pharisees had made two mistakes. They were not distinguishing between ceremonial uncleanness and dirt. And they were not distinguishing ceremonial uncleanness from sin.

In Peter's famous rooftop vision of the sheet full of clean and unclean animals (Acts 10:9-16), it was made very clear to him that the old covenant rules of ceremonially clean and unclean were no longer necessary. They had their place in teaching the people what it means to be pleasing to God, but now that Christ has revealed the reality of true Christian holiness, we no longer need that kind of instruction. Everything was made good and fit for proper human use.

In this gospel age we must not call any person *unclean*, meaning that they are unfit for the gospel. The good news must be preached to all, and those who accept it can be made God's own people. Sin is what defiles a person, and sin can be cleansed away by God in Christ Jesus so that no one is inherently incapable of being made a Christian.

Old Testament rules like these were good, but not permanent. We teach a small child never to cross the street without an adult. But when the child is older, the rule is no longer necessary. When the spiritual reality appeared in Christ and his death and resurrection, the old ceremonial rules became unnecessary.

Holy means Belonging to God

In the Old Testament, the people of Israel were called holy because they were God's own people whom he had chosen for himself (Exod. 19:5-6). But this was done in an anticipatory sense. The fact is that at times God did not claim them as his own because of their sin (Hos. 1:9). In this gospel age, we know that the individual Christian is not holy because he or she was born into a particular nation. One is holy because the person as an individual has accepted the spiritual cleansing offered in Christ Jesus, and has voluntarily let God make him or her holy.

Meaning of Belonging to God

Everything in the universe belongs to God by right of creation. He made it all, and it is his. But much more than this is meant when we are talking about the Bible meaning of holiness. All people are under the dominion of God, but not all admit it. They do not belong to God in the special sense of being his people. God does not claim them as his. This is because he has given each person some freedom of choice. We can choose whether or not we want to put ourselves under God's control and let him have his way with us. Only *persons* can be holy in the sense of the New Testament. And persons cannot be holy in this sense unless they themselves choose to allow God to cleanse them, break the power of sin, and make them holy to the Lord. Thus the word has a far deeper and richer meaning in the New Testament age than in the Old.

This concept of belong to God as the essence of Biblical holiness, was spelled out by C. E. Brown in one of the last articles he published on the subject.

> The very first thing we can say about the holy man is that he belongs to God. And just as certainly we can say with the absolute assurance of stating a mathematical axiom: Every man who belongs to God is holy. .

Let us not insist too much upon how good we may be (not denying it), but let us emphasize this truth that we have only the minimum standard for any Christian: We belong to God. No Christian can fall short of that. No person who is such can fail to be holy"[62]

Holiness is Positive

Holiness is not a thing which is added to a person, just as sin is not a thing. Sin is not something which can be in a person and which must be removed. So holiness is far more than the lack of sin. If holiness were merely the lack of sin, it would be purely negative in nature, as some seem to believe. Holiness would then be an emptiness which would remain when all sin had been dropped off. But it is far more than that.

Holiness is a positive, committed covenant relationship with God, and sin is the lack of that. As darkness is the absence of light, so holiness is covenant love for God, and sinfulness is the absence of it. As we saw in our study of sin, it is the basic orientation of the person away from God, and sins are those things a person does because one is facing away from God. The individual acts of sin follow from that wrong orientation of the soul.

It is essential for us to escape from the atomistic view of sins as isolated incidents. The sinner sins because of a sinful condition. The Christian has made a covenant with God and by the grace of God is no longer in that sinful condition.

If sin is isolated events, then holiness is seen to be impossible for human beings, since it is so easy for us to the something that is less than our best. We can then feel as though we have lost all the goodness and holiness we ever had and feel that the whole attempt to be holy is hopeless.

However, if holiness is covenant-love to God and sin is the absence of that love, we have a far different situation. If holiness is being turned in love toward God, and sin is turning away from God, then surely we can know whether or not we still love God! We can know whether or not we have turned our hearts away from him. We can know his continued and continuing forgiveness of our failings. We can forgive ourselves more easily when we know that he forgives. "For he knows how we were made; he remembers that we are dust" (Ps. 103:14).

This does not mean that we can casually go on living in sin and feeling that God forgives all we do (Rom. 6:1-2). It simply means that God for knows what we can do by his grace and what we cannot do because of our human ignorance or lack of maturity. God is at least as merciful with us as we parents are with little children. We do not expect them to act like adults, for we know they cannot. We do not expect a baby to know better than to cry while the preacher is preaching. We do expect the child to learn—in time. If the child brings a handful of weeds as a gift of love to us, we accept it as the loving gift it is and say nothing of the lack of beauty. We are happy for the love. We know that God can see the love in our hearts, even when our actions do not measure up to the standard of maturity he hopes to help us to attain in time. [63]

Positive Love for God

If holiness is merely the total absence of sin or wrong, then we must look very carefully at a person and every aspect of the life before we dare to say that the person is holy. We must be very sure that some little sin somewhere in his or her live has not been overlooked. We would have the problem of proving a universal negative, which is impossible.

On the other hand, since holiness is positive, committed love for God, we can see that love shining in the person's heart and life. And the person involved knows of the love in the heart for God, and is sure of the covenant made with God. We can have the constant assurance that we belong to him. We may get discouraged at times about ourselves, and may wonder if we are still pleasing to God, but we can be sure we have made that commitment of ourselves to God, and that we have never gone back on it. This gives assurance.

Perfect?

"Be perfect, therefore, as your heavenly Father is perfect" (Mat. 5:48). These words of Jesus startle us. *Perfect*? How could that be?

One cannot grow in the Lord without learning that one's past life has been less than perfect. Every parent knows what it is to look back and see how the training of the children could have been better accomplished. Every Christian knows what it is like to look back and see how we could have done better at one point or another. That is the result of growing maturity, and it is a part of being a Christian, and of being able to see the past better than the present.

We make mistakes and blunders of all kinds. We spell words incorrectly, use less-than-perfect grammar, forget names, drop things, stumble, and unintentionally hurt the feelings of others. So why did Jesus say for us to be perfect?

Did Jesus mean for us to *try* to be perfect? If so, why did he not say it that way?

Some insist that the Greek word τελειος means "mature, full-grown, completely finished." But this makes the problem more difficult. Maturity is a matter of growth and age. How can a person be mature when he or she is immature? What good does it do to tell us to be completely finished. We cannot be what we are not, simply because we are to be.

When Jesus said for us to be perfect, he was speaking of the love we should have for others. He said that God showed love to all persons, whether they loved God or not. So Jesus said that showing love to all, whether we are loved in return or not, is the way to be like God. It is not easy, but it can be done by the grace of God. This is what Jesus told us to do. Since love is not a feeling, but a way of acting, we can do this by the grace of God. This perfection is not beyond the reach of one who is aided by the Holy Spirit. It is not divine perfection. It is simply that we reach out in love to all people, as God does.

Relative Perfection

God alone is absolutely perfect. Any perfection we human beings may have is relative perfection. Yet relative perfection is real perfection. The word *perfect* always means "relatively perfect" when applied to anything but to God.

Human beings could not define, describe or recognize absolute perfection in anything. When we call a line "perfectly straight" we know that it is not absolutely perfect in straightness. Any microscope will show that it is not even a line, since it varies in width, and a line has no width at all. What we draw simply represents a straight line. Some lines are better representations than others, but judged by absolute standards, they are not lines at all and are far from perfect. Yet if they are straight enough for our purpose we can call them "perfect."

Here, then, is the clue to the meaning of perfection. To call anything perfect means that it is "good enough for the purpose for which it is to be used." Or that it "meets the standards of the maker." It may not be good enough for other purposes. It may not meet the standards of some other person. It is perfect if it meets the needs of the maker or user.

What the Christian must do is to meet the standards of the Creator God for that particular person. God judges each person individually. God know the heart, the mind, the soul, the body of that person, and does not expect more of that one than is possible for that person at that time. God expects us to grow and learn. But God knows what we know and can do at a particular time. Yet we must judge ourselves far stricter than we judge others (Mat. 7:1-2).

The Christian will not presume on the love and mercy of God but will regret any failure and beg for forgiveness. We must not overlook failure and depend on the love of God to forgive. We must ask for forgiveness and seek for grace so as not to fail again in that same way. This is the way of growth. This is the way to keep the path clear between the soul and God. This is the way to continue walking in the highway of holiness. This is the adventure of holiness.

CHILDREN OF GOD

It is depressing to hear some say that we are "all miserable sinners." If we are, then what is the point of seeking to be Christians? Jesus said to his disciples, "Rejoice that your names are written in heaven" (Luke 10:20). We read in Philippians 4:4, "Rejoice in the Lord always; again I will say, Rejoice." Such commands are found so often in Philippians that it can be considered almost the theme of the book. This does not sound as though Christians are deprived and miserable!

Christians are children of God and call God "Father."
They have been made children of God by faith in Jesus Christ (John 1:12; 1 Jn. 3:2). So they have boldness to pray for the grace of God to live the kind of lives which will please God, and know that God cares and will do what needs to be done to help us (Heb. 4:15-16; 11:6; Jas. 1:5).

Right Relationship with God

If we consider the history of the Old Testament, as told in the thirty-nine books, we see how God worked especially with certain persons in many ages to teach them to know him. He worked with them in an unusual close fellowship. This made it possible for such persons to become leaders in their generations and to show others the will of God more perfectly. All this was the work of the Holy Spirit in the hearts of these people. For the work of the Holy Spirit did not begin at Pentecost. Before Pentecost, he did the same work, but concentrated in doing for the few what he wills to do for all today. As Jeremiah 31:34 says, "For they shall all know me, from the least of them to the greatest, says the Lord."

God's plan from the beginning of creation was to have a people with a special covenant-relationship with him, who would love and serve him and with whom he could have constant close fellowship and communion. God set his love upon human beings. It was not because of our greatness, but because of God's love that he wants us to belong specially to him (Deut. 7:6-8). He did not want us to be robots who would do his will from necessity. He has longed for people with a free will to choose to love and serve him in response to his love for them. After sin wrecked the plan in the beginning, God did not give up. He prepared the way, by the Holy Spirit, for the coming of Jesus Christ, who would complete a plan of salvation from sin for those who would accept it.

This right relationship with God is the essence of holiness, just as a wrong relationship is the essence of sin. The nature of holiness is determined by the nature of God's perfection. His holiness determines what we must be like in order to please him with our lives. No matter how much he loves us, he cannot tolerate sin or rebellion in us. So if we are to live in a right relationship with him, we must give up all that displeases him. He has loved us, and we must love God in return.

Victory Over Sin

Holiness includes victory over sin and temptation. "For sin will have no dominion over you, since you are not under law but under grace" (Rom. 6:14).

We Christians do not have to live in constant guilt. God does not plan for us to live in sin all through this life, wishing we could do better, but knowing that we cannot. We can live in this present world lives that are pleasing to God because of our love for God. What a blessing it is for us to be able to say with Paul: "There is therefore now no condemnation for those who are in Christ Jesus. For the law of the Spirit of life in Christ Jesus has set you free from the law of sin and of death. For God has done what the law, weakened by the flesh, could not do: by sending his own Son in the likeness of sinful flesh, and to deal with sin, he condemned sin in the flesh, so that the just requirement of the law might be fulfilled in us, who walk not according to the flesh but according to the Spirit" (Rom. 8:1-4).

He had already explained in Romans 6 that the Christian has died to sin and can no longer continue to live in it. Now he shows that all this victory over sin is due to the way Jesus Christ has died for us so that we can die to sin and rise to a new life in Christ Jesus. The "Just requirement of the law" can now be fulfilled in us, since we are no longer under the power of the purely human desires of the flesh, but are enabled to walk according to the Spirit (Rom. 8:8-14). In the last part of the chapter we find a list of things which might be too much for the Christian to bear, and exclaims "No, in all these things we are more than conquerors through him who loved us" (Rom. 8:37).

Contrast this victory over sin with the statement in the Westminster Catechism: "No man even by the aid of Divine grace, can avoid sinning, but daily sins in thought, word and deed."

If this declaration is true, what is the difference between a sinner and a Christian? What is the advantage of being a Christian? Does the Christian sins as much as the sinner? Are these "Christian" sins forgiven as they are committed? How can one claim to be "saved from sin" (Mat. 1:21) if sin continues to rule the whole life?

Dead to Sin

Look once more at Romans 6:1-2: "Are we to continue in sin that grace may abound? By no means! How can we who died to sin still live in it?" This seems perfectly clear, but some are so involved in their theories of sinning Christians that they cannot accept the concept of victory over sin.

J. Sidlow Baxter created a complicated interpretation which avoids the conclusion above. He claims that Paul does not mean that we die to sin, but that we die to law.[64] This interpretation seems most difficult to support, especially if we follow Paul a little further: "We know that our old self was crucified with him so that the body of sin might be destroyed, and we might no longer be enslaved to sin. For whoever has died is freed from sin. . . . So you also must consider yourselves dead to sin and alive to God in Christ Jesus" (Rom. 6:6-7, 11).

In this last verse we meet the strange but common paradox that Paul tells Christians to be what they are. You are dead to sin, therefore be dead to sin. Consider yourself dead to sin. You are holy; therefore be holy. This mixture of the indicative and the imperative points up the fact that we must be ever diligent to remember what we are, and to keep what we have. It is not the one who makes a good start who wins in the end, but the one who continues steadfast to the end.

You are dead to sin; therefore persist in this condition. Consider yourself dead to sin, because you are. Do not respond to sin and temptation. Keep on considering yourself dead to sin, because you are, by the grace of God.

The Christian must never forget that temptation comes to all, so the Christian must be diligent in guarding against it. Christ himself was tempted (Heb. 4:15; Mat. 4, etc.) so we too will be tempted repeatedly as long as we live, and must resist the attraction to sin. We do not lose our freedom of choice when we die to sin. The possibility of sinning is always present.

John Wesley once said that holiness does not mean that we are unable to sin, but that we are *able not to sin!* We could go further. It is not freedom from temptation, but power to overcome temptation. It is not infallible judgment, but sincere seeking for the will and wisdom of God. It is not freedom from conflict, but victory through conflict. It is not the end of progress, but constant and diligent seeking for progress in the grace of God.

Sometimes one uses 1 John 1:8 to prove that no one can live in this world without sinning regularly. Holiness of life is therefore impossible, they believe. If this is true, it would contradict some of the teachings of Jesus and Paul which we have already considered. So a careful study of the whole passage is necessary.

The theme of the paragraph is stated in verse 5, in the statement that "God is light and in him there is no darkness at all." Then three false ideas are stated and refuted. 1. If we claim to be in fellowship with God while walking in the darkness of sin, we are not true (vs. 6). "But if we walk in the light as he himself is in the light, we have fellowship with one another, and the blood of Jesus his Son cleanses us from all sin" (7). 2. But if we say that we have no sin from which to be cleansed (8), we are deceiving ourselves. Wesley, in his "Notes," explained this as a sinner who claims he needs no salvation. Ray Dunning applies it to the depravity caused by sin.[65] Either way makes sense of this verse and the verse which follows. If we say we have no sin to be cleansed, we are deceiving ourselves. But if we confess our sins, he will forgive and cleanse (9). 3. We must be honest enough to confess our sins, and must never feel that we have never committed sin. No one can live to maturity without sinning. If some could live without ever sinning, this would make the Savior less necessary, and would make a lie of the statement that "all have sinned" (Rom. 3:23).

What If I Do Sin?

Twice when Jesus healed someone, he said to the person "Sin no more" (John 5:14; 8:11). How could Jesus have given such a firm command if he knew that it was impossible for that person to live without sinning? The expression Jesus used means, "Stop sinning" or "do not go on sinning."

It is sure, then, that Jesus tells us we do not have to go on sinning. But what if we do find that we have committed a sin? Should we just give up and say that we cannot live for God? Or should we just decide to call our sins "mistakes" and say they do not matter all that much? 1 John deals with that very problem:

> "My little children, I am writing these things to you so that you may not sin. But if anyone does sin, we have an advocate with the Father, Jesus Christ the righteous; and he is the atoning sacrifice for our sins, and not for ours only but also for the sins of the whole world" (1 John 2:1-2).

Here we read that we should never sin. That is the way we should live, with no sinning at all. Yet we are immediately told that if we do commit a sin, God still loves us and is willing to forgive. We have an Advocate with the Father, and Jesus will forgive again, as he did before. We must never treat our sin casually, but immediately ask God to forgive us, and go on trusting in his forgiveness and help. One must never give up. And we must never let sin go unforgiven.

What if we think we have sinned, and are not sure whether we have or not? Ask God to forgive, anyway. It is far better to ask forgiveness for what is not really a sin, than to let sin go on unforgiven. It is wiser to ask for forgiveness for careless mistakes or failings than to fail to ask often enough. One does not have to decide each time whether this act was really sinful or not before deciding what to do about it. If we truly love God we will ask forgiveness if we even imagine that he might be grieved by what we did or did not do. Simply ask forgiveness, accept it, and go on your way rejoicing in God's grace. Never feel you must be defeated by sin. By the grace of God you can have the victory always."Whatever is born of God conquers the world. And this is the victory that conquers the world, our faith" (1 John 5:4). You can sing with Barney E. Warren:

> The victory is mine, the victory is mine
> Through Jesus my Lord, obeying his Word;
> He conquers the foe wherever I go,
> I'm living with him in holy accord.

Chapter 15

The Holy Spirit

> "But the Advocate, the Holy Spirit, whom the Father will send in my name, will teach you everything, and remind you of all that I have said to you" (John 14:26).
> **Who is the Holy Spirit? What is He like, and what does He do? Is He God? Why is he called "Holy"? Or is he just a power? How can we get him and his power to work for us?**

When Jesus promised to send another Helper like himself, he called him the Holy Spirit. We believe in the Father, and in Jesus Christ, the Son of God. Yet the Holy Spirit is just as truly God as the other two members of the Trinity and is just as important. So we need to understand what we can of his nature and work. Even though we have looked at a few basic facts about him in our consideration of the Trinity, we need more details.

Spirit in the Old Testament

The phrase "Holy Spirit" occurs 93 times in the New Testament, but only three times in the Old Testament (Ps. 51:11 and Isa. 63:10-11). The Old Testament stresses the work or activity of the Holy Spirit without any definition of his being. Yet we see in his works much of his nature and power.

It is most regrettable that the person and work of the Holy Spirit was sadly neglected in the first two-thirds of this century. Some theology books have been written with no section on the Spirit. Note Thomas Oden's trenchant remark: "It remains a mixed blessing that modern charismatic and Pentecostal voices have so stressed special aspects of the work of the Spirit that some other Protestant voices have tended to back away completely from all teaching concerning the Spirit." [66]

The neglect of one of the members of the Trinity is tragic, and it is all the more tragic as the Holy Spirit is the One through whom the mercy and message of the gospel is mediated to the world. Where nothing much is said about the Spirit, room is left for false concepts of the Spirit and spirituality to grow. That is exactly what has happened lately, and the neglect of proper teaching by the church has some responsibility for it. In the public mind in the United States, "spiritual" means almost anything emotional or vaguely religious. When a word means almost anything, it means nothing in particular.

Spirit in the Old Testament

Both of the biblical words for "Spirit" (Heb. רוח, Gr. πνευμα) can be translated "breath," "wind," "storm," or "life." The exact translation must be determined by the context and use of the word.

The work of the Holy Spirit in the Old Testament is described in a variety of actions in regard to persons. First of all, he was present and working in the creation. "And the Spirit of God was moving over the face of the waters" (Gen. 1:2b, RSV). The translation "a mighty wind" (NEB) or "a wind from God" (NRSV) is possible, but not commendable. It is true that in the Old Testament times the Spirit of God may have been thought of in more impersonal ways than after the coming of Christ, and that the idea of divine Trinity was not understood. Yet we know that both the Son and the Spirit were present in the creation, and that the work of creation can be attributed to the Three, as the New Testament makes clear (cf. John 1:3). Further, this is not the poetic context in which we usually find the word רוח *(ruach)* used as wind with the Tetragrammaton as an adjective. Further, the Holy Spirit in the New Testament is identified in the New Testament as the same as the Spirit of God in the Old Testament (Acts 2:16-21; 4:25; 7:51; 28:25; 1 Pet. 1:11; 2 Pet. 1:19-21). The use of the term "Holy Spirit" in the New Testament may serve to emphasize the full New Testament revelation of the personhood of the Spirit as a member of the Divine Trinity. Since God alone is holy in and of himself, it may also stress his deity.

He is said in the Old Testament to be entering into a person (Ezek. 2:2;

3:24), resting on a person (Num. 11:17,25-29; 1 Sam. 19:20-23), coming upon a person (Num. 24:2; Judg. 3:20; 1 Chron. 12:18; 2 Chron. 24:20); and lifting up a person (Ezek. 3:12, 14). Note that in these cases, the work of the Spirit of God was usually momentary and for a specific purpose of working in that situation. Nothing is said in these cases of a permanent abiding of the Spirit, as we find in the New Testament.

The Spirit is spoken of as working with select individual persons. Note further that the goal of his work was either to enable the person to do what was needed, or to reveal the will of God through the person. Thus the Spirit of God was most evident in the Old Testament prophets, as they preached in the guidance and power of the Holy Spirit.

Predictions of Better Things

On the Day of Pentecost, in Acts 2, Peter declared that what had happened was a fulfillment of Joel 2:28-29, which had predicted that the Holy Spirit would be poured out on all the people, high and low, old and young, male and female. The prediction in Joel was prefigured in Isaiah 44:3b: "I will pour out my spirit upon your descendants, and my blessing on your offspring."

Ezekiel predicted, "A new heart I will give you, and a new spirit I will put within you; and I will remove from your body the heart of stone and give you a heart of flesh. I will put my spirit within you, and make you follow my statutes and be careful to observe my ordinances" (Ezek. 36:26-27).

What happened at Pentecost was also wished for by Moses, according to Numbers 11:29. Moses had chosen seventy men, as God had commanded, and they had gone out of the camp and had briefly prophesied as the Holy Spirit had come on them. But two, Medad and Eldad, had stayed in the camp and had also prophesied. So one young man had told Moses about it and wanted them stopped. Moses said to him, "Would that all the Lord's people were prophets, and that the Lord would put his spirit on them."

Instead of the Holy Spirit coming upon certain individuals for select tasks, the wish was that He would be available to all God's people. This wish, and Joel's promise, are seen to be fulfilled in the New Testament, beginning especially at Pentecost, as Peter declared.

New Testament Terms

In the New Testament the major chapters in regard to the Holy Spirit are: John 14--16; Acts 2, 4; Romans 8, 12; and 1 Corinthians 12--14. The chapters in John report the last long discourse of Jesus with his disciples before his arrest, trial and death. The passage in 1 Corinthians is in Paul's letter to the church in Corinth, attempting to help them with serious problems that had arisen in the church.

We can learn much about the Holy Spirit from the terms that are used for Him in the New Testament. Even in the Old Testament there are hints that the Spirit of God is more than an impersonal power or force. For example, we are told that the wickedness of the people "grieved his holy Spirit" (Isa. 63:10, cf. Ps. 78:40, where God is grieved in the same way). Yet there is the full revelation of his divinity and personality in the New Testament. Some of this can be seen in the terms by which he is called.

Expressing his relationship to the Father. "Spirit of God" (Mat. 3:16). "Spirit of the Lord" (Acts 5:9; 8:39; Luke 4:18). "Spirit of our God" (1 Cor. 6:11). "Spirit of the living God" (2 Cor. 3:3). "Spirit of the Father" (Mat. 10:20). "Spirit of glory which is the Spirit of God" (1 Pet. 4:14). "The promise of the Father" (Acts 1:4).

Expressing his relationship to the Son. "The Spirit of Christ (Rom. 8:9). "The Spirit of Jesus Christ" (Phil. 1:19). "The Spirit of Jesus" (Acts 16:7). "The Spirit of his (God's) Son" (Gal. 4:6). "Another Advocate" or Helper—like Jesus (John 14:16).

Expressing His own Godhood. "The Lord the Spirit" (2 Cor. 3:18). "The eternal Spirit" (Heb. 9:14). "The Holy Spirit" (Mat. 28:19 and 90 other places). "The Holy One" (1 John 2:20). In regard to the last two terms, we know that only God is holy in and of himself.

Expressing the gifts he gives. "The Spirit of life" (Rom. 8:2). "The Spirit of holiness" (Rom. 1:4). "Spirit of wisdom and revelation" (Eph. 1:17). "The Spirit of Truth" (John 14:17; 16:13), "The Spirit of Grace" (Heb. 10:29; 12:10); "The Spirit of Faith" (2 Cor. 4:13), "Spirit of Adoption" (Rom. 8:15), "Spirit of Power and Love and Discipline" (2 Tim. 1:7).

The variety of terms applied to the Spirit tells us something of our needs and of God's power to fill them. They also tell us something of the whole scope of the fullness of the Holy Spirit.

We should point out that some of the older translations used two terms: "Holy Spirit" and "Holy Ghost." This has led readers to wonder if there is a difference between the two. There is no justification in the original languages for using two words, as they both represent the Greek πνευμα in every case. Possibly there was a desire for variety. But since the word "ghost" has taken on some undesirable connotations in English, it is better now to use only the one word "Spirit."

The Power of the Spirit

"The earth was without form and void, and darkness was upon the face of the deep; and the Spirit of God was moving over the face of the waters" (Gen. 1:2 RSV). Thus the Spirit participated in the creation, bring order out of the unformed earth. Whenever the Spirit of God is given control, there is beauty, purity and holiness. He has power to change things and make them what they ought to be.

The Holy Spirit has bower to change people and to make them what God wills for them to be. He uses this power to change those who yield to him completely.

All through the Old Testament the Spirit of God has fought evil by revealing God's will to the prophets and leaders. He spoke to Amos, Hosea, Joel, Isaiah, Jeremiah, Ezekiel and all the rest. Through them he revealed his will to human beings. He gave them a message to deliver to the people, a message of God's love for them, and of God's hatred of sin.

God gave the prophets the power of the Spirit to strengthen them for their work. He gave them boldness to declare the truth whether the people liked it or not. He told Isaiah that the people would destroy the nation because of their continued disobedience, but that he must go on with the preaching of the message in spite of that stubbornness (Isa. 6:11-13). When he called Jeremiah to preach to the same sinful nation later on, he told him "Do not be afraid of them, for I am with you to deliver you, says the Lord" (Jer. 1:8). When he called Ezekiel he said something similar, but more elaborately in chapters two and three. "Mortal, I am sending you to the people of Israel, to a nation of rebels who have rebelled against me, they and their ancestors have transgressed against me to this very day . . Whether they hear or refuse to hear (for they are a rebellious house), they shall know that there has been a prophet among them . . . O mortal, do not be afraid of them" (Ezek. 2:36).

It was in the power of the spirit that these prophets were able to speak with boldness the message of God. They had no fear of death for speaking the truth, as they would rather please God than the people. Like Abraham, Moses, Elijah and Micaiah, they were not afraid to stand before kings and declare the truth they had learned from God.

The Spirit of the living God was with the prophets. They preached in the power of the Spirit, and they changed the course of human history.

Jesus came "In the power of the Spirit" (Luke 4:14) as he began his ministry in Galilee. Thus his ministry astonished the people who heard him preach. Not only was his ministry enabled by the Spirit, but he is the Giver or Sender of the Holy Spirit to the church (Luke 24:29; John 15:26; 16:7). This means that there was a two-fold relationship between Christ and the Spirit. The Holy Spirit enabled the ministry of Jesus, and Jesus sends the Spirit to the church.

The power of the Spirit in which Christ came was the same power which worked in creation. Speaking of all living things in the world, a psalmist wrote, "When you send forth your spirit, they are created" (Psa. 104:30). In Job we read, "The Spirit of God has made me, and the breath of the Almighty gives me life" (Job. 33:4).

The Spirit of God gave skills to people for the building the tabernacle (Exod. 31:3-5), and wisdom to leaders of God's people (Deut. 34:9).

One fact which cannot be over-emphasized is that the Holy Spirit in the New Testament is the same Spirit as in the Old Testament. He plays a more prominent role in certain respects in the New Testament than in the Old. Christ had to come and explain his role before he could act as he does now.

The Holy Spirit worked freely in the Old Testament times, but he was able to work most clearly in certain individuals. After Pentecost he chooses to work in all Christians just as he did with the prophets and leaders of the Old Testament. Yet he is the same Spirit all the way through the Bible. There is only one Holy Spirit.

The Spirit is Personal

We must not think of the Holy Spirit as an impersonal force, for he is personal. He is not merely a force, or the power of God, but a thinking, reasoning and loving member of the Divine Trinity on the same level with God the Father and God the Son. He is always referred to in the New Testament with personal pronouns. We are baptized "in the name of" the Spirit, just as we are baptized "in the name of the Father and of the Son" (Matt. 28:19). Paul wrote of the "grace of the Lord Jesus Christ and the love of God and the fellowship of the Holy Spirit" (2 Cor. 13:14).

The personal aspect of the Spirit is shown in the fact that he feels love. "I appeal to you, brethren, by our Lord Jesus Christ and by the love of the Spirit" (Rom. 15:30). It is this love of God that he pours into our hearts "through the Holy Spirit, which has been given to us" (Rom. 5:5). He can feel grief at our stubbornness or rebellion (Eph. 4:30. He sent Barnabas and Paul on their missionary tours (Acts 13:4), and directed where and when they went.

PREVENIENT GRACE

It is the Holy Spirit who works in the hearts of sinful people to bring them to salvation through faith in Christ. No sinner can conquer sin without the aid of God. The power of sin is great, and "everyone who commits sin is a slave to sin" (John 8:34). Since no one is capable of breaking that slavery alone, how can anyone be saved? It is possible only through Jesus Christ

If Christ died only for the elect few, how could the rest of humankind be condemned for not accepting a salvation which was not purchased for them? But if Christ died for all (2 Cor. 5:14), because he loved the whole world (John 3:16), then he can truly and sincerely offer salvation to all, and "whosoever will" may be saved by his grace. So the atonement is not limited to a few.

If the prevenient grace of God, mediated through the Holy Spirit, makes it possible for a sinner to choose to accept the salvation of God, and if that choice is freely made, then we cannot say that God's grace is irresistible. It is possible for the sinner to accept the justifying grace of God, or to refuse it. The prevenient grace of God's convicting Spirit simply lifts the sinner up to the point where the choice is possible. The saving grace of God can be resisted. Thus, the election of God is not unconditional, for it is conditioned on the sinner's freely chosen acceptance.

Ray Dunning has pointed up this vital importance of Wesley's concept of prevenient grace:

> Wesley only avoided the morass of Calvinism by a 'hair's breadth,' to use his own words. But that 'hair' was enough to stand as a continental divide so that the two theologies (perspectives) lie miles apart in their fully developed expressions. The truth that holds them but a hair's breadth apart at the point of the watershed is the doctrine of *prevenient grace*. It could even be argued that this teaching was the most far-reaching and pervasive aspect of Wesley's thought.[67].

Meaning of Prevenient Grace

Prevenient grace is all the work of the Holy Spirit in the person before conversion. It is like the work of the Spirit in the person after conversion, except for the difference in the person. Jesus described this work when he said of the Spirit: "And when he comes, he will convince the world of sin and of righteousness and of judgment: of sin, because they do not believe in me; of righteousness, because I go to the Father, and you will see me no more; of judgment, because the ruler of this world is to be judged. (John 16:8-11, RSV)."

This work in the heart of a sinner is difficult because the sinner is not oriented toward God, and may at various times so act as to become hardened against the work of the Spirit. We are sure the Spirit begins this work as soon as the child can understand anything, so as to lead the child to a knowledge of God and his will. The Spirit's work is made easier and speeded along by any Christian teaching the child may get, so parents and Church teachers have their responsibility to do what they can to lead the child in the way of the Lord.

HIS WORK IN CHRISTIANS

In John 14—16, we find the longest discussion of the Holy Spirit in the whole Bible. This was the last discourse of Jesus with his disciples before he was crucified the next morning. In it he spoke to them about the fact that he would soon be leaving them, but that he would send them another "helper" like himself to be with them in his stead.

The Greek word Jesus used for the Spirit was παρακλητος, which is difficult to translate into one clear English word. The King James uses "Comforter" which used to have the meaning of strengthener, but which now gives some wrong impressions. The Revised Standard Version usually uses "Counselor." This is sometimes close to the meaning, but the Greek word has a broader range of meanings than this. Others have suggested words such as *Strengthener, Helper, Advocate,* and *Convincer.* If we have to use one word, probably "Helper" fits most occasions.

Our Personal Helper

The doctrine of the Holy Spirit is not some esoteric idea far removed from the lives of most of us. It is vital to every one of us. The Holy Spirit is personal, and works with us as persons. His work in our minds and hearts is indispensable if we are to learn how to live for God.

Nothing is more important to us than to know how to work with the Holy Spirit. How can we hear his voice? How can we know for sure what he wants to teach us? How can we follow his leading day by day? There is no way except through careful obedience. We know God's general will through conscientious study of the Bible, but we need daily guidance as we work out the constant decisions we must make in our personal lives. We can learn from the thinking of others, but we need the personal help of the Holy Spirit as we make our own decisions. This is the Person-to-person work of the Holy Spirit in our minds and hearts.

He is our personal strengthener (Jn. 14:16). One of the primary works of the Holy Spirit in the heart of the willing follower is to give power to do all that God wants done. He will never leave us to our own resources in doing the work of God. We can always depend on the help of the Spirit as we try to do what God wills. We can be certain that if God wants us to do something, the Holy Spirit will make it possible for us to do just that.

Not only will the Spirit give power to do things for God's glory, he gives power to resist temptation, to fight evil in high places, to know and do the right things to help others. He will seek to protect you from evil and temptation and to guide you in the paths of righteousness.

He is our personal companion (Jn. 14:17). "He abides with you and he will be in you." No Christian need ever feel totally alone, because we have the constant companionship of the Spirit of God. He is our companion for life. What a blessing this is for us when others are no longer present. The elderly, who have lost their companions, and the young who often feel that no one knows or cares, can all learn to feel and enjoy the constant companionship of the Holy Spirit.

How often we feel that there is no one with whom we can share our deepest concerns or our greatest fears. We have to make such important decisions without finding anyone with whom we can discuss them as we would like. We have to make them all alone. Yet we are not alone. We never have to make unaided decisions. Through prayer we can learn to lean upon the guidance and companionship of the Holy Spirit as we make decisions and act upon them. The Spirit never leaves us. He is always present to guide us, encourage us and help us.

He is our personal Teacher (Jn. 14:26). One of the greatest problems with our schools is that there are not enough teachers for the students. Even in small classes, it is not possible for the teacher to spend as much time with individual students as they may need. So the student may have to puzzle out what a good teacher could quickly make clear. There is value in figuring out something for yourself, but some things must be explained carefully or we may never come to understand them fully. So it is wonderful to know that the Spirit can be a personal teacher for each of us. He never leaves us completely on our own. He knows the trouble we are having and knows exactly when the time is right for him to teach us something more, and he knows how and when to let us think something through for ourselves. He is the perfect personal Teacher.

The Spirit has ways of teaching us what we need to know, even if we never understand that he was doing the teaching. The best teacher I ever had in graduate school was a master at guiding our thinking so that when we learned something important we thought it was our own idea. He was so skillful at leading us along in our thinking that we hardly realized where to draw the line between our thinking and his teaching. The Holy Spirit is an even better teacher than that.

As we pray, the Holy Spirit helps us to pray for the right things and in the right way (Rom. 8:26). If we pray for the wrong things, or in the wrong way, He knows how to guide our praying so that we come to understand how we ought to be praying. Knowing this, we can pray in perfect confidence and boldness. If we are wrong, He can help us to see that, though with some of us, it may take a lifetime! If we do not learn fast, we simply make our way harder than it ought to be. But the Spirit is a patient teacher.

One problem with thinking of the Spirit as our teacher is that some come to feel that they are never wrong, as they have the perfect teacher. This attitude makes true learning difficult, if not impossible. Learning requires humility. If we think we know it all, we will learn nothing, no matter how great the teacher.

Further, learning requires listening. It requires careful listening. As a college professor, I came to feel that I could say nothing which was not misunderstood by someone! This is probably an exaggeration, but there were many times when it seemed true to me. I learned never to judge any teacher by what the students said the teacher believed. We will be wise to be slow to believe what someone says "God told me." As 1 John 4:1 warns us, "Do not believe every spirit, but test the spirits to see whether they are from God." Even if it is the Holy Spirit speaking to us, we can so often misunderstand. So we have to work at our listening to the Spirit for his guidance.

He is our personal co-witness (John 15:26-27). When we witness to others about the life, death and resurrection of Jesus Christ, the Holy Spirit witnesses along with us. When we seek to persuade others that they can and should be saved by the power of God in Christ Jesus, we can be sure that while we speak to their minds, the Holy Spirit is speaking to their hearts. We can be sure that he has already been working in their hearts to lead them toward the point of acceptance of the gospel. We can also be sure that he will be working with us to help us say the right things in the right way.

There is no one to whom we can speak of Christ, to whom the Spirit has not been speaking already. No matter where we go in the world, we can know for sure that the Spirit has been working in hearts there before our arrival. He is always doing his work of convicting the world of sin, and of righteousness, and of judgment (John 16:7-8). With those who have never heard of the gospel, whether in a civilized land or not, he may not be able to do much except the preliminary work of preparing the heart for the gospel, but that is vital.

What an encouragement this is for us who seek to work for God. The efficacy of our witness does not depend on us alone. We can do our best, but then we have to leave the results to God. We are not alone in this work. The Holy Spirit works before our witness, and continues to work in the hearts after we are gone. We can save no one! He alone can bring about results.

At the same time, the Spirit needs to work through us. As our witness cannot stand alone, neither can that of the Spirit. He wants to work through our work as he seeks to bring people to Christ.

He is personal convictor (John 16:8-11). We have discussed this above in our discussion of prevenient grace, but need to note further what this means to the Christian working to bring sinners to Christ. We can and must do our best, but the Holy Spirit does the real work. Nothing we do for God can be effective without his blessing and ministry. No preacher can be what God chooses unless the Spirit works in and through the preaching. No sermon or gospel song can be effective without the anointing of the Holy Spirit. Neither can a church school teacher be effective without Him. But with the blessing and anointing of the Holy Spirit, we can do all that God wants us to do.

He is our personal guide (John 16:13). We need the Spirit to guide us into truth because we do not yet know all truth. We need him to guide us in the ways of righteousness, because we do not yet know all the ways God would have us go. How wonderful it is to have a personal Guide to help us through the difficulties and to show us the way to live.

Even though we have the guidance of the Spirit all the time, we must never imagine that we are beyond the possibility of being mistaken. The hardest person to teach is the who thinks he or she already knows. If we are to be guided by the Spirit, we must admit we do not know the way ourselves. Then he will be able to guide us, step by step, into more truth.

The Spirit as Sanctifier

At least twenty-five adjectives or nouns are used in combination the with the word *spirit* to describe him in the New Testament. He is called "Spirit of truth," "Spirit of love," "Spirit of power." He is also called the "Spirit of God," "Spirit of the Lord" and the "Holy Spirit." But he is most often called "The Holy Spirit." Once he is called the "Spirit of holiness" (Rom. 1:4). This latter term is applied to the resurrected Christ, who is now Spirit, as he was before the incarnation, and who is mediated to us through the Holy Spirit.

The primary reason for calling him the Holy Spirit is that he is the member of the Trinity who sanctifies Christians. He makes them holy. He is the sanctifier.

The Holy Spirit is no more holy than the Father and the Son. But when we speak of the Trinity we must always remember that we cannot fully comprehend anything about God. So far as that goes, we cannot fully comprehend anything on the earth, much less heavenly things. God knew we could not, and therefore reveals to us what is necessary for our eternal salvation. What we do learn from the Bible is that the Holy Spirit is now the administrator of the whole plan of salvation purchased by the blood of Christ according to the will of the Father. Whatever one member of the Trinity does is done with the full concurrence of the other two.

So we can think of the Holy Spirit as the sanctifier. He imparts to us the holiness that enables us to please God. In the next chapter we must consider what is meant by "entire sanctification." Still later we will deal with the Holy Spirit working in the church as a whole.

Paul took this work of the Spirit "leading us into all truth" a step further when he said that he was praying for Christians, that "with the eyes of your heart enlightened, you may know. . . ." (Eph. 1:17-19). It is not enough for us to have a rote memory of some words which express a spiritual truth. We must come to have a "heart knowledge" of the truth which sees its relevance for our living. Nothing less than this will do, and the Holy Spirit seeks to give us just this.

It is the work of the preacher to declare the truth of God to the hearers, but only the Spirit can move the hearts of the people to accept the truth. While the sermon is preached, the Spirit is working in the hearts of the hearers to help them not only to understand the message, but to feel its relevance. The work of the Holy Spirit includes not only instruction but even more importantly illumination.

Chapter 16

Entire Sanctification

> May the God of peace himself sanctify you entirely, and my your spirit and soul and body be kept sound and blameless at the coming of our Lord Jesus Christ (1 Thess. 5:24).
> **If entire sanctification is possible in this life, how would anyone achieve it? When we are saved, are we sanctified at the same time? What is meant by a "second work of grace?"**

A classic definition of the term was written by A. M. Hills, and is often falsely attributed to John Wesley:

> Entire sanctification is a second definite work of grace wrought by the baptism with the Holy Spirit in the heart of the believer subsequently to regeneration, received instantaneously by faith, by which the heart is cleansed from all corruption and filled with the perfect love of God[68]

Sanctification is the work of the Holy Spirit in a person after conversion, by which one is made holy, filled with love, and empowered to live a life fully pleasing to God. It is the completion of the work of Christ in salvation. Christ is our sanctifier, and the work is mediated to us through the Holy Spirit.

This is a Wesleyan definition, although it was not written by Wesley, nor did John Wesley write a concise definition of it. He did not seem to like the idea of such formulations of doctrine. He felt that such things did little for the unlearned, and sounded to them like a foreign language. He sought to preach the Bible truths in simple language and make practical applications so that anyone could understand. Yet there comes a time, if we are to do clear thinking, when we have to define our ideas, drawing lines around the truth so as to leave out false concepts. This we must do if we are to make any progress in theological understanding.

Wilber T. Dayton, in an attempt to do just this, made an expanded definition of sanctification:

> Entire sanctification is the act of God by which the human heart is cleansed from all sin and filled with love by the holy Spirit who is given, through faith, to the fully consecrated believer. The resultant life of Christian holiness is known as perfect love or Christian perfection;. Entire sanctification is distinct from the beginning of holiness or sanctification that comes in the new birth (or regeneration).[69]

Note that entire sanctification is clearly distinguished from what happens to a person in conversion, though that, too, includes something called sanctification. To distinguish the two, it is common to say that conversion includes "*initial* sanctification" rather than "*entire* sanctification." Such a distinction means that we need to take a further look at what happens to a person when converted.

As we have seen, the New Testament uses a variety of terms for this first great crisis by which one becomes a Christian: *Salvation, conversion, redemption, ransom, forgiveness, justification, reconciliation, regeneration, new birth* and *adoption.* We have also seen that these are not separate actions or experiences, but ways of looking at or describing the work of salvation from sin. Human languages are human inventions and are based on human experiences. No words in any human languages can express all that God does when he saves a soul. So we have to use a variety of words, each of which expresses some aspect of the work of God in the human soul.

A Crisis

By calling conversion the first crisis in Christian experience, we are saying that it is a *spiritual* crisis. It is a spiritual crisis in which one comes to belong to God. Some do not like to call it a crisis because their own conversion was so quiet and smooth a transition that they feel "crisis" is too strong a word. Nevertheless, there is a basic difference between an unconverted person who does not truly know and obey God, and the person after conversion. This change is accompanied by a decision to accept God's offered salvation and to live for him. Just as in a serious illness, there is some point of crisis at which one begins to get better. One may not know at the time just what happened or when, nevertheless, there comes a time when one knows that the crisis is past, and one is getting well.

We will be speaking of two crisis points, or points of critical change in the person. By doing so, we are not denying the fact of general experience that there are many times in a person's life when major decisions have to be made, and which may be called life-changing crises. But we are speaking of the two major points of change when the Holy Spirit brings us to the point of decision about our submission to God and his will for us. There are many other times of decision, but these are the two major decision points in our relationship with God. Wesley usually called these "two moments" in Christian experience. He used the word "moment" to mean "a time of notable or conspicuous consequence."

The First Crisis

Look at some of the wonderful changes wrought in a person at the moment of conversion. All past sins are forgiven by the grace of God (1 John 1:9). The believer in Christ is no longer bound by her or his fleshly weakness to sin (Rom. 6:1-2) but has set the mind on higher things, heavenly things, the things of the Spirit (Rom. 8:1-17; Col. 3:1-2). There is no longer the weight of condemnation of sin (Rom. 8:1). The law of the Spirit of life in Christ Jesus has set you free from the law of sin and of death" (Rom. 8:2). As a result, the Christian does not any longer live in sin (Rom. 6:8; 1 Cor. 15:34). The Christian is being protected by the Spirit from the power of evil (Rom. 8:31-39) and is being led by the Spirit into more Christlike living (Rom. 8:18-27; 2 Cor. 3:18). The whole life and way of living has been changed by the grace of God, and the Christian knows the love of God and loves God in return (1 John 4:19). The Christian has been reconciled by God to God (2 Cor 5:18) and is now a new creation (2 Cor. 5:17). All this and much more result from the transformation that we call conversion, or salvation.

The crisis that brings all this about is precipitated by the convicting power of the Holy Spirit. The first work of the Holy Spirit in the sinner is to convict the sinner of sin, and of the possibility and necessity of righteousness (John 16:8). The Holy Spirit continues this convicting work until the sinner either accepts the salvation offered by God or dies. It is possible for the sinner to reject the Spirit so completely and finally that the Spirit will withdraw (Mat. 12:31-32). Such a person would no longer care about God or goodness and would no longer feel any desire to turn to God, because that desire is a result of the Spirit's work in the heart. That person's heart and mind would be fully and permanently set against God so that God's Spirit could no longer have any effect on the person. So if anyone says, I want to be saved, but cannot because I have committed the unpardonable sin against the Spirit, that is clearly not true of this person. If it were, the person would no longer desire to be saved.

So when one is converted in what we call this first crisis experience with God, it is the result of the work of the Spirit in bringing the person to that point. The work of conversion, which cannot be brought about by human power, is done by the Spirit. We are saved by the blood of Christ, but the power is applied to our hearts by the Holy Spirit. All this is done by the grace of God, by the unmerited favor of God so we call this a work of grace.

Initial Sanctification

This first major work of grace is often called "initial sanctification." This is not a bad term since conversion initiates the process of sanctification, which is continued in growth in grace and is brought to a climax in the second major work of grace, entire sanctification, after which the spiritual growth can continue with less hindrance.

Another way of considering this is to sum up all the manifold work of God in conversion in the two words "justification" and "regeneration." Justification includes the forgiveness of sin, redemption, reconciliation and atonement. All these have to do with a change in relationship with God. Regeneration is the new birth by which the nature of the person is changed so that one can live a life pleasing to God. By the new birth, the person who has died to sin is raised up by God's power to live a new kind of life (Rom. 6:6-12). This spiritual resurrection is regeneration, new birth, or new creation (2 Cor. 5:17). It is the beginning of holiness of heart and life.

Holy People

The primary meaning of holiness or sanctification is belonging to God. The sinner does not really belong to God, though he or she was created by God and is totally answerable to God for all he or she does. But every Christian belongs to God and has been purchased by the blood of Jesus Christ. The Christian has forsaken sin, been forgiven, and has accepted by faith the salvation made possible by the death and resurrection of Christ. The Christian can thus be called holy. Yet this holiness is not complete, as we shall see, and must be considered initial, or preliminary.

All Christians are called holy in the New Testament, in spite of the fact that they sometimes had much to learn about living for God and had yet many changes to be made in their lives. The Christian may have much to learn about the ethical implications of conversion, but cannot continue doing what he or she knows is sinful.

The Christian does not continue living in sin, for she or he has died to sin (Rom. 6:12). The new convert does not know all about what God requires and may therefore make many blunders. Some actions may grieve the heart of God, but the convert cannot go on doing what is known to be displeasing to God. So the Christian does not go on sinning but is required to be holy in every intention of the heart and will.

Growing Sanctification

It is possible to use the term "positional sanctification" for conversion, as George Allen Turner does and call this growing sanctification "actual sanctification."[70] Yet this can be misleading, as "positional holiness" is used by Keswick theologians and some others to mean that the person is not truly holy, but is in such a position in Christ that his sins are not counted against him. This use is in effect a denial of human holiness. It is based on the assumption that God simply *imputes* holiness to the sinner, rather than *imparting* holiness to the person.

It may be better to call it "growing sanctification," or "growing in grace." The new Christian begins immediately to grow in grace and in understanding the requirements of God both ethically and spiritually. Much intellectual, ethical and spiritual growth begins to take place. Just as the newborn infant must begin to grow physically and intellectually, so the newborn Christian must grow or die. One can grow *in* grace, but cannot grow *into* grace.

This spiritual and ethical growth is described in part in 2 Peter 1:5-11. Just as we, like Jesus as a child, have to grow in wisdom, stature, and in favor with God and others (Luke 2:52), so the young Christian has to grow (1 Pet. 2:2). All Christians thus should recognize that we must continue to grow, but can we ever come to the point of completion of sanctification in this life? This seems to be implied in the term "entire sanctification."

ENTIRE SANCTIFICATION

Entire sanctification refers to the completed process by which the Holy Spirit makes his home in the human soul. It is not the completion of the process of growth, for one cannot grow into this grace. It does not mean that the process of spiritual growth has been completed, for growth is speeded up at this point. Rather, it means that the person is wholly committed to God, and that the Holy Spirit has accepted the invitation to dwell in the soul and to do all he comes to do.

This is most important for us to understand as it is so common in non-Wesleyan theologies to think of sanctification always as a process of growth towards entire sanctification. As long as one considers the subject with this presupposition, it will be impossible to think of it as being complete in this life. If it is growth toward perfect Christlikeness, it is never complete until after death.

It is therefore vital that we see that we are considering entire sanctification as a special work of Christ in us by the Spirit, which makes it possible for us to live as he wishes. The Holy Spirit wishes to make his home in us and to dwell in us. Listen to the words of Jesus in that wonderful promise: "Those who love me will keep my word, and my Father will love them, and we will come to them and make our home with them (John 14:23).

So God the Father, Christ the Son, and the Holy Spirit want to have a close relationship of love with every Christian. This is a covenant relationship in which the person agrees with God's plan and requirements for letting God live within.

Meaning of the Term

The term "entire sanctification" comes from the statement, "May the God of peace himself sanctify you entirely; and may your spirit and soul and body be kept sound and blameless at the coming of our Lord Jesus Christ" (1 Thess. 5:23). This expresses the idea of the completeness of the holiness the Christian experiences after the so-called "second work of grace" by the Holy Spirit.

"Entire sanctification," expresses the completeness of the relationship one has with God. It is not saying that the Christian is now perfect, but that the relationship with God is perfectly clear, unhindered by any voluntary resistance on the part of the Christian.

This relationship with God is one of love, as John Wesley always insisted. God loves us, and we love God in return. This love had its beginning in conversion but could not come to completion until we had presented our saved selves to God in unconditional surrender and commitment. Then the Holy Spirit could complete the work of sanctification and seal in us a depth of relationship with God that we were unable to know before.

John and Charles Wesley, after 1739 rarely used the term "baptism of the Holy Spirit." They called this second experience by a variety of terms: purity of heart, perfect love, full salvation, entire sanctification and full restoration of the divine image. Since then, these terms and a few others have been widely used by writers and preachers of holiness.

Cleansing

At times the discussion of entire sanctification has been an attempt to decide just how to describe what is cleansed out of the heart in order to make the person pleasing to God. This is fruitless. What is cleansed is the heart, soul, mind and will. The cleanser is the Holy Spirit. We do not have to know exactly what he does or how he does it. All we have to do is to turn ourselves over to him in unconditional, unreserved surrender and let him do for us, to us, and in us exactly what he chooses.

It is necessary to be as clear as possible on this point because of much misunderstanding. Some of this misconception originates in a tendency to reify sin. To reify sin is to think of sin as a *thing* that is separate from the self, and which causes our actions. Sin is not something separate from the self. Sin, as we have seen is the whole self oriented in the wrong direction, away from God. It is love turned away from God.

R. R. Byrum insisted that "depravity can not properly be thought of as a physical entity. . . . It is rather a state or condition of the moral nature."[71] "It should be understood that depravity is not a root, a stump, a germ, or any other physical entity, but a change in man's nature."

Yet there has been a tendency to think of depravity as a substance which could be rooted out. Though it has not been a part of systematic theologies, it has been common in holiness preaching since the nineteenth century to use the illustration of sin as a tree. In salvation the tree is cut down, and in sanctification the root is taken out. This can be traced at least as far as the early nineteenth century. Like so many homiletic illustrations of spiritual matters, it lead to distortion. It at least implies that sin is a thing which can be *rooted out* (which is the meaning of the Latin verb from which it is formed).

Without retracting any of the warning against making sin a thing added to a person, it must be admitted that some have sought to use the term "eradication" without yielding to the temptation to reify sin[72]. Yet there are problems with this use of the term. The tree and root illustration shows sin as something separate from the person which can be removed. The appeal to Hebrews 12:15 as support for it shows skimpy exegesis. Both this passage and Deuteronomy 29:18 from which it is quoted are dealing with a sinful person in the midst of the group, not with something in one individual heart. The major problem with the illustration is that those who hear may remember the tree and its roots more than they remember any warning against taking it literally.

When all our study is completed, we understand that we can have different methods of explaining what none of us fully comprehend. John Miley closed his discussion of some of these points with these words: "Who shall say that the only permissible or profitable preaching of sanctification is that which prescribes an exact mode of its attainment? The doctrine itself, and not any rigid form into which we may cast it, is the real interest; the privilege itself, the great privilege; the actual attainment, the highest aim."[73]

The Spirit does have to cleanse our hearts of all the depravity which our sins have made in our hearts and minds during the time we have been living in sin. Only the work of the Holy Spirit is able to give us complete victory over the habits of mind and heart which have grown and hardened.

From the human standpoint the cleansing of the heart can be seen as "The expulsive power of a new love." This love for God is "poured into our hearts through the Holy Spirit that has been given to us" (Rom. 5:5). This is perhaps the most important single verse in the Bible about the work of the Holy Spirit. He gives us divine power to love both other people and to love God in a way never known before. What we may find difficult or consider impossible, the Spirit gives us power to do.

This love that God gives us drives out all other loves, so that the heart is purified. It is not some surgical process which puts some foreign matter in our beings. It is God freeing us from all that would keep us from him. This is part of the work of restoring us to the image of God. He restores our lost freedom for God and freedom to love others with godly love. He restores the created freedom for self so that the Christian is at peace with self and able then to use all powers of mind, body and soul for God and others and for the earth as well.

A Second Work

When we speak of the converted person as "holy" we have shown that we mean that the Christian belongs to God, separated from all else to belong to God[74]. Yet there is a new and deeper relationship with God is established in entire sanctification. God is able to do more in and through the person as that person is fully yielded to God and submits to the work of the Spirit.

In the examples in Acts of people being filled with the Spirit or baptized with the Spirit, they were first Christians and then had this experience. The disciples were accepted by Christ as having their names written in heaven (Luke 17:20), and told them that the Holy Spirit was dwelling with them (John 14:17). Yet he told them in the same verse that they could expect the Spirit to be in them later. In his high priestly prayer for them he prayed that God would sanctify them (John 17:17; Acts 1:4-5). Paul at Damascus had already been converted and was obeying God before receiving the Spirit (Acts 9). The same can be said of Cornelius and his household (Acts 10:1-2; 15:8-9). The Samaritan disciples were converted under Philip and baptized in the Spirit under Peter's preaching (Acts. 8:15-17). The Thessalonian church is another example (Acts 17:1-4; 1 Thess. 5:23). This is not actual proof that conversion has to come first, but they point in this direction.

However we consider the proof by example, which Gordon D. Fee rightly states is not conclusive proof[75], there is other evidence for a second special work of God's grace. Jesus said to his disciples: "This is the Spirit of truth, whom the world cannot receive, because it neither sees him nor knows him. You know him, because he abides with you and he will be in you" (John 14:17). When John speaks of the world, he means those who are yet in sin. He regularly uses the term for the world of sin and sinners. Sinners are not ready for the holy Spirit to do his complete work in them. They need forgiveness, conversion, regeneration. Only then can he do more.

Cherem Again

The major reason for the dual work of the Spirit in the person is found in this previously discussed word. As we have seen earlier, that which is dedicated to the worship of an idol is cherem to God. The only way it can be given to God is for it to be cleansed first. Otherwise it must be "utterly destroyed." In the Old Testament, this was true of both things and people.

The sinner is *cherem* to God, and certainly unfit for God's service. So the sinner is not fit to give self to God as a sacrifice, and cannot be accepted as such by God. It is only by the grace of God, and God's love even for sinful people that any sinner can be cleansed from sin and made fit to offer self to God in complete surrender. Thus the world (sinners) are not able to receive the Holy Spirit in his full control of their lives. Sinners must be cleaned up first.

CONDITIONS FOR SANCTIFICATION

There are two conditions which must be met if the Christian is to be sanctified: Consecration and faith. By consecration is meant the unrestrained dedication of the whole saved self to God, so that the Holy Spirit may do with the person all he chooses. Paul makes this clear in Romans 6:12-22 and 12:1.

Notice that in verse 12 he points out that since the Christian has died to sin, the person must no longer let sin rule over the life, but rather refuse to obey sinful desires. This is said to Christians—converted persons, those who are born anew. He makes this point most forcefully in verse 13 when he shows one what the next step ought to be: "No longer present your members to sin as instruments of wickedness, but present yourselves to God as those who have been brought from death to life, and present your members to God as instruments of righteousness."

Note the verb "present" which is used three times in this verse and repeatedly in the rest of the chapter. This word has a number of uses in the Bible, but one of them is in regard to sacrifices. A person "presents" a sacrifice to God at the altar. The one who presents the sacrifice gives up possession and control over the sacrifice to God. The word is also used in Romans 12:1 of presenting the saved self to God as a sacrifice for God to use as he pleases. In both Romans 6 and 12, the result is sanctification. "For just as you once presented your members as slaves to impurity and to greater and greater iniquity, so now present your members as slaves to righteousness for sanctification." (Rom. 6:19). "I appeal to you therefore, brother and sisters, by the mercies of God, to present your bodies as a living sacrifice, holy and acceptable to God, which is your spiritual worship" (Rom. 12:1).

In the latter passage there are three characteristics of the person offering self to God: Living, holy, acceptable to God. These are the same three requirements listed in Leviticus for the animal to be offered to God as a sacrifice. The animal had to be alive, acceptable to God as a "clean" animal, and passed upon by the priest as not sick or injured. God wants our best, and nothing but our best and our all.

Consecration, Dedication

For us to present our selves to God for sanctification on the altar of God, we must be already made alive in Christ (Eph. 2:1-4), not still dead in our sins. We must be "acceptable to God" (Rom. 12:1) Then we can present our saved selves to God on the spiritual "altar" and believe that he accepts our sacrifice.

It was Phoebe Palmer, the camp meeting evangelist and holiness theologian of nineteenth century America, who built up what has been called this "altar theology." She insisted that when one puts all of self on the spiritual altar as a sacrifice, then one ought simply to believe that God sanctified the gift. Trust God to do what he promised to do. No special signs are necessary. No proof of sanctification is to be looked for. Simply believe that God keeps his word. She insisted that one should not look for any special feelings or emotions, but simply trust God to do what he said he would do.[76]

This altar theology has been most influential throughout the Wesleyan holiness movement since 1837. It simplified the whole process of seeking for sanctification into three steps: Commitment of self on the altar to God, believing God does give the Holy Spirit, and testimony to entire sanctification. Testifying to the work strengthens the faith and resolve of the Christian, and helps others as well.

Phoebe Palmer's "altar theology" is scriptural and simple enough for anyone to understand and practice. It has therefore been most helpful to the spread of holiness. That is why we love to sing such songs as "Have Thine own way, Lord," and "Is your all on the altar?"

> You have longed for sweet peace,
>   and for faith to increase,
> And have earnestly, fervently prayed;
> But you cannot have rest,
> Or be perfectly blest,
> Until all on the altar is laid.
> Is your all on the altar of sacrifice laid?
> Your heart, does the Spirit control?
> You can only be blest and have peace and sweet rest,
> As you yield him your body and soul.
>   Elisha A. Hoffman (1900)

Faith

As we have seen, the other condition for sanctification, or the baptism of the Spirit, or being filled with the Spirit, is to believe that God does what he promised. If we have done what he said, we can know for sure that he does what he promised. It can be as simple as that. Faith is the condition for sanctification, and dedication is the foundation for faith.

While this is simple, it is not uncommon for some to have trouble believing for sanctification. This problem can happen to some because they have false expectations. They have heard some other person tell about the thrilling emotions they felt when they were sanctified, and want to have the same feelings. But this is always wrong. Each of us reacts in a way that may be far different from the reactions of others. No one should ever trust in feelings, but trust in God. Emotions are not the work of God but only our reaction. That reaction depends not only on what happens to us, but on our personalities, our expectations, and our perceptions.

Since sanctification is a gift of God, it cannot be achieved by human effort. Since it is by grace, it is accepted by faith, and can therefore be completed in a moment. One does not have to be a "seeker after holiness" for years, as some have thought, or even for weeks.

One does not need to "renew their consecration" every year, as some seem to feel. When a couple is married, they do not need to renew their vows whenever some problem arises. They only need to carry out the vow they made at their wedding. When one joins the army, it is not necessary to renew that decision before every battle, but only act upon it. so it is with dedication to God. It can be done once, and last for a lifetime. One never needs to renew that consecration unless the person has renounced it, either in word or in deed.

It is true that in a time of trouble, one may need to pray for a special gift of power to face the trouble like a real Christian. And at such a time one may receive a new surge of power like being filled with the Spirit. Yet that is different from feeling that the decision to dedicate self to God needs to be reviewed and renewed. You made the dedication; now act on it.

It is more important to know that you are totally committed to God, so far as you can know, than to point to some day in the past when you were entirely sanctified. As Mildred Bangs Wynkoop used to say, the "secondness" of the experience is not so important as to know one's dedication, and to keep on living for God by his grace.

Results of Sanctification

The Holy Spirit dwells within. Jesus had promised this would happen (John 14:17; Acts 2:1-4). This is the real benefit of the experience of being filled with the Spirit. He then becomes a personal Helper in all of life, and one who will never leave us. As Christians, we knew Jesus Christ before, but now he is more personal to us. He can have more complete control over us, and can help us better because of our dedication of our saved selves to God.

The Holy Spirit pours God's love into our hearts (Rom. 5:5). This means not only that the person is more sure of God's love in all situations. It means also that the Holy Spirit enables the sanctified person to manifest the special kind of love which brought Jesus into the world to save the world from sin (John 3:16). This love is so special that the early Christians used a special word for it (agape). As a result, Christians are enabled to be "perfect" in love as Jesus commanded (Mat. 5:48). They can reach out in love to all kinds of people, not just to the most lovely (Mat. 5:43-48).

The Sanctified person grows the fruit of the Spirit (Gal. 5:22-23). All the other fruit of the Spirit flows from love. Love for God and for others brings joy in service. And the love for God gives peace. Before leaving the disciples, Jesus said to them: "Peace I leave with you; my peace I give to you. I do not give to you as the world give. Do not let your hearts be troubled, and do not let them be afraid" (John 14:27). He was saying he would give us his own peace—the peace which he had the next morning when he stood before Pilate who sentenced him to be crucified! A study of the nine fruits of the Spirit listed in Galatians 5 can show how all the fruit flows from love.

It has often be pointed out that Paul writes of the "works of the flesh" as plural, and the "fruit" of the Spirit as either singular or collective. It is true that just as sin divides the person and separates the person from others, the Spirit unifies. The Spirit makes the divided personality whole, and makes it easier for the person to unite with others.

The Spirit gives power (Acts 1:8). A basic part of the work of the Spirit in a person is to give the person the power needed to be a faithful and more effective witness for Christ. The same disciples of Christ who followed him afar off as he went to trial were so bold after Pentecost that their judges were astonished at their boldness (Acts 4:13).

Through the Holy Spirit, Christ gives us the power to live and to work for him. He does not give us more power than we need, but he does fill our needs. His power upholds us in our troubles, and helps us to be overcomers in all our trials and temptations. We have to do the work he wants us to do, but he furnishes all the power we need to do it. So we can be sure that whatever Christ wants us to, he can make us able to do. The power he gives through the Holy Spirit eventuates in what Paul called "gifts of the Spirit." Since these gifts are given to the church for the building up of the whole church, we shall leave their study until that point where we study the church and its work.

The power Christ gives us through the Spirit, as individual persons, is the power to witness to Christ and his salvation. We are enabled to be effective witnesses. This does not mean that we will win every person to whom we witness to saving faith in Christ. Some will reject our witness because they reject God (Ezek. 3:4-8). God told Ezekiel to preach to the people to whom he sent him, even though he knew the bulk of them would not respond. God wants everyone to hear the gospel of salvation in Jesus Christ well presented, whether they obey or not. Every person in the world has a right to hear the message and make an informed decision.

Chapter 17

Holy Living

> I therefore, the prisoner in the Lord, beg you to lead a life worthy of the calling to which you have been called, with all humility and gentleness, with patience, bearing with one another in love, making every effort to maintain the unity of the Spirit in the bond of peace (Eph. 4:1-3).

Does being a Christian make much difference in the way one lives? Did not Christ come to suspend all the laws and rules so that we are free to live as we please? If we love one another, why do we need to think about how we should live? Isn't love enough to guide us?

This chapter is not on the theory of ethics, but rather on the practical guidance in the Bible as to the way a Christian ought to live. It is not enough for us to know that we Christians are supposed to live holy lives. We really need more guidance than that because of the kind of world we inhabit.

There are many misconceptions about the Bible and modern life. Some feel that since the Bible is so old, it is irrelevant to the twentieth and twenty-first centuries. Some think that the New Testament canceled out the Old Testament, and that the Sermon on the Mount replaced the Ten Commandments. Still others have concluded that anything is good so long as it is done in love, or that there are no rules at all in Christianity, and we are free to do whatever we think we want to do. such distortions of Christian freedom have distorted the whole concept of Christian ethics.

If we imagine that the Sermon on the Mount has for us replaced the Ten Commandments, we have not paid attention to what Jesus said in it. The sermon is found in its longest form in Matthew 5, 6, 7. A similar sermon is found in its longest form in Matthew 5, 6, 7. A similar sermon is found in Luke 6, though that may be a different sermon with some similarities. In Matthew 5:17-19 Jesus said: "Do not think that I have come to abolish the law or the prophets; I have come not to abolish, but to fulfill. For truly I tell you, until heaven and earth pass away, not one letter, not one stroke of a letter, will pass from the law until all is accomplished. Therefore, whoever breaks one of the least of these commandments, and teaches others to do the same, will be called least in the kingdom of heaven."

Though we shall look again at the rest of what Jesus said about this, it is enough for at this point to see that he did not wish to annul the teachings of the five Mosaic books.

THE BIBLICAL TEACHING

Rules?

One way to consider Christian ethics is to seek to list all the different situations in which one needs to choose an action, and show what a Christian ought to do in that case. But this casuistic approach leaves much to be desired. First, to write such a list would require a library of books, and no one would have time to look up a particular situation and see what to do. Second, It is hard to see how such a list could ever be all-inclusive, as there are so many changing situations, and no two are exactly alike. Third, how could such a list be updated often enough to keep up with changing times?

Such a method will not work. However, some sincere Christians are so hungry for this kind of detailed guidance that they fall prey to a teacher or preacher who loves to tell them just what to do. Such a pastor or preacher becomes as God to the person, and the person becomes totally dependent on the guide. This is a most unhealthy situation, and accounts for some of the tragedies we have seen in cults. Some dominating pastors of churches have developed many of the characteristics of a cult through this kind of relationship.

Jesus did not seek to give us rules or laws for each life situation. He came to set us free from sin, make us God's children, and give us the kind of love for God that our strongest desire will be to find, understand, and do the will of God. The heart, Jesus insisted, is the source of good or evil (Mat. 12:34-35). So following all possible rules would not make the person good. A deeper change is needed than to make the outward actions conform to rules.

Once the heart is transformed by the power of God, the person is able to do what is right. One will not automatically know and do the right thing, for that requires a growing understanding, but will do what is known to be right, and feel remorse for every failure. The heartfelt spirit of love and obedience to God make it easy to learn the truth. And the love of others God puts in the heart determines a different attitude toward them. This new love causes more Christlike actions toward those with whom one associates.

Godly Love is the Key

The new kind of love which Jesus revealed by his life and death is the key to Christian holy living. God puts his love in the hearts of Christians (Rom. 5:5), and this love makes it possible for the person to have a right relationship with God and with other people. God's love is a new kind of love, for it is the kind of love which reaches out to the worst of people. It is not placed merely on the lovely, but on the unlovely (Mat. 5:44 those-48). Jesus told us that our love ought to be like God's love in this respect, so that we love even who act like enemies.

We must be careful not to confuse sexual desire or lust with godly love.[77] The English word "love" is so broad in its use that it would be good if we had an alternative. Sometimes the Greek word *agape* is added as though to make that distinction, but this does not assist the average person much. Godly love is the kind of love Jesus Christ demonstrated in laying down his life for rebellious sinners. "But God proves his love for us in that while we still were sinners Christ died for us" (Rom. 5:8). This is a self-giving, unselfish love which respects the other person, not for what that person is, but for what that person could become. Such love is not common, and can be known only through God working in the human heart.

Love for God and love for others is the key to holy living. Yet we must seek earnestly to learn how to express this love in ways which will please God and help others. As we work with others in loving ways, we hope that the love we show will help them in two ways: Help make their lives easier and happier, and help them see the love of God and want to know him for themselves.

The Ten Commandments

What we call the Ten Commandments are in Exodus 20 and Deuteronomy 5. The first four have to do with our love and loyalty to God, and the last six have to do with our relationships with others.

Those who believe that the New Testament cancels out these commandments usually feel that love makes them unnecessary. Others have a vague feeling that for Christians only the New Testament has authority for us, and that the Old Testament is completely outmoded. The fact that the Old Law is not canceled out by Christ is seen in the passage quoted above by Jesus in the Sermon on the Mount.

The Ten Commandments are ratified more than once in the New Testament. Four of them are listed by Paul as samples of the fact that Christian love fulfills the commandments. That they are not abolished when they are fulfilled in Christ is seen by the way Jesus continues in his Sermon, as recorded by Matthew.

The Sermon On The Mount

Let us examine what Jesus did with the Old Testament commandments in the Sermon on the Mount (Matt. 5—7). After saying that it was not his purpose to abolish but to fulfill, he took up first the law against murder: "You have heard that it was said to those of ancient times, 'You shall not murder'; and 'whoever murders shall be liable to judgment.' But I say to you that if you are angry with a brother or sister, you will be liable to judgment" (Mat. 5:21-22).

Murder. Far from abolishing the law, Jesus filled it with deeper meaning. He showed that murder begins with hatred or anger, and that if we are to please God, we must control not only our actions, but our hearts and emotions. Always Jesus pointed to the heart as the source of actions. "Blessed are the pure in heart, for they will see God" (Mat. 5:8).

In one sense it was not new to say that sin begins in the heart of the person, and that nothing but overt action is sinful. The last of the Ten

Commandments says "You shall not covet. . ." This is clearly a sin of the heart, or the emotions. Coveting is not an overt act, but a sin of the heart. And when Jesus was asked about the most important commandment of the Law, Jesus did not choose any of the Ten Commandments, as the lawyers of his day usually did, nor any of the other hundreds of commandments. He chose two commandments having to do with the heart. The first, he said is to love God, and the second greatest is to love other people.

Even though it was not strictly new to make sin a thing of the heart, it was not the usual way it was done by the Jewish leaders. Jesus made the same approach to the other rules he discussed.

Adultery. Jesus turned next to the sin of adultery. "You have heard that it was said, 'You shall not commit adultery.' But I say to you that everyone who looks at a woman with lust has already committed adultery with her in his heart." (Mat. 5:27-28).

Jesus makes it perfectly clear that adultery begins in the heart. It is not merely the act of adultery which is sin, then, but we must be diligent to control the emotions which lead to adultery. He follows here the general principle which he had first laid down about the Old Testament. This should have been seen by all readers of the Old Testament, but it is always easier to look at such things superficially. This commandment should be interpreted in terms of the last of the Ten, "You shall not covet" which clearly puts the emphasis on the desires of the heart. It is superficial to make it merely an overt action.

The person Jesus has in mind is not the one who merely *sees* an attractive person of the opposite sex. Otherwise no one could live in the world without sinning regularly. It is one who *looks at*, or *gazes at* one for the purpose of lusting after that person. It is not the seeing, but the continued lustful gazing, which is evil. Adultery begins in the mind and heart.

Surely it goes without saying that this saying applies to women as well as to men. Matthew never speaks of the woman being adulterous by divorcing, for example (Mat. 19:3-9). Yet Mark (10:12) in the same context, does quote Jesus as applying the same to a woman. Jesus is not spelling out rules in legalistic fashion, where one would have to specify every detail so that it could be defended in court. Instead he was illustrating the fact that sin is always in the heart before it becomes action.

It is the heart that one must guard (Mat. 5:8; Prov. 4:23).

Be Perfect

Without looking at the other illustrations of the general principle in this chapter, note that Jesus closed with that amazing admonition, "Be perfect, therefore, as your heavenly Father is perfect" (Mat. 5:48).

How can any human being be perfect? No matter how we try, we must know that our human love is finite, while God's love is infinite. Yet the love we have for others can be the same *kind* of love that God shows in Christ Jesus. It is like God's love because God gives it to us. But even so, we must keep praying and working to cultivate this love.

Jesus did not say that we must be "as perfect as" God. But rather that we should be like God in loving all persons, regardless of race, religion or morals, as God does. That is the immediate context in which he made the statement. Our love must be the kind of love that God has for us. And it must reach out to every person we contact. Nothing less than that will do.

Christian perfection must not be misinterpreted as meaning that one is not improvable. Christian perfection is constantly growing and improving as one learns how to do the will of God. Paul M. Bassett has some cogent remarks on this command to be perfect:

> If *we* define perfection, we may be sure that we shall never attain it, for any such definition as we may seek to realize comes from fallen intellects and imaginations.... The heart of the matter is love. Perfection is perfect love. It is love that does not need love to prime itself or to maintain itself. Perfection is love that initiates, love that loves in the midst of the unlovely, love that neither hatred, nor selfish imposition, nor egotism can quell."[78]

If we apply the last verse of the chapter to all the rest, we see that it is not enough to control all our actions, but we must seek constantly to guard against any attitudes, thoughts, or emotions which could lead to sin. The best way to do this is to feed our minds and hearts on the word of God, on uplifting literature and music, on Christian friendships, and on everything which will draw us closer to God. Memorize Scriptures that will help you live for God. Memorize the words of great songs and hymns of the faith. Fill your mind and heart with the kinds of things which will be morally uplifting and will help you love God more.

Do Right for the Right Reason

"Be careful not to do your righteousness before others to be seen by them, for if you do, you will receive no reward from your Father in Heaven" (Mat. 6:1, author's translation).

We see here another important principle. Jesus insists that we must not only watch our hearts so as to prevent the desires and feelings which can lead to evil. When we do righteous deeds, we must not do them to receive the applause of others. We must do them for the approval of God, and because of the love we have for the righteousness of God.

Jesus illustrated this general principle with the actions of giving to charity, praying and fasting. When we do these things, we must not do them in public for the praise of others, or so that others will see how saintly we are. If we do them for that reason, that will be the only reward we will get.

Following this principle is not as easy as it might seem. It is easy for us to be subconsciously all to happy to hear the praise of others. Every preacher knows the temptation to rejoice in the praise of others for a sermon or prayer well-delivered. A singer or other musician can feel the same temptation.

At the same time, we can recognize that this is further elucidation of the general moral principle of love. If we love others we will do the right thing for them whether they praise us or not. If we love God we will seek to please him whether or not others recognize or approve our actions.

This general moral principle of love is stated by other writers in the New Testament also. Four of the major statements are found in Romans 13:8-10; 1 Corinthians 13; Ephesians 5:1-2; and 1 John 4:7-21.

This principle is not a complete guide to Christian living of holy lives, but it is essential. For most of us, we need to be given many examples of the way Godly love works, and things it will not do. Even with examples, we need time to "work out your own salvation with fear and trembling; for it is God who is at work in you, enabling you both to will and to work for his good pleasure" (Phil. 2:12b-13).

Christian Stewardship

A fundamental application of the principle of love to God is that of our stewardship of time, abilities, energy, and money. All that we have comes as a gift from God, whether it is much or little. It is what God has given us, and we never know when we will be called to give account of our use of them.

Our time belongs to God, and we ought to use it for him. This does not mean that we must give all our time to "religious matters." But it does mean that when we are working out the way we will prioritize and use our time, we must recognize that we owe it all to God, and must never use it in ways that will grieve God.

We need to pray daily about the way we will use our time, our energy and health. Taking care of our health means that we need to give some time to play, rest, sleep, and careful eating of healthful food.

We need to plan time for serious Bible study and prayer (1 Thess. 5:17). These are easy to neglect, but most rewarding. There is no other way to build a strong Christian character. If Jesus spent nights in prayer alone with God the Father, we mere mortals must not neglect this work.

All of our physical, intellectual and spiritual abilities must be used for the glory of God. This includes our talents or abilities, our money, and whatever degree of health and strength God gives us day by day.

We need to pray seriously about God's will for marriage. Sincere prayer must be coupled with study of the Scriptural study to know the will of God in this matter, since marriage affects all of life. It is the will of God for one man and one woman to leave their parents and cling to one another for life (Gen. 2:24; Mat. 19:3-12). Divorce is harmful to all concerned, even if the marriage is one which should not have been consummated.[79]

This means that one should pray for guidance, and possibly consult with trusted friends and advisors, including some older person, before marriage, so as to avoid the problems which the wrong choice could cause. Some will be better off not to marry at all, for a variety of reasons.

It should go without saying that honesty in business is surely the will of God. Living holy lives affects every part of life, and cannot be omitted from business dealings with impunity. We can illustrate this fact by considering what the Bible says about work.

Work

God worked at creation (Gen. 2:1-3; Ps 8:3; 19:1), and is still at work in the world (Jn 5:17; 9:4). He made human beings for work (Gen. 1:26-27).

The ancient Greeks felt that work was beneath the dignity of citizens. They felt that it should be left to slaves. Aristotle described his ideal man as one who would not soil his hands with work.

But the Hebrews knew that God had commanded work. Saul was plowing in the field when he was called to be anointed King (1 Sam. 11:5). David was tending sheep when Samuel had him called to be anointed king (1 Sam. 16:11-13). Amos said that he was "a herdsman and a dresser of sycamore trees, and the Lord took me from following the flock, and the Lord said to me, 'Go, prophesy to my people Israel'" (Amos 7:14-15). Jesus worked as a carpenter for most of his life (Mat. 13:55). Paul often supported his ministry by making tents (Acts 18:3; 1 Thess. 2:9). Christians remembered that since God worked in creation, it is right for us to work.

Work is not a curse laid on us because of sin, as it was commanded before the Fall (Gen. 2:15). It is neither a curse nor a punishment, but was part of God's original plan for us. But sin, and the guilt it brings, makes work laborious. It is not really the kind of work we do which makes it hard to bear, but rather the self-centered attitude of the worker. Christians should seek to work for the glory of God. As Paul explained to the slaves who were Christians, we should work as servants of God, knowing that if we please him, we can be happy in our work (Eph. 6:5-8). He himself gave that example (2 Thess. 3:6-13).

God planned for Adam and Eve to work (Gen 2:15). But sin corrupted work and made it laborious (Gen 3:17). God commanded work, rest and recreation (Exod. 20:8-11), and lazy idleness is condemned (2 Thess. 3:10-12).

But what if illness or age make it impossible to work? This brings real problems to the Christian who has been seeking to do everything possible for God. Older Christians often feel guilty that they can no longer do what they used to do for God.

David understood this problem (Ps 71:9). We need to understand that

God will never forsake us (Heb 13:5). God understands our weakness and inability (Ps. 103:13-18). It is right for us to do what we can for God. But when we can do nothing, for reasons beyond our control, we need to learn to trust in God's love, mercy, and grace.

The Christian and the Old Testament

Jesus made it clear that he did not come to destroy the Old Testament and its law. He came rather to fulfill it all (Mat. 5:17-20). He said that none of it would pass away until it was all fulfilled. We would be wrong, then, to say that the Old Testament has no value for Christians.

Jesus proceeded to give six illustrations of his point that the Old Testament must be fulfilled. From these illustrations we can see that he fills each of the commands with more meaning. He makes it clear that we are not to live below the commands of the Old Testament, but must live *above* them. It is not just that we must never break any of the commandments, but that we must go beyond the literal meaning of the words, and stop the beginnings of sin.

For example, when the law says that we must not murder (Mat. 5:21), Jesus says that we must be careful not even to hate another person. We must not treat anyone hatefully. Still later he points out that we must love even those who act like enemies to us (Mat. 5:43-48). We must have the kind of love that God has, which reaches out to the worst of people with love. This is the only kind of love that will please God (Mat. 5:48). In this way he shows us that since murder begins with hatred, we must guard ourselves against hatred or enmity. The sin of animosity is the beginning of hurting another. This is where we must work on our own hearts. We can sin even though this sin may never eventuate in an action which hurts the other person. So we must guard not only against the acting out of bad feelings toward another, but against the feelings of animosity.

Jesus did the same thing with the other commands, showing that sin does not begin with actions, but with the heart. In another context Jesus explained even more emphatically that it is what is in the heart that defiles (Mat. 15:10-20; Mark 7:14-23). "For it is from within, from the human heart, that evil intentions come" (Mark 7:21). In this he was stressing what the Old Testament had said: "Keep your heart with all vigilance, for from it flow the springs of life" (Prov. 4:23). "I treasure your word in my heart,

Holy Living 249

so that I may not sin against you" (Ps. 119:11). The Psalmist was right in saying that we can guard our hearts by treasuring up the word of God in our minds and hearts. At the same time, we must be most careful what we look at (Mat. 5:28), listen to, or think about (Phil. 4:8).

The Old Law

The Ten Commandments and other rules for living in the Old Testament are not irrelevant to Christians. The ceremonial laws of sacrifice were fulfilled when Jesus gave himself as the perfect sacrifice for sin. Temple worship is no longer required since our own bodies are the temple of God (1 Cor. 6:19-20). And obeying the Ten Commandments will not save anyone (Luke 18:18 ff). The Old Testament *as a way of salvation* has been superseded in Christ. But the Christian will seek to obey the will of God, wherever he finds it expressed, because of the grace of God received. You are not saved by obeying rules, but if you are saved you will do your best to obey the rules of God.

The Christian Life

The Christian who sincerely wants to learn all about pleasing God will search the Scriptures for the further guidance to be found there. There is much more in the Gospels, both in the teachings of Jesus and his example. Many of the epistles have both a section of doctrine, and a section on the way the Christian ought to live. In Romans, it begins with chapter twelve.

One of the most instructive longer passages is in Ephesians 4—5. Here we find the Greek word περιπατεω, which is often translated "walk." It points rather to what is now called in English "a life-style," and refers to the whole way of living. It is used five times in these two chapters, and each time refers to a different aspect of the Christian way of living. 1. "Lead a life worthy of the calling to which you have been called" (4:1-16). 2. Not like the sinful world (4:17-32). 3. Live in love, not selfish lust (5:1-7). 4. Live as children of light, not darkness (5:8-14). 5. Live most carefully (5:15-21). This bare outline should be filled in by every Christian in prayerful study of the whole section. And this should be supplemented by the same prayerful study of the rest of the Bible, daily. One should seek to saturate the mind with the Bible, so as to know and do

God's will more and more perfectly.

Prayer

The old hymn says, "Prayer is the soul's sincere desire, unuttered or expressed." It is the response of the soul to God, and should be as natural as breathing. It is a gift of God's grace that we can commune with God anywhere and anytime. God did not have to make this possible, but he did. He loves to hear us pray. The prayers of the people of God are compared to a sweet-smelling incense before God (Rev. 5:8). So we need to learn to come boldly, though humbly, to the throne of God in prayer (Heb. 4:14-16).

Prayer does not have to be limited to praise and thanksgiving, as some believe. Requests are proper, even if they are often repeated (Luke 18:1-8). "Pray without ceasing" (1 Thess. 5:17)

Prayer for Healing

There were healings in the Old Testament in answer to prayer. Yet when Jesus came, he did far more than had been done before. It is said in some places that Jesus healed all who came (Mat. 4:23; 9:35). In many other places individual healings are mentioned (Mat. 8:14-15; John 5:5-9). On one visit to his hometown he could not heal many because of their unbelief (Mat. 13:58; Mark 6:5-6).

After Pentecost the disciples healed just as Jesus had done (Acts 3:2; 6:8; 8:7; 14:10). There is evidence in the rest of the New Testament that this healing ministry continued through the lives of the apostles.

Some today believe that healing miracles ceased with the apostles, along with all other manifestations of the miraculous gifts of the Spirit. However, we continue to find them described in the writings of such writers as Justin Martyr, Origen, Tertullian, and Augustine. So they continued through the first five centuries, at least. And though some medieval stories have been exaggerated beyond belief, miraculous healings are attested down to the present time.

It is reasonable to suppose that God can heal the body as well as the soul. He does so in answer to scriptural promises found in Mark 16:18;

1 Corinthians 12:9-30, James 5:14-15, and elsewhere.

Mark 16:18 is mentioned here, although it must be noted that the last eleven verses of this chapter are not found in the very oldest manuscripts, and may have been added to the Book of Mark near the end of the first century or the beginning of the second. Yet they are very old, and can hardly be omitted completely from our study. But one should notice that it cannot bear the interpretation that any one of the "signs" listed is proof of the work of the Holy Spirit. The Spirit is not mentioned here, and it is wrong to place one of them above the others. They simply illustrate the working of God in the lives of believers, when necessary, and do not prove anything except that God is present.

The passage in James is unique in that it speaks of anointing the person and praying the prayer of faith for healing. There are two explanations for the practice of anointing. One is that oil was used for a curative agent. The second is that oil is used as a symbol of the Holy Spirit. Both are biblically attested, and it is not possible to be sure which James had in mind. The two are not incompatible. If we take it as curative, it shows us that it is not wrong to do whatever we can do to aid our healing, and that does not rule out the miraculous work of God in our bodies. If we take it as symbolic of the work of the Holy Spirit, we still know that both God and human effort can be at work in the same person at the same time.

God Loves Us

God's love for us makes him want to heal us, but he does not always heal us. Some in the New Testament were not healed (Epaphroditus, Phil. 2:25-27; Trophimus, 2 Tim. 4:20; and Timothy, who was often ill, 1 Tim. 5:23).

It is God's general will to heal the sick. Yet God cares more about our spiritual and moral excellence than about our physical health. Therefore God may try us through allowing us to remain afflicted for a longer or shorter period.

Healing, in this particular, is not parallel with salvation. God's will is always to save the repentant soul. But it is not always God's will to heal the individual body. God is not in the business of spoiling us by answering every prayer, but is in the work of building spiritually strong people. How could our faith grow if it is not tested? How can we learn to comfort others in their suffering if God never let us suffer?

God Heals

It is God who heals, not faith. "Faith healing" is only part of the truth. Psychologists agree that faith and confidence can aid in healing the body. But this is not what "divine healing" is all about. Our faith must be placed in the love and power of God, so that God can bring about the healing. If we have this kind of faith in God, our faith cannot be shattered if God does not heal. We trust in his love, even when he does not heal.

Trustful Living

We can live a life of faith in God for guidance and help in finding the right way. And we can trust him to give us strength to do whatever ought to be done for his glory.

Chapter 18

The Church of God

> Simon Peter answered, 'You are the Messiah, the Son of the living God.' And Jesus answered him, 'Blessed are you, Simon son Jonah! For flesh and blood has not revealed this to you, but my Father in heaven. And I tell you, you are Peter, and on this rock I will build my church, and the gates of Hades will not prevail against it.' (Mat. 16:16-18).
>
> **What really is the church, and how did it originate? Is it purely a human invention? If it was planned by God, is it today the kind of church God planned? How can anyone say there is one church, when we know of hundreds? Is it hopeless to talk about the unity of the church and how it can be achieved? How can anyone say the church is holy, when so many sinners go to church?**

Before we consider the origin and nature of the church, we should seek to define it. The church is the people of God, called out from the world to belong only to God in Christ Jesus, so as to continue to do the work of Christ: To declare the gospel and call others to accept the salvation of God and live for him.

ORIGIN OF THE CHURCH

When Jesus asked the disciples, late in his ministry with them, just who they themselves thought he was, Peter answered for the rest by declaring that he was the Messiah, the son of God. It was after this that Jesus made his only clear statement about the church, according to Matthew. He said that he would build his own church. This must have been said in this way to state that he would replace the old people of God with a new one. The difference in the new people of God is that they would be those redeemed by his own sacrifice, and thus a new kind of people. This new people of God had been predicted by Jeremiah (31:31 ff) and others in the Old Testament. Jesus brought it to pass.

Jesus then built his church as a refinement of the old Israel, the people of God. God had promised that Israel would be his people so long as they would obey him and worship him only (Gen. 12:1-3; Deut. 28). This conditional aspect of the promises of God is emphasized in other places in the Old Testament (Exod. 29:9 compared with 1 Sam. 2:30; Jer. 18:1-11). The passage in Exodus made an eternal promise, and did not mention any conditions, yet God told Samuel that it was conditional upon continued faithfulness by the nation. Jeremiah plainly said that this was true, whether the conditions were stated or not. God has a right to withdraw his blessing upon a nation if that nation does not continue to be faithful to him.

What this means to our consideration of Israel is that the promises to that nation were conditional. God's promise to them did not mean that they were free to depart from true worship and living. God could not continue to bless them if they did. So when Christ was preaching to them what they would not accept, they had no right to believe God would continue to bless them. They had come to the crucial point for which God had been preparing them, and they refused to accept any Messiah except the kind they wanted. By that time they had come to believe the Messiah would be a military leader who would free them from Rome. They sought to make Jesus Christ their king to lead them against the Romans, and he refused (John 6:14-15). Jesus said that he would build "my church" (Mat. 16:18), not an earthly, militant kingdom. For this reason, Paul went so far as to call all Christians "the Israel of God" (Gal. 6:14-16).

Called Out

In the Old Testament the people of God are called by the Hebrew term, qahal (קהל), meaning "called to assembly" and in the New Testament the Greek word is εκκλησια. These words refer to the fact that God's special people are called together to worship God and live for

Him.

Abraham was called out from among his country, his kindred and his father's house to go where God would lead him (Gen. 12:1). A primary reason he had to leave was that he lived among idol worshipers, and God wanted to get him away from this influence. This was necessary if God were to teach him to know and serve the one God who created all things. So he was called out.

In Isaiah we find another call to come out and be separate, this time from the exile in Babylon. "Depart, depart, go out from there! Touch no unclean thing; go out from the midst of it, purify yourselves, you who carry the vessels of the Lord" (Isa. 52:11). Jeremiah echoes the same call (Jer. 50:8; 51:6, 9). Still another verse is used more than once in the New Testament: "Come out of her, my people! Save your lives, each of you, from the fierce anger of the Lord (Jer. 51:45).

In the New Testament these calls are addressed to the church, the people of God. One quotes from both Isaiah and Jeremiah: "Do not be mismatched with unbelievers. For what partnership is there between righteousness and lawlessness? Or what fellowship is there between light and darkness? . . . Therefore come out from them, and be separate from them, says the Lord, and touch nothing unclean, then I will welcome you, and I will be your father, and you shall be my sons and daughters, says the Lord Almighty" (2 Cor. 6:14, 16-18).

It should be noted that verse 14 does not refer to marriage of a believer to an unbeliever, as some have thought. To apply it in this way is to overextend the principle involved. Paul is further speaking of the same matter he addressed in 1 Corinthians 5:9, where he admonished the church for accepting an arrogant sinner as a Christian. Later, he spoke of the legitimate mingling of Christians and pagans (1 Cor. 8--10). Now he points out the folly of permanent religious partnership with pagans. Christians must make a clear distinction between their way of life and that of pagans. We must avoid any relationship which would tend to blur that distinction.

In Revelation 18:4, the same call is given in the same words as a call to leave "Babylon," which in Revelation is used for the opposite of the "holy city, the new Jerusalem," which is the church. This church is called out from "Babylon the Great," as Nebuchadnezzar had called it. But it was not so great as his pride had thought. So it fittingly represents the city of sin, the whole world of sin, and the realm ruled by Satan and human pride. The church is called to be separate from the world of sin. This does not mean that we must not associate with sinners outside of the church, but that we must not treat as Christians those who are immoral in the congregation (1 Cor. 5:9-11).

The church, then is called out of the world of sin to belong only to God in Christ Jesus. Yet it is not enough to say that the word for church (εκκλησια *ekklesia*) means "called out." This would mean that being a Christian is primarily negative—separated *from* sin. However, as we saw in our study of holiness, being separated *from* sin is not sufficient to make us holy. We are separated *from* sin *to* God. We are called to belong only to God. We are to be his people alone. This is what it means to be part of the church Jesus built.

Church is "called together"

It is true that the church is people who are "called out" from sin to belong specially to God, but the word "out" is not emphasized in the Greek word. By the time of Christ it simply meant an "assembly" of people called together for some purpose. The word is used for a political meeting in Acts 19:39, 41, as was common in secular writings. In the other 112 uses of the word in the New Testament it refers to the church built by Jesus. God had a special people in the Old Testament, and they were referred to by the same word later use for the church. God called Abram out of Ur (Gen. 12:1-3; Heb. 11:8-10), and promised that his descendants would be a great people for God if they would live for him. The rest of the Old testament tells how God worked with this people to help them belong to him and be the kind of people he could claim and bless.

The Intention of Jesus

The church is neither an accident nor a purely human invention. The intention of Jesus in his earthly sojourn was to build the church. This is true in spite of the fact that in his recorded words Jesus used the word "church" only three times, in contrast to the 109 times the word is used in the rest of the New Testament. Two of these three occurrences are in the same verse, Matthew 18:17, and the other is in the famous passage containing Peter's confession of faith in Christ--Matthew 16:18.

When Jesus made these two statements, there was of course no New Testament church. We must ask ourselves what Jesus meant when he used the word "church." In Matthew 18:17, Jesus could have been referring either to the future Christian church or to the present Jewish synagogue. The latter inference is possible because in the Septuagint, the Bible of the New Testament church), the words "synagogue" and "church" are used interchangeably.

It is clear, however, that in Matthew 16:18 when Jesus said, "I will build my church," he was speaking of the future church which he intended to build to replace the old people of God—Israel. But this one verse is not by any means the only proof that the intention of Jesus was to build the church.

Result of Jesus' life and teachings

We can see in the gospel records that the intention of Jesus was to build the church, even though such an intention is stated only once in the four gospels. We can do it by noting that the church is the inevitable consequence of the life and teachings of Jesus.

While Jesus was living and teaching, the disciples became accustomed to a close fellowship in prayer and in eating together. They thought of themselves as friends of Jesus, living as he taught them, and looking forward to the establishment of the kingdom.

After Jesus left them, they continued to live and worship together as he had taught them, and were conscious of his living presence among them. New believers were added to the company from time to time until, because of their great numbers, they had to develop some sort of organization. All this was done under the guidance of the Holy Spirit.

So it was that the church was built by Jesus Christ as he, through the agency of his Holy Spirit, enabled his followers to perpetuate the church which he had begun during his earthly ministry.

It will pay us now to examine carefully some of the words of Jesus in the light of the church which he later built. In doing so, we can see that while he was on earth, he was in the process of building the church. At the very least, we can say that he was laying the foundation, drawing the plans, and preparing the materials.

The Foundation. Jesus prepared the foundation for the church by his very life and death. Jesus is himself the foundation of the church, and it was by his incarnation, life and teaching, and his vicarious death for all men that he became that foundation. The church is built on the faith of men and women everywhere that Jesus, being God, voluntarily "emptied himself" of divine glory, left his home in heaven, took upon himself the form of sinful human beings, died to save us from sin, and rose to die no more so that we might have life eternal with him. So the church is ultimately built on Jesus, and his whole life was the preparation of that foundation.

The Plans. Jesus, by his teachings, drew the plans for the church which he was to build. He described the people who would be members of the church. Part of the description, for instance, is found in the Beatitudes and in the rest of the Sermon on the Mount. Further description is found in most of the parables, sermons and sayings of Jesus.

Jesus commanded his disciples to preach the gospel all over the world, which would provide a perpetual membership for the church. If Jesus had not intended to build a church, what possible reason could he have had for telling his disciples to evangelize? Obedience to this command is the very thing which brought the church into being, and which has kept it growing through two millenniums, until it has spread all over the world.

The Materials Jesus prepared the materials for the church he was to build. First, he prepared his followers for membership in the church. He did this by the way he lived among them as a heavenly example and by the way he taught them. And he not only taught them the right and best ways, but he helped them to learn by reproving their wrong and childish ways.

Second, Jesus taught ways of living which make for peaceful and effective growing and working within the church. If we Christian people could translate the teaching of Jesus more adequately into our lives, we could get far more done in the church and do it more effectively.

Third, Jesus trained and prepared preachers to build up the church, both in numbers and in height of spiritual attainment. The disciples were with him almost constantly during all of his public ministry. They heard him preach, ate with him, lived with him, and walked long distances with him. During these common experiences Jesus was teaching them the things he wanted them to know, and was training them to continue the great work he could only begin.

Future Continuance

Jesus promised to send the Holy Spirit to build the church together into a holy institution and to guide the believers into all truth. This promise and its fulfillment assured the eternal triumph of the church, and precluded any possibility that Jesus' work would be either vain or transitory. Since that first day of Pentecost, that promise has been fulfilled. All through the Book of Acts we see the work of the Holy Spirit in the church. This is true to such an extent that the book has often been called "Acts of the Holy Spirit." And He is still at work today in the church, as he has been for two thousand years.

Jesus called himself the "good shepherd" and his disciples "little flock." These terms on the lips of the Son of God show that he considered himself the leader of a group of people. Unless he intended to build an eternal church, we must conclude that his crucifixion brought an ignominious end to a glorious beginning. This cannot be true. All Christian history denies it. The intention of Jesus was to build and establish the church.

NATURE OF THE CHURCH

The church is made up of all those who believe in Jesus Christ as the supreme revelation of God, who are committed to him as Lord and Savior, and who seek to follow his teachings and way of life. This means that the church includes all Christians and excludes all sinners. It is not limited to those who have joined any particular church, or all those in all the churches, as one can be a Christian without having joined any church.

Although the Gospel of John does not mention the church, Jesus was speaking of the people of God, which is the same thing, when he said "I am the gate for the sheep" (John 10:7). He meant that he is the way of entrance into the "sheepfold," by which he meant the church. His thought is made clear by the context. In the previous chapter the blind man had been healed, and then excommunicated from the synagogue because he was healed on the Sabbath and sought to defend that fact to the Pharisees. Now Jesus says that no matter what people may do about the synagogue, Jesus is the door or gateway to what is really important.

> Very truly, I tell you, anyone who does not enter the sheepfold by the gate but climbs in by another way is a thief and a bandit. The one who enters by the gate is the shepherd of the sheep. The gatekeeper opens the gate for him, and the sheep hear his voice. He calls his own sheep by name and leads them out (John 10:1-3).

This is the background for his statement that he is the gate, or the door, the way of entrance. If Jesus is the gate, no one can get in without his approval. This means that all who are in the church is a converted person, born from above. It also implies that there is no Christian who is not one of God's people, in the church.

The fact that the church is the people of God is basic to understanding the various aspects of the church. It is not some purely human institution invented by human beings. When it was first set up, the church was a new kind of fellowship made up of God's chosen people. The very fact that they are all the redeemed people of God makes the church different, for they have all died to sin and been raised up to live for God.

In the New Testament, "church" is used for all the people of God, or for local groups of them as they meet together in one place. It speaks of any such group as the church of God, not as a part of the church. Any time two or more meet together, there is the church.

BIBLICAL FIGURES OF THE CHURCH

Body of Christ

Paul introduced this important figure (Col. 1:24; Eph. 1:22-23). It is most important because it shows the organic nature of the church, and that all the members work together to make the church the whole that it is. This was one of Paul's greatest contributions to the understanding of the church.

Christ is the Head of the body (Col. 1:18). He is thus both source and guide, but primarily the source. The church is the body of Christ through whom He works, and in whom He dwells among worldly people.

It is the whole universal church which is the body, not a single congregation. No congregation is ever spoken of as a member of a larger body. Each congregation is the church. Wherever two Christians meet together, there is the church.

Bride of Christ

This comparison of the church and Christ with a bride and her bridegroom is a beautiful one. The prophets in the Old Testament had spoken of Israel as the bride of God, so this was a natural way for the church to think of itself. This is another indication of the church being a new Israel in the sense of being a new people of God.

As the bride of Christ, the church seeks to be useful, and beautiful, a holy people for the Lord. And the church seeks to be fully pleasing to God in Christ Jesus. The church seeks both to be and to do what is pleasing to God.

Temple of God

The temple represents the immanence of God on earth. Although the apostles had appointed places for worship, they never lost sight of the fact that God does not dwell in man-made buildings. Neither are there any priests in the New Testament church. Christ is our High Priest, and all Christians are priests who need no other mediator than Christ to approach God.

The church is a building "fitly framed together" (Eph. 4:16). Not a building in the sense of an institution, but as a worshiping people in whom God dwells. It is a center from which flows the healing Gospel (Ezek. 47:1-12; Isa. 2:1-3).

Family of God, or People of God

No Hebrew or Greek term exactly corresponds with the English word, "family". This fact needs to be considered when building on this figure of speech.

The modern concept of family as father, mother and children may cause us to read too much into certain passages. It is true that God is our

Father, and that we are all brothers and sisters in Christ. The term "brothers" is the term for Christians (174 times). "All ye are brethren" (Mat. 23:8). "No longer a slave, but a brother beloved" (Phm 16). Christ is "the firstborn among many brethren" (Rom. 8:29).

But the church is not our mother in the same sense as God is our Father. God is our Father because He is our Creator and the One who saves us from sin through Jesus Christ. But the church is our mother only in an instrumental sense. The church can neither create nor save, but can only be the instrument through which the gospel comes to us.

Greek *patria* means clan, tribe, nation, or people, not family in our modern sense. So it may be best to use little of this figure, and speak of the church as the people of God. In this sense, it is the "Israel of God" (Gal. 6:16).

Salt of the earth

The church, the people of God, are the salt of the earth, not servants of the world. The church is made up of servant-Christians, but is never said to be serving the world. The church serves God, as Jesus Christ did. The church must never be subservient to the world, nor conform itself to the world. The church will serve God by being kind and helpful to the sinful world, by living as much like Christ as possible, by the grace of God, and by declaring the gospel of salvation by Christ to the world. The last is the best and finest way of rescuing the world from sin, thus doing its best for the world.

MODELS OF CHURCH

These are based on the study by Avery Dulles.[80] They are only suggested in Scripture. They are an attempt to understand the church as described in Scripture, especially as related to the functions of the church.

Church as an Institution

It is not truly helpful to think of the church as an institution, but rather dangerous. It puts the focus on obedience to the human leaders, and detracts from concentration on the relationship with the triune God.

Church as a Mystery

The purpose here is to stress the fact that the church is not a human structure or institution, but is built by God. The emphasis is on communion, fellowship, and being the body of Christ. The church was not a human invention, but is a manifestation of eternal life that now exists through the grace of God.

Church as Herald

The point of this model is to stress the importance of the church as proclaiming the word of God to the world. This is good, and has support in Scripture. But it can lead to distortion in two ways. First, the church must not only proclaim the word, but must live it. It must live as it preaches, or the world will not listen. Second, if the church is to preach the word, what must it do with all the different interpretations of the word which it preaches? What word will it preach? Surely it gives an uncertain sound to the world. This model has something to say to the church, but it fails to be an overall view of what the church really is.

Church as Servant

As noted above, it may be logical to think of the church as a servant, but not as servant to the world. The church is a servant only to God. The church is not to be reconciled to the world. The world is rather to be reconciled to Christ as served by the church. The church cannot afford to seek to be reconciled to this wicked world. The church can help the world most by living for God, and by demonstrating to the world what it is like to have freedom and life in Christ.

Jesus declared that he came to serve, but he did not serve the interests and needs which the world perceived. He rather did for the world what God sent Him to do. Jesus served the world by doing the will of his Father. This is not to deny that there are social results of the gospel, for there are. Christian people have a compassion and love for the people of the world that causes them to serve people. But this service is always guided by their love for God and their desire to please Him.

Church as a "Pilgrim People

Jesus prayed for his followers to be kept in the world, but "not of the world, even as I am not of the world (John 17:14). Paul declared that while we live in this world, "our citizenship is in heaven" (Phil. 3:20), and warned us not to live like the Gentiles (unbelievers) around us. Peter wrote of the way we ought to live lives which are far different from the people among whom we travel as strangers on earth (1 Pet. 4:1-5).

The author of Hebrews shares some strong remarks on this concept of the church as a pilgrim people (Heb. 11:13-16). He speaks of God's people as "strangers and exiles on the earth," who are seeking for a heavenly city in which to make their home. The church is that kind of people, living in the world, but knowing that they belong to another world.

Here we have an exciting and helpful model of the church in relation to the world in which the church lives. We cannot afford to become too attached to the world or the things in it. We do not belong to this present age, and are just passing through it. This gives the church a new way to serve the Lord while helping the people of this world to live a higher way, if they only will. We are not walking alone through this world, as Jesus Christ has promised to go with us every step of the way. He is the Suffering Servant who has trod the way before us, and who will never leave us nor forsake us.

MARKS OF THE CHURCH

Since the fourth century after Christ it has been common to speak of the four marks, or notes, of the church. By this is meant the distinguishing characteristics of the church. Early creeds have spoken of the church as "one, holy, catholic and apostolic." So we have come to think of the marks of the church as: Holiness, Apostolicity, Catholicity, and Unity. We will look at them in the latter order.

Apostolicity

In saying that the church is apostolic, we are saying that the church ought to be like that described by the apostolic writers of the New

Testament. This is not a mere matter of imitation of all the details of the church and it organization and work. That would mean that we could not apostolic and be a part of the modern world. We do not have to dress like the people of the New Testament, nor do we need to leave off the modern amenities of life. Those things are peripheral and are not what made the church what it was. If the church is to be apostolic, it must follow the principles laid down in the New Testament. We live two thousand years later, but we can seek to restore the glory of the early church and be like the church they described as the ideal.

It is true that the individual churches described in the New Testament were not perfect in organization, doctrine, or work. They all had their faults and failings, but the apostolic preachers labored hard at the task of correcting their failings. Many of the letters to the churches were written because the local churches needed correction and much instruction. Galatians was written to help the churches of Galatia to see that they were slipping away from basic principles of the gospel. The Thessalonian letters were written to correct some serious faults in the thinking of those people. But the worst example of all was the church in Corinth, which was recognizing as Christians some who were far from living for God.

The apostolicity of the church means that we seek to apply the Christian principles of belief and practice which the apostles wrote down. In this way we seek to be a "New Testament church." Note these words by Charles E. Brown:

> We are under a most heavy responsibility, so far as possible, to reproduce the spiritual life, the truth, the doctrine, the holy equality of the universal priesthood of believers; the warm, rich, deep fellowship; and the burning message of redemption, as well as the overwhelming experiences of the Spirit's complete control of our lives, which were know so well in the apostolic church.[81]

Now we must admit that the best of the characteristics which Brown listed were not found in all the believers in each congregation of that time. There was a mixture of good and less worthy people in the church then as there are now. That fact does not change our desire to be like the best ideals described in the New Testament. We must not seek to be like the least Christlike persons, but like the best. No one who understands the situation would want a local church today to be like the church in Corinth when Paul wrote his first letter to it. Paul had himself lived there for a year and a half to plant the church, but it was far from what the church ought to be. We should not seek to be like that church. Yet we should seek earnestly to be the kind of church Paul presented to them in the letter.

The church is now about two thousand years old, and cannot be a new church again. When we say we want to be a New Testament church, we are not wanting to go back to the infancy of the church, but we wish to have the spiritual health of the first century church. Even more importantly we want to follow the guidance of the New Testament as to the kind of people we ought to be.

The point of apostolicity, then is that the church today ought to be in harmony with the principles laid down in the New Testament. The church should be seeking to be like the best ideals we find in the New Testament. This is the way to be a New Testament, apostolic church.

Holiness

The church is holy because the members of the church, being Christians, born from above, are holy. They are holy since they belong to the holy God. Yet the statement that the church is holy has caused much discussion and confusion in the church through the centuries. A major question is about the fact that sinners come to worship with the church.

If sinners are in the congregation, how can the church be holy? Augustine declared that the holiness of the church was really the holiness of Christ, even though the church itself was made up of unholy persons. But rather than go into the controversies which brought him to this concept, we will look at the New Testament ideas which may throw light on the whole subject.

Jesus is the door. This is stated by Jesus in John 10:9. He is the means of entrance to the people of God, which is the church. We read also that God adds people to the church as they are converted (Acts 2:47). Since this is true, and since it is by being born anew by faith in Him, that one becomes a member of the church, sinners cannot get into the church and still live in sin. Sinners can be in the congregation, and should be, but they are not members of the church until they enter by Christ.

All Christians belong to the church of God. God places the members in the church, the body of Christ (1 Cor. 12:27-28). This means that all Christians belong to God's church. We see that if we are speaking of the church as made up of Christians whom God recognizes, then all Christians are in the church. No sinners are in the church.

Admittedly, this is not the usual Protestant concept of the church, but it is Scriptural. The church is all the people of God. Some of them may have joined some denomination, but if they are Christians, they are members of the same church as all other Christians.

Catholicity

If this discussion of the holiness of the church is based on the true Scriptural concept of the church, then of course the church is the sum of all the Christians in the world, and all those who have already died in the Lord. This makes the church truly catholic.

We are here using the word *catholic* in the sense of "universal" but not in the sense of Roman Catholic or Greek Catholic. If the church includes all the Christians in heaven and earth, then it is truly universal and catholic.

It was when the idea of the church was narrowed down to mean only those who belonged to a particular group, or who acknowledged the supreme authority of some one person, that confusion entered. At that point it could no longer be said that all Christians belonged to the church or that no sinners were in the church. When human conditions were laid down for membership, the church became something different from the New Testament description. It then included all who had joined that particular church, or who had been placed in it by parents as an infant. This brought new problems along with a different concept of the nature of the church.

Unity of the Church

If we accept the description of the catholicity of the church, then the unity of the church logically follows. It cannot be catholic and not be single. There cannot be two universal churches. If the church is the people of God, there is only one church, since it includes all the people of God. Since there are no Christians outside the universal church, there can be no other people of God. By its very nature the church is only one, not many (Rom. 12:4-5).

In New Testament times there was only one church, with no other churches for anyone to join. The word εκκλησια is singular in 108 times and four times in the plural. The word refers either to the universal church, meaning all the people of God, or to a congregation in some location. The four times it is used in the plural (1 Cor. 11:16; 1 Thess. 2:14; 2 Thess. 1:4; Rom. 16:16) refer either to all the congregations of the church of God, or to the congregations in a particular area.

The fact that the church is spoken of as not only one body, but the body of Christ (Eph. 2:21-22; Col. 1:24) makes the singleness and the unity of the church even more emphatic. He has only one body, and he is the one head of the body.

When Jesus was speaking of himself as Shepherd and Christians as his flock, he strongly emphasized the unity of the flock of God. He knows his sheep and they know him (John 10:5), so they go where he wants them to go. "I know my own and my own know me. . .And I lay down my life for the sheep" (vss. 14-15). And he immediately explains: "I have other sheep that do not belong to this fold. I must bring them also, and they will listen to my voice. So there will be one flock, one shepherd" (vs. 16). As Leon Morris says of this verse: "It is difficult to interpret 'not of this fold' other than as indicating those who are not to be found within Judaism. The words look to the world-wide scope of the gospel.[82]

The intention of Jesus, then, was to bring all his people together into one church, from all nations, races and peoples, under his direction. When we are converted, we become the special people of God, and are joined together in the love of God with all the rest of his people everywhere. For this reason, Jesus prayed in Gethsemane: "The glory that you have given me I have given them, so that they may be one, as we are one. I in them and you in me, that they may become completely one" (John 17:22-23). The unity of the people of God in the church ought to be like the unity of the Trinity! This is what God planned for the church, though it is easy to see that is not the case in our world. There are so many churches, and so very many Protestant denominations that most Christians see no hope of any real unity.

Can Christians Be One? Jesus' great desire was for unity (John 10:16). He prayed earnestly for unity (John 17:11, 20-22), and died that we all may be one John 11:49-52). So Jesus must have believed that it was possible for all Christians to be one.

There is a strong doctrinal basis for the unity of all Christians. We are all saved by the same process (John 10:9). All Christians serve the same Lord and have the same Bible (Eph. 4:5; 2 Tim. 3:16). There is only one heaven for all Christians of all the ages, all nations (Eph. 4:4; Rev. 7:9). All have the same Holy Spirit to guide us (1 Cor. 12:13). And according to the Bible there is only one church for all Christians (Rom. 12:4-5; 1 Cor. 12:13, 18). All these facts make it scriptural for us all to belong to one church, with loyalty only to Christ.

Yet there are difficult problems to overcome if we are to be one in the way Jesus longed for us to be. There is such a variety of churches or denominations, with so many kinds of organizations, and different methods and traditions of worship. And there are strong denominational loyalties from which people find it hard to break away.

The Call to Be One. For the last century and a half there have been calls for all God's people to be one. After the American Civil War, these called increased. Some of the strongest came from missionaries who found new Christians in mission churches were so confused by the variety of churches that they could not understand what was true. Mission work was greatly hindered by the wastefulness of mission work being carried on in the same places by competing churches.

In America, as we near the twenty-first century, we see that there has been a weakening of denominational loyalties. There are some bad aspects of this, but there is some reason to hope for a revival of eagerness for one church, with no competition.

As for differing sets of beliefs which separate Christians, there is hope that we can learn to differ in beliefs, but not allow these differences in doctrine to stand in the way of true Christian unity. We all have the same Bible, and the more we study it together, the more we see that we are truly one in Christ. If we let the Bible actually work in our hearts, and are determined to let God lead us into all truth, God can draw us together in spite of our theological differences.

Warner's Vision of Unity. In the last quarter of the nineteenth century Daniel Sidney Warner began to see and preach a new vision of the unity of God's church. He began with the concept of the sinfulness of a divided church. This was a concept which had been advocated by others in the nineteenth century, in various ways. At the same time Warner was preaching, some strong appeals for an end to the division of denominations was coming from mission fields.

Daniel Warner not only came to love unity so much that he determined to do whatever he could to bring it about. He wanted to get rid of all that divided Christians, and came to see a way by which he believed it could be ended. He felt sure that the New Testament supported a view of the church as being made up only of those who were redeemed by Christ, and therefore identical with all of God's people. In writing about the followers of D. S. Warner, and their vision of the church, John W. V. Smith wrote:

> Seeing the light on the church" was, for them, more than a mere intellectual understanding of it. In their vision they saw the Church as a visible universal spiritual fellowship of all the redeemed. It is visible, they said, because it is made up of living people who are redeemed by the atoning work of Christ--recognizable saints whose lives are a witness to their experience of rebirth. It is universal in that it includes all the redeemed, regardless of whatever churchly affiliations they might or might not have. It is spiritual in that its true membership is limited to the spiritually reborn; the Church can include only those who are truly "saved."[83]

It follows from this that God's church cannot be identified with any denomination, nor with all of them. Denominations are composed of both sinners and genuine Christians, because of the way they are made up according to standards set by leaders. Since the Church of God is made up of those whom God has placed in it (Acts 2:47; 1 Cor. 12:13, 18), all Christians belong to the same church, even if they have joined some other church also. Warner believed then that all we had to do to have unity is for us to give up our membership in other churches, and simply be one in Christ. This simply we could exhibit the unity for which Christ longed (John 10:16), for which he prayed (John 17:21), and for which he died (11:52).

C. E. Brown used Augustine's expression of the visible and invisible church although Augustine used the terms in a different context and for a far different purpose.[84] Warner simply believed that in every congregation there are both sinners and Christians. The visible church consists of both, but only the Christians are in God's church, which might be called invisible, since the line of demarcation between them can only be seen clearly by God. Warner believed that it is better for us not to decide who is in the church and who is not, but to leave that to God. We can live in harmony with all Christians who are willing to fellowship with us. And we can do this best if we do not divide Christians from Christians by joining any church.

This was the reason for the call for all Christians to give up their allegiance to all denominations and simply belong to Christ, as members of God's church. The purpose of this is to bring about the kind of unity for which Christ prayed: "I ask not only on behalf of these, but also on behalf of those who will believe in me through their word, that they all may be one. . . . so that the world may believe that you have sent me." (John 17:20-21).

It is not the size of the church which will rightly impress the world and help them to believe in God. It is rather the unity and harmony of the church as they abide in Christ and live for him. This alone will fulfill God's plan and purpose for the church.

It is thus that we see the twin truths of Unity and Holiness to which Warner committed himself. If we are to be the kind of church Jesus seems to have intended, then we must hold fast to these twin truths, and determine to do all in our power, by the grace of God, to be God's holy people, and to make "every effort to maintain the unity of the Spirit in the bond of peace" (Eph. 4:3). (The whole paragraph, Eph. 4:1-6, strongly emphasizes the unity which we ought to have.)

The Church of God

The group, or reformation movement, which grew out of the preaching of Warner and others of like convictions, is called the Church of God, which is a term found a dozen times in the New Testament. It is not used to claim that this group is all the people God has in the world. It is used to refer to the fact that we are determined not to belong to any church except God's church.

In this century many groups have come to call themselves by this same term. This has led some to feel that we ought to change the name to something more distinctive or descriptive. Yet this name expresses the fact that all Christians should belong only to the church God built, and is therefore a good one.

It has become a tradition in the Church of God movement to capitalize the word Church in writing of the movement, but not when referring to the universal people of God. The Church of God is not the same as the church of God. The church of God includes all the Christians in heaven and on earth. The Church of God is only a group of people who are seeking to represent the church of God in a visible form. We should long for the time when we will never need to Capitalize the word, but simply speak and write of the church of God -- God's church, which is all the people God has on earth. May God speed the day!

ORDINANCES OF THE CHURCH

An ordinance is a Christian ceremony, commanded by Jesus, with a spiritual meaning. It is an outward act symbolizing an inward work of God in the heart. Augustine defined "sacrament" in words we could apply to an ordinance: "an outward and visible sign of an inward and spiritual grace." However, he included many acts which would not be considered sacraments even by Roman Catholics today. The sixteenth century reformers narrowed the list to baptism and the Lord's Supper. The sacramental Protestants of the seventeenth century emphasized the power of sacraments to bring the grace of God. The preference for the word ordinance may stem from a reaction against this tendency. Like some other nineteenth century holiness people, we also include foot-washing as a third ordinance.

Baptism reminds us that we died to our old ways, and came to life as servant of God and of people. The Lord's Supper reminds us that all God's servants eat at the same table of the same spiritual food-- Christ. The washing of feet reminds us that we gladly serve one another.

Baptism we normally observe only once, since it speaks of our entrance into the Kingdom. It shows the world we have forsaken its ways. We have died to our old goals and lesser ideals, and rose to a new kind of life in Christ Jesus, a life of service to God and people.

The Lord's Supper reminds us that our new life comes through Christ, who died for us. He is our bread of life, who sustains us.

Washing the feet of the saints is a picture of our humble willingness to serve.

Baptism for Believers Only. Baptism is for believers only. John the

Baptist evidently refused to baptize those who were not truly penitent (Matt. 3:8-9). Peter said, "Repent and be baptized, every one of you" (Acts 2:38). All those who were baptized were believers (Acts 8:12; 18:8). Paul and Cornelius were converted and filled with the Holy Spirit before they were baptized. This is the basic reason infants are not proper subjects of baptism, for they are not capable of believing so as to be converted.

Baptism as an Ordinance. We could call baptism a sacrament, but in the Church of God we avoid that. Our major point about baptism is that it is only an outward sign of what God has done within. R. R. Byrum expressed it this way: "But neither the Scriptures nor reason furnish any ground for supposing salvation may be obtained by any physical means. The common sense of mankind instinctively repudiates the idea than any magical efficacy exists in any outward rite that of itself can confer spiritual grace."[85]

Byrum later explains why baptism does not save us (574-575). Salvation is not dependent on any outward rite. This is one of the differences between the Old Testament and the New Testament. "Our sins are not washed away by the baptismal waters, but by the blood of Christ (Rev. 1:5; 7:14). That blood is applied on the conditions of repentance and faith (John 3:18; Acts 13:39; 1 John 5:1)." He also points out that this would make our salvation dependent on another person, who would perform the baptism. Baptism is a ceremonial cleansing, and not the true inward cleansing from sin (Acts 26:13-18; 1 Pet. 3:21).

The Lord's Supper, or Eucharist

The first written description of the Lord's Supper is in 1 Corinthians 11:23-26, where the rest of the chapter is given over to some instructions for doing it properly. Paul wrote this because of some of the unworthy practices which the church in Corinth had adopted. There are other records in the Gospels (Mat. 26:26-28; Mark 14:22-24; Luke 22:19-20). The Roman Catholic, Eastern Orthodox, Anglican churches and some others, teach that the elements used, when they are properly blessed, are the real body and blood of Christ. Most others believe that they only represent the body and blood of Christ. A problem with the belief in the real body and blood of Christ is that some came to believe that it was a repetition of the sacrifice of Christ on the cross. Yet Jesus died once for all (Heb. 9:27-28). That sacrifice never needs to be repeated.

There is no instruction given as to how often this should be observed. Some read the words "Do this, as often as you drink it, in remembrance of me" (1 Cor. 11:25), and emphasize the word "often." They feel then that it ought to be a part of every Sunday morning worship. The rest of us take it to be simply a way of saying that whenever we do it we should do it in remembrance of Jesus and what he did for us.

The Lord's Supper is often called by the Greek term "Eucharist," which means "giving thanks." The term originated because Jesus gave thanks for the bread and the wine before giving it to others. This has become a customary part of the observance. It is our way of giving thanks to God for his gift of salvation and eternal life.

The Lord's Supper reminds us that this new life comes through Christ Jesus and his death for us. He is our bread of life, who sustains us. His body was broken for our salvation and his blood was shed that we might have life. We servants of God cannot live without our Lord. All servants alike are dependent on Him. None of us is so great as to live without him. In him we live and move and have our being. "Just as the branch cannot bear fruit by itself unless it abides in the vine, neither can you unless you abide in me" (John 15:4).

Some churches use wine, while the rest use grape juice. There are good reasons for using grape juice in modern times. We have better ways of getting juice in these days, and keeping it fresh. There is no value in its fermentation, and there is reason not to let it ferment. It is wise for some recovering alcoholics to refrain from participation in the communion service, or Eucharist, if they suspect it might be performed with wine. So why cause a problem for anyone? It is better that the juice be unfermented.

Washing of Feet

The record of Jesus washing the feet of the disciples, including Judas, and commanding his disciples to continue doing this, is found in John 13:1-17. It is not described in the other Gospels, but is mentioned in 1 Timothy 5:10 as a requirement.

When Jesus came, he came both as King and as Servant of all. He told

Pilate that his kingdom was not of this world. He told his disciples: "You know that the rulers of the Gentiles lord it over them, and their great ones are tyrants over them. It will not be so among you; but whoever wishes to be great among you must be your servant. And whoever wishes to be first among you must be your slave; just as the Son of Man came not to be served, but to serve, and to give his life a ransom for many " (Mat. 20:15-28).

Jesus built a kingdom of servants. In other kingdoms, people seek for power and authority. In God's kingdom, we seek to serve God and to serve one another. In God's kingdom the greatest person is the one who serves most faithfully. The ceremony of washing one another's feet is a picture of our humble willingness to serve.

Some object that Christ did not intend for us to take him literally as he commanded us to wash one another's feet. They do not believe that he intended to institute an ordinance or ceremony. They say that Jesus was simply doing for the disciples what no servant had done for them. Their feet were dusty from their walk, and since there was no servant to wash them, he did it for them.

There are good reasons for believing that Jesus was doing far more than the usual act of a custom of that day. First of all, they were already eating, and it would have been most improper for them to proceed this far into the meal with dirty feet. They had bathed before beginning to eat this annual Passover Meal.

Second, Jesus said that they were clean because they had bathed, but he insisted that it was necessary for him to wash their feet. Thus he reminded them that they had already bathed and were clean (except for Judas, who had a different kind of uncleanness). He was not doing this because they were dirty, but because they needed a spiritual lesson.

Third, Jesus implied that they did not understand what he was doing (John 12:13). They understood very well the common custom. But they did not understand this. So this was not the customary washing of feet to wash off the dust of walking. This was something far different.

It is objected by some that Jesus did this to teach humility. That is true, and the object lesson he gave them was effective. But just as we need the repetition of the Lord's Supper to remind us of our dependence on God for continued life, so we need the repetition of the humble service of one another in the washing of feet to remind us of our servanthood.

The ceremony symbolizes the lifelong attitude of Christians to one another. It shows us how we ought to feel about others all the time in all circumstances. It is a wonderful demonstration of the way we love one another. This physical act can reinforce and determine emotions. "If you know these things, you are blessed if you do them" (John 13:17).

Chapter 19

The Spirit in the Church

> Repent, and be baptized every one of you in the name of Jesus Christ so that your sins may be forgiven, and you will receive the gift of the Holy Spirit (Acts 2:38).

If the Spirit is given to individuals, is it for the benefit of the individual? Or for the church? What does it mean for the Spirit to be given as a gift to the church? What happens to the person as a result of receiving the Holy Spirit? How can we make the fruit of the Spirit grow?

The Holy Spirit works in and through the church to do God's will in the world. It is the work of the Holy Spirit to preside over the whole work of God on earth, to infuse with power, and to invest with authority.

The Holy Spirit seeks to rule the church. This is why the Book of Acts has so often been called "The Acts of the Holy Spirit." The leaders of the early church knew that this church was the building of God, and that he must lead them in all their work if they were to please God and have the kind of success he wanted. In this work, the Holy Spirit gives to the church individuals with abilities to do what is needed. These abilities are sometimes called "gifts."

The gifts of the Spirit are often made to sound like something mysterious and superhuman, totally foreign to anything we could hear about otherwise. They are superhuman in that they involve God's power, but they are ordinary abilities which are further enabled by God.

THE GIFT OF THE SPIRIT

First we need to recognize that the gift of the Spirit is the Holy Spirit himself (Acts 2:38; 10:45; 11:17; Rom. 5:5). The most mportant thing is not to seek for some special gift from the Spirit, but to receive the Spirit. He had promised this gift of the Spirit in the Old Testament (Ezek 36:27; 37:14; Joel 2:28-29). John the Baptist and Jesus had both repeated the promise and made it more specific. Since the Day of Pentecost the gift can be received by any who will meet the conditions. It is all too common for us to be careless of the value of this great gift from God. It is amazing and almost beyond belief that the Creator of the universe would care enough about these insignificant human beings that he would come to live within us (1 Kings 8:27; Isa. 57:15).

We do not lightly claim that the Holy Spirit can and does live within us. This is the greatest gift we could possible imagine. No other religion has imagined such a gift. Some pagans have thought that a god of speech, or a god of some other part of creation could come into a person, at least for a time. But not the great God of all creation. This gift of the Holy Spirit living within us is what makes life such a wonderful adventure. Even pain and sorrow can be borne with some equanimity when we know that he is there, and that he cares. But this is not the end of the story. Christ came to the earth where he lived and died and ascended to the Father, and gives gifts to human beings. "But each of us was given grace according to the measure of Christ's gift. Therefore it is said, 'When he ascended on high he made captivity itself a captive; he gave gifts to his people" (Eph. 4:7-8).

GIFTS OF THE SPIRIT

In the verses immediately following these words it is made clearer that it is Christ who did all this and that it is Christ himself who gives the gifts of the Spirit to the church for building up the church. The gifts are such things as apostles, prophets (preachers), evangelists, pastors and teachers.

One vital point to note here is that these workers are gifts given to the church. So the gifts of the Spirit which makes these kinds of work possible, are gifts to the church. They are given by God so that the work of the church can be done as he pleases.

The only extended discussion of the "gifts of the Spirit" is in First Corinthians 12—14. Like the other topics in this letter, the gifts are discussed because of the troubles caused by the false understanding of them by the Corinthian Christians. He had discussed the unity of the church because of the disunity in the Corinthian church. He discussed spiritual wisdom in chapter two because the Corinthians had argued over who of them had the most of it. In chapter five, he spoke of immorality because the church had been condoning it in a leader. He wrote about lawsuits, because some of the Corinthians were suing others in the church. The discussion of marriage and divorce in chapter seven was motivated by distortions of the subject by some in Corinth. He wrote about the eating of meat and about worship because of some serious problems with these matters.

After dealing with each of these problems, in chapter 12, Paul turns to the matter of the gifts of the Spirit, on which the Corinthians were so divided. They made so much of the more spectacular gift that they sought for what they called "tongues" and neglected to seek for what would build up the church. They were seeking for what would exalt the individual instead of what would exalt Christ, glorify God, and strengthen others. They felt that those who could utter words or sounds that others could not understand were more spiritual than those who could not do this.

In response to the situation in Corinth, Paul began by putting the gifts in proper perspective and showing their purpose. He then points out the value of the love of God which is given by the Spirit. Finally he spoke directly to the point of the "tongues" which seemed to mean so much to the church in Corinth.

Growing the fruit of the spirit is far more important than having all the "gifts" of the Spirit. This is the gist of chapter 13, so beautifully placed in the center of the whole discussion.

Meaning of Gifts (Charismata)

The Greek word for gifts is χαρισμα (pl. χαρισματα), and is often used by some in the tranliterated forms—charisma and charismatic. The word charisma has taken on a much weaker meaning in English, as has the related word "charismatic." We need to deal with the Greek word as used in the New Testament. The Greek word is derived from the word for "grace" and "graciousness." It is not the common word for "gift Its basic meaning is a "gift graciously given."

Paul and Peter are the only ones in the New Testament to use the word. Paul uses it 16 times and it is found otherwise only in 1 Peter 4:10. Eight of Paul's uses of the word have nothing to do with what are generally called today "gifts of the Spirit." It is worthwhile to look at these eight times.

Paul seems to be thinking of his whole ministry as a gracious gift of God in Romans 1:11-12. He wishes that he could be with the church in Rome for a while for the mutual encouragement of both himself and the church, and that the church might be more firmly established by the Holy Spirit working in and through both. In Romans 5:15-16, Paul speaks of justification as the "gracious gift" of God. He uses the word also of eternal life (Rom. 6:23). He uses the same word to refer to God's mercy in choosing salvation (Rom. 11:29), a particular position in life (1 Cor. 7:7), answered prayer (2 Cor. 1:11), and ability for ministry in general (1 Tim. 4:14; 2 Tim. 1:6).

These passages can help us to see that life itself is a gracious gift of God. The troubles we find along the way can also be gracious gifts by which God can lead us, and help us grow. By the time we enter eternity, we may come to feel that even our physical ailments have been blessed gifts of God's grace, and that they have helped to make us what we are for God.

God is a God Who Gives. One of the things Jesus teaches us about God is that He is a God who gives gifts to human beings because He loves us so. God has given us our very existence. We would not be if God had not created us, and the world in which we live. He has given us all the beauty and order which surrounds us daily. He has given us the materials and powers which we use by the aid of our sciences to create comfort and health for ourselves.

We sometimes feel proud of our achievements and may feel that we have no need for God any longer, as we can make for ourselves anything we need. But that is totally false, since it is God who has given us the ability to do these things, and the brains with which to do them. It is God who continues to give us life and breath each day so that we can go on with our work in this world in which he has placed us. As Paul pointed out to the Athenians, "He himself gives to all men life and breath and everything" (Acts 17:25).

It is for this reason that we Christians know that we must give thanks every day for life, health, shelter, and all that we have. We cannot eat without first thanking God for food and the ability to eat it. We cannot go to sleep at night without thanking God for the day we have had, and for the night in which to sleep and regain our strength. We know that we have nothing which we have not been given. It is all given to us by the giving God.

God Gave Us Jesus. That most familiar passage, John 3:16, tells us that Jesus Christ himself is a gift to mankind: "For God so loved the world that he gave his only Son, that whoever believes in him should not perish, but have eternal life." So Jesus is himself the gift of God to the world of human beings. He is the greatest gift we could possibly know, since he saves us from our own sinfulness and makes us children of God. He restores what sin has torn down and destroyed.

Since Jesus Christ is God, and voluntarily came to this world as the gift of God, we can say that he gave himself. So Paul wrote to the Galatian churches: "Grace to you and peace from God the Father and our Lord Jesus Christ, who gave himself for our sins to deliver us from the present evil age, according to the will of our God and Father" (Gal. 1:3-4).

Jesus is like God in being a giver of gifts. So he gave himself for our salvation. In this way he gave his all for us, the greatest gift we could possibly have. He gave his life as a ransom for us, to redeem us from sin (Mark 10:45, Matt. 20:28; Luke 22:19). No greater gift could be given, as he held back nothing which was for our good. He gave his all.

God Gives All Good Gifts. In describing the willingness of our heavenly Father to give to us, Jesus compared our giving to that of God: "If you then, who are evil, know how to give good gifts to your children, how much more will your Father who is in heaven give good things to those who ask him!" (Matt. 7:11). In this, God is like the best of earthly fathers, only infinitely better.

As James puts it, God is the giver of all good gifts: "Every good endowment and every perfect gift is from above, coming down from the Father of lights with whom there is no variation or shadow due to change" (James 1:17).

The Spirit A Gift of God

In Luke's version of the statement quoted above from Matthew 7:11, Jesus says more specifically what "good things" God gives to us: "If you then, who are evil, know how to give good gifts to your children, how much more will the heavenly Father give the Holy Spirit to those who ask him!" (Luke 11:13). After salvation from sin, the greatest gift God gives to us on earth is the Holy Spirit himself. When Peter preached on the Day of Pentecost and the convicted crowd asked what they should do, he told them: "Repent, and be baptized every one of you in the name of Jesus Christ for the forgiveness of your sins; and you shall receive the gift of the Holy Spirit" (Acts 2:38).

Paul wrote to the Corinthians in his second letter and said that God has given Christians this great gift of the Spirit. "But it is God who establishes us with you in Christ and has commissioned us; he has put his seal upon us and given us his Spirit in our hearts as a guarantee" (2 Cor. 1:22-23; Compare 1 Thess. 4:8 and Rom. 5:5).

The Holy Spirit is never simply the giver of gifts or powers to human beings. He is Himself the Gift of God. He is a greater gift than any gift He might give us. So the gift of the Spirit is the Holy Spirit himself!

This fact has important consequences. Since the Holy Spirit is the gift of God, and we have his abiding presence with us, then it would not be right for us to want what he can do for us more than we want his own presence. We should love the Giver more than any of his gifts. We should want his presence with us more than we desire anything he can do for us. We should be satisfied with having him with us, whether he gives us gifts or not.

THE BAPTISM WITH THE SPIRIT

There are several ways in which the New Testament writers describe the outpouring or reception of the Holy Spirit. "Baptized with" or "in" the Holy Spirit (Matt. 3:11; Mark 1:8; Luke 3:16; John 1:33; Acts 1:5; 11:16; 1 Cor. 12:13). "Receive" the Holy Spirit (John 7:39; 14:17; 20:22; Acts 2:38; 8:15, 17, 19; 10:47; 19:2; Gal. 3:2, 14). "Filled with" the Holy Spirit (Acts 2:4; 9:17; 13:52).

A study of these passages shows that the terms are used synonymously, to describe the same experience. The baptism with the Spirit is the same as being filled with the spirit, or receiving the Spirit. This can be seen also from the way Christ speaks of "being baptized with the Spirit" (Acts 1:5), which is the "promise of the Father" (Acts 1:4), and was fulfilled by the disciples being "filled with the Spirit" (Acts 2:4). In the same way, Peter equates "being baptized with the Spirit" (Acts 11:16) with the "gift of the Spirit" (vs. 17), with the Spirit "being poured out" (Acts 10:45), and with "receiving" the Spirit (vs. 47). These are all the same experience.

THE FRUIT OF THE SPIRIT

In the familiar passage in Galatians 5 Paul listed the works of the flesh, by which he meant the results of living without the daily guidance and help of the Holy Spirit. Living without the Spirit is living "in the flesh" and leads to death in the end. One who is living "in the flesh" is dead, because life without God is no life at all.

After listing some of the works of the flesh, Paul lists what he calls the "fruit" of the Spirit. By this he means the moral, spiritual fruit which grows in the personality when that person is filled with the Spirit and living according to the guidance of the Holy Spirit. "But the fruit of the Spirit is love, joy, peace, patience, kindness, goodness, faithfulness, gentleness, self-control" (Gal. 5:22-23).

It has often been noted that the "works" of the flesh are plural, while the "fruit" of the Spirit is singular or collective. Sin is always divisive, and makes a variety of troubles. Yet the work of the Spirit is always harmony and peace. Sin disrupts, but the Holy Spirit builds up. Sin destroys, but the Spirit gives life.

Any pastor knows of people whose lives have been torn apart by sin, and who have felt that their very personalities were divided by the sinful things they have done. This is the way sin works, and Paul was right to use a plural term which expressed this idea.

On the other hand, Paul was surely inspired of God to use a singular term to express the results of the Spirit in one's heart and life. It does not matter whether we think of "fruit" as being singular or collective, the truth is the same. If it is singular, we realize that each of the varieties of fruit he lists can be seen as love in various expressions. The joy and peace we have come from the new love for God and for others. The same is true of patience, gentleness, meekness and all the rest. They are present because God-given love is in our hearts. But if we think of "fruit" as collective, the truth is the same. The fruit of an apple tree is apples. The fruit of a peach tree is peaches. The fruit of a pear tree is pears. The fruit of the Spirit is love, joy, peace, etc. They are all the same kind of godly fruit - the growth caused by the indwelling Holy Spirit.

There is another side to the contrast between works and fruit. Paul seems to make a sharp distinction between them in that "works" are what man does on his own. But "fruit" grows by the power of God. Where the Spirit of life is, fruit grows. And the fruit of the Spirit cannot be manufactured or worked up, by human will alone. Only God can make the fruit grow. Only God can cause true Christian love to grow in the human heart. Only God can grow the fruit of real joy, peace and patience in the human heart.

The Fruit

Love. Christian love comes only from God, so that no one can truly love except a Christian. Is this not what John was implying in 1 John 3-4? "We know that we have passed out of death into life, because we love the brethren" (1 John 3:14). This is one way to know whether we are Christians or not, by our godly love for others. There is a kind, or quality, of love which can only come from the work of the Holy Spirit in the heart. It is this love which is impossible for non-Christians.

The problem stems from the fact that the English word "love" can mean so many different things. Think about these statements: "I love chocolate cake." "I love God." "I love arithmetic." "I love my wife." "I love my husband." "I love everybody." "I love blue." "I love my children." "I love my neighbor."

Love does not mean the same thing in each of these statements, though the same word is used. In some cases perhaps we should say "I like," but we tend to say "love" for all of them. We should have at least a half-dozen different words for these various kinds of feelings or actions expressed, but we do not have such a variety in English.

In the Greek in which the New Testament was written there were many words for love, not all of which are used in the New Testament. *Eros* is passionate love, and is only used once in the New Testament (Gal. 6:14), where it means "passionate love for the sinful world." *Storge*, which is strong affection is used only in a compound word in the New Testament, but not by itself. *Philia* is the common word for love of friends, and by New Testament times seems to be synonymous with *Agapao* (verb form), though the noun had not yet been used in Greek, so far as we know. *Philia* was used in many compound nouns, and some of these are found in the New Testament. So Greek had a much richer vocabulary of love than we do in English, and did not have to make one word do for all the different meanings. Yet the Christians had found in Jesus a new kind of self-giving, self-sacrificing love for which they needed a new word. So they appropriated one. They took the verb *agapao*, which was not so commonly used by non-Christians, and used the noun form of it (agape) to express the godly love which they had seen in Christ, and which they knew to be the love of God. It is so scarce outside of the New Testament until the Second Century A.D. that we are not sure whether it was used or not. At any rate, it had not been contaminated by pagan feelings and ideas, as had some of the other words. So they used it to express the new kind of godly love which they had learned in Christ.

This Christian love is given to us by the Holy Spirit, as Paul plainly said: "Because God's love has been poured into our hearts through the Holy Spirit which has been given to us" (Rom. 5:5b). So far as the result of being filled with the Spirit is concerned, this is the most important passage in the New Testament. Christian love is more important than any miraculous power God might give us through the Holy Spirit. Paul made this clear in 1 Corinthians 13, which we shall examine in chapter five. For now, it is enough to see that Christian love is different from all else that is called love.

Joy. There is a difference between the joy given by the Spirit and the happiness which comes from feeling good. The happiness which comes from physical and emotional well-being can not carry one through much trouble, but the joy of the Holy Spirit can do just that. We can be happy when everything is going our way, but we can have the joy of the Spirit when everything seems to be against us. Happiness is transient; the joy of the Spirit is eternal. Happiness depends too much on circumstances; Christian joy can persist in the worst of circumstances.

The word "joy" occurs sixty times in the New Testament and the word "rejoice" seventy-four times. Paul wrote a letter to the Philippians a letter in which he used the Greek words for "joy" and "rejoice" 26 times in four chapters. One could almost say that the theme of the book is "rejoice." Yet he wrote this from prison! So the joy of a Christian, the joy which is the fruit of the indwelling Holy Spirit is not dependent on good outward circumstances. Since it grows from within, it is there in spite of the circumstances.

This joy can be seen as closely related to love. True love brings with it a quality of love previously unknown. Love for God brings with it a joy in knowing God's love and God's presence. Out of this love for God grows a love for others which also produces a joy which has a deeper source than pleasure in pleasant circumstances.

Peace. The English word can never do justice to the Biblical concept represented by *shalom* in the Old Testament, and by *eirene* in the New Testament. The English word is primarily negative - expressing the absence of war or turmoil. But the Biblical concept is positive, and refers to physical, mental and spiritual well-being which comes from the blessing of God. This peace can come only from God. It cannot be produced by our human striving, nor achieved by the unconverted. It is truly a fruit of the Spirit, and grows as one lives for God over the years.

Arlo Newell was right on target when he said: "The true peace revealed in God's Word is not simply the absence of frustration, faults, and failures. It is not the state of being freed from all anxieties and worries. Rather, it is produced by the presence of the Holy Spirit, abiding as the dove of peace. It's a peace that comes only when we cease striving to be righteous in our human goodness and allow the Prince of Peace to possess us completely."[86] This is why it is a fruit of the Spirit, rather than a matter of human attainment.

Longsuffering. The word comes originally from Tyndale, the Sixteenth Century translator. In one place, Coverdale, who got the word from Tyndale, translated "longe-wrath" (his spelling), which almost exactly corresponds to the Greek and Hebrew words. It means bearing up a long time under trouble or opposition without responding in anger or despair.

The meaning of the word is seen in 2 Peter 3:9, where Peter is explaining why God has so long refrained from destroying the world because of its wickedness: "The Lord is not slow about his promise as some count slowness, but is forbearing (KJV "longsuffering") toward you, not wishing that any should perish, but that all should reach repentance." Since this is the attitude of God, it should be ours as well. But if we are to be godly in this sense, it can only come from the working of God's Spirit within us. It is a fruit of the Spirit.

Kindness. it has been said that some people "suffer long" but are not "kind" to others during their suffering. There is some truth in this. We all know what kindness is, but it is hard to practice at times. We find it easier to recognize the unkindness of our actions than to control our actions in the midst of responding to the unkindness of others. Yet kindness, a fruit of the Spirit, must be cultivated if we are to grow more and more like Christ. In such times the best cultivation must include watering with the tears of repentance. The Holy Spirit can cause kindness to grow within us over the months and years if we will allow Him to work.

Goodness. Not only must we show kindness to others, but if we are to be like God, we must shower goodness on others as God pours out good things on us. God does not limit himself to the goodness we deserve, but gives us far more than we desire. He does not always give us what we desire, but gives us what we would desire if we knew as much as he does about what we need, or ought to have. He does this out of the goodness of his love for us. We ought to be good to others as God is good to us.

This goodness of the Christian is also a fruit of the Spirit. We can seek to imitate our highest ideal of goodness, but only the Holy Spirit can grow the real thing in our hearts.

Faith. Faith, in the Bible, always includes the idea of faithfulness. It is more than merely believing certain facts, but is belief in God. The one who believes in God is made faithful because of the firmness God causes to grow in the soul. This can only come as fruit grown in the Spirit. It is not something we can create in ourselves. That is why Paul lists it as a fruit of the Spirit.

Gentleness. As God is gentle with us, so we must learn to be gentle with others, so as not to hurt them. We must seek to help everyone we contact, not ever to hurt. One way to understand what is hurtful to others is to think of the things which hurt us. Do we want others to speak sharply to us, and say they are doing it for our good? Then we should seek to be kind and gentle in our seeking to work with others. This is the way the Holy Spirit will seek to lead us to act.

Self-control. This is what is meant by the King James term "temperance." It requires one to have the inner strength given by the Spirit, so that one does not have to react to others in unkind, cruel ways, but can control emotions enough to treat others as they should be treated, no matter what they do. Surely this is not the natural, easy way, but it is the Christian way. This kind of self-control can be cultivated, but it must be grown by the Spirit working in us.

SPIRITUAL WORSHIP AND WORK

A major work of the Spirit is to build up the church. This entails building us together in a fellowship, or communion which is more real than any other communion could ever be. For this reason the Spirit gives gifts to the church.

Israel, the Old Testament people of God, was built on the deliverance from Egypt. The church, the New Testament people of God, is built on deliverance from sin through Jesus Christ (Mat. 1:2; Acts 2:47). In Ephesians, chapter two begins with the description of this deliverance from sin, and chapter three shows how God seeks to bring about the unity of his people. The prayer at the end of chapter three is that Christ may "dwell in your hearts through faith," as you are being rooted and grounded in love (vs. 17). This can come about as we are strengthened by his Spirit (vs. 16). Then the suggestion is made that God is "able to accomplish abundantly far more than all we can ask or imagine" (vs.20). Is it possible that God could, through the continued work of the Holy Spirit, bring about some real unity in the church? That would surely be beyond the belief of many!

The Two-Fold Work of the Church

Under the direction of the Holy Spirit, the church has a two-fold work—to strengthen itself, and to build up society. The church itself must be strong, and this involves worship, instruction and nurturing Christians. The responsibility to society is fulfilled by evangelism and all the means we have to make the world a better place. We can consider each of them briefly in turn.

Worship. Group worship, wherever it is conducted, is an important part of the work of the church. Worshiping God with other people can be vitally important to the life of the individual Christians. This is why the disciples, after Pentecost began meeting together in the temple and in their homes for worship, praise and testimony (Acts 2:42-47; 4:23-31). Singing is important in worship, as it was in the early church. "As you sing psalms and hymns and spiritual songs among yourselves, singing and making melody to the Lord in your hearts, giving thanks to God the Father at all times and for everything in the name of the Lord Jesus Christ" (Eph. 5:19-20).

We should never neglect or denigrate the public, corporate worship of the church. There has come into the church in some quarters a tendency to say that this is just "talking to ourselves" when we ought to be speaking to others. Yet this work of gathering together to worship the Lord who saved us is a vital part of the task of the church. We should help each other in this way to grow in our own spiritual development, and learn the things which will help us to do the work of evangelism. If we do not go to church services, we neglect the most effective means we have of encouraging one another and helping one another live the holy, victorious lives we must live before the world.

Nurturing. In thinking of the value of gathering together for worship, we need to remember that we are first "babes in Christ" and need much help and encouragement from other Christians. This, then, is a vital part of the work of the church, which is all too often neglected. The church needs to plan ways of nurturing new Christians. Every Christian needs to be taught how to live for God, and how to teach others to do the same.

Instruction. The need for instruction in the deeper things of God and his will for us is easy to neglect. We need more of the spirit of Priscilla and Aquila, who took Apollos and taught him more about the word of God, so he could be a better worker (Acts 18:24-28). All of us need to be more like the people of Beroea, who were called "more noble" since they daily searched the scriptures to learn the truth of the gospel (Acts 17:10-12). Instruction is not merely for children.

Evangelism/Missions.

The task of reaching the lost around the church is the work of evangelism. This cannot be achieved by "evangelistic meetings" alone, as we know. But those can be very much a part of the work of evangelism;. We need to preach to the world, as well as to one another.

But the work of evangelistic preaching must be coupled with the holy lives of the people in the congregation. Each Christian must live in such a way as to be like "Stars in a dark world" (Phil 2:15, Moffatt translation). We are "People of the light," not night" (1 Thess. 5:1-8).

The church needs to be working to change the nation for Christ. It is not always fitting for the church as a whole to take certain political actions which the individual members ought to be taking. But if the Christians do not seek to make the world a better place, who will? We can see the problems of our politics, and need to make our voice heard on the side of right and godliness.

World-wide missions is a necessary part of our church task. We know today that we cannot neglect this task, or put it off until our own nation is fully Christian. That may never come to be, but it cannot stop us from doing the work of God wherever we have the opportunity.

Christians in every country must feel the need and necessity for giving of our means to spread the gospel to all who have not heard it, or who have not heeded it. No one is exempt from the urgency of this task. If we have little, we can give little, but we must do what we can, in response to Matthew 28:19-20.

Work in Society

David F. Wells, in his analysis of the church at the end of the century, said, "The provision of social relief is a largely neural activity, however, and it often looks much the same regardless of the disparate theological springs from which it arises. As a matter of fact, it can also serve as a substitute for theology"[87]

This means that social work in the community is not the primary work of the church, though it is part of it. The church needs to be sure to do the work that only the church can do, while not neglecting to do what is possible of other work. The work of feeding, housing and clothing the poor must be done by every person in the community who has any compassion for others. We do not lose that compassion, but gain more, when we become Christian. However, this is not the primary task of the church. Not every church can or should set up a soup kitchen, a day care facility, housing for the homeless or a free clothing shop.

The church, as a church, has an obligation to itself, to God, to other Christians, to the community, to the nation, and to the world. Blessed is the congregation of Christians who know how to balance these responsibilities and give them the proper priorities.

CHAPTER 20

Gifts of the Spirit

> The gifts he gave were that some would be apostles, some prophets, some evangelists, some pastors and teachers, to equip the saints for the work of ministry, for building up the body of Christ, until all of us come to the unity of the faith and of the knowledge of the Son of God, to maturity, to the measure of the full stature of Christ (Eph. 4:11-14).

To whom are the gifts given? Why are they given? Are the gifts given to individuals for their pleasure and use? How do the gifts of the Spirit compare with the fruit of the Spirit? If one receives a gift, can it be lost? Which is the most important gift?

We have seen in the previous chapter that the gift of the Spirit is the Holy Spirit himself. But the giving God gives not only the Holy Spirit, but also a variety of abilities, which are in 1 Corinthians 12 called "gifts" (Gr. χαρισματα).

The only extended discussion of the "gifts of the Spirit" is in First Corinthians 12. Like the other topics in this letter, the gifts are discussed because of the troubles caused by the false understanding of them by the Corinthian Christians.

MANY GIFTS FROM ONE SPIRIT

There are five lists of spiritual gifts (χαρισματα): Romans 12:4-6, 1 Corinthians 12:8-10; 12:28; 12:29-30; Ephesians 4:11. Each list is different. Since no two of the lists are alike, one wonders how many Paul would have listed if he had written about them in one more place. One gets the impression that the Holy Spirit simply qualifies and empowers each person to do the task at hand, whatever it might be. There is then no set list of gifts. The Holy Spirit can do in and through each of us just what is needed, even if it is something which has never been done before.

Those writers are unscriptural, then, who speak of the "nine gifts of the Spirit." They do this by looking at one list only. Yet Paul listed 19 or 20. (The total number depends on whether we count them in the original Greek, where we find 20, or in one of the common English versions, which may give more or less).

Only "prophecy" is in all five lists. "Teachers" is in four lists. In three lists are: "Healings," "miracles," "tongues," "apostles." In only two lists: "Translating." Eight are in one list only.

Yet all of the gifts have the same source. As Paul says repeatedly, the gifts are different, but they all come from the same Holy Spirit. The unity of the church is assured by the unity of the Spirit who puts it together and works in it. "For just as the body is one and has many members, and all the members of the body, though many, are one body, so it is with Christ. . . . Now you are the body of Christ and individually members of it" (1 Cor. 12:12, 27).

Furthermore, the equal validity of all the gifts is assured by the fact that the same Holy Spirit gives all of them. In every case, the same Holy Spirit is working all things in all the people (vs. 6). "All these are inspired by one and the same Spirit, who apportions to each one individually as he wills" (vs. 11). "Now there are varieties of gifts, but the same Spirit; and there are varieties of service, but the same Lord; and there are varieties of working, but it is the same God who inspires them all in everyone. To each is given the manifestation of the Spirit for the common good" (verses. 4-7).

All of the gifts are equally valid. No one is to be exalted above the others, since all are useful in the church. Whatever God does in and through us, he does for the good of the church, and he knows what he is doing. He does not work in us needlessly or carelessly. He knows how to build up the church by working in us as individuals. He knows how to use each of us in such a way as to accomplish in the whole church just what he desires.

There is no reason for us to tell God what to do in us. He knows just what to do and how to do it. If he chooses to use us in a prominent position, or in one which seems useless to us, it is not our business to complain, or to seek for a higher position. Our business is to submit gladly to his will for us, and do what we can where we are in the church. Only in this way can we be of service to God. Whatever we do that is to glorify ourselves, cannot truly glorify God. Our work must be to exalt Christ, not ourselves. Our purpose must be to glorify God. "Like good stewards of the manifold grace of God, serve one another with whatever gift each of you has received. . . . so that God may be glorified in all things through Jesus Christ" (1 Pet. 4:10-11).

It is not by accident that Paul's prose-poem on love is found between the discussion of the Spirit in the Church, and that of the abuse of the gift of languages. Love for the church, which binds the individuals together in the church, supersedes every form of spiritual individualism. Paul's constant emphasis is on the fact that our first desire should be to build up and strengthen the church.

Paul puts the stress on the church, not on the individual person in the church. He makes it clear that the work of the Spirit is not to build up the individual, but to build up the church. This emphasis is strong in both chapter 12 and chapter 13, and is the very reason for chapter 13. It is part of the foundation of chapter 14. As human beings we have a tendency to be self-centered in many ways. But the Holy Spirit working within us seeks to counteract this tendency and help us see that the best work we can do is for others.

This does not minimize either the importance of the individual persons, or the variety of the contributions each can make to the church as a whole. But it is the church which is important, not the individual alone. The importance of the individual is seen in his contribution to the whole. God loves me, but the fellowship of the Christians is more important and valuable than I am. So I cannot afford to seek my own pleasure, but the good of the church. "Love does not insist on its own way" (1 Cor. 13:5). Love seeks for the good of the church and the glory of God.

The Gifts Listed

Not all of these are referred to as "gifts" (*charismata*) in Paul's writings. For example, the Bible never speaks of a "gift of tongues." And we must understand that the Greek word *charisma* does not mean just the same as the English word "gift". The Greek word used by Paul puts the stress on the fact that it is the grace of God which is working in the person to help the church. The English word seems to be used to mean that one has been born with a special talent or ability. As when we say that one has a gift for speaking, meaning that from childhood the person has been more fluent in speaking than the average. This is not at all what Paul had in mind. He writes, not of innate abilities, but of special working of the grace of God in the person through the Holy Spirit, to do the will of God in the church.

Every person has some natural abilities, and these are all given by God, in a very general sense. We do not invent our own innate potential abilities, though we can cultivate them. Every Christian has the responsibility to use and develop whatever abilities one has, and to use them to the glory of God.

It cannot be overemphasized that the *charismata* are not natural abilities, but the working of God's grace in the individual Christian. They are "grace-gifts." They are not necessarily permanent. If one backslides, for instance, he loses both the saving grace of God in Christ Jesus, and the special grace of God in the Holy Spirit by whom he was enabled to work in the Kingdom of God. There is no indication in the New Testament that one can always do what is possible at one time. Paul stresses in his discussion that each "grace-gift" is the result of the work of the Holy Spirit in that person. God's Spirit can work in and through the committed Christian in whatever way is needed at the moment. Paul gives lists of some of these special ways.

Prophecy. This is the only gift which is in all five lists. It refers to the proclamation of God's truth under the anointing of the Spirit. In other words, it means preaching. The Greek word (*prophemi*) means "speaking for" someone. The prophet speaks for God, by declaring the gospel. Contrary to popular thought, prediction is not the basic aspect of prophecy. The Old Testament prophets predicted the coming of Christ and his Kingdom, and those events which helped prepare the nation for Christ. Prophecy is not a crystal ball, to satisfy our curiosity about future events. If God reveals something of our future, it is for a specific purpose, to help us to carry out his will. The essential aspect of the work of the prophet is preaching the word of God in the power of the Holy Spirit. Prophecy is in all the lists, and is emphasized by Paul because it is the means by which the Gospel is given to others.

Teaching. Teaching is found in four of the five lists. It is the essential work of instructing people in the meaning of the Bible. Twenty-four times in the Gospels, Jesus is described as teaching. Paul, in his missionary work, spent much of his time in teaching. Every preacher and teacher needs to have the help of the Holy Spirit in teaching. Some are better at it than others, but each has to do the best he can with the ability God has given.

Apostle. In the New Testament the word "apostle" is applied chiefly to the Twelve, and to Paul, who were not only preachers of the gospel, but independent witnesses to Christ in his earthly ministry. They were the pioneer missionaries of the gospel. In this strict sense, there could never be any others. In any case, they performed their ministry in the power of the Spirit, by whom they had been chosen.

Miracles. Healings. These may be considered together, since they are so closely related. Each is in three lists, and they are much alike. There are people through whom God has chosen to bring healing to the sick, and to perform other miracles of mercy. Any Christian is able to pray for the sick with the result that they are healed. But God is able to work in and through some Christians in a special way. Healing can be miraculous, but so can many other works of God be called miracles.

Tongues. Meaning "languages." This is in three lists, (1 Cor. 12:10, 28, 30), though the wording is slightly different. It is explicitly stated in verse 31 that all do not speak in tongues. It is clear from the only description of this work (Acts 2:4-11) that it means speaking in a recognizable human language which one has not learned, but which can be easily understood by one who knows that language. If I were to speak in Swahili, it would have to be by the help of the Holy Spirit. But I have had students who speak it as their native language. If they heard me speaking in Swahili, they would understand me clearly. But that is not necessary, as they also speak English. We shall consider this in more detail later.

Translating. This is only in one list, as are all the following. It is the anointing of the Spirit in the translation of what is spoken in another language. Anyone who has preached through an interpreter knows that it is one thing for the interpreter to have an understanding of both languages, and quite another for the interpreter to be able to translate both accurately and effectively from one language to another. At such a time, one prays for a God-given, Spirit-filled interpreter. Without such a one, the best delivered sermon can be rendered ineffective.

Distinguishing between spirits. Every Christian ought to be able to distinguish between good and evil spirits in people. Yet some are enabled by the Spirit to see more clearly and quickly that a person is not what he seems to be, or claims to be. This is a valuable gift.

Utterance of wisdom. It is one thing to know what to say, and it is quite another to be able to speak the right words of wisdom at the right time. In my experience, Elsie Egermeier was one who had this gift. But she did not feel that it was a gift, since she worked and prayed to find just the right thing to say to others to help them.

Word of knowledge. This is closely related to teaching, and is also closely related to wisdom. But knowledge tends to imply that the person has studied and researched to learn what he now says. Yet some have much knowledge without being able to express it clearly in words. This is the gift of God.

Faith. All Christians have faith as the gift of God, since it is a prerequisite to salvation. But to some is given special faith to trust even when others have given up.

Helping. There can be no gift more needed than the gift of helping others in the Kingdom of God. Blessed is the church in which one or more Christians have the gift of helping. It may seem more desirable to be the big worker, but every worker must have many helpers.

Administrators. Many want to be leaders, but no one can be a leader if one has no followers. Some are better at planning and administering plans than others. Some find it easier to inspire others to follow their leadership. And the Spirit gives some few a gift of leadership which is sorely needed. The worst problems arise because of some who are determined to be leaders, and seeks to put down all other leadership in order to rise to the top. This is not a gift, but a sin.

Evangelism. This Greek word simply means telling the gospel to those who need to hear it. It may mean preaching to vast crowds, but it may also mean a quiet witness over the back fence, or across the lunch table.

Pastor. The Greek word literally means "shepherd". The great pastor may be a good preacher, or may not be. But the pastor knows how to help the people in his care. He knows how to feed them good spiritual food, to encourage them to do the work of God, and to give them spiritual rest.

Serving. This is closely akin to "helping." It means exactly what it says, simply serving the needs of others. This requires true humility and love, but we all ought to pray for the ability to do it well.

Encouraging. Most of us remember someone who had the gift of encouraging Christians who were about to give up, or felt they could not go on. This requires close observation of others, and caring enough to see when they need a spiritual lift. What a blessing this can be at the time.

Giving. We are made to feel ashamed when we see how freely and joyfully some Christians give of themselves to the church and to anyone in need. It is not only the giving of money, but of self.

Showing compassion. The gift of both feeling and showing compassion is one we all need at some time in our life. It is good that the Holy Spirit knows how to lead certain persons to be especially good at this.

Exhorting. This is the ability of persuasive appeal. God gives some the gift of teaching the gospel, others the gift of effective preaching, and to still others the gift of persuading sinners to do what they ought to do - come to Christ. It is also the gift of persuading Christians to move forward in their life and work for God.

Probably over the centuries, God has given many special gifts which are not in these five lists. The Holy Spirit is able in any situation, to enable a Christian to do what needs to be done at that time, in the way in which it needs to be effected. New inventions, like radio and television, may call for special abilities, but the Holy Spirit is always able to provide them for the church.

Each of these gifts is an enhancement of ordinary human abilities. The Holy Spirit works with what we already have, and makes us capable of doing more than we could never do without him.

Nature Of the Gifts

They are given to the church. As we have said before, the gifts are not given to the individual Christian for his benefit. They are given to the church, for the building up of the body of Christ. This is especially seen in Ephesians 4:11-12.

They are given as God chooses. "All these are inspired by one and the same Spirit, who apportions to each one individually as he wills" (1 Cor. 12:11). "God arranged the organs in the body, each one of them, as he chose" (vs. 18). "And God has appointed in the church . . ." (vs. 27). It is good for us to pray for gifts, but it is not proper for us to demand or seek a particular gift. Neither must we seek to manufacture a gift for ourselves. God is Lord, and decides just what to give each person. The choice is his, not ours.

There is a variety of gifts. There is no hint in the Bible that any one congregation ought to have all of the gifts, or that one person ought to expect more than one. Some of us may wonder if we have even one. But if the Spirit is given freedom to work in and through us, He will do in us just what he sees best.

Since there is such a variety, there is no Scriptural support for seeking to receive any particular gift. There is no gift which makes one more spiritual, or closer to God, than other gifts. No gift makes one more fit for heaven than those who do not have that gift. No one gift is the proof of the presence of the Holy Spirit. No one gift is proof of the approval of God. No gift is *the* sign that the Holy Spirit is working in us. The proof of the Spirit is the Spirit himself. If he is in us, we know him and he knows us, and that is all the proof we need. It is all we can ever have.

There is variety because many kinds of work are necessary if the church is to be built up and strengthened. And this is the purpose of the Holy Spirit in giving them. His objective is not to make us feel good, or to assure us of his presence, but to help us build up others. And this is not to edify individuals only, but to strengthen the whole church, as it is made up of individual Christians.

One of our problems is that we take the short view instead of the eternal view. If we can study the history of the church for the last 2,000 years, we will begin to see how slowly but surely the church has been brought to its present state. There are more Christians on earth now than there have ever been before. There are more preachers, preaching to more sinners, than ever before in the history of the world. By means of modern technology one preacher can preach the Gospel to more people than Jesus preached to in his whole earthly ministry. Granted that some are abusing that privilege, and preaching something less than the gospel. But we can rejoice that it can be done, and is being done. God's Holy Spirit is working in the world now to build up the church in ways beyond our comprehension.

No one of us can do much, but we must do what God enables us to do, and leave the rest to God. It is his church, and he will take good care of it. So we do what we can, and trust God to continue the work through others.

There Is Unity In Diversity. There are a variety of gifts, but they all come from the one Spirit. He works in and through all of us to bring about a heavenly unity in the church. It is the Holy Spirit who works to bind us together in one. As each of us does what we can in the Lord, the Spirit builds us up together into one body, the body of Christ (1 Cor. 12:14-27). All of us are necessary, if the church is to be what God wills. So none of us should feel more important, or less necessary because of the work we are doing, or the abilities we have or do not have.

It is not wise for us to be too introspective about our gifts. To be overly concerned with finding out what gift we have, or what gifts others have or do not have, leads to trouble in the church. It makes us more concerned with analyzing ourselves than with doing the work of God. Let us simply pray and work to fit into the church in a useful way, and let God take care of the final results.

There is no hint in the Bible teaching that we should find out what gift we have, and no Christian should be concerned about that. Use your abilities for God as you have opportunity, and have no concern about deciding whether these abilities are natural or supernatural. Every good gift comes from God (James 1:17), so do what you are able to do in such a way as to glorify God. If God wants you to do more, he will make that possible.

It is not the number of gifts one has that is important, but what one does for the Lord. No one should announce "I have a gift of the Spirit, and I must use it now." No person should announce the possession of a certain gift. If this is true, the church will recognize it in due time. The gifts are for the church, and we must find ways of using them so as to edify the church.

Blessed is the Christian who is just as willing to listen as to speak or sing; to be taught as to teach; to be helped as to help.

God governs the church. It is clear from the New Testament that God is in control of the church. This does not mean that his control is absolute, for individuals can so easily get outside the will of God. Yet Jesus built the church in the first place, and is continuing to build it according to his plan. Through the work of the Holy Spirit in individuals, he seeks to direct the organization and operation of the church at all times.

It is He who chooses whom to empower to do a particular work for Him. We have no right to demand that he give us any special power or ability. He will never do so for our exaltation or satisfaction.

Speaking in Tongues

We have been considering the gifts in general, but because of the present interest in "the gift of tongues" we will give it some special consideration. Perhaps we can do this best in seven propositions summing up what the New Testament teaches about it.

1. What was spoken in tongues, or with tongues, was intelligible to those who were familiar with the particular language being spoken, as we can see from Acts 2:11. It was not a meaningless babbling, ecstatic utterance, or heavenly language, but real, human languages.

2. What was spoken conveyed messages of prayer, praise, thanksgiving, and the gospel of Jesus Christ (Acts 2:11; 1 Cor. 14:14-17).

3. True tongues edified the person uttering them, therefore they were understandable to the speaker.

4. The fact that they were capable of interpretation also indicates that they were actual human languages. There is nothing in the New Testament about a "prayer language" or "heavenly language." God understands all the languages any human being understands, but when he speaks to human beings, he uses whatever language they use. There is no example in the Old Testament or the New Testament of anyone needing an interpreter to understand what God had said to that individual. When we speak, we should seek to speak with the mind as well as with the heart (1 Cor. 14:15).

5. Even though the speaker knew what he was saying, and certain foreigners could also understand if they were present, others could not understand. Therefore, speaking in foreign languages was not suitable for public worship except in the special circumstance of a foreigner not being

able to speak the language of the others. There is no point in speaking Chinese to one who only understands French. The hearers were not helped. Paul rebuked the spirit of emulation which caused this (1 Cor. 14:19-20).

6. That these are human languages is consistent with what is said in the New Testament. Luke makes it clear that this is what is meant in Acts, and what Paul says is consistent with this. The basic rule of exegesis is that we must choose the explanation which is consistent with plain teachings of the Bible. Difficult passages must be interpreted in the light of those which are clear. Paul points out to the Corinthians that it is possible and preferable to speak under the inspiration of the Holy Spirit and at the same time speak so as to be understood by those who hear (1 Cor. 14:15.

This discussion by Paul implies that some of the Corinthians believed that unless they were speaking what could not be understood, they were not speaking "in the Spirit." They had gotten this idea from the worship of certain Greek gods. Paul assures them that it was not only possible to speak understandably "in the Spirit" but that it was profitable to the church, and therefore preferable.

7. Some ask why there is a separate gift of interpretation, if it is true that the speaker knows what he is saying. Why cannot the speaker himself interpret what he had said? Consider the example of a person who is learning a new language. Such a one may write the message so as to deliver it accurately and understandably. Such a one could speak the message clearly and forcefully in their native language, and could then give the interpretation in the language of the hearers. But the interpretation is halting and flat as the speaker is trying to remember how to pronounce the words written out. It would be better to have someone with the gift of interpretation to translate for the hearers in their language.

The natural difficulty of making a good and effective translation is known only by those who have tried to preach through an interpreter. Missionaries, for this reason, often find it frustrating to speak through an interpreter. Even if the interpreter has the words right, the spirit is lacking. On the other hand, a missionary may understand what is spoken in a language one is learning, and yet be unable to preach in that language. Paul, who had much experience in this way, in spite of the variety of languages he spoke, no doubt had often prayed for the interpreter to have the gift of the Holy Spirit for interpretation.

Tongues in Corinth

In writing this first letter to the church in Corinth, Paul condemns the church for a variety of distortions of the gospel, one of which was the speaking in tongues. They were using this in a way that did not glorify God nor build up the church (1 Cor. 12—14). The whole letter was dealing with problems, and this was one of them. If it had not been causing division and trouble there, it probably would not have been mentioned in the New Testament, except in the textually difficult Mark 16:17.

The key to the discussion of the gifts of the Spirit in 1 Corinthians 12--14 is seen in the central chapter on love. Paul first shows clearly that what one is able to do does not make that person superior to any other, since we are all parts of the same body and equally necessary. He then explains that the far better way is to bind the whole church together in the love of God. It is the love of God in our hearts, put there by the Holy Spirit (Rom. 5:5) which Paul emphasizes in this whole passage. Everything else is subordinate to that.

Paul states that the way of love for one another is a far better way than the search for exotic powers of speech or action. "But strive for the greater gifts. And I will show you a still more excellent way" (12:31). As he had indicated before, preaching and teaching were much higher gifts than others. But now he shows that to desire love is to desire the very best gift of all. In doing this, he wrote one of the most beautiful chapters in the whole Bible, and placed it in the center of the discussion of spiritual gifts (1 Cor. 13).

The greatest gift the Holy Spirit can give us is the gift of loving God and loving others. It is the love of God in us which binds us together into a church. It is love which can bear up under all the pressures of living and working together for God. No matter what other "gifts" we may think we have, if we do not have the kind of love for others which only God's Spirit can give, then we are worthless to God.

God's Command

The New Testament does not anywhere command us to speak in tongues, but does give us four basic commandments concerning the Holy

Spirit.
  1. Be filled with the Spirit (Eph. 5:18). The ideal is not self-control, or control by some irrational motivation, but control by the Spirit of God. The Holy Spirit is a rational Spirit, and what he leads us to do will make sense;, and edify.
  2. Grieve not the Holy Spirit (Eph. 4:30).
  3. Quench not the Spirit (1 Thess. 5:19). However, this does not mean that we are to do everything we feel like doing. We often have to quench our own spirits. So we need to learn to distinguish our own spirits from the Spirit of God.
  4. Walk in the Spirit (Gal. 5:16).

Concluding Thoughts

You cannot receive the gifts of the Spirit without being first yielded or committed to the Holy Spirit.

If one loses salvation and goes back into sin, that person loses the gifts of the Spirit, who will not live in a sinner. No one can have the gifts of the Spirit who does not make a holy dwelling for the Spirit of God.

Only imitations of the gifts are demonstrated by sinners.

Gifts of the Holy Spirit are always accompanied by and overshadowed by the fruit of the Spirit. One who does not bear the fruit of the Spirit *does not have the gifts*, though one may have either imitations of the gifts, or great natural abilities.

Chapter 21

Church: Organization and Work

> And to make everyone see what is the plan of the mystery hidden for ages in God who created all things; so that through the church the wisdom of God in its rich variety might now be made known to the rulers and authorities in the heavenly places (Eph. 3:9-11).

What should the church be like in the twenty-first century? Should it look just like the church of the first century? Or should it be whatever we want to make it in our day? What kind of ministry will be needed for the future? What kind of organization?

Any organization can be known by its membership, its reason for being, and its regulations or laws. When we consider the church in the light of these factors we have a beginning for understanding the polity of the church.

First, the control of its membership. The church consists of all who are born again through faith in Jesus Christ. Faith in Him is the requirement for entrance. Jesus is the door (Jn. 10:9). God sets the members in the body as it pleases Him (1 Cor. 12:18). By one Spirit we are baptized in one body (1 Cor. 12:13).

Second, its purpose or rationale for being. It is the servant of God in the world. Its purpose is to do the will of God, and to serve Him by preaching the gospel of salvation in Christ.

Third, its regulation or laws. The law of the church is the law of love. The church is to obey God implicitly. Jesus said we are to do the will of God, just as He came to do the will of God. Members of the church are led by the Spirit of God (Rom. 8:14-16). So the whole church is governed by and through the Holy Spirit.

BIBLICAL PRINCIPLES

It is best to begin our search for Biblical models of church organization and government by gathering up the facts we find in the New Testament. Then we can seek to classify them in modern terms.

General Facts

Church order is not a matter of indifference, as it part of the Gospel. That is, it is part of the witness of the church to the world. What the church is, and the way it operates, is part of the witness of the church to sinners. Since this is true, we need to ask what polity will most fit and facilitate the message of this reformation movement.

If we search the New Testament for the theological concepts and concerns which caused the church to operate as it did, and not in any other way, we find such things as freedom in the Spirit, the importance of the individual, love in Christ for others, and concern for the lost.

The fact that the New Testament church was organized is clearly seen in the fact that there were stated times for meetings (Acts 20:7; Heb. 10:25). Further, we see indications that the work was organized: They chose workers for special needs, as in Acts 6:1-6. They recognized that the apostles had their own work, and should be left free from other responsibilities. and there were qualifications for church work.

God calls to ministry. This call comes through the Holy Spirit, who both calls and enables the person to do the work He chooses for that one. The church only recognizes that call.

God's gifts qualify for leadership (Eph. 4:1-16; Rom. 12:5-8). The church supports those whom the Holy Spirit has called, equipped and used (1 Cor. 16:16; 1 Cor. 9:4 ff.; 1 Thess. 2:7; 2 Thess. 3:9; Gal. 6:6).

Ministers

Deacons. This is the general term for ministers. The Greek word διακονια is used thirty times in the New Testament. The KJV translates it "deacon" three times, "servant" seven times, and "minister" 20 times. A minister is a servant of the church, serving God by serving the church. The "seven" in Acts 6 were not called deacons. Just as they gave themselves to the service (διακονια *diakonia*, anglicized as *deacon*) of tables, so the others gave themselves to the service (διακονια) of the word. To be a deacon was simply to be a helper or worker in the church, and might entail any of a number of kinds of work. We have no example of "ordination" of deacons in any official sense, as has developed since. Jesus was called a deacon, as were others who served in a variety of capacities. It was a function, not an office. The word was used in New Testament times to refer to any worker or helper. So the term may refer to anyone who serves the church in any capacity, from Christ on down to the most humble worker.

Christ himself is called a διακονια in Romans 15:8, where the word is often translated "servant." The very idea of Christian service derives from Christ and the way he served all mankind (Mat. 20:28, Mark 10:45). Since Jesus set the example of loving service, he assures us that the person who wishes to be honored in the kingdom of God should be servant of all others (Mat. 20:27).

Elders, bishops, pastors. Luke first used the term Christians (Acts 11:26), and also was first to speak of Christian "elders" (Ac 11:30; 21:18). The term may have been borrowed from the synagogue. In the Synoptic Gospels, and in the beginning and end of Acts, "elders" is used of the Jewish synagogue elders. They were lay leaders closely associated with the priests. There are no Christian priests in the New Testament.

Since Lightfoot's famous essay "The Christian Ministry" in his commentary on Philippians, 1890, most scholars have agreed that "elders" and "bishops" are used by Paul to refer to the same persons. Elders are never mentioned in the four major books of Paul (Romans, 1 and 2 Corinthians, Galatians).

A. C. Grant says that elders and bishops are the same. "That 'elders' and 'bishops' were in apostolic and subapostolic times the same is now almost universally admitted; in all New Testament references their functions are identical. The most probable explanation of the difference of names is that 'elder' refers mainly to the person and 'bishop' to the function; the name 'elder' emphasizes what he is, while 'bishop,' i.e., 'overseer,' emphasizes what the elder or presbyter does.[88]

Note that in Acts 20:28 the elders are said to be bishops over the churches. So 'elders' and 'bishops' are identical. "Take heed to yourselves, and to all the flock (*poimnio*) over which the Holy Spirit has made you overseers (*episcopous*), to shepherd (*poimainein*) the church of God." Note also that Luke had called these persons "elders" (*presbyteroi*) in 20:17. So the elders = bishops = pastors (shepherds). Compare also John 21:16, where Jesus tells Peter to "feed (*poimaine*) my sheep" = "shepherd, (pastor) my flock." In 1 Peter 5:1-4 Peter instructs the "elders" in the Christian way to "pastor" (shepherd) the flock of God. 1 Peter 2:25 Jesus is the "Shepherd" (*Poimena*) and "Bishop" (*Episkopon*).

Pastoral Authority

The pastor does have authority over the churches, which is related to the pastoral responsibility. Peter speaks of the pastor as exercising oversight (1 Pet. 5:2). Christians are to obey them that rule (Heb. 13:17). But this is not blind submission. It cannot say "Amen" unless it understands what is said, and what this means (1 Cor. 14:16). It is not dictatorial.

> The minister does not own a congregation, although we might infer the opposite from the way some pastors refer to 'my church.' Theologically stated, the congregation belongs to God for God's mission of reconciliation in the world. The congregation. . . calls the minister to help the congregation better serve that mission.
> "In India, I once heard a seminarian describing the power a village healer had over his followers. The seminarian spoke enviously: 'With authority like that, think what we could do to build up a church.' A wise critic. . .said, 'A pastor has some of that mystique. The question is whether to exploit and increase it or try to dispel it. Perhaps you would be usurping the place of Christ in a man's life, to have that power.'[89]

Since the authority of a pastor is coupled with responsibility for the spiritual lives of those in the congregation, it is not something to be taken lightly. The wise pastor will be slow to exercise any authority over the lives of others beyond the clear teachings of the Bible. Even this will be after sincere prayer for guidance. It is all too easy for one to be following personal desires rather than God's guidance.

The Foundations of Ministry

Note that Paul does not appeal to a pastor or leader in the Corinthian church who is able to straighten out the problems of the church, but appeals to the church as a whole. The authority of the pastor is "authority within" the church, not "authority above" it. Peter describes the way in which the authority of the overseer is to be exercised (1 Pet. 5:2).

Ministers are to train the laymen to do the work of the ministry. (Eph. 4:11. J. I. Packer speaks of the "Calamitous Comma" which the King James Version inserts after "saints.") Both ministers and laymen are led by the Spirit of God (Rom. 8:14-16).

Choosing ministers

The church did not choose ministers, though they chose some committees. The Seven were chosen by the church (Ac 6:3-13). These were never called "deacons," but were simply good men chosen to meet a need by doing a particular work. Some of them later went out as preachers. So this was a temporary appointment of an ad hoc committee. In the same way, the church chose to send a committee to Antioch (Acts 15:22), and one to take money to Jerusalem (1 Cor. 16:3).

Timothy had hands laid on him by Paul 2 Tim. 1:6), and by some elders (1 Tim. 4:14). Titus was to appoint elders in every city (Titus 1:5).

Yet in every case, the church seems to be approving and blessing what God has already done. It is the Holy Spirit who chooses and calls ministers of all kinds. This includes even such "natural" ministries as helpfulness, giving, faith, and wisdom. Some of these would not normally be thought of as workings of the Spirit, but Paul says they are.

Not offices, but functions

Many scholars feel that, except for "apostle", there were no official positions or titles in the New Testament church. Any function could be performed by any Christian. To some extent this is due to the fact that there are no Christian priests. The priest in the church is Jesus Christ. The Old Testament priest had to be officially qualified and placed in office. But the priesthood of all believers in Christ obviates the necessity for such "office."

In the Church, all who serve as God chooses are on the same level. God decides what he wants each person to do. So there should be no feelings of superiority (1 Cor. 12:21-25, or of inferiority (12:15-20). Each Christian should rejoice in the gift of the other.

This is strongly supported by Donald Guthrie in discussing the church in the Synoptic Gospels: "The character of the ethical teaching of Jesus excludes the notion of hierarchy among the disciples. . .(Mat. 18:1 ff.; Mk. 9:33f.; Lk. 9:46f.). He also criticized the use of status titles like 'Rabbi'. (Guthrie 1981, 708). In discussing church officials in the Pastoral Epistles, he states: "Clearly in addressing the Thessalonians Paul is more concerned about the function than the office, and it would be true to say that this is generally evident in what we might call his theology of church government." [90] These statements sound even stronger when we recognize that Guthrie seeks in one or two places to find support for official positions in the New Testament.

We must not make the mistake of reading institutionalism into the New Testament list of ministers (*diakonoi* = servants). All of the servants of the church are placed in their work by the Holy Spirit - "charismatic government." One person may perform several functions, or only one. (See the discussion by John Knox, (in Niebuhr and Williams 1956, 10 ff). Every Christian was bound to serve the community according to his abilities and his gifts and there was, at this period, no 'office', to which a man had to be appointed or ordained and which was the prerequisite of service to the community (see 1 Cor. 12:28; Rom. 12:4 ff.). . .They all had to perform a service, that of building up the community of Christ and of considering those outside the community (1 Cor. 14), and the universal Christian service of love (1 Cor. 13), which is a 'still more excellent way' for all.

No "ordination" in the New Testament

There is no specific example or instruction in the New Testament about ordination of ministers in the sense in which it is used today. Modern "ordination" may be a later invention. "Laying on of hands" was associated, not so much with the beginning of a ministry, but with a new work. So it may have been more like "installing" a minister in a new task. The church at Antioch thus laid hands on Paul and Barnabas as they sent them out as missionaries. It is also associated with healing of sickness, benediction, and baptism. What seems to be common to all these uses is the imparting of God's power.

Discipline in the church

Discipline, in the New Testament, is exercised by the church. In the case of Matthew 18:17, Jesus probably refers to the synagogue, but the discipline is in the hands of the group. But, the Corinthian church was urged to settle its own disputes and to maintain internal discipline (1 Cor. 5:5 and in 2 Cor. 2:2). However, Paul may have thought of the church as the sum of all the congregations in a city or locality.

Models of church government

There are three theories about the New Testament and governance today: First, that the New Testament prescribes a form of governance. But those who hold this differ on the form they think is prescribed, so this could scarcely be supported by Scripture. Second, that nothing is said about a form of governance in the New Testament, and that it is left to our discretion. Third, that principles are laid down, and we have to work out our form of governance to suit our needs and desires, based on those principles.

Models as sketched by Leon Morris[91]

The fact is that the New Testament gives some guidance as to the governance of the church, but does not present models which can be easily adopted by the church today. The church was in its infancy, and did not use the same model in each congregation. Rather, the congregations used forms which were familiar to them as a result of their background, and developed organization as it was needed to accomplish their task.

There are three major forms of church government in use today: Episcopal, presbyterian, and congregational. None of these is exclusively prescribed in the New Testament as the only acceptable form. Rather we can discover in the New Testament a prototype of each of the three common forms of government. But that prototype may be only the germ of that principle or form of polity.

Episcopal

This is the system in which the chief ministers of the church, those who have the most authority, are bishops. Others are presbyters (elders) or deacons. Thus the three kinds of ministers are a mark of this model of governance.

Leon Morris, "Those who see an episcopal system in the New Testament point to the function of the apostles (which some feel was passed on to the bishops they ordained), to the position of James of Jerusalem (which is not unlike that of the later bishop), to the function of Timothy and Titus as revealed in the Pastoral Epistles." [92]

Actually, in Jerusalem it was natural for the church to organize itself on the familiar pattern of the synagogue. This was not so natural after that in the Gentile churches. It is interesting to note that the church in Antioch, founded by Hellenistic Jews, refugees from the persecution in Jerusalem, did not make the synagogue their pattern of organization. B. H. Streeter suggests that this may have been deliberate. He bases this conclusion on the fact that five 'prophets and teachers' are named, but no elders."[93] In support of this model, it is said that Peter acted like a bishop in Acts 2--5, and that the apostles ordained others (Acts 6:6 and 1 Tim. 4:14). Yet there is nothing so formal as the later development of ordination, but only appointment and a prayer of dedication, with the laying on of hands.

It is true that there was some ministerial authority, but there was no bishop over other ministers until the second century. Further, there is no evidence that bishops differed from elders, as the terms are used synonymously.

Presbyterian (rule by elders)

This is usually rule by clergy and laity alike. That is, it is the rule by elders (presbyters) and laymen in session. Presbyterianism does not generally hold that only this form is taught or practiced in the New Testament. Some of the reformers in the sixteenth century held this, but few would do so today. Bo Reicke suggests that the apostles served as a collegium in Acts 15.[94] It is clear that the elders held an important place in the New Testament churches. They are identical with the overseers (bishops) and were the pastors of the churches. There were elders in every church.

Yet the same reasons brought against the episcopalian model as the complete understanding of the New Testament militate against the presbyterian. So does what is said below.

Congregational

As the name implies, the whole church votes democratically to decide issues. A second characteristic is the autonomy of the local church. In regard to the first, C. E. Brown wrote that the church is in reality a theocracy, but that from a human standpoint it looks like a democracy.[95] That is, God can only work through individual Christians, by His Holy Spirit. So when we seek to make decisions, each Christian has a right to express his opinion through voting, or through the Quaker way of seeking through prayer and discussion to find the "consensus of the group" before deciding.

Congregational government is chiefly supported by the concept of the priesthood of all believers (1 Pet. 2:9), coupled with the fact that Christ is head of the church (Col. 1:18, etc). It is also true that the most humble believer can come boldly to the throne of God (Heb. 10:19). No priest is necessary.

A caveat needs to be inserted here. While God loves all people alike, and while the Holy Spirit works in all Christians, there are two facts that cause some people to be more able to lead than others. The first is that we are not all equal in natural abilities—physical, intellectual, and emotional. Second, the Holy Spirit's work in each person is limited by the natural abilities and development of that person. One with a well-trained mind may be able to grasp the leadership of the Spirit much more quickly and accurately than one who is illiterate. This extreme illustration may help us to see that though each may be filled with the Spirit, all are not equally able to take advantage of his work within.

What we are saying about democracy in the church is that being filled with the Spirit is like a bundle of possibilities. Some people are able to make more of those possibilities than others. Two men may have equally sharp axes, but one can cut down a number of trees with the axe while the other is trying to get one down. So it is with the Spirit, who does not do our work for us, but rather helps us and leads us. But one is more able to understand and follow the leading of the Spirit than another, and therefore may be more helpful and useful in the church than others. Yet all must have the spirit of meekness and humility to work together in good harmony with all the rest. No one person is to dictate to all the rest.

Theocratic?

The church is not truly a democracy, though it may look like one at times. Jesus Christ is the head of the church, and the church must always work hard at the task of finding his will. We must seek to be aware of our own feelings and desires, and learn what God would have us do. It is not easy to do, but we must learn as much as we can about God, ourselves and others, so that we can understand more and more about how to do the right and Christian thing in all the work of the church.

Real troubles arise when ungodly people gain control of the church, as they sought to do in Corinth. Paul had to write a strong and disturbing letter to the church to persuade them to see what had happened. Part of what he said is in 1 Corinthians 5, and there are indications that he wrote them a letter which we do not have, dealing with the same problem. They had allowed a man guilty of sexual immorality to be considered a part of the church, and trouble ensued. No doubt he had friends and family who supported him in his false pretension to be a Christian. And No doubt the church people were slow to condemn, because they did not want to hurt his feelings. In his self-centered boldness he and his friends were no doubt arrogant (1 Cor. 5:2) and determined to have their way. Paul said they should not be considered a part of the church while continuing in sin so insolently. They were to do this for the sake of the sinner, and for the sake of the church.

As when Israel chose to have a king, like others around them, the church can easily choose either a dictator/pastor or let unspiritual people lead them. It is difficult for loving, godly people to be strong against friends who are sinful and determined to lead.

Each local congregation needs to be taught "the way of God more accurately" (Acts 18:26) so that they can know how to understand the ways of God. This requires a pastor who knows the Bible and theology, and who is humble enough to know that pastors make mistakes too. Such a pastor can lead the church into seeking hard to be a theocracy.

Churches: Autonomous, but Interdependent

The churches of the New Testament seem to be autonomous. But it is still true that the congregational autonomy is never taught, nor is democratic decision-making prescribed. It may be that the old Quaker meeting is closer to the New Testament practice.

Congregations were interdependent, rather than totally independent of one another. "Paul expects one church to serve another with the gifts that have been specially bestowed on it. If Jerusalem has served the Gentile churches with the 'spiritual gifts of preaching, it has been served by them with the 'fleshly' gifts of the collection (Rom. 15:27). On the other hand, the faith of the Gentiles is to stir up Israel on its part to take the way of faith (Rom. 11:11)."[96]

In the New Testament, then, there is no one form of government. Each of these forms arose at times when that form of secular government was commonly known in the world: The Roman Catholic Papal rule arose in medieval times, and later the Episcopal government. Presbyterianism arose in Scotland in the Sixteenth Century, and the congregational form in America. None of them can claim to have exclusive New Testament support.

IMPLICATIONS FOR GOVERNANCE AND POLITY TODAY

First we must consider the theoretical question: How is modern polity related to that of the New Testament? Several possible ways have been suggested.

It has been thought that it may be imitative. That is, we should find out how the early church was organized, and organize today in exactly the same way. But this would not allow for progress of any kind, or adaptation to different kinds of situations, different cultures, different needs, or different problems. Yet we find the New Testament church adapting in just those ways.

Second, there is Newman's theory of development. This is the ingenious theory that Jesus created the church, just as we know it in later history, but he left everything in miniature. The task of the church organizers who came afterwards was to educe the larger picture which was latent in what seemed to be nothing but a blur. All was there, down to the minutest detail, but it took centuries to disclose fully what was hidden. But it would be difficult to support this either Biblically or historically. Third, we may consider that there has been development of methods, but the same principles. This makes more sense, but what are the principles we can deduce from the New Testament? Let us summarize some of them from what has been said.

Concluding Summary

1. The Triune God rules the church. Surely this is a basic principle. God originated the church. Jesus is King, and the Holy Spirit is Administrator.
2. Christ is the head of the church. No Christian should act without first earnestly seeking to know His will.
3. The priesthood of all believers. (This is one of the factors contributing to congregationalism.)
4. Freedom in the Spirit. This means that we have equal freedom to follow the Spirit's guidance, with equal responsibility to seek to know and follow the Spirit's guidance, and equal responsibility to have a Christlike spirit of obedience and humble service.
5. Two key concepts are servanthood and sacrifice.
6. All Christians are servants of God and of one another.
7. All have equal rights and equal responsibility.
8. There is no place in the church for a political type of maneuvering.
9. There is no place in the church for love of money, love of things, or love of power.
10. In all organization stress should be on function, not office. No office should be self-perpetuating, but should exist only so long as it is the best way to fulfill the mission of the church.
11. Organization should be democratic, so as to allow each person to

make his full contribution to the work.

12. The most efficient organization is as simple as possible and as complex as necessary to do the work.

13. Organization should be flexible enough to change as conditions and needs change. This requires periodic, if not constant, reevaluation and restructuring, but not so as to hinder the work being done or to disrupt functioning.

14. Organization should aim to make full use of every gift of every Christian.

15. The organization must always be open to the guidance of the Holy Spirit.

Chapter 22

Final Things: Eschatology

> In the presence of God, who gives life to all things, and of Christ Jesus, who in his testimony before Pontius Pilate made the good confession, I charge you to keep the commandment without spot or blame until the manifestation of our Lord Jesus Christ, which he will bring about at the right time (1 Tim. 6:13-15a).

Can we be sure that Christ will ever return? If he does, what will he come to do? By what signs can we know when he is about to come?

When is the kingdom of God established? Is Christ now King? Or must he wait until he comes again? Did Jesus try to set up his kingdom when he came the first time? Or did he fail, and must come again to try to establish it?

What will heaven and hell be like? Can we know anything about them? How much does the Bible say about the pleasures of heaven and the suffering of hell?

We come now to the whole question of the future and what it will be like. Life in this world is short. It may seem long to one who has lived one hundred years. But when we compare that century to the thousands of years of human history, it seems short. Then when we compare the whole history of mankind to the time it has taken the light to come from the nearest stars, it is seen to be insignificant. And when we compare that time to the time for light to come from the farthest nebulae yet discovered by astronomers, the comparison is staggering.

We believe that God so far transcends even the whole universe that he made it all, and is beyond it all. If we meditate on this fact, we wonder how he can have any concern for such insignificant creatures as we are. How can he have any love for us? Yet he does, and has made plans for our eternal salvation.

It requires true humility for us to speak of knowing anything about the plans of God. Yet it is true that we can know the will of God as he reveals it to us in some positive way. Since we cannot know the future in and of ourselves, we need to be careful as we seek to learn the will of God. We must not too freely announce that God wants us to do a certain thing. God's Spirit can reveal to us what we ought to do, but we can so easily be mistaken that some of us need to be more humble about what we say we know.

Humility in Eschatology

If any aspect of theology requires humility, it is this subject of eschatology. We can see how the New Testament points out certain events as fulfilling Old Testament predictions. But if we look closely at all of those, we see that the fulfillment makes sense of the prediction, but that one could hardly read the prediction and know exactly what the fulfillment would be like.

Consider the predictions of the coming of the Messiah. They were fulfilled in Jesus Christ, but who could know that he would come into the world as a helpless baby? Even Mary, his mother, had trouble learning about this unique son of hers. When Jesus told his disciples about his coming death and resurrection, they did not really understand what he meant until after the resurrection. If they had know just what the future would be like, they would not have followed him at a distance (Mat. 26:58). Thomas was willing to die for Jesus (John 11:16), and heard him more than once predict his resurrection, yet had such a problem believing it after it happened (John 20:24-25).

No totally new event can be fully comprehended until one has experienced it. Reading a book about flying a plane may make it easier to learn, but you cannot know what it is like until you get in the plane. Feeling the sudden drop of the nose of the plane throws a blinding light on what the book said about "stalling!"

If this is true of the common things of earth, how much more is it true of such experiences as death, resurrection, judgment and eternity! Yet the

Christian life is a life of hope in the Biblical revelation of these very events of the future.

The Christian Hope

Today we sometimes use the word hope when a situation is hopeless. In the New Testament the words for hope, both noun and verb, never point to a vague or fearful anticipation. It is always a sure expectation of something good. The verb is used thirty-one times in the New Testament, and the noun fifty-four times, making eighty-five altogether. They are used only eight times in the Gospels, but are important in the rest of the New Testament. It is never selfish hope for a blessing, but is always centered in Christ Jesus.

This hope of the Christian is a sure anchor to the soul (Heb. 6:19). The hope of the Christian is a heavenly hope, built on the word of Christ, which is sure to be true. Note the way in which Jesus' promise of his return was made personal for each Christian. "And if I go and prepare a place for you, I will come again and will take you to myself, so that where I am, there you may be also" (John 14:3).

Even if we knew nothing more about our eternal future than that we would be with Christ, it would be a wonderful hope to have. We do not need to know anything about where heaven will be or what it will be like. We know that we shall be with him, and that is enough.

The Hope of His Coming

"Blessed be the God and Father of our Lord Jesus Christ! By his great mercy he has given us a new birth into a living hope through the resurrection of Jesus Christ from the dead . . . kept in heaven for you, who are being protected by the power of God through faith for a salvation ready to be revealed in the last time" (1 Pet. 1:3-5).

The hope of the Christian is never a selfish hope for a great blessing, but is always centered in Christ. This hope is for a final salvation from the troubles, suffering, and temptations of this world. It will be revealed at the coming of Christ to us. It is the assurance that Christ will come again and take us to be with him forever.

Jesus Is Coming Again

Almost every book in the New Testament speaks of the second coming of Christ. The only ones which do not are Galatians, which was written for a very specific purpose, and the very short books of Philemon and Second and Third John. It is mentioned 318 times in the 216 chapters of the New Testament. It is the center of the hope of the Christian, though it will seal the doom of the sinner who rejects Christ in this life. "I will come again and will take you to myself, so that where I am, there you may be also" (John 14:3). "For the Son of Man is to come with his angels in the glory of his Father, and then he will repay everyone for what he has done" (Mat. 16:27; cf. Mk. 8:38; Luke 9:26).

Jesus spoke of his return and of the judgment which would take place at that time (Mat. 16:27; Mk. 8:38; Luke 9:26). According to Luke, the birth of Jesus was announced by angels (Luke 2:8-14), and so was this prediction of his return (Acts 1:9-11).

Since we have the word of Jesus Christ himself that he will come again, and since this is confirmed through the rest of the New Testament, we are sure of this. The next thing we would like to know is what will happen when he comes.

The Time of His Coming

An amazing amount of ink has been used in explaining just when Jesus Christ will return. Some of the best minds have tried to figure it out, mainly from the Books of Daniel and Revelation, and from Matthew 24. There has hardly been a century since the time of Christ that someone has not predicted that it would come in that century! In the twentieth century many dates have been set by preachers claiming to have full information.

On October 18, 1992, a large, unsigned advertisement appeared in a city newspaper stating that the "rapture" of all the church secretly from the earth will take place October 28, 1992 and listing such scriptures as 1 Corinthians 15:49-55 and Matthew 24. In large print, the date is mentioned three times in the ad. The strange thing is that there was never another ad in the paper apologizing for the mistaken date published in such lurid terms! The same kind of ad appeared in 1994, as others have done for two centuries.

Another strange thing is that the rapture of the saints is said in the ad to be a secret departure of millions of saints from the earth, yet two of the passages listed state that it will be accompanied by the "trumpet of God." How could it then happen secretly?

Another strange thing is that Matthew 24 is emphasized as telling us just when the end will come.. Yet in that chapter Jesus stated four times that it will be at a time when it is not expected (36, 42, 44, 50). "But about that day and hour no one know, neither the angels of heaven, nor the Son, but only the Father" (Mat. 24:36). "Keep awake therefore, for you do not know on what day your Lord is coming. But understand this: if the owner of the house had known in what part of the night the thief was coming, he would have stayed awake and would not have let his house be broken into. Therefore you also must be ready, for the Son of Man is coming at an unexpected hour" (42-44).

Most of those who seek to predict the time make major use of the Book of Daniel. Yet Jesus knew the Book of Daniel thoroughly, and he said he did not know! How much more clearly could Jesus have said that no one will know ahead of time when the end will come?

At the other extreme, there are those who say that he cannot come yet because of Matthew 24:14, "And this good news of the kingdom will be proclaimed throughout the world, as a testimony to all the nations, and then the end will come." Some seem to feel that Jesus is saying that he will not return as long as there is a person anywhere who has not heard the gospel.

Yet Jesus is speaking of preaching to all nations, not necessarily to all individuals. This verse is like the Great Commission (Mat. 28:19-20) and the final command of Jesus to his disciples in Acts 1:8. In both he told them to preach to all the nations, the gentiles. This was a command which the disciples and all Jews had a hard time taking literally. They had always been taught that gentiles were not acceptable to God. If they came to God, they would have to become Jewish proselytes first. Peter had to be shown the same vision three times before he would go to the house of Cornelius to preach the gospel (Acts 10, 11, 15). As in Titus 2:11, we must recognize that the good news has come into the world for all nations, and for all individuals. We must not withhold it from anyone on the grounds of nationality.

One further point is important in this regard. Paul stated in Colossians

1:6, 23 that the gospel had already been preached in all the world. This statement gives meaning to the statement of Jesus about preaching to the whole world. It means that it must not be withheld from anyone on account of nationality or race, or religion. The Jews who had been converted must, in spite of their early teaching, preach to all the gentiles.

WHAT WILL HAPPEN WHEN HE COMES?

The New Testament does not draw us a picture of what it will be like when Jesus returns. In the same way, the Old Testament dis not describe the birth of Jesus in Nazareth, with the angels, shepherds and Wise Men. Yet it was made clear that He would come. After the event, we can look back and see some foreshadowings of some of the details. Predictive prophecy is not give to satisfy our curiosity about the future, but to help us prepare for the future work of God. A study of the New Testament shows that we can expect certain things to happen at the Second Coming of Christ, though details of the event are not given.

Resurrection of all the dead

The universal resurrection of the dead was taught by Jesus as clearly as was the New Birth and the resurrection from death in sin to a new life in Christ."Very truly, I tell you, the hour is coming, and is now here, when the dead will hear the voice of the Son of God, and those who hear will live" (John 5:25).

This is the way he described the resurrection from death in sin, which he declared was already going on at the time he spoke. Immediately after making this statement, he declared: "Do not be astonished at this; for the hour is coming when all who are in their graves will come out——those who have done good, to the resurrection of life, and those who have done evil, to the resurrection of condemnation" (John 5:28-29).

By this Jesus clearly predicted the resurrection of all the dead, whether sinners or righteous. The resurrection of both Christians and sinners are described as simultaneous, as in the statement of Paul (Acts 24:15).

In John 6:39-54, within these few verses, Jesus said four times that he would raise us up "at the last day" (39, 40, 44, 54). That is what we know about when it will take place. It is on the day which will bring human history as we know it to an end. There will not be another day after the last day, although Dwight Pentecost wasted several pages trying to explain why the last day is not the last day. He insisted that there would be at least one thousand and three and one-half years after the last day! (J. Dwight Pentecost, *Things to Come*, Findlay, Ohio: Dunham Publishing Co., 1958).

We know that we shall rise again from the grave, but we know nothing about what we shall be like after the resurrection. Paul dealt briefly with the resurrection body in his major study of the resurrection, 1 Corinthians 15. Verses 35-57 say almost all that we know about the resurrection body. But that is not much. We know that it will not be like this physical body, which is subject to sickness, pain and decay. It will be a spiritual body 44). It will be immortal (53).

One problem is that when we say we will have a spiritual body, we do not know what a spiritual body is. But that does not bother us, since we know that we shall be like Christ. "Beloved, we are God's children now; what we will be has not yet been revealed. What we do know is this: when he is revealed, we will be like him, for we will see him as he is" (1 John 3:2).

Final judgment of all

The Final Judgment is predicted by Jesus and supported by the rest of the Bible. It is spoken of as the Day of Judgment (2 Pet. 3:7), the judgment of the great day (Jude 6), and the day of wrath (Rom. 2:5; Rev. 6:17). It will take place on the day appointed by God (Acts 17:31; Rom. 2:16). We will not know before when it will come (Mark 13:32).

The Old Testament also speaks of the universal judgment in many ways (Ps. 50:1-6; 96:13; Eccl. 3:17; 12:14, etc.). Jesus himself gave the most dramatic picture of the judgment, in Matthew 25:31-46. This passage describes the final judgment in terms of a shepherd separating sheep and goats. He then sends each of the two groups to their eternal reward.

This picture of the final judgment is not a literal depiction of the way it will be, as it has many aspects of parable. No details are given as to where it will take place, or just how the separation will be done. Nothing is said of the length of time the separation will involve. It is parabolic in that all the people are represented by animals. It is absolute truth in that all of us will be judged by Christ after our resurrection, and he will assign us our eternal destiny.

The Basis of Judgment. One problem with the interpretation of this passage is that of the basis of the judgment. Since the work of Walter Rauschenbush, it is often stated that God will judge us only on the basis of the way we have treated others. So the primary work of Christians and the church is social work. It is true that the passage only mentions such things as feeding the poor, visiting the sick and imprisoned, and other social welfare matters. It is also true that this is important. Yet this is not the only basis of judgment given by Jesus in this chapter.

There are three parables of judgment in Matthew 25: The wise and foolish bridesmaids, the talents, and the sheep and goats. The first indicates that we must be ready to meet our Maker, who is compared to the bridegroom. The second shows that we must make sure of our right use of our God-given abilities. The third speaks of our relationship with others. We must be right with God, right with ourselves, and right with others.

Jesus presented a balanced basis for the final judgment. We must beware of emphasizing one or more of these three to the exclusion or minimizing of the others. It is wrong to minimize any one of the three.

Jesus Christ, the Judge. No one of us can ever be saved by the things we do in this life. Salvation is only from God through the death and resurrection of Jesus Christ. Apart from Christ there is no salvation for anyone at any time (Acts 4:12; John 3:16; 14:6; 1 Cor. 3:11). Therefore it is reasonable for Christ to be the one to decide our eternal fate. Jesus himself said that he would repay each for what one has done (Mat. 16:27; 25:31-32; John 5:22-23; Acts 10:42; 17:31; 2 Cor. 5:10). "For all of us must appear before the judgment seat of Christ, so that each may receive recompense for what has been done in the body, whether good or evil" (2 Cor. 5:10).

It is true that Christians will stand in the judgment before Christ, but they do not need to fear judgment (2 Cor. 5:8; Rom. 8:1; 1 John 4:18). Our faith in Jesus Christ as our Savior leaves no room to fear him as our Judge.

Reason for the Judgment. God knows us very well while we are still living, and knows whether we are trusting in Christ for salvation and living for him. Why does he need to set a day to judge us? Some seem to feel that a final judgment day makes no sense. And that might be true if the only purpose of the judgment were to determine our fate. God knows that already. But there are other reasons for the final judgment, though it would be speculative to say we know all of them or even the most important of them.

Yet some reasons are apparent. The Judgment Day will reveal to each of us the justice of God. It will also show us his grace and mercy in a final revelation. It will reveal the real character of each person. It will be the final vindication of God's justice and mercy. It will reveal the awful sinfulness of sin, which people have sought to hide from themselves. It will reveal even to sinners the glory of God whom they have rejected. And it will show each sinner that the final reward is deserved.

When we consider the fact that the judgment of God will be the final estimation of the life lived here, we see even more that it will do. No one's life can be fairly judged until it is over. Only then can the extent of good and evil be seen. The effects of a life, whether good or evil, go on even after death. Only at the end of history can all the effects of a person's thoughts and deeds be fully known. God's Final Judgment can reveal all this in a final summation.

End of the World

The second coming of Christ will mark the end of history as we know it, and the beginning of eternity. This is clear from the statements of the Bible, but we do not know just what it will be like. Most of what we know is speculation, though it is based on certain Scriptures.

A major problem is that of the continuity or discontinuity between the world we know and the new world into which we shall be resurrected. 2 Peter 3 stresses the discontinuity: "But the day of the Lord will come like a thief, and then the heavens will pass away with a loud noise, and the elements will be dissolved with fire, and the earth and the works that are upon it will be burned up. Since all these things are thus to be dissolved, what sort of persons ought you to be in lives of holiness and godliness" (2 Pet. 3:10-11).

This sounds like utter destruction of the earth and all the elements of which it is composed (as in Mat. 24:35; Isa. 51:6). Yet we are warned against being too sure of our concept when we see that in verses 5-6 of this same chapter similar words are used about the destruction in the day of Noah. The latter took place by water, and the former by fire. Does he mean to say that all the universe will cease to exist, or that it will cease to exist in its present form? It must also be affirmed that there is a serious textual problem in the end of verse 10, which makes us even less dogmatic about the exact meaning.

The discontinuity between this age and the age to come is strongest in 2 Peter 3. This needs to be balanced against the continuity of the two ages as found in Romans 8:18-25, where it is implied that the whole creation will be redeemed from the "futility caused by sin. Revelation 21 can be read in the same way, emphasizing continuity between the present and future ages. What did Jesus mean by saying "Blessed are the meek, for they will inherit the earth" (Mat. 5:5)? Surely he means at least that Christians can fully enjoy all the good things God gives in this age, and also in the age to come. Yet he does not explain what that new age will be. Will it be in a renewed earth, or in a totally new earth?

The Christian hope does not require the destruction or the dissolution of this universe. There will be an end of this age, and the beginning of a new age, but what will happen to physical things we do not know.

We do not need to know such details. The things of this world are temporary (2 Cor. 4:18), so we ought to sit lightly on the *things* we may seem to possess. The created world is not eternal, and will cease to exist if God ceases to hold it together. This does not mean that the world and the universe of which it is a part is meaningless. Temporary things can have value. Our bodies are temporary, but they are valuable, and we need to take care of them.

If the earth and sky cease to exist, we need not be concerned, for "we wait for new heavens and a new earth, where righteousness is at home" (2 Pet. 3:13; cf: Isa. 65:17; 66:22; Rev. 21:1). The old must go so that the new can come.

It is not clear what is mean by the old and new "heaven and earth." We can understand this as referring to the present universe and a new one, but that is not necessarily the meaning. We know that the present sinful world order will pass away, to make room for a new age without sin.

Personal Death and Resurrection

Death is universal

All who live, die. No one needs a Scripture passage to prove this, for it is a fact we can observe. The death rate is one hundred percent. The great question is about life after death.

The Bible does not answer all our questions about life after death, so we have to enter the experience for ourselves. Books have been written on the experience of death, but these seem to be based, not on the experience of death, but on near-death experiences.

As we have seen, we shall all be raised up from death at the second coming of Christ. But what happens to us between death and the resurrection of all? Where will we be? Will we know anything, or will we be just dead or sleeping?

Intermediate State

Theologians have spoken of the time between death and the resurrection as the "Intermediate State." The Bible does not use this term, and does not discuss this period of time. So it is an inference, and may be based on some false assumptions. Yet we can feel rather sure of some statements we can make about it.

We can be sure that it is a state of conscious existence, and that we will still be alive. The fact that we are alive after the body dies is seen from the answer Jesus gave to the Sadducees who did not believe in the resurrection from the dead. "And as for the resurrection of the dead, have you not read what was said to you by God, 'I am the God of Abraham, the God of Isaac, and the God of Jacob'? He is God not of the dead, but of the living" (Mat. 22:31-32).

The fact that we shall be conscious after death can be inferred from the story Jesus told of Lazarus and the rich man who both died (Luke 16:19-31). Both were alive and conscious after they died, though one was in torment and the other in a place of peace with Abraham and God.

Some have said that this is a parable, and that we cannot build a doctrine on a parable. But, though this story is like a parable in some ways, it is different. It was told for the purpose of teaching something about life after death, and must have a strong element of truth in it. It tells us emphatically that sinners and Christians are separated after death, and are in an existence which is related to their eternal state. It may be an incomplete state (Phil. 3:10-11; 2 Cor. 5:3-4).

While Jesus was hanging on the cross, he said to the repentant thief on another cross near him, "Truly I tell you, today you will be with me in Paradise" (Luke 23:43). The thief had just made an astounding request to Jesus, who was also dying. This showed the kind of saving faith he had in Christ, and received this encouraging reply. Jesus assured him that they would be together after death, and that they would be in Paradise, the Garden of God. If we are with Christ after death, that is enough for us to know. To say more than this is to speculate.

Resurrection, Judgment, Eternity

We have already discussed the resurrection as it applies to all, and it will apply to us as individuals in the same way. Then we shall appear before God in Judgment, then eternity will begin. If we have lived for God in this life, trusting in the grace of God in Christ Jesus, we shall enter into life with God forever. If not, we shall be apart from God forever.

Future judgment is often mentioned in the Bible, but never described in detail, so we do not know what it will be like. It would be fruitless for us to speculate on what we cannot know. But we know it will come.

Millennium?

It would require a large book to give adequate attention to the many theories about the exact nature of the second Advent, and what will happen after that. Most of these speculations have to do with the kingdom and reign of Christ. Premillennialists say that Christ will set up his kingdom on earth at his second advent, and reign for one thousand years before ending history and ushering in eternity. The post-millennial theory is that the world will gradually be transformed by the gospel so that it will become the kingdom of God, and then Christ will come again. Dispensationalism is a complicated form of premillennial theory, with so many variations that it is hardly safe to be dogmatic about what they believe. Basically, they believe that all the Old Testament prophecies about the people of Israel must be literally fulfilled on earth, and that Jesus will come again to set up his kingdom with the Jews at the center. He will reign for one thousand years on earth, and at the end of that time there will be a horrible uprising against him. He will destroy his enemies in a great battle, and then the judgment will be held for the wicked nations before eternity begins. But before he sets up his kingdom, he will come secretly and take away all the righteous saints in a secret "rapture," so that they will not be here in the time of troubles which will last either three and a half years, or seven years before the millennium.

These are the theories, in brief form. The dispensational theory, with its dramatic concept of a secret rapture of the church leads to such fascination that it is often preached. Books are written about this great event when all the righteous suddenly disappear from the earth. It is easy to be dramatic about such a concept as this! Books on the subject sell as quickly as any other exciting stories.

The Kingdom

At the heart of all these millennial theories is the idea of the kingdom of God, and the question about when it is established. In regard to the time, post-millennialists believe it will be set up gradually by the influence of the gospel, and then Christ will come. The second coming of Christ will be *after* the millennium, hence the name of this concept. Premillennial teaching is that Christ will come to set up the kingdom for one thousand years on earth. So Christ will come *before* the millennial reign.

It may be fair to say that Dispensationalism has zoomed off into a never-never land of fantasy and speculation, and has lost touch with the real life of both individuals and nations. It has developed a most complicated scheme of interpretation of Old Testament prophecy and of the future which has little in common with what Christians have believed from the beginning. As to the prophecies of the Old Testament, it is asserted that there are many which have never been fulfilled with respect to the nation of Israel, and which will be fulfilled literally in the future. For example, a large part of the concept is that Israel will return to Jerusalem and the land around it, where Christ will reign over the whole world with their help. His kingdom will be a Jewish kingdom, ruling over the whole world. This will be the primary reason for his coming back to earth. But before that there will be a great tribulation, from which the church will be saved by being secretly taken out of the world at the time of the "secret rapture." It is said by some that they will come back to earth after the tribulation, and reign with Christ for one thousand years.[97]

Progressive Dispensationalism

What has been said above is true of the dispensationalism of Darby in the middle of the nineteenth century, of the Scofield Bible of 1909 and 1917, and of the Systematic Theology of Lewis Sperry Chafer in 1948. It is also true of many who preach it and teach it in some Bible schools.. Some find it exciting to preach their imagined concepts of what will happen when Jesus returns "to rule the world for 1,000 years." And they love to preach about what God will do with Israel and the whole middle east as Christ sets up his earthly kingdom there, as they think. For the theory is that there are two peoples of God, Israel is one, and the church is the other. So they think of the church as having a temporary purpose, but the real plan of God for Israel is far different. This is dispensationalism as it has been known. It is regularly preached and elaborated on the radio and television. It is easy to make such a theory exciting. But is it true?

Beginning in the 1950s and 1960s some leaders in dispensational thinking began to move toward a more universally acceptable exegesis. This lead to the revision of the Scofield Reference Bible in 1967. Certain of the more radical ideas were not found in the notes of this revised Bible.

In 1986 a "Dispensational Study Group" began annual meetings, and this has led to further modifications. Some changes have come so that there is more emphasis on the eternal salvation of both Israelites and the church, and this is good. The older distinction between Israel and the church has been minimized.. All this gives us hope that dispensationalists will move forward into the mainstream of conservative Biblical exegesis.

Kingdom is Eternal

In contrast to the millennial theories, the Bible states in thirty passages that the kingdom of God is eternal, not one thousand years! A list of

passages will help anyone who wishes to know more about this concept.
  2 Samuel 7:16, 28, 29
  Ps. 89:3-9, 34-37; 45:6; 72:5, 17
  Isa. 9:6-7; 51:6-8; 55:3; 60:19-26; 61:18
  Jer. 32:46; 33:14-17, 20-24; 37:24-28
  Ezek. 16:60; 43:7-9
  Dan. 7:13-14, 27; 9:24
  Hosea 2:19
  Joel 3:20
  Amos 9:15
  Luke 1:30-33
  1 Tim. 1:17
  Rev. 11:15

One thousand years may seem like a long time to us who can barely hope to live a tenth of that time. But a millennium is far too short a time for Christ to reign. He will reign forever.

Realized Millennium

What is often called "amillennial" might be more accurately called the "Realized millennial" position. Instead of waiting for God to set up his kingdom on the earth some time in the future, we see that Jesus established his kingdom when he came the first time. This is seen clearly from the plain statement of Jesus in Luke 11:20, quoted above. The same statement, with a slight variation, is found in Matthew 12:28 "But if it is by the Spirit of God that I cast out demons, then the kingdom of God has come to you."

The notes in the Scofield Bible insist that Jesus sought to establish his Jewish kingdom before he was crucified, but that they refused his offer. Yet there is no passage of Scripture which cites either his offer or their refusal. Instead we read: "When Jesus realized that they were about to come and take him by force to make him king, he withdrew again to the mountain by himself" (John 6:15).

Jesus absolutely refused to set up a political kingdom on earth as some wanted him to do. They hoped that he would drive out the Romans and make them a free nation. But what Jesus wanted to do was to set them free from their slavery to sin (John 8:31-34). They were seeking for the wrong kind of freedom. Jesus was not concerned about ruling over Jerusalem, but in the hearts of those who love the Lord. His is a spiritual kingdom (1 Cor. 4:20; Rom. 14:17). "Once Jesus was asked by the Pharisees when the kingdom of God was coming, and he answered, 'The kingdom of God is not coming with things that can be observed; nor will they say, "Look, here it is!" or "There it is!" For, in fact, the kingdom of God is among you" (Luke 17:20-21).

The Greek word here translated "among" is usually translated "within" or "inside." It should be so translated here. Either way, it is clear that Jesus was saying that the kingdom was then present, but that it is not to be looked for as some great political power. (The word used here is only used one other time in the New Testament, Matthew 23:26, where it is used of the inside of the cup. It is used in the Old Testament to mean "inside," as in Psalm 103:1 and 39:3.)

Christ is Now King

Jesus spoke frankly to Pilate when asked if he was really the King of the Jews: My kingdom is not from this world. If my kingdom were from this world, my followers would be fighting to keep me from being handed over to the Jews. But as it is, my kingdom is not from here" (John 18:36).

Here Jesus admitted that he had a kingdom, but insisted that it was not the kind of worldly kingdom that is based on the power of the sword. In Revelation 1:5 he is called "the ruler of the kings of the earth."

King Over Heaven and Earth

Before leaving this earth in his physical form, Jesus said to the disciples, "All authority in heaven and on earth has been given to me" (Mat. 28:18). I Peter 3:22 states that Christ is "at the right hand of God, with angels, authorities, and powers made subject to him." Jesus is reigning now in the hearts of those who trust in Him and live for him in this world. He is now King.

To look for some time in the future when Jesus will return and set up his kingdom is to continue the mistake of the Jews in his time who wanted him to be their political ruler. It disparages the accomplishment of his life. It makes a tragedy of the crucifixion and resurrection, and denies that the plan of salvation was finished as he died and rose again. It turns the cry "It is finished" (John 19:30) from a report of the completion of that work to a cry of defeat. It implies that Jesus was wrong when he declared to the Father "I glorified you on earth by finishing the work that you gave me to do" (John 17:4).

The Church

One of the great problems with Dispensationalism, which is now the most popular form of millennialism, is that it does not give full place to the church in the plan of God. According to the theory, the church is temporary, and will be removed from the earth while Christ carries out his final plans for the Jews. It is insisted that the church is not foretold in the Old Testament, and had no place in prophecy.

Some good persons have defended the whole idea of Dispensationalism, but it seems hard to defend in the light of plain Scriptures. Jesus said that the Old Testament spoke of him and his work (Luke 24:25-27). And establishing the church was a part of his work. On the day of Pentecost, which is considered the real beginning of the church, Peter declared that the events of that day were the fulfillment of Joel 3. Yet it is common for dispensationalists to insist that Pentecost was not the real fulfillment of the passage in Joel. They declare that it will have some literal fulfillment in the future.

Prophecy

The dispensational view is that prophecy is a picture of the future, telling exactly what will happen in the future, and must be fulfilled literally, and in detail. If prophecy speaks of David's throne, then David will someday come back to life and sit on his throne in Jerusalem. If it says that the people of Israel will return to Jerusalem, then they will do that sometime in the future. Even though there was a great return from Babylon to Jerusalem hundreds of years before Christ, they say it is still in the future. They say this in spite of the fact that no prophet after the fifth century before Christ ever mentioned it. These did not speak of a return to Jerusalem for the simple reason that it had already taken place.

Some dispensational writers like to read the prophecies which they say speak of the destruction of the Roman Empire and the Babylonian Empire and Egypt. Since the Roman Empire has not existed for fifteen hundred years, there are some who say it will be rebuilt before the second coming of Christ, so that it can be destroyed. They say the same of the Temple in Jerusalem. So they find ways to declare that Old Testament prophecies, which were long ago fulfilled, will be fulfilled in the future.

This brief discussion is about the type of dispensationalism which has built on the work of C. I. Scofield, as seen in the notes in the Scofield Bible. Dispensationalism is taking new forms, discarding some of the less defensible concepts. Yet the older dispensationalism is still popular, being preached on the radio and television, and presented in popular books.

Prophecy is not a crystal ball to satisfy our natural curiosity about the future. It is rather the proclamation of the sovereign, gracious will of God for all people to bow the knee to Him, and serve him in covenant faithfulness to the Lord of heaven and earth.

Signs of His Coming

Millennialists like to talk about the signs by which we can know that Christ is about to come. Some of these they find in Matthew 24: Wars and rumors of wars (6); persecution (9); men hating one another (10); lawlessness (12); eating and drinking (38).

Several things need to be noted about these so-called signs. First, they are not called "signs" by Jesus. He emphatically stated that "the end is not yet" (24:6). Second, these are all things which were happening at the time Jesus said these words. There have been wars and rumors of wars almost since people were created. Jesus simply said that the world would continue to be as it was then until the sudden end.

Jesus insisted that now one know when the end will come, and that he himself did not know (24:36). He discouraged speculation about the time of his coming. He said instead that we must "be ready, for the Son of Man is coming at an unexpected hour" (24:44). How much clearer could he say that no one will get any advance warning?

Consider further the idea of the "rapture" of the church seven years before the second advent of Christ. If it were true, then all who were left in the world would know that Jesus would come in exactly seven years. He would not be unexpected, as he said he would be.

Jesus said for us to be ready "for you know not the hour" (Matt. 24:42, 44; 25:13; Mark 13:35).

What Rapture?

The idea of a secret rapture of the church before a "great tribulation" was born about twenty years before the Civil War in America. The purpose is to get the church out of the world so that they will not have to go through the period of tribulation which will come upon earth, according to the theory of Darby which has been adopted by some.

It will be a secret rapture, quiet, noiseless, sudden as the step of the thief in the night, so some say. But does the Bible teach such a thing?

The major passage used to support the idea is 1 Thessalonians 4:16-18: "For the Lord himself, with a cry of command, with the archangel's call and with the sound of God's trumpet, will descend from heaven, and the dead in Christ will rise first. Then we who are alive, who are left, will be caught up in the clouds together with them to meet the Lord in the air; and so we will be with the Lord forever. Therefore encourage one another with these words."

It is clear here and in other places that all Christians will be taken from the earth to be with the Lord forever. But it is just as clear that all the sinners will be taken at the same time, and that the world will be destroyed (2 Pet. 3:10-12).

Instead of describing a secret coming, verse 16 is one of the noisiest verses in the Bible! There is nothing quiet or secretive about the cry of command, the call of the archangel and the trumpet of God!

Instead of saying that the dead in Christ will rise first before the dead unbelievers, it says plainly that the dead Christians will rise first before the living ones go to meet the Lord. The whole passage says nothing about unbelievers because they have nothing to do with the subject Paul was discussing in verses thirteen and following. All will be able to go together to meet the Lord.

Instead of saying that we shall be with the Lord in the air for seven years, while the wicked on earth are undergoing tribulation, Paul says plainly "and so we will be with the Lord forever."

"Look! He is coming with the clouds; every eye will see him, even those who pierced him; and on his account all the tribes of the earth will

wail. So it is to be. Amen." (Rev. 1:7). Sinners will mourn when he comes, but believers are eager to see him. "For as the lightning comes from the east and flashes as far as the west, so will be the coming of the Son of Man" (Mat. 24:27).
The Bible clearly teaches that Christ will come again, and that all the people on earth, dead and alive, will see him. Let us be
ready for his coming.

Armageddon

Millennialists differ as to when the Battle of Armageddon will take place, but some of them love to describe its horrors. The fact is that there is no battle of Armageddon in the Bible. It is true that in Revelation 16:16, which is the only place the term "Har-Megiddo" is used, it is said that the nations gathered for battle against God and his people. But there is no battle. The angel poured his vial on the air and cried "It is done!" The battle ended before it began. No contest!

"Har-Megiddo" is explained as Hebrew, but no translation or geographical explanation is offered. As Hebrew, it means the "Mountain of Megiddo." But Megiddo is not a mountain, but a plain. So Zechariah 12:11 speaks of the "plain of Megiddo." There is no mountain there except Mount Carmel. If he had meant Carmel why did he not say so? The simplest explanation is that he meant neither Megiddo nor Carmel, but that he used the term as a symbol of conflict between good and evil.

Even so, there was no battle. God stopped them with trouble that reminds us of another of the plagues of Egypt. No human beings can stand against the word of God. "Even the nations are like a drop from a bucket, and are accounted as dust on the scales; see, he takes up the isles like find dust. Lebanon would not suffice for fuel, nor are its beasts enough for a burnt offering. All the nations are as nothing before him, they are accounted by him as less than nothing and emptiness" (Isa. 40:15-17).

Rev. 20:1-6

Millennial teachers know that this is the only passage in the Bible which mentions anything about one thousand years (millennium) reign of Christ. The foundation for the theory is this passage of Revelation. With that in mind we can notice that the whole passage does not say anything about the coming of Christ, the rapture of the church, or Christ reigning on earth over all the nations. It says nothing of resurrected bodies, but only of the "souls of those who had been beheaded for their testimony to Jesus" (20:4). There is nothing here about universal peace and prosperity on earth. Nothing is said of a throne or capital on earth, nor of Jerusalem. There is nothing about a world government, nor of Jewish preeminence.

In other words, the whole passage on which the theory of a thousand year reign of Christ on earth is based, does not mention any of the important points of the concept. The point is that this key passage is no foundation for the theory constructed on it.

The first three verses of this passage tell of the binding of Satan "so that he would deceive the nations no more" (20:3). But this happened at the first advent of Christ. Satan had "deceived the nations" so that Gentiles could not hear the word of God. But now Jesus said "Go therefore and make disciples of all nations" (Mat. 28:19).

Jesus conquered Satan so he was able to cast out demons (Mat. 12:24 ff; Mark 3:22 ff.) He said, "I watched Satan fall from heaven like a flash of lightning. See I have given you authority to tread on snakes and scorpions, and over all the power of the enemy; and nothing will hurt you. Nevertheless, do not rejoice at this, that the spirits submit to you, but rejoice that your names are written in heaven" (Luke 10:18-20).

Before the Great Commission, as we call it, Jesus said, "All authority in heaven and on earth has been given to me" (Mat. 28:18). On the cross "He disarmed the rulers and authorities and made a public example of them, triumphing over them in it" (Col. 2:15). Jesus had come as a mortal human being "so that through death he might destroy the one who has the power of death, that is, the devil, and free those who all their lives were held in slavery by the fear of death" (Heb. 2:14-15).

This means that the binding of Satan is not something which will take place in the future, but which did occur long ago, before Jesus set up his kingdom in the hearts of his people. We are able to resist the devil by the grace of God, and live lives which please God. The devil is now bound, so that we can have the victory over him. He was bound so that Gentiles like us can hear the gospel and be God's people. We can now reign with

Christ in this present evil world.

> "One we hail as King immortal,
> He did earth and hell ;subdue;
> And, bequeathing us his glory,
> We are kings anointed, too.
>
> Shall we then, by sin be humbled?
> Must we yield to any foe?
> No, by heaven's gift we're reigning
> Over all this world below.
>
> I am reigning, sweetly reigning.
> Far above this world of strife;
> In my blessed loving Savior
> I am reigning in this life.
>
> Daniel Sidney Warner

No Millennium When Jesus Comes

NO NEED for a millennial reign. Christ has already established his kingdom in the hearts of believers. So God's people are reigning now in this wicked world. Christ will come only once more, and that will be to bring an end to history and usher in eternity. His work of preparing salvation is finished, and he did what he came to do. Christ is now King, and when he comes again he will offer up the kingdom to the Father (1 Cor. 15:24).

NO TIME for a millennium when Jesus comes again. He will come at the LAST day (John 6:39, 40, 44, 54). He will judge all people at the LAST day (John 12:48). There will be no days after the LAST day.

NO PLACE for a millennium. The earth will be destroyed (2 Pet. 3:10-11; Heb. 1:10-11; Rev. 20:11; 21:1).

Heaven and Hell

The word for "heaven" in the Old Testament sometimes refers to the sky (Gen. 1:8; 7:11). In other places it means the atmosphere, where the clouds and birds are (Gen 8:2; Josh. 10:11; Ps. 147:8). It sometimes means what we call outer space, where the stars, planets, sun and moon

Final Things: Eschatology   341

are (Deut. 4:19; Isa. 47:13; Gen. 1:14). It can also be used to refer to the abode of God (Isa. 63:15; Ps. 33:14; 61:4). In the New Testament it is used in these same ways, and also is a substitute for the word "God," as when the prodigal son said he had "sinned against heaven" (God) (Luke 15:21). Today, we tend to use it primarily in the special sense of the dwelling place of God. We do this, even though we know that God is everywhere. We mean that God is "above" us in power, majesty, knowledge, holiness, and love. So we are using the term heaven here in this special sense of the abode of God and the eternal abode of his people.

Most of what we know of heaven and hell is speculation. It is apt to be based not on the Bible, but on such writings as those of Dante, and other medieval writers. The usual pictures described, then, are not Biblical but medieval. The Bible itself tells us almost nothing about their nature.

This is as it should be. Jesus told Nicodemus that if he could not understand such earthly matters as the new birth, how could Nicodemus believe if he told him about heavenly things? (John 3:12).

Paul speaks humbly and cautiously about his own (presumably) experience of being "caught up into Paradise and heard things that are not to be told, that no mortal is permitted to repeat" (2 Cor. 12:4). "Not to be told" represents a Greek word which literally means "unspeakable," or things for which there are no words. The word translated "permitted" also means "able," so that it can mean things of which human speech is not capable of describing.

We can only describe things of which we have some sort of knowledge. New things demand new words. Heaven and hell are both beyond our experience, and therefore we would not understand what they were like if Jesus had tried to tell us.

Reinhold Niebuhr was right to warn us that: "It is unwise for Christians to claim any knowledge of either the furniture of heaven or the temperature of hell."[98] Taking this warning seriously, and refusing to go beyond what the Bible teaches us, there is still a little that we can say about both heaven and hell.

Hell

We will give our attention to hell first in order to end on a more encouraging note. We point out first that no specific details are given about hell at all. The Bible does not tell where it is, or if it is a place at all, in our sense of the word. Jesus came to show us the love of God and his salvation from sin. Yet Jesus told more about the danger of hell than the rest of the Bible together. The primary fact about hell is that it is final separation from God (Mat. 7:23; 8:12; 22:13; 25:12, 30). Jesus described this as "outer darkness" (Mat. 8:12), and in other places as fire (Mat. 13:42, 49-50). The two ideas seem incompatible, but both are used to mean the separation from all that is good. "Every generous act of giving, with every perfect gift, is from above, coming down from the Father of lights" (James 1:17). When one is separated permanently from God, the person is separated from every good gift. Since God is light (1 John 1:5), separation from him is to be in darkness.

"Fire" represents the wrath of God. Wrath is one of the characteristics of which many would like to deny, but which is common in both Testaments. "For the wrath of God is revealed from heaven against all ungodliness and wickedness of those who by their wickedness suppress the truth" (Rom. 1:18). "Much more surely then, now that we have been justified by his blood, will we be saved through him from the wrath of God" (Rom. 5:9). "Let no one deceive you with empty words, for because of these things the wrath of God comes on those who are disobedient" (Eph. 5:6; cf.. Col. 3:6). "And to wait for his Son from heaven, whom he raised from the dead--Jesus, who rescues us from the wrath that is coming" (1 Thess. 1:10).

It is impossible to take the wrath of God out of the Bible without destroying the message of both Testaments.

The Suffering of Hell

With this background, we can probably be safe in suggesting that the suffering of hell will involve the loss of all earthly good. It will be the banishment from the presence and love of God. The person in hell will suffer the eternal withdrawal of the Holy Spirit, and the consequent unrestrained rule of sin and sinful passions.

There will also be the sting of conscience telling you that you deserve your fate. This should bring total despair. The inhabitant of hell will have nothing but evil associates.

There will be the suffering of whatever punishment God has prepared, and of which we are totally ignorant. But we do know that there will be the loss of all hope.

With all of this, we recognize that hell does not have the place in God's planning that heaven holds. Jesus said that at the judgment, "he will say to those at his left hand, 'You that are accursed, depart from me into the eternal fire prepared for the devil and his angels" (Mat. 25:41). This is not the desire of God, but is the obverse of his love. God is "not wanting any to perish, but all to come to repentance" (2 Pet. 3:9b).

With all of this to cause suffering, there is no need to think of literal fire. Hell is the final separation from all that is good, and from God. There are references to a "lake of fire" but also "outer darkness." It is the loss of all that is good and pleasant. It is the eternal loss of the loving presence of God. Nothing could be worse.

Joys of Heaven

If we think of heaven as the place of the eternal reward of Christians, we may be astonished to learn that the Bible does not speak of it. In the Old Testament the word "heaven" is used in four senses: 1. The sky, in the sense of a more or less solid separation of earth and whatever is beyond (Gen. 1:8; 7:11). 2. The atmosphere, where the clouds and birds are (Ps 147:8; Zech. 6:5). 3. Outer space, where the stars, planets, sun and moon are (Deut. 4:19; Jer. 44:17-25. Isa. 47:13). 4. The abode of God. "Look down from heaven and see, from your holy and glorious habitation" (Isa. 63:15).

All of the figures which say anything about the pleasures of heaven are just that—figures of speech. The best things of this world are as nothing in comparison with heaven, the eternal abode of those who live for God in this life.

It must be stated that the word "heaven" is usually used in the Bible to mean the sky or the air. We know little about the worldviews of the first century, but it seems most likely that they thought of three heavens (though sometimes seven). The three heavens seem to include the air (birds and clouds, the starry heavens, and the third heaven as the abode of God.

When we speak of heaven as the abode of God, we are speaking metaphorically, not literally. God is not above the clouds nor beyond the stars. God is everywhere. There is no place where God is not. There is no place one can go from the presence of God (Ps. 139:7-12).

Some Reasons for Joy in Heaven

The great joy of heaven will be to see God as he is (John 14:3; 1 John 3:2). This "beatific vision" has occupied the minds of Christians since the time of Christ. We cannot imagine what it is like, but know that it will better than anything we can know in this world. As the song says, "Just one glimpse of Him in glory will the toils of life repay."

Charles Hodge gives a list of reasons for the joy we shall experience in heaven, besides the vision of God as he is. There will be the direct experience of God's infinite love. If what we know here is good, what will this be like? The enlargement of all human faculties is not stated in the Bible in this way, but it is reasonable to suppose, since we will not be shackled by our physical frailness.

There will be no temptation to sin, and this should be a great relief. There will be no sorrow, separation, or death.

We shall enjoy the endless communion with the redeemed of all ages. What a blessed thought. For some of us especially, there will be the joy of eternally growing knowledge. We have to work so hard here to learn what we can in our short lives, what a blessing it will be to have time to learn. Oliver Buswell, Jr. once spoke for one hour in a seminary chapel on the blessing of not being limited for time in heaven! He was the kind of man who was so conscious of the shortness of time that he wore a wrist-watch, a pocket watch, and laid an alarm clock on the desk as he taught a class! Eternity will have no time limits.

Then, too, we will enjoy the secure and eternal possession of all possible good. And whatever Jesus meant by preparing a place for us (John 14:3), we know that God who made such a beautiful world for us here, will have much more beauty for us to enjoy. For it will not be spoiled by sin.

Heaven will be worth all it costs to get there. If you miss heaven, you will have missed everything.

Endnotes

1. A helpful classified list of theologians can be found in Garrett, James Leo. *Systematic Theology*, I, 25-39.
2. Dunning, H. Ray. *Grace, FAith and Holiness*, 77.
3. WTJ, Spring 1985, p. 9.
4. The reader who wishes to get a quick bit of information about any or all of these theologies could begin by looking them up in a dictionary of theology, such as the *Beacon Dictionary of Theology*, or the *New International Dictionary of the Christian Church.*.
5. Coppedge, Allan. *John Wesley in Theological Debate*. Wesley Heritage Press, 1987, 36-37.
6. John W. V. Smith, *The Quest for Unity and Holiness*.
7. Oden, *The Living God*, 142-143.
8. On the problems of evil in nature, see Thomas Oden, *The Living God*, 294-315.
9. W. A. Visser 't Hooft, *The Fatherhood of God in an Age of Emancipation*. Philadelphia: Westminster Press, 1982, 119-127.
10. Ibid, 132.
11. The indeterminacy and consequent unpredictability in subatomic physics can not negate the harmony and predictable order of the visible universe.
12. Robert B. Sloan, "Unity in Diversity: A Clue to the Emergence of the New Testament as Sacred Literature" in *New Testament Criticism and Interpretation*, Zondervan, 1991, 437-470.
13. WTJ 20:159.
14. *Answers to Questions*, Zondervan, p. 217.
15. Kenneth E. Jones, *Let's Study the Bible*. Anderson, IN: Warner Press, 1962, 1982, Chapter 2.
16. Dunning, 307-308, note 13.
17. Wiley I, 394.
18. Young, Edward J., *Studies in Genesis I*, Grand Rapids: Eerdmans, 1964, 102.
19. R. K. Harrison in ISBE, II, 427-428.
20. Augustine, *City of God*, XI, 6.
21. Byrum, R. R. *Christian Theology*, 1925, 239.
22. H. L. Ellison, in IBC, 116-117.

23. Hoekema, Anthony A., *The Four Major Cults,* Grand Rapids: Baker, 1963. Also see the chapter in my *Strange New Faiths*. Anderson, IN: Warner Press, 1953.
24. Wesley, *Notes*, on 1 Thess. 5:23.
25. See Collins, Kenneth J., *A Faithful Witness: John Wesley's Homiletical Theology*, Wilmore, KY: Wesley Heritage Press, 1993, 108-109.
26. Dunning, 278-279.
27. Dunning, 282.
28. *The Missionary Nature of the Church*. New York: McGraw-Hill, 1962.
29. Erickson, *Christian Theology*, 568
30. Temple, *Nature, Man, and God*, 367
31. Dunning, 280.
32. Quoted in Albert C. Outler, *John Wesley*. New York: Oxford University Press, 1964. 287.
33. Kenneth E. Jones, *Commitment to Holiness*, 39-56.
34. On the depth of the Wesleyan concept of sin, see Harald Lindstrom, *Weslely and Sanctification*. Stockholm: Almqvist and Wiksells, 1946. 19-26.
35. Berkouwer, *Sin*, 14.
36. John Wesley, *Works*, 10:123.
37. Wiley, *Christian Theology*. 2:123.
38. Brown, C. E., *Meaning of Sanctification*, 99.
39. *Right Conception of Sin*, 112.
40. WBC, 5:38.
41. Taylor, *Exploring Christian Holiness*. 3:60.
42. Kenneth E. Jones, *The Word of God*, 93-100. A longer survey is the first 318 pages of Geerhardus Vos, *Biblical Theology*, Grand Rapids: Eerdmans, 1948.
43. NIDNT, 2:725
44. NICNT, "John" 473, n. 116.
45. For a helpful discussion, see Leon Morris, NTT. 104-105.
46. I. H. Marshall, DJG, "Son of Man."
47. Augustine, *Letters*, 3;
48. Oden, *Word*, 117. (Italics by Oden).
49. The New Testament insists that Jesus Christ was truly God, and not some demi-god, as ancient Gnostics believed.
50. Baillie, D. M., *God Was in Christ*, 109.
51. On the theories of the atonement, see Brown, C. E., *We Preach Christ*, 75-80. Kenneth Grider, *A Wesleyaan-Holiness Theology,* 322-335, has a good discussion of the four theories of atonement. This is helpful. Yet not all

Wesleyan scholars are as enamored as he of the governmentaal theory. It has advantages, which he describes, but it is not the whole answer.
52. Brown, *Meaning of Salvation*, 97.
53. Ibid, 116.
54. K. Jones, *Commitment to Holiness*, 115-127. Brown, *The Meaning of Sanctification*, 37-57.
55. Wesley, *Works*, 5:133.
56. I Howard Marshall, *Kept by the Power of God*, 211.
57. N. H. Snaith, *The Distinctive Ideas of the Old Testament*, 24.
58. On *cherem* there is a brief article in ISBE under "Devote." A more complete discussion of the word and concept can be found in N. H. Snaith, *Distinctive Ideas of the Old Testament*. The Septuagint trnaslates the word with the Greek word *anathema,* which is sometimes transliterated and sometimes rendered "accursed." It is found in the New Testament in these forms. It never means that one is to be punished by others, but to be turned over to God for destruction or conversion. On the New Testament use of the concept, see the discussion under "curse" in NIDNTT, 1:413-415.
59. "A New Approach to Sanctification" in Gospel Trumpet (Now *Vital Christianity*), Nov. 6, 1954.
60. A careful study of Mildred Bangs Wynkoop, *A Theology of Love*, will be most helpful on this whole subject of holiness, sin, entire sanctification, and holiness as love.
61. J. Sidlow Baxter, *A New Call to Holiness*, Grand Rapids, Zondervan, 1967, 73-88.
62. Dunning, "1 John" ABT, 1209.
63. Thomas Oden, *Life in the Spirit*, 3.
64. Dunning, GFT, p. 49.
65. A. M. Hills, *Fundamental Christian Theology*, Pasadena, CA: C. J. Kinne, 1931, 1:373-382.
66. Wilber T. Dayton, "Entire Sanctificaation" in *A Contemporary Wesleyan Theology*. Charles W. Carter, Ed., p. 28.
67. *Vision Which Transforms*, 120-121.
68. R. R. Byrum, *Christian Theology*, 327. He stated it even more emphatically in *Holy Spirit Baptism and the Second Cleansing*, 86.
69. J. Kenneth Grider, *Entire Sanctification: the Distinctive Doctrine of Weslleyanismm*. Kansas City: Beacon Hill Press, 1980, 28.
70. John Miley, *Systematic Theology*. Peabody, Mass: Hendrickson Publishers [1893] 1989, 2:371.
71. Brown, *Meaning of Sanctification,* 138ff; Jones, *Commitment*, 28-29.
72. Fee, Gordon D., *Gospel nd Spirit, Issues in New Testament Hermeneutics*. Peabody, Mass: Hendrickson Publisheers, 1991, 89-92.

73. On Phoebe Palmer, it is well worth while for any Christian to read Thomas C. Oden, editor, *Phoebe Palmer, Selected Writings*. New York: Paulist Press, 1988. The thrilling story of her own successful search for the baptism of the Holy Spirit is told on pages 114-122, in excerpts from her diary. Probably no other preacher of holiness in the nineteenth century affected the thinking of the American holiness movement more than Mrs. Palmer.

74. Ephesians 5:1-7 is a warning against this very confusion. We are told there to "live in love," but we are also wrned that what the world calls love must be distinguished from godly love and avoided at all costs. Christians must have no part with the worldly customs of joking about sex, as thaat is not suitable.

75. "Jesus' Call to Perfection" in H. Ray Dunning, ed. *Biblical Resources for Holiness Preaching*, Vol. 2, Kansas City: Beacon Hill Press, 1993, 40-41.

76. Kenneth E. Jones, *Divorce and Remarriage in the Bible*. Anderson: Warner Press, 1989.

77. Avery Dulles, *Models of the Church*. Garden City, NY: Doubleday, 1974.

78. Brown, *Apostolic Church*, 1947, 31.

79. NICNT, "John" 512.

80. Smith, *Quest for Unity and Holiness*, 89.

81. Brown, *When Souls Awaken*, 63-65.

82. R. R. Byrum, *Christian Theology*, 556.

83. Newell, *Receive the Holy Spirit*, 67.

84. David F. Wells, *No Place for Truth: Or Whatever Happened to Evangelical Theology*. Grand Rapids: Eerdmans, 1993, 131.

85. ISBE, "elder."

86. Noyce, 1988, 34 ff.

87. Guthrie, Donald. *New Testament Theology*, 1961, 761.

88. BDT, 126-127.

89. BDT, 126

90. B. H. Streeter, 1929, 78-79.

91. Purkiser, Taylor nd Taylor, 1977, 601-602.

92. Brown, *Apostolic Church*, 126.

93. E. Schweizer, *Church Order in the New Testament*, 123.

94. J. Dwight Pentecost, *Things to Come*. Findlay, OH: Dunham Publishing Co., 1958.

95. Ibid.

96. The word used here is only used one other time in the New Testament, Matthew 23:26, where it is used of the inside of the cup. It is used in the Septuagint to mean "inside," as in Psalm 103:1 and 39:3.

97. Reinhold Niebuhr, *Nature and Destiny of Man*, 2:294.

Bibliography

Baillie, Donald M. *God Was In Christ*. London: Faber and Faber, 1955. A valuable study of the New Testament teaching about Christ. Begins with a review of some history of Christology.

Bassett, Paul M., and William M. Gr4eathouse. *Exploring Christian Holiness, Vol. 2, The Historical Development*. Kanss City, MO: Beacon Hill Press, 1985. History of the doctrine from Apostolic Fathers to Early Protestantism by Bassett. From Wesley to the American Holiness Movement by Greathouse.

Bright, John. *Authority of the Old Testament, The*. Grand Rapids: Baker, 1967 1978. A thought-provoking study of major problems of the Olld Testament, with some helpful suggestions toward their solution.

Bromiley, Geoffrey W. "Church." In *International Standard Bible Enclyclopedia*, edited by G. W. Bromiley, 1:693-698. Grand Rapids: Eerdmans, 1979.

Brown, Charles Ewing. *The Church Beyond Division*. Anderson, IN: Warner Press/Gospel Trumpet Co., 1939. An important step in the ecclesiology of the Church of God.

------. *The Meaning of Salvation*. Anderson, IN: Warner Press, 1944.

------. *The Meaning of Sanctification*. Anderson, IN: Warner Press, 1945. One of the best studies of the meaning of entire sanctification and holiness. This book haas been widely used as a textbook in holiness colleges and seminaries

------. *We Preach Christ*. Anderson, IN: Warner Press, 1957. A brief, but careful study of the doctrines of the Church of God.

------. *When The Trumpet Sounded*. Anderson, IN: Warner Press, 1951. The first attempt to write a full history of the Church of God.

Brown, Colin, Ed. "NIDNTT." In *The New International Dictionary of New Testament Theology*, edited by Colin Brown. Grand Rapids: Zondervan, 1975.

Bruce, F. F. *Answers to Questions*. Grand Rapids: Zondervan.

Brunner, Emil. *The Misunderstanding of the Church*1953.

Byers, A. L. *Birth of a Reformation*. Andeerson, IN: Gospel Trumpet Co. (Warner Press), 1921. Quotes largely from the diaries of D. S. Warner

Byrum, Russell R. *Christian Theology*. Anderson, IN: Warner Press, 1925. The classic statement of the theology of the Church of God.

Calvin, John. *Institutes of the Christian Religion*. Philadelphia: Westminster Press, 1960. This copy was edited by John T. McNeill from the 1559 Latin text.

Carter, Charles W. *Life's Lordship Over Death, A Study of Immortality and the Heaeafter from a Wesleyan Perspective*. Indianapolis: Wesley Press, 1988. A valuable study of a nneglected aspect of theology: Death, resurrection, eternal life.

------. *The Person and Ministry of the Holy Spirit*. Grand Rapids: Baker Book House, 1974.

Cell, George Croft. *The Rediscoovery of John Wesley*. New York,: Henry Holt and Co., 1935.

Coppedge, Allan. *John Wesley in Theological Debate*. Wilmore, KY: Wesley Heritage Press, 1987. An excellent study of some of Wesley's writings. Helpful.

Denney, James. *Studies in Theology*. Ann Arbor: Baker Book House, 1895, 1976. Old, but by a good conservative theologian.

Dulles, Avery. *Models of the Church*. Garden City: Doubleday, 1974. Comparative study of some of the various concepts of the church and of church government.

Dunning, H. Ray. *Grace, Faith and Holiness: A Wesleyan Systematic Theology*. Kaansas City, MO: Beacon Hill Press, 1988. A Systematic theology. Biblical, philosophical, and theological. Has a valuable appendix on "Speculative eschatology." A most valuable, insightful, aand helpful theology. Thoroughly Wesleyan. Shows a strong background in philosophy. His Ph.D. was in theology with a minor in philosophy. Nazarene

Gaulke, Max R.. *May Thy Kingdom Come—Now!* Andersson, IN: Warner Press, 1959. A valluable book on the Kingdom of God and against millennial theories.

Gray, Albert F. *Christian Theology*. Anderson, IN: Warner Press, 1944, 46. A good theology written by the founding president of Warner Pacific College, who also taught theology there. Originally two volumes.

Grider, J. Kenneth. *Entire Sanctification: The Distinctive Doctrine of Wesleyanism*. Kansas City, MO: Beacon Hill Press, 1980.

------. *A Wesleyan-Holiness Theology*. Kansas City: Beacon Hill Press of Kansas City, 1994. An excellent new holiness theology book, by a gracious scholar.

Guthrie, Donald. *New Testament Theology*. Downers Grove, IL: InterVarsity Press, 1981. A valuable survey of New Testament Theology, written by a British Methodist professor. Unlike most such books, it is organized around topics, rather than the now usuaal study of the various books of the New Testament. 990 pages + bibliography

Harrison, Everett F. *Baker's Dictionary of Theology*. Edited by Everett F. Harrison. Grand Rapids: Baker Book House, 1960. Useful for its many Scripture references.

Jones, Kenneth E. "Babylon and the New Jerusalem: Interpreting the Book of Revelation." In *Listening to the Word of God*, edited by Barry L. Callen, 133-50. Anderson, IN: Warner Press, 1990.

------. *Commitment to Holiness*. Anderson, IN: Warner Press, 1985.

------. "Study." In *Let's Study the Bible*. Anderson, IN: Warner Press, 1962, 1982.

------. *The Word of God.* Anderson, IN: Warner Press, 1980. On the nature and authority of the Bible.

Ladd, George Eldon. *A Theology of the New Testament.* Graand Rapids: Eerdmans, 1974. A much-used conservative NT Theology, by a well-trained scholar. In eschatology, Ladd took a position against traditional dispensationalism which displeased both dispensationalists and their opponents.

Lightfoot, J. B. *The Christian Ministry.* London: Macmillan and Co., 1903.

Manson, T. W. *The Churche's Ministry.* London: Hodder and Stoughton, 1948.

Marshall, I. Howard. *Kept by the Power of God.* Minneapolis: Bethany Fellowship, Inc., 1969, 1975. A most valuable study of the teaching of the New Testament about the assurance of salvation and eternal security. He concludes that we can be safely kept from sin by grace, but that we mast "take heed lest we fall". Well balanced.

Martin, Earl L. *Towaard Understanding God.* Anderson, IN: Waarner Press, 1942. A survey of the main topics of theology, as seen by a teacher at Anderson University. Does not deal with some of the more thorny problems.

McGrath, Alister E. *Christian Theology, An Introduction.* Cambridge, Mass: Blackwell, 1994. Especially valuable as an introduction to the historical origin and development of the basic concepts of theology.

Minear. *Images of the Church.* Philadelphia: Westminster Press, 1960.

Morris, Leon. *New Testament Theology.* Grand Rapids: Zondervan (Academie Books, 1990. By a thoughtful Australian Methodist. Wesleyan

Newell, Arlo F. *Receive the Holy Spirit.* Anderson, IN: Warner Press, 1978. Clear exposition of the work of the Holy Spirit.

Oden, Thomas C. *After Modernity... What?* Grand Rapids: Zondervan, 1990. Evaluation and answer to many aspects of modern theology.

------. *John Wesley's Scriptural Christianity.* Grand Rapids: Zondervan, 1994. "A Plain Exposition of His teaching on Christian Doctrine. A study of the teachings of John Wesley in an attempt to show that Wesley was a systematic theologian, contrary to a common opinion. Valuable resource for understanding John Wesley.

------. *Life in the Spirit.* Systematic Theology, vol. 3. San Francisco: Harper, 1992. (See on The Living God)

------. *The Living God.* Systematic Theology, vol. 1. San Francisco: Harper, 1987. Most exciting and helpful . Unique in its reliance on the writing Fathers of the first four centuries, with many quotations. Oden says he determined not to present anything new, but only what could be found to be the concensus of the Apostolic Christians. No one wlse gives such a complete picture of the Apostolic theology. It is an excellent introduction and guide to the writings of the first four centuries.

------. *The Word of Life.* Systematic Theology, vol. 2. San Francisco: Harper,

1989. (See on The Living God)

Outler, Albert C. Ed. *John Wesley.* New York: Oxford University Pess, 1964. Selected reading s from Wesley, with thorough introductions by Outler. The author explains much of the background of the various readings, and gives valuable advice on understanding them. In one case, his insistence that Wesley depended on Macarius, his judgment has proved to be questionable, as new evidence has come to light on some of Wesley's sources, and on the authorship of that collection of writings known aas Macarius.

Purkiser, W. T. *Exploring Christian Holiness, Vol. 1, The Biblical Foundations.* Kansas City, MO: Beacon Hill Press, 1983. Holiness as taught in the OT, Gospels, Acts, Pauline, General epistlles, with a chapter on each. Good bibliography.

------, Richard S. Taylor, and Willard H. Taylor. *God, Man and Salvation.* Kansas City: Beacon Hill Press, 1977. Studies in Old and New Testament Theology, by Nazarene scholars.

Rice, Hillery C. *Tell Me About the Church.* Anderson, IN: Warner Press, 1956.

Richardson, Alan, ed. *A Theological Word Book of the Bible.* New York: Macmillan Co., 1951.

Ridderbos, H. N. *Paul: An Outline of His Theology.* Grand Rapids: Eerdmans, 1975.

Ridout, S. *The Church and Its Order According to Scripture.* Neptune, N. Y.: Loizeaux Brothers, 1915, 1976.

Riggle, Herbert McClellan. *The New Testament Church: Spiritual, Practical.* Anderson, IN: Gospel Trumpet Co./ Warner Press, 1937.

Robinson, William. *The Biblical Doctrine of the Church.* St. Louis: Bethany Press, 1948.

Schmidt, K. L. "Ekklesia." In *Theological Dictionary of the New Testament,* edited by Kittel. Gerjard and Trans. Geoffrey W. Bromiley. Grand Rapids: Eerdmans, 1942, 1967. Translated from the German and published in English in 10 volumes.

Schweizer, Eduard [Trans by Frand Clalrlke. *Church Order in the New Testament.* Naperville, IL: Alec R. Allenson, Inc, 1959, 1961.

Shelton, R. Larry. ""Nature, Character and Origin of Scripture."" In *Asbury Bible Commentary,* edited by Eugene Carpenter and Wayne McCown, 19-37. Grand Rapids: Zondervan, 1991. One of the helpful articles in this commentary.

Sloan. "Unity in Diversity: A Clue to the Emergence of the NT as Sacred Literature." In *New Testament Criticism and Interpretation,* edited by David Alan Black and David S. Dockery, 437-70. Grand Rapids: Zondervan, 1991. Collection of papers by conservative scholars who uphold the authority of the New Testament.

Smith John W. V. *I Will Build My Church.* Anderson, IN: Warner Press, 1985. Basic doctrines of the Church of God Movement

Smith, John W. V. *The Quest for Holiness and Unity.* Anderson, IN: Warner Press, 1980.

Snaith, Norman H. *The Distinctive Ideas of the Old Testament.* London: Epworth Press, 1944.

Stafford, Gilbert W. "Frontiers in Contemporary Theology." In *A Contemporary Wesleyan Theology,* edited by Charles W. Carter, 1:15-50. Anderson, IN: Warner Press, 1983. By the professor of theology at the Graduate School of Theology, Anderson University.

Taylor, Richard S. *Exploring Christian Holiness, Vol. 3, The Theological Formulation.* Kansas City, MO: Beacon Hill Press, 1985. Excellent study of the theology of holiness by one of the great Nazarene theologians.

------. "Historical and Modern Significance of Wesleyan Theology." In *A Contemporary Wesleyan Theology,* edited by Charles W. Carter, 1:51-71. Anderson, IN: Warner Pess, 1983.

------. *A Right Conception of Sin.* Kansas City, MO: Beacon Hill Press, 1945. A help in understanding the difference betwen Calvinistic and Wesleyan concepts of sin and holiness.

Trueblood, D. Elton. *Philosophy of Religion.* New York: Harper, 1957. Most valuable.

Turner, George Allen. *The Vision Which Transforms.* Kansas City, MO: Beacon Hill Press, 1977. Revised version of a Ph. D. dissertation. on the question of Wesley's interpretation of the Bible teaching on holiness.

Wesley, John. *Explanatory Notes Upon the New Testament.* London: Epworth Press, 19441.

------. *A Plain Account of Christian Perfection.* Kansas City, MO: Beacon Hill Press, 1950. Wesley's mature view of Christian holiness.

Wiley, H. Orton. *KChristian Theology, 3 Volumes.* Kansas City, MO: Beacon Hill Press, 1940-1943.

Wynkoop, Mildred Bangs. *The Foundations of Wesleyan-Arminian Theology.* Kansas City, MO: Beacon Hill Press, 1967. Good comparison of Wesleyand and Calvinistic concepts.

------. *A Theology of Love: The Dynamic of Wesleyanism.* Kansas City: Beacon Hill Press, 1972. A most valuable study of the theology of John Wesley.

Index

Agnosticism 26
Arguments for God 23-24
Armageddon 338
Assurance 170-173
Atonement 176
Authority, Biblical 45ff
Baptism 272ff
Cherem 196, 232
Christ, humanity 168ff
Christ, return of 322
Christ, divinity 161, 164
Christ 149ff
Church of God 13, 272ff
Church organization 305ff
Church, marks of 265ff
Church, work of 288
Creation, date 86
Creation 85ff
Criticism, Biblical 10ff
Day in Genesis 1 88
Deism 24
Depravity 132ff
Deprivity 135-136
Dispensationalism   332ff
Eschatology 319ff
Evangelism 290ff
Evil, problem of 20, 93ff
Evolution, naturalistic 87
Exegesis 59ff
Experience 3, 30, 55
Footwashing 274
Fundamentalism 9
God, attributes 64
God, image of 105ff
God, personal 17, 37, 65-66
God, holy 64ff
God, love 1, 67ff
Grace, prevenient 34, 215
Heaven 341ff

Hell 341ff
Holiness, human 191ff
Holy Spirit 209ff, 277ff
Holy Living 239ff
Human beings 101ff
Humanism, secular 26
Incarnation 172ff
Inspiration. 47
Intermediate state 329
Interpretation, biblical 56ff
Judgment 325
Judgment 325
Kingdom of God 331ff
Language, theological ... 30-31
Liberal 9
Lord's Supper 273ff
Millennium 330ff
Ministers 307-311
Miracles, gift of 275
Missions 290
Naturalism 25, 85
New Age 27
Ordinances 272ff
Ordination 310
Pantheism 26
Pastors 307ff
Pastors, authority 308
Perfection, Christian ... 201, 244
Personal Helper 217-220
Prayer 250
Prevenient grace 215ff
Providence 93, 150
Quadrilateral 7
Rapture, secret 337ff
Reason 34-38, 54
Resurrection, universal 324ff
Revelation, necessity 33
Salvation 177ff
Salvation, tenses of 189ff
Salvation, conditions 169ff

Index

Sanctification, conditions ... 232
Sanctification, entire .. 223ff, 228
Science, limits of 91
Second Advent 322ff
Signs of the end 336
Sin, corporate 122
Sin, effects of 143ff
Sin, freedom from 121
Sin, nature of 113ff
Sin, original 130
Sin, universal 129ff
Sin, victory over 121
Sin, what it is not 110ff
Spirit, gifts of ... 278-282, 291ff
Spirit, fruit of 262-267
Stewardship 246-247
Theodicy 96
Theology, Wesleyan 14
Tongues, gift of 300
Trinity 75ff
Unity of church 267-271
Worship 288